R. F. Chapman.
107 N. C.
Yale
"

THE PHILOSOPHY OF THE ACTIVE AND MORAL POWERS OF MAN.

BY

DUGALD STEWART, F. R. SS. LOND. AND ED.

REVISED, WITH OMISSIONS AND ADDITIONS,

BY JAMES WALKER, D. D.,
PROFESSOR OF INTELLECTUAL AND MORAL PHILOSOPHY IN HARVARD COLLEGE.

Seventh Edition.

BOSTON:
PHILLIPS, SAMPSON, AND COMPANY.
1859.

PREFACE

BY THE EDITOR.

Sir James Mackintosh has said of Mr. Stewart, — "Perhaps few men ever lived, who poured into the breasts of youth a more fervid, and yet reasonable, love of liberty, of truth, and of virtue. How many are still alive, in different countries, and in every rank to which education reaches, who, if they accurately examined their own minds and lives, would ascribe much of whatever goodness and happiness they possess to the early impressions of his gentle and persuasive eloquence!"

The Philosophy of the Active and Moral Powers of Man was the last of his publications; it came from the press in the spring of 1828, a few weeks before the author's death. An unfriendly and severe critic in the *Penny Cyclopædia* admits, in respect to this treatise, that it is "by far the least exceptionable of his works. It is more systematic, and contains more new truths, than any of his metaphysical writings; and his long acquaintance with the world and with letters enabled him to suggest many obvious but overlooked analyses." Only two editions of it have appeared in this country, — one separately in 1828, the other in a collection of his works in the following year; the former has long been out of print.

The author begins his Preface by apologizing for "the large and perhaps disproportionate space" allotted by him to the evidence and doctrines of natural religion. This part, making nearly one third of the whole, has been omitted in the present edition, as being out of place here, however excellent in itself. Other retrenchments have also been made in respect to unimportant details, in order to find room, without transgressing the prescribed limits, for some additional notes and illustrations. The latter, which are indicated by brackets, or otherwise, as they occur, consist almost exclusively of extracts from living or late writers, or references to them, and are inserted with a view to mark whatever progress has been made or attempted in ethical speculation since Mr. Stewart's day.

Some changes have been made in the distribution and numbering of the chapters and sections, and sub-sections have been introduced for the first time. The use of the latter in giving a more distinct impression of the successive steps in the argument or exposition, no practised teacher will fail to appreciate. The Latin and Greek citations in the text are translated in the present edition, where this had not been done by the author. The translations are taken, for the most part, from common sources, without particular acknowledgment, the only object being to fit the work for more general and convenient use as a text-book.

CAMBRIDGE, August 16, 1849.

CONTENTS.

BOOK I.

OF OUR INSTINCTIVE PRINCIPLES OF ACTION.

BOOK II.

OF OUR RATIONAL AND GOVERNING PRINCIPLES OF ACTION.

CHAPTER I.

CHAPTER II.

OF THE MORAL FACULTY.

APPENDIX TO CHAPTER II.

CHAPTER III.

CHAPTER IV.

CHAPTER V.

CHAPTER VI.

OF MAN'S FREE AGENCY.

BOOK III.

OF THE VARIOUS BRANCHES OF OUR DUTY.

CHAPTER I.

CHAPTER II.

CHAPTER III.

BOOK IV.

OF THE NATURE AND ESSENCE OF VIRTUE.

CHAPTER I.

CHAPTER II.

CHAPTER III.

APPENDIX TO BOOK IV.

THE

PHILOSOPHY

OF THE

ACTIVE AND MORAL POWERS OF MAN.

INTRODUCTION.

1. *Connection between the Intellectual and the Active Powers.*] In my former work on the Human Mind I confined my attention almost exclusively to man considered as an *intellectual being;* and attempted an analysis of those faculties and powers which compose that part of his nature commonly called his *intellect* or his *understanding.* It is by these faculties that he acquires his knowledge of external objects; that he investigates truth in the sciences; that he combines means in order to attain the ends he has in view; and that he imparts to his fellow-creatures the acquisitions he has made. A being might, I think, be conceived, possessed of these principles, without any of the active propensities belonging to our species, at least without any of them but the principle of curiosity; — a being formed only for speculation, without any determination to the pursuit of particular external objects, and whose whole happiness consisted in intellectual gratifications.

But, although such a being might perhaps be conceived to exist, and although, in studying our internal frame, it be convenient to treat of our intellectual powers apart from our active propensities, yet, in fact, the two are very intimately, and indeed inseparably, connected in all our mental operations. I have already hinted, that, even in our speculative inquiries, the principle of curiosity is necessary to account for the exertion we make; and it is still more obvious, that a combination of means to accomplish particular ends presupposes some determination of our nature which makes the attainment of these ends desirable. Our active propensities, therefore, are the motives which induce us to exert our intellectual powers; and our intellectual powers are the instruments by which we attain the ends recommended to us by our active propensities: —

"Reason the card, but passion is the gale."

It will afterwards appear, that our active propensities are not only necessary to produce our intellectual exertions, but that the state of the intellectual powers, in the case of individuals, depends, in a great measure, on the strength of their propensities, and on the particular propensities which are predominant in the temper of their minds. A man of strong philosophical curiosity is likely to possess a much more cultivated and inventive understanding than another of equal natural capacity, destitute of the same stimulus. In like manner, the love of fame, or a strong sense of duty, may compensate for original defects, or may lay the foundation of uncommon attainments. The intellectual powers, too, may be variously modified by the habits arising from avarice, from the animal appetites, from ambition, or from the benevolent affections; insomuch that the moral principles of the miser, of the elegant voluptuary, of the political intriguer, and of the philanthropist are not, perhaps, more dissimilar than the acquired capacities of their understandings, and the species of information with which their memories are stored. Among the various external indications of character, few circumstances will be found to throw more light on the ruling passions of individuals than the habitual direction of their studies, and the nature of those accomplishments which they have been ambitious to attain.

When Montaigne complains of "the difficulty he experienced in remembering the names of his servants; of his ignorance of the value of the French coins which he was daily handling; and of his inability to distinguish the different kinds of grain from each other, both in the earth and in the granary";* his observations, instead of proving the point which he supposed them to establish (an original and incurable defect in his faculty of memory), only afford an illustration of the little interest he took in things external, and of the preternatural and distempered engrossment of his thoughts with the phenomena of the internal world. To this peculiarity in his turn of mind he had himself alluded, when he says, "I study myself more than any other subject. This is my metaphysic; this my natural philosophy." A person well acquainted with the peculiarities of Montaigne's memory might, I think, on comparing them with the general superiority of his mental powers, have anticipated him in this specification of the study which almost exclusively occupied his attention.†

Helvetius in his book *De l'Esprit* (a work which, among many paradoxical and some very pernicious opinions, contains a number of acute and lively observations) has prosecuted, with considerable success, this last view of human nature, and has collected a variety of amusing facts to illustrate the influence of the passions on the intellectual powers. "It is the passions," he observes, "that rouse the soul from its natural ten-

* Montaigne's *Essays*, Book II. Chap. xvii.

† The following remarks of the learned and ingenious Dr. Jortin are not unworthy of the attention of those whose taste leads them to the observation and study of character.

"From the complexion of those anecdotes which a man collects from others, or which he forms by his own pen, may, without much difficulty, be conjectured what manner of man he was.

"The human being is mightily given to assimilation, and, from the stories which any one relates with spirit, from the general tenor of his conversation, and from the books or associates to which he most addicts his attention, the inference cannot be far distant as to the texture of his mind, the vein of his wit, or, we may add, the ruling passion of his heart." — Jortin's *Tracts*, Vol. I. p. 445.

dency to rest, and surmount the *vis inertiæ* to which it is always inclined to yield; and it is the *strong* passions alone that prompt men to the execution of those heroic actions, and give birth to those sublime ideas, which command the admiration of ages.

"It is the strength of passion alone that can enable men to defy dangers, pain, and death.

"It is the passions, too, which, by keeping up a perpetual fermentation in our minds, fertilize the same ideas, which, in more phlegmatic temperaments, are barren, and resemble seed scattered on a rock.

"It is the passions which, having strongly fixed our attention on the object of our desire, lead us to view it under aspects unknown to other men; and which, consequently, prompt heroes to plan and execute those hardy enterprises which must always appear ridiculous to the multitude till the sagacity of their authors has been evinced by success." *

To this passage, which is, I think, just in the main, I have only to object, that, in consequence of the ambiguity of the word *passion*, it is apt to suggest an erroneous idea of the author's meaning. It is plain that he uses it to denote our active principles in general; and, in this sense, there can be no doubt that his doctrine is well founded; inasmuch as, without such principles as curiosity, the love of fame, ambition, avarice, or the love of mankind, our intellectual capacities would for ever remain sterile and useless. But it is not in this sense that the word *passion* is most commonly employed. In its ordinary acceptation it denotes those animal impulses which, although they may sometimes prompt to intellectual exertion, are certainly on the whole unfavorable to intellectual improvement. Helvetius himself has not always attended to this ambiguity of language; and hence may be traced many of the paradoxes and errors of his philosophy.

To these slight remarks it may not be useless to subjoin an observation of La Rochefoucauld, which is

* *De l'Esprit*, Discours III. Chap. vi.

equally refined and just; and which, in its practical tendency, calls the attention to a source of danger in a quarter where it is too seldom apprehended. "It is a mistake to believe that none but the violent passions, such as ambition and love, are able to triumph over the other active principles. Laziness, as languid as it is, often gets the mastery of them all; overrules all the designs and actions of life, and insensibly consumes and destroys both passions and virtues." *

From the foregoing observations it appears, that, in accounting for the diversities of genius and of intellectual character among men, important lights may be derived from an examination of their active propensities. It is of more consequence for me, however, to remark at present the intimate relation which an analysis of these propensities bears to the theory of morals, and its practical connection with our opinions on the duties and the happiness of human life. Indeed, it is in this way alone that the light of nature enables us to form any reasonable conclusions concerning the ends and destination of our being, and the purposes for which we were sent into the world: *Quid sumus, et quidnam victuri gignimur.*† It forms, therefore, a necessary introduction to the science of ethics, or rather is the foundation on which that science may rest.

II. *Object and Plan of the Work.*] In prosecuting our inquiries into the Active and the Moral Powers of Man, I propose, *first*, to attempt a classification and analysis of the most important principles belonging to this part of our constitution; and, *secondly*, to treat of the various branches of our duty. Under the former of these heads, my principal aim will be to illustrate the essential distinction between those active principles which originate in man's rational nature, and those which urge him, by a blind and instinctive impulse, to their respective objects.

In general, it may be here remarked, that the word

* *Sentences et Maximes*, cclxvi.

† Persius, *Sat.* III. l. 67.

action is properly applied to those exertions which are consequent on volition, whether the exertion be made on external objects, or be confined to our mental operations. Thus, we say the mind is active when engaged in study. In ordinary discourse, indeed, we are apt to confound together action and motion. As the operations in the minds of other men escape our notice, we can judge of their activity only from the sensible effects it produces; and hence we are led to apply the character of activity to those whose bodily activity is the most remarkable, and to distinguish mankind into two classes, the active and the speculative. In the present instance, the word *active* is used in its most extensive signification, as applicable to every voluntary exertion.

According to the definition now given of the word *action*, the primary sources of our activity are the circumstances in which the acts of the will originate. Of these there are some which make a part of our constitution, and which, on that account, are called active principles. Such are hunger, thirst, the appetite which unites the sexes, curiosity, ambition, pity, resentment. These active principles are also called powers of the will, because, by stimulating us in *various* ways to action, they afford exercise to our sense of duty and our other rational principles of action, and give occasion to our voluntary determinations as free agents.

III. *Difficulty of the Study.*] The study of this part of our constitution, although it may at first view seem to lie more open to our examination than the powers of the understanding, is attended with some difficulties peculiar to itself. For this various reasons may be assigned; among which there are two that seem principally to claim our attention.

1. When we wish to examine the nature of any of our intellectual principles, we can at all times subject the faculty in question to the scrutiny of *reflection;* and can institute whatever experiments with respect to it may be necessary for ascertaining its general laws

It is characteristic of all our operations purely intellectual to leave the mind cool and undisturbed, so that the *exercise* of the faculties concerned in them does not prevent us from an analytical investigation of their theory. The case is very different with our active powers, particularly with those which, from their violence and impetuosity, have the greatest influence on human happiness. When we are under the dominion of the power, or, in plainer language, when we are hurried by *passion* to the pursuit of a particular end, we feel no inclination to speculate concerning the mental phenomena. When the tumult subsides, and our curiosity is awakened concerning the past, the moment for observation and experiment is lost, and we are obliged to search for our facts in an imperfect recollection of what was viewed, even in the *first* instance, through the most troubled and deceitful of all *media*.

Something connected with this is the following remark of Mr. Hume: — "Moral philosophy has this peculiar disadvantage, which is not to be found in natural, that, in collecting its experiments, it cannot make them purposely, with premeditation, and after such a manner as to satisfy itself concerning every particular difficulty that may arise. When I am at a loss to know the effects of one body upon another in any situation, I need only put them in that situation, and observe what results from it. But should I endeavour to clear up, after the same manner, any doubts in moral philosophy, by placing myself in the same case with that which I consider, it is evident that this reflection and premeditation would so disturb the operation of my natural principles, as must render it impossible to form any just conclusion from the phenomenon. We must therefore glean up our experiments in this science from a cautious observation of human life, and take them as they appear in the common course of the world, by men's behaviour in company, in affairs, and in their pleasures." *

* *Treatise of Human Nature*, Vol. I., Introduction.

2. Another circumstance which adds much to the difficulty of this branch of study is the great variety of our active principles, and the endless diversity of their combinations in the characters of men. The same action may proceed from very different, and even opposite, motives in the case of two individuals, and even in the same individual on different occasions; — or an action which in one man proceeds from a single motive may, in another, proceed from a number of motives conspiring together and modifying each other's effects. The philosophers who have speculated on this subject have in general been misled by an excessive love of simplicity, and have attempted to explain the phenomena from the smallest possible number of data. Overlooking the real complication of our active principles, they have sometimes fixed on a single one, (good or bad, according as they were disposed to think well or ill of human nature,) and have deduced from it a plausible explanation of all the varieties of human character and conduct.

Our inquiries on this subject must be conducted in one of two ways, either by studying the characters of other men, or by studying our own. In the former way, we may undoubtedly collect many useful hints, and many facts to confirm or to limit our conclusions; but the conjectures we form concerning the motives of others are liable to so much uncertainty, that it is chiefly by attending to what passes in our own minds that we can reasonably hope to ascertain the general laws of our constitution as active and moral beings.

Even this plan of study, however, as I have already hinted, requires uncommon perseverance, and still more uncommon candor. The difficulty is great of attending to any of the operations of the mind; but this difficulty is much increased in those cases in which we are led by vanity or timidity to fancy that we have an interest in concealing the truth from our own knowledge.

Most men, perhaps, are disposed, in consequence of these and some other causes, to believe themselves better than they really are; and a few, there is reason to suspect, go into the opposite extreme, from the influence of false systems of philosophy or religion, or from the gloomy views inspired by a morbid melancholy.

When to these considerations we add the endless metaphysical disputes on the subject of the will, and of man's free agency, it may easily be conceived that the field of inquiry upon which we are now to enter abounds with questions not less curious and intricate than any of those which have been hitherto under our review. In point of practical importance some of them will be found in a still higher degree entitled to our attention.

IV. *Division of the Active Principles.*] In the further prosecution of this subject, I shall avoid, as much as possible, all technical divisions and classifications, and shall content myself with the following enumeration of our Active Principles, which I hope will be found sufficiently distinct and comprehensive for our purposes.

1. APPETITES.
2. DESIRES.
3. AFFECTIONS.
4. SELF-LOVE.
5. THE MORAL FACULTY.

The first three may be distinguished (for a reason which will afterwards appear) by the title of INSTINCTIVE OR IMPLANTED PROPENSITIES; the last two by the title of RATIONAL AND GOVERNING PRINCIPLES OF ACTION.*

* In the above enumeration I have departed widely from Dr. Reid's language. See his *Essays on the Active Powers*, Essay III., Parts I, II., and III. This great philosopher, with whom I am always unwilling to differ, refers our active principles to three classes, the *mechanical*, the *animal*, and the *rational*; using all these three words with what I think a very exceptional latitude. On this occasion I shall only observe, that the word *mechanical* (under which he comprehends our *instincts and habits*) cannot, in my opinion, be properly applied to any of our active principles. It is indeed used, in this instance, merely as a term of distinction; but it *seems* to imply some theory concerning the nature of the principles comprehended under it, and is apt to suggest incorrect notions on the subject.

If I had been disposed to examine this part of our constitution with all the minute accuracy of which it is susceptible, I should have preferred the following arrangement to that which I have adopted, as well as to that proposed by Dr Reid: — 1. Of our *original* principles of action. 2. Of our *acquired* principles of action.

The *original* principles of action may be subdivided into the *animal* and the *rational;* to the former of which classes our *instincts* ought undoubtedly to be referred, as well as our *appetites* In Dr. Reid's arrangement, nothing appears more unaccountable, if not capricious, than to call our appetites *animal* principles, because they are common to man and to the brutes; and, at the same time, to distinguish our *instincts* by the title of *mechanical;* — when, of all our active propensities, there are none in which the nature of man bears so strong an analogy to that of the lower animals as in these instinctive impulses. Indeed, it is from the condition of the brutes that the word *instinct* is transferred to that of man by a sort of figure or metaphor.

Our *acquired* principles of action comprehend all those propensities to act which we acquire from habit. Such are our artificial appetites and artificial desires, and the various factitious motives of human conduct generated by association and fashion.

At present, it being useless for any of the purposes which I have in view to attempt so comprehensive and detailed an examination of the subject, I shall confine myself to the general enumeration already mentioned. As our appetites, our desires, and our affections, whether original or acquired, stand in the same common relation to the Moral Faculty (the illustration of which is the chief object of this volume), I purposely avoid those slighter and less important subdivisions which might be thought to savour unnecessarily of scholastic subtilty.

[For later classifications of our Active Principles, see Upham's *Elements of Mental Philosophy*, Vol. II., Introduction, Chap. ii., and Whewell's *Elements of Morality*, Book I. Chap. ii.]

BOOK I.

OF OUR INSTINCTIVE PRINCIPLES OF ACTION.

CHAPTER I.

OF OUR APPETITES.

I. *Their Nature, Use, and Abuse.*] This class of our Active Principles is distinguished by the following circumstances: —

1. They take their rise from the body, and are common to us with the brutes.

2. They are not constant, but occasional.

3. They are accompanied with an uneasy sensation, which is strong or weak in proportion to the strength or weakness of the appetite.

Our appetites are three in number, *hunger*, *thirst*, and the *appetite of sex*. Of these, two were intended for the preservation of the individual; the third for the continuation of the species; and without them reason would have been insufficient for these important purposes. Suppose, for example, that the appetite of hunger had been no part of our constitution, reason and experience might have satisfied us of the necessity of food to our preservation; but how should we have been able, without an implanted princi ,le, to ascertain, according to the varying state of our animal economy, the proper seasons for eating, or the quantity of food that is salutary to the body? The lower animals not only receive this information from nature, but are, moreover, directed by instinct to the particular sort of food that is proper for them to use in health and in sickness. The senses of taste and smell, in the savage state of our species, are subservient, at least in some degree, to the same purpose.

Our appetites can, with no propriety, be called *selfish*, for they are directed to their respective objects as ultimate ends, and they must all have operated, *in the first instance*, prior to any experience of the pleasure arising from their gratification. *After* this experience, indeed, the desire of enjoyment will naturally come to be combined with the appetite; and it may sometimes lead us to stimulate or provoke the appetite with a view to the pleasure which is to result from indulging it. Imagination, too, and the association of ideas, together with the social affections, and sometimes the moral faculty, lend their aid, and all conspire together in forming a complex passion, in which the animal appetite is only one ingredient. In proportion as this passion is gratified, its influence over the conduct becomes the more irresistible, (for all the *active* determinations of our nature are strengthened by habit,) till at last we struggle in vain against its tyranny. A man so enslaved by his animal appetites exhibits humanity in one of its most miserable and contemptible forms.

As an additional proof of the misery of such a state, it is of great importance to remark, that, while habit strengthens all our *active* determinations, it diminishes the liveliness of our passive *impressions*; — a remarkable instance of which occurs in the effects produced by an immoderate use of strong liquors, which, at the same time that it confirms the active habit of intemperance, deadens and destroys the sensibility of the palate. In consequence of this law of our nature, the evils of excessive indulgence are doubled, inasmuch as our sensibility to pleasure decays in proportion as the cravings of appetite increase.

In general, it will be found, that, wherever we attempt to enlarge the sphere of enjoyment beyond the limits prescribed by nature, we frustrate our own purpose.

A man so enslaved by his appetites may undoubtedly, in one sense, be called *selfish*; for, as he must necessarily neglect the duties he owes to others, he may be presumed to be deficient in the benevolent affections. But it cannot be said of him that he is actuated by an inordinate *self-love*, (meaning by that word an excessive regard for his own happiness,) for he sacrifices to the meanest gratifications all the noblest pleasures of which he is susceptible, and sacrifices to the pleasure of the moment the permanent enjoyments of health, reputation, and conscience. This is true even when the desire of gratification is combined with the original appetite; for no two principles can be more widely at variance than the desire of gratification and the desire of happiness.

Of the errors introduced into morals, in consequence of the vague use of the words *selfishness* and *self-love*, I shall afterwards take notice. What I wish chiefly to remark at present is, that in no sense of these words can we refer to them the origin of our animal appetites; and that the active propensitics comprehended under this title are ultimate facts in the human constitution.

II. *Acquired Appetites.*] Besides our natural appetites we have many *acquired* ones. Such are our appetites for tobacco, for opium, and for other intoxicating drugs. In general, every thing that stimulates the nervous system produces a subsequent languor, which gives rise to a desire of repetition.

The universality of this appetite for intoxicating drugs is a curious fact in the history of our species. "It seems," says Dr. Robertson, "to have been one of the first exertions of human ingenuity to discover some composition of an intoxicating quality; and there is hardly any nation so rude, or so destitute of invention, as not to have succeeded in this fatal research. The most barbarous of the American tribes have been so unfortunate as to attain this art; and even those who are so deficient in knowledge as to be unacquainted with the method of giving an inebriating strength to liquors by fermentation can accomplish the same end by other means. The people of the islands of North

America and of California used for this purpose the smoke of tobacco, drawn up with a certain instrument into the nostrils, the fumes of which ascending to the brain, they felt all the transports and frenzy of intoxication. In almost every part of the New World the natives possessed the art of extracting an intoxicating liquor from maize, or the manioc root, the same substances which they convert into bread. The operation by which they effect this nearly resembles the common one of brewing, but with this difference, that, instead of yeast, they use a nauseous infusion of maize or manioc chewed by their women. The saliva excites a vigorous fermentation, and in a few days the liquor becomes fit for drinking. It is not disagreeable to the taste, and, when swallowed in large quantities, is of an inebriating quality. This is the general beverage of the Americans, which they distinguish by different names, and for which they feel such a violent and insatiable desire, as it is not easy either to conceive or describe." *

Many striking confirmations of this remark occur in the voyages of Cook and of later navigators.

III. *Other analogous Propensities.*] Our occasional propensities to *action* and to *repose* are, in many respects, analogous to our appetites. They have, indeed, all the three characteristics of our appetites already mentioned. They are common, too, to man and to the lower animals, and they operate, in our own species, in the most infant state of the individual. In general, every animal we know is prompted by an instinctive impulse to take that degree of exercise which is salutary to the body, and is prevented from passing the bounds of moderation by that languor and desire of repose which are the consequences of continued exertion.

There is something, also, very similar to this with respect to the mind. We are impelled by nature to the exercise of its different faculties, and we are warned,

---

* *History of America*, Book IV. § 100.

when we are in danger of overstraining them, by a consciousness of fatigue. After we are exhausted by a long course of application to business, how delightful are the first moments of indolence and repose! *O che bella cosa di far niente!* We are apt to imagine that no inducement shall again lead us to engage in the bustle of the world: but, after a short respite from our labors, our intellectual vigor returns; the mind rouses from its lethargy "like a giant from his sleep," and we feel ourselves urged by an irresistible impulse to return to our duties as members of society.

The active principles already mentioned are common to man and to the brutes. But besides these, the latter have some instinctive impulses, of which I do not know that there are any traces to be found in the human race. Such are those *antipathies* which they discover against the natural enemies of their respective tribes. It is probable, I think, that their existence is guarded entirely by their appetites and antipathies; for the desire of self-preservation implies a degree of reason and reflection which they do not appear to possess. Even in the case of man, this desire is probably the result of his experience of the pleasures which life affords; and, accordingly, as Dr. Beattie very finely remarks, Milton has, with exquisite judgment, represented Adam, in the first moments of his being, as contemplating, without anxiety or regret, the idea of immediate annihilation:—

> "While thus I called and strayed I knew not whither
> From where I first drew air, and first beheld
> This happy light, when answer none returned,
> On a green, shady bank profuse of flowers
> Pensive I sat me down. There gentle sleep
> *First* found me, and with soft oppression seized
> My drowzied sense; UNTROUBLED, though I thought
> I then was passing to my former state
> Insensible, and forthwith to dissolve." *

* *Paradise Lost*, Book VIII. 283.

CHAPTER II.

OF OUR DESIRES.

Our desires are distinguished from our appetites by the following circumstances: —

1. They do not take their rise from the body.
2. They do not operate periodically after certain intervals, nor do they cease after the attainment of a particular object.

The most remarkable active principles belonging to this class are, —

1. The *Desire of Knowledge*, or the principle of *Curiosity.*
2. The *Desire of Society.*
3. The *Desire of Esteem.*
4. The *Desire of Power*, or the principle of *Ambition.*
5. The *Desire of Superiority*, or the principle of *Emulation.*

Section I.

THE DESIRE OF KNOWLEDGE.

I. *Early and various Manifestations.*] The principle of curiosity appears in children at a very early period, and is commonly proportioned to the degree of intellectual capacity they possess. The direction, too, which it takes, is regulated by nature according to the order of our wants and necessities; being confined, in the first instance, exclusively to those properties of material objects, and those laws of the material world, an acquaintance with which is essential to the preservation of our animal existence. Hence the instinctive eagerness with which children handle and examine every thing which is presented to them; an employment which we are commonly apt to consider as a mere exercise of their animal powers, but which, if we reflect on the limited province of sight prior to experience, and on the early period of life at which we are able to judge by the eye of the distances and of the tangible qualities of bodies, will appear plainly to be the most useful occupation in which they could be engaged, if it were in the power of a philosopher to have the regulation of their attention from the hour of their birth. In more advanced years curiosity displays itself in one way or another in every individual, and gives rise to an infinite diversity in their pursuits, — engrossing the attention of one man about physical causes, of another about mathematical truths, of a third about historical facts, of a fourth about the objects of natural history, of a fifth about the transactions of private families, or about the politics and news of the day.

Whether this diversity be owing to natural predisposition, or to early education, it is of little consequence to determine, as, upon either supposition, a preparation is made for it in the original constitution of the mind, combined with the circumstances of our external situation. Its final cause is also sufficiently obvious, as it is this which gives rise in the case of individuals to a limitation of attention and study, and lays the foundation of all the advantages which society derives from the division and subdivision of intellectual labor.

II. *Neither Selfish nor Moral in itself.*] These advantages are so great, that some philosophers have attempted to resolve the desire of knowledge into self-love. But to this theory the same objection may be stated which has already been made to the attempts of some philosophers to account, in a similar way, for the origin of our appetites; — that all of these are active principles, manifestly directed by nature to particular specific objects, as their ultimate ends; — that as the object of hunger is not happiness, but food, so the object of curiosity is not happiness, but knowledge. To this analogy Cicero has very beautifully alluded, when he calls knowledge the natural food of the understanding. "Est animorum ingeniorumque nostrorum na turale quoddam quasi pabulum consideratio contemplatioque naturæ." We can indeed conceive a being prompted merely by the cool desire of happiness to accumulate information; but in a creature like man, endowed with a variety of other active principles, the stock of his knowledge would probably have been scanty, unless self-love had been aided in this particular by the principle of curiosity.

Although, however, the desire of knowledge is not resolvable into self-love, it is not in itself an object of *moral approbation.* A person may indeed employ his intellectual powers with a view to his own moral improvement, or to the happiness of society, and so far he acts from a laudable principle. But to prosecute study merely from the desire of knowledge is neither virtuous nor vicious. When not suffered to interfere with our duties it is morally innocent. The virtue or vice does not lie in the desire, but in the proper or improper regulation of it. The ancient astronomer, who, when accused of indifference with respect to public transactions, answered that *his* country was in the heavens, acted criminally, inasmuch as he suffered his desire of knowledge to interfere with the duties which he owed to mankind.

III. *But superior in Dignity and Use to the Appetites.*] At the same time, it must be admitted that the desire of knowledge (and the same observation is applicable to our other desires) is of a more dignified nature than those appetites which are common to us with the brutes. A thirst for science has been always considered as a mark of a liberal and elevated mind; and it generally coöperates with the moral faculty in forming us to those habits of self-government which enable us to keep our animal appetites in due subjection.

There is another circumstance which renders this desire peculiarly estimable, that it is always accompanied with a strong desire to communicate our knowledge to others; insomuch, that it has been doubted if the principle of curiosity would be sufficiently power ful to animate the intellectual exertions of any man in a long course of persevering study, if he had no prospect of being ever able to impart his acquisitions to his friends or the public. "Si quis in cœlum ascendisset," says Cicero, "naturamque mundi et pulchritudinem siderum perspexisset, insuavem illam admirationem ei fore, quæ jucundissima fuisset, si aliquem, cui narraret, habuisset. Sic natura solitarium nihil amat, semperque ad aliquod tamquam adminiculum annititur, quod in amicissimo quoque dulcissimum est."* And to the same purpose Seneca: — "Nec me ulla res delectabit, licet sit eximia et salutaris, quam mihi uni sciturus sum. Si cum hac exceptione detur sapientia, ut illam inclusam teneam, nec enuntiem, rejiciam: nullius boni, sine socio, jucunda possessio est." †

A strong curiosity, properly directed, may be justly considered as one of the most important elements in philosophical genius; and, accordingly, there is no circumstance of greater consequence in education than to keep the curiosity always awake, and to turn it to useful pursuits. I cannot help, therefore, disapproving greatly of a very common practice in this country, that of communicating to children general and superficial views of science and history by means of popular introductions. In this way we rob their future studies of all that interest which can render study agreeable, and reduce the mind, in the pursuits of science, to the same state of listlessness and languor as when we toil through the pages of a tedious novel after being made acquainted with the final catastrophe.

---

* *De Amicitia*, 23. Thus translated, or rather paraphrased, by Melmoth: — "Were a man to be carried up to heaven, and the beauties of universal nature displayed to his view, he would receive but little pleasure from the wonderful scene, if there were none to whom he might relate the glories he had beheld. Human nature, indeed, is so constituted as to be incapable of lonely satisfaction: man, like those plants which are formed to embrace others, is led by an instinctive impulse to recline on his species; and he finds his happiest and most secure support in the arms of a faithful friend."

† Seneca, *Epist. Mor.*, Lib. I. Ep. 6. "Nor, indeed, would any thing give me pleasure, however excellent and salutary it might be, were I to keep the knowledge of it to myself. Were wisdom offered me under such restriction as to be obliged to conceal it, I would reject it. No enjoyment whatever can be agreeable without participation."

It would contribute greatly to the culture and the guidance of this principle of curiosity, if the different sciences were taught as much as possible in the order of the *analytic* rather than in that of the *synthetic* method;* a plan, however, which I readily admit it is not so practicable to carry into effect in a course of public as of private instruction. Such a mode of education, too, would be attended with the additional advantage of accustoming the student to the proper method of investigation; and thereby preparing him in due time to enter on the career of invention and discovery. Nor is this all. It would impress the knowledge he thus acquired, in some measure by his own ingenuity, much more deeply on his *memory* than if it were passively imbibed from books or teachers; — in the same manner as the windings of a road make a more lasting impression on the mind when we have once travelled it alone, and inquired out the way at every turn, than if we had travelled along it a hundred times trusting ourselves implicitly to the guidance of a companion. I am happy to be confirmed in this opinion by its coincidence with what has been excellently remarked on the same subject by Miss Edgeworth, in her treatise on Practical Education; a work equally distinguished by good sense and by originality of thought. The passage I allude to more particularly at present is the short dialogue about the steam-engine, as improved by Mr. Watt.†

Section II.

THE DESIRE OF SOCIETY.

I. *An Instinctive Principle.*] Abstracted from those affections which interest us in the happiness of others,

---

* *Analytically* we discover, by a sort of decomposition, the simple laws which are concerned in the phenomenon under consideration; *synthetically* taking the laws for granted, we determine *à priori* what the result will be of any hypothetical combination of them. — Ed.

† *Essays on Practical Education*, Chap. XXI.

and from all the advantages which we ourselves derive from the social union, we are led by a natural and instinctive desire to associate with our species. This principle is easily discernible in the minds of children long before the dawn of reason. "Attend only," says an intelligent and accurate observer, "to the eyes, the features, and the gestures of a child on the breast when another child is presented to it; — both instantly, previous to the possibility of instruction or habit, exhibit the most evident expressions of joy. Their eyes sparkle, and their features and gestures demonstrate, in the most unequivocal manner, a mutual attachment. When further advanced, children who are strangers to each other, though their social appetite be equally strong, discover a mutual shyness of approach, which, however, is soon conquered by the more powerful instinct of association." *

In the lower animals, too, very evident traces of the same instinct appear. In some of these we observe a species of union strikingly analogous to political associations among men: in others we observe occasional unions among individuals to accomplish a particular purpose, — to repel, for example, a hostile assault; — but there are also various tribes which discover a desire of society, and a pleasure in the company of their own species, without an apparent reference to any further end. Thus we frequently see horses, when confined alone in an inclosure, neglect their food and break the fences to join their companions in the contiguous field. Every person must have remarked the spirit and alacrity with which this animal exerts himself on the road, when accompanied by another animal of his own species, in comparison of what he discovers when travelling alone; and, with respect to oxen and cows, it has been asserted, that even in the finest pasture they do not fatten so rapidly in a solitary state as when they feed together in a herd.†

* Smellie's *Philosophy of Natural History*, Chap. XI.

† One of the best accounts of the social principle in animals is found in Swainson's *Habits and Instincts of Animals*, Chapters IX. and X. — Ed.

What is the final cause of the associating instinct in such animals as have now been mentioned it is not easy to conjecture, unless we suppose that it was intended merely to augment the sum of their enjoyments. But whatever opinion we may form on this point, it is indisputable that the instinctive determination is a strong one, and that it produces striking effects on the habits of the animal, even when external circumstances are the most unfavorable to its operation. Horses and oxen, for example, when deprived of companions of their own species, associate and become attached to each other. The same thing sometimes happens between individuals that belong to tribes naturally hostile; as between dogs and cats, or between a cat and a bird.

If these facts be candidly considered, there will appear but little reason to doubt the existence of the social instinct in our own species, when it is so agreeable to the general analogy of nature, as displayed through the rest of the animal creation. As this point, however, has been controverted warmly by authors of eminence, it will be necessary to consider it with some attention.

II. *The Theory of Hobbes stated and refuted.*] The question with respect to the social or the solitary nature of man seems to me to amount to this; whether man has any disinterested principles which lead him to unite with his fellow-creatures, or whether the social union be the result of prudential views of self-interest, suggested by the experience of his own insufficiency to procure the objec s of his natural desires. Of these two opinions, Hobbes has maintained the latter, and has endeavoured to establish it by proving, that, in what he calls the state of nature, every man is an enemy to his brother, and that it was the experience of the evils arising from these hostile dispositions that induced men to unite in a political society. In proof of this he insists on the terror which children feel at the sight of a stranger; on the apprehension which, he says, a person naturally feels when he hears the tread of a foot in the dark; on the universal invention of locks and keys and on various other circumstances of a similar nature.*

That this theory of Hobbes is contrary to the universal history of mankind cannot be disputed. Man has always been found in a social state; and there is reason even for thinking, that the principles of union which nature has implanted in his heart operate with the greatest force in those situations in which the advantages of the social union are the smallest. As society advances, the relations among individuals are continually multiplied, and man is rendered the more necessary to man: but it may be doubted, if, in a period of great refinement, the social affections be as warm and powerful as when the species were wandering in the forest.

Besides, it does not seem to be easy to conceive in what manner Hobbes's supposition could be realized. Surely, if there be a foundation for any thing laid in the constitution of man's nature, it is for family union. The infant of our species continues longer in a helpless state, and requires longer the protecting care of both parents, than the young of any other animal. Before the first child is able to provide for itself, a second and a third are produced, and thus the union of the sexes, supposing it at first to have been merely casual, is insensibly confirmed by habit, and cemented by the common interest which both parents take in their offspring. So just is the simple and beautiful statement of the fact given by Montesquieu, that "man is born in society, and there he remains."

From these considerations, it appears that the social union does not take its rise from views of self-interest, but that it forms a necessary part of the condition of man from the constitution of his nature. It is true, indeed, that before he begins to reflect he finds himself connected with society by a thousand ties; so that, in-

* *Leviathan*, Part I. Chap. xiii. *De Corpore Politico*, Part I. Chap. i.

dependently of any social instinct, prudence would undoubtedly prevent him from abandoning his fellow-creatures. But still it is evident that the social instinct forms a part of human nature, and has a tendency to unite men even when they stand in no need of each other's assistence. Were the case otherwise, prudence and the social disposition would be only different names for the same principle, whereas it is matter of common remark, that although the two principles be by no means inconsistent when kept within reasonable bounds, yet that the former, when it rises to any excess, is in a great measure exclusive of the latter. I have hinted, too, already, that it is in societies where individuals are most independent of each other as to their animal wants, that the social principles operate with the greatest force.

III. *The Wants and Necessities of Man help to develop, but do not create, his Social Principles.*] According to the view of the subject now given, the multiplied wants and necessities of man in his infant state, by laying the foundation of the family union, impose upon our species, as a necessary part of their condition, those social connections which are so essential to our improvement and happiness. And therefore nothing could be more unphilosophical than the complaints which the ancient Epicureans founded upon this circumstance, and which Lucretius has so pathetically expressed in the following verses: —

"Tum porro puer, ut sævis projectus ab undis
Navita, nudus humi jacet, infans, indigus omni
Vitali auxilio, cum primum in luminis oras
Nixibus ex alvo matris natura profudit:
Vagituque locum lugubri complet, ut æquum est,
Cui tantum in vitâ restat transire malorum." *

* Lib. V. 223.

"As when wild, wrecking tempests sweep the skies,
Cast on the shore the naked sailor lies;
So the weak infant, when he springs to light,
Thrown on the strand of life in helpless plight,
With mournful cries the joyful mansion fills,
The unheeded omens of a life of ills."

The philosophy of Pope is in this respect much more pleasing and much more solid: —

"Heaven, forming each on other to depend,
A master, or a servant, or a friend,
Bids each on other for assistance call,
Till one man's weakness grows the strength of all.
Wants, frailties, passions, closer still ally
The common interest, or endear the tie.
To these we owe true friendship, love sincere,
Each home-felt joy that life inherits here." *

The considerations now stated afford a beautiful illustration of the beneficent design with which the physical condition of man is adapted to the principles of his moral constitution; an adaptation so striking, that it is not surprising those philosophers who are fond of simplifying the theory of human nature should have attempted to account for the origin of these principles from the habits which our external circumstances impose. In this, as in many other instances, their attention has been misled by the spirit of system from those wonderful combinations of means to particular ends, which are everywhere conspicuous in the universe. It is not by the physical condition of man that the essential principles of his mind are formed; but the one is fitted to the other by the same superintending wisdom which adapts the fin of the fish to the water, and the wing of the bird to the air, and which scatters the seeds of the vegetable tribes in those soils and exposures where they are fitted to vegetate. It is not the wants and necessities of his animal being which *create* his social principles, and which produce an artificial and interested league among individuals who are naturally solitary and hostile; but, determined by instinct to society, endowed with innumerable principles which have a reference to his fellow-creatures, he is placed by the condition of his birth in that element where alone the perfection and happiness of his nature are to be found.

---

* *Essay on Man*, Ep. II. 249. See on this subject *The Moralists* of Lord Shaftesbury.

IV. *Man's Nature adjusted beforehand to the Condi tion in which he is placed.*] In speaking of the lowe animals, I before observed, that such of them as are in stinctively social discover the secret workings of nature even when removed from the society of their kind. This fact amounts in *their* case to a demonstration of that mutual adaptation of the different parts of nature to each other which I have just remarked. It demonstrates that the structure of their *internal* frame is purposely adjusted to that *external* scene in which they are destined to be placed. As the lamb, when it strikes with its forehead while yet unarmed, proves that it is not its weapons which determine its instincts, but that it has preëxistent instincts suited to its weapons, so when we see an animal deprived of the sight of his fellows cling to a stranger, or disarm, by his caresses, the rage of an enemy, we perceive the workings of a social instinct, not only not superinduced by external circumstances, but manifesting itself in spite of circumstances which are adverse to its operation. The same remark may be extended to man. When in solitude, he languishes, and, by making companions of the lower animals, or by attaching himself to inanimate objects, strives to fill up the void of which he is conscious. "Were I in a desert," says an author, who, amidst all his extravagances and absurdities, sometimes writes like a *wise* man, and, where the moral feelings are at all concerned, never fails to write like a *good* man,—"were I in a desert, I would find out wherewith in it to call forth my affections. If I could not do better, I would fasten them upon some sweet myrtle, or seek some melancholy cypress to connect myself to; I would court their shade, and greet them kindly for their protection. I would cut my name upon them, and swear they were the loveliest trees throughout the desert. If their leaves withered, I would teach myself to mourn, and when they rejoiced, I would rejoice along with them."

The Count de Lauzun was confined by Louis XIV. for nine years in the castle of Pignerol, in a small room where no light could enter but from a chink in the roof. In this solitude he attached himself to a spider, and contrived for some time to amuse himself with attempting to tame it, with catching flies for its support, and with superintending the progress of its web. The jailer discovered his amusement, and killed the spider; and the Count used afterwards to declare, that the pang he felt on the occasion could be compared only to that of a mother for the loss of a child.

This anecdote is quoted by Lord Kames in his *Sketches*, and by the late Lord Auckland in his *Principles of Penal Law*. It is remarkable that both these learned and respectable writers should have introduced it into their works on account of the shocking incident of the jailer, and as a proof of the pure and unprovoked malice of which some minds are capable, without taking any notice of it as a beautiful picture of the feelings of a man of sensibility in a state of solitude, and of his disposition to create to himself some object upon which he may rest those affections which have a reference to society.

It will be said that *these* are the feelings of one who has experienced the pleasures of social life, and that no inference can be drawn from such facts in opposition to Hobbes. But if they do not prove in man an instinctive impulse towards society prior to experience, they at least prove that he feels a delight in the society of his fellow-creatures, which no view of self-interest is sufficient to explain.

It does not belong to our present speculation to illustrate the importance of the social union to our improvement and our happiness. Its subserviency to both (abstracted entirely from its necessity for the complete gratification of our physical wants) is much greater than we should be disposed at first to apprehend. In proof of this, it is sufficient to mention here its connection with the culture of our intellectual faculties, and with the development of our moral principles. Illustrations of this may be drawn from the low state in which both these parts of our nature are generally found in the deaf and dumb, and from the effects which a few months' education sometimes has in unfolding their mental powers. The pleasing change which in the mean time takes place in their once vacant countenances, when animated and lighted up by an active and inquisitive mind, cannot escape the notice of the most careless observer.*

SECTION III.

THE DESIRE OF ESTEEM.

I. *An Original Principle of our Nature.*] This principle, as well as those we have now been considering, discovers itself at a very early period in infants, who, long before they are able to reflect on *the advantages* resulting from the good opinion of others, and even before they acquire the use of speech, are sensibly mortified by any expression of neglect or contempt. It seems, therefore, to be *an original principle of our*

---

* For an additional illustration of the same thing, see a remarkable case of recovery from deafness and dumbness in the history of the Royal Academy of Sciences at Paris for the year 1703.

A doctrine similar to that which I have now been controverting, concerning the origin of society, was maintained by some of the ancient sophists, and has found advocates in every age among those writers who wished to depreciate human nature, as well as among many who were anxious to represent man as entirely the creature of education and government, with the view of inculcating implicit and passive obedience to the civil magistrate. In Buchanan's elegant and philosophical Dialogue *De Jure Regni apud Scotos*, the question is particularly discussed between the two interlocutors, one of whom ascribes the origin of society to views of utility, meaning by *utility* the private interest or advantage of the individual. On the contrary, Buchanan himself, who is the other speaker, contends with great warmth for the existence of social principles in the nature of man, which, independently of any views of interest, lay a foundation for the social union.

Part of this Dialogue is curious, as it shows how completely Buchanan had not only anticipated, but refuted, the very far-fetched argument which Hobbes was soon after to draw from his supposed state of nature in support of his slavish maxims of government.

[See the subject of man's natural sociality still further illustrated, in connection with experiments in prison discipline, in De Beaumont and De Tocqueville's *Penitentiary System of the United States;* and in F. C. Gray's *Prison Discipline of America.*]

nature; that is, it does not appear to be resolvable into reason and experience, or into any other principle more general than itself. An additional proof of this is the very powerful influence it has over the mind,— an influence more striking than that of any other active principle whatsoever. Even the love of life daily gives way to the desire of esteem, and of an esteem which, as it is only to affect our memories, cannot be supposed to interest our self-love. In what manner the association of ideas should manufacture, out of the other principles of our constitution, a new principle stronger than them all, it is difficult to conceive.

In these observations I have had an eye to the theories of those modern philosophers who represent self-love, or the desire of happiness, as the only original principle of action in man, and who attempt to account for the origin of *all* our other active principles from habit or the association of ideas. That this theory is just in some instances cannot be disputed. Thus, in the case of *avarice*, it is manifest that it is from habit alone it derives its influence over the mind; for no man surely was ever brought into the world with an innate love of money. Money is at first desired, merely as the means of obtaining other objects; but in consequence of being long and constantly accustomed to direct our efforts to its attainment on account of its apprehended utility, we come at last to pursue it as an ultimate end, and frequently retain our attachment to it long after we have lost all relish for the enjoyments it enables us to command. In like manner, it has been supposed that the esteem of our fellow-creatures is at first desired on account of its apprehended utility, and that it comes in time to be pursued as an ultimate end, without any reference on our part to the advantages it bestows. In opposition to this doctrine it seems to me to be clear, that as the object of hunger is not happiness, but food; as the object of curiosity is not happiness, but knowledge; so the object of this principle of action is not happiness, but the esteem and respect of other men. That

3*

this is not inconsistent with the analogy of our nature appears from the observations already made on our appetites and desires; and that it really is the fact may be proved by various arguments. Before touching, however, on these, I must remark, that I consider this as merely a question of speculative curiosity; for, upon either supposition, the desire of esteem is equally the work of nature; and consequently, upon either supposition, it is equally unphilosophical to attempt, by metaphysical subtilties, to counteract her wise and beneficent purposes.

Among the different arguments which concur to prove that the desire of esteem is not wholly resolvable into the association of ideas, one of the strongest has already been hinted at, — the early period of life at which this principle discovers itself, — long before we are able to form the idea of *happiness*, far less to judge of the circumstances which have a tendency to promote it. The difference in this respect between avarice and the desire of esteem is remarkable. The former is the vice of old age, and is, comparatively speaking, confined to a few. The latter is one of the most powerful engines in the education of children, and is not less universal in its influence than the principle of curiosity.

II. *The Desire of Posthumous Fame represented by Wollaston as Illusory.*] The desire, too, of *posthumous* fame, of which no man can entirely divest himself, furnishes an insurmountable objection to the theories already mentioned. It is, indeed, an objection so obvious to the common sense of mankind, that all the philosophers who have leaned to these theories have employed their ingenuity in attempting to resolve this desire into an illusion of the imagination produced by habit. This, too, was the opinion of an excellent writer, and still more excellent man, Mr. Wollaston, who, from a well-meant, but very mistaken, zeal to weaken the influence of this principle of action on human conduct, has been at pains to give as ludicrous an account as possible of its origin. As I differ widely from Wollaston on this point, both in his theoretical speculations and in the practical inferences he deduces from them, I shall quote the passage at length, and then subjoin a few remarks on it.

" Men please themselves with notions of immortality, and fancy a perpetuity of fame secured to themselves by books and testimonies of historians; but alas! it is a stupid delusion when they imagine themselves *present* and *enjoying* that fame at the reading of their story after their death. And beside, in reality, the man is not known ever the more to posterity, because his name is transmitted to them. *He* doth not live, because his *name* does. When it is said, 'Julius Cæsar subdued Gaul, beat Pompey, and changed the Roman commonwealth into a monarchy,' it is the same thing as to say, 'The conqueror of Pompey was Cæsar'; that is, Cæsar and the conqueror of Pompey are the same thing, and Cæsar is as much known by the one designation as by the other. The amount, then, is only this, that the conqueror of Pompey conquered Pompey, or somebody conquered Pompey; or rather, since Pompey is now as little known as Cæsar, *somebody* conquered *somebody*. Such a poor business is this boasted immortality; and such as has been described is the thing called glory among us! The notion of it may serve to excite them who, having abilities to serve their country in time of real danger or want, or to do some other good, have yet not philosophy enough to do this upon principles of virtue, or to see through the glories of the world (just as we excite children by praising them, and as we see many good inventions and improvements proceed from emulation and vanity); but to discerning men this fame is mere air, and the next remove from nothing, which they despise, if not shun. I think there are two considerations which may justify a desire of *some* glory or honor, and scarce more. When men have performed any *virtuous* actions, or such as sit easy on their memories, it is a reasonable pleasure to have the testimony of the world added to that of their own consciences, that they have done well. And more than that, if the reputation acquired by any qualification or action may produce a man any *real* comfort or advantage (if it be only protection from the insolence and injustice of mankind, or if it enables him, by his authority, to do more good to others), to have this privilege must be a great satisfaction, and what a wise and good man may be allowed, as he has opportunity, to propose to himself. But then he proposes it no further than it may be *useful*, and it can be no further useful than he wants it. So that, upon the whole, glory, praise, and the like, are either mere vanity, or only valuable in proportion to defects and wants." *

It appears from this passage, that Wollaston does not consider the desire of posthumous fame as an ultimate fact in our nature, for he proposes a theory to account for it. "It is," says he, "a stupid delusion, when men imagine themselves *present* and enjoying that fame at the reading of their story after death." Mr. Smith, too, in his *Theory of Moral Sentiments*,

---

* Wollaston's *Religion of Nature Delineated,* Sect. V. § xix. A thought substantially the same with that of Wollaston occurs in Cowley's ode entitled *Life and Fame.*

"Great Cæsar's self a higher place does claim
In the seraphic entity of fame.
He, since that toy, his death,
Doth fill each mouth and breath.
'T is true, the two immortal syllables remain;
But, O ye learned men, explain,
What essence, what existence this,
What substance, what subsistence, what hypostasis
In six poor letters is?
In those alone does the great Cæsar live.
'T is all the conquered world could give."

Notwithstanding the merit of these lines, I should hardly have thought it worth while to quote them, if Dr. Hurd (a critic of no common ingenuity as well as learning) had not shown, by his comment upon them, how completely he had misapprehended the reasoning both of the poet and of the philosopher. He remarks: —

"This lively ridicule on posthumous fame is well enough placed in a poem or declamation; but we are a little surprised to find so grave a writer as Wollaston diverting himself with it. 'In reality,' says he, 'the man is not known ever the more to posterity because his name is transmitted to them. *He* does not live, because his *name* does.' When it is said, 'Julius Cæsar subdued Gaul,' &c., &c., the sophistry is apparent.

seems to think that the desire of a posthumous fame is to be resolvable into an illusion of the imagination. "Men," says he, "have often voluntarily thrown away life to acquire after death a renown which they could no longer enjoy. Their imagination, in the mean time, anticipated that fame which was thereafter to be bestowed upon them. Those applauses which they were never to hear rung in their ears, the thoughts of that admiration whose effects they were never to feel played about their hearts, banished from their breasts the strongest of all natural fears, and transported them to perform actions which seem almost beyond the reach of human nature." * But why have recourse to an illusion of the imagination to account for a principle which the wisest of men find it impossible to extinguish in themselves, or even sensibly to weaken; and none more remarkably than some of those who have employed their ingenuity in attempting to turn it into ridicule? Is it possible that men should imagine themselves *present* and enjoying their fame at the reading of

---

Put Cato in the place of Cæsar, and then see whether that great man do not *live* in his name *substantially*, that is, to good purpose, if the impression which these two *immortal syllables* make on the mind be of use in exciting posterity, or any one man, to the love and imitation of Cato's virtue."—Hurd's Cowley, Vol. I. p. 179

In this remark, Hurd plainly proceeds on the supposition, that Wollaston's *sophistry* is directed against the *utility* of the love of posthumous glory, whereas the only point in dispute relates to the *origin* of this principle, which Wollaston seems to have thought, if it could not be resolved into the rational motive of self-love, must be the illegitimate and contemptible offspring of our own stupidity and folly.

How very different must Cowley's feelings have been when he wrote the metaphysical ode referred to by Hurd, from those which inspired that first burst of juvenile emotion which forms the *exordium* to his Poetical Works!

"What shall I do to be for ever known,
And make the age to come my own?
I shall, like beasts or common people, die,
Unless you write my elegy.

. . . . .

What sound is 't strikes mine ear?
Sure I fame's trumpet hear.
It sounds like the last trumpet, for it can
Raise up the buried man."

* Part III. Chap. ii.

their story after death, without being conscious of this operation of the imagination themselves? Is not this to depart from the plain and obvious appearance of the fact, and to adopt refinements similar to those by which the selfish philosophers explain away all our disinterested affections? We might as well suppose that a man's regard for the welfare of his posterity and friends after his death does not arise from natural affection, but from an illusion of the imagination, leading him to suppose himself still present with them, and a witness of their prosperity.* If we have confessedly various other propensities directed to specific objects as ultimate ends, where is the difficulty of conceiving that a desire, directed to the good opinion of our fellow-creatures (without any reference to the advantages it is to yield us either now or hereafter), may be among the number?

III. *Vindication of this Principle.*] It would not, indeed, (as I have already hinted,) materially affect the argument, although we should suppose, with Wollaston, that the desire of posthumous fame is resolvable into an illusion of the imagination. For, whatever be its origin, it was plainly the intention of nature that all men should be in some measure under its influence; and it is perhaps of little consequence whether we regard it as a principle originally implanted by nature, or suppose that she has laid a foundation for it in other principles which belong universally to the species.

* The two cases seem to be so exactly parallel, that it is somewhat surprising that no attempt should have been made to extend to the latter principle of action the same ridicule which has been so lavishly bestowed on the former. So far, however, from this being the case, I believe it will be *universally* granted, that, where the latter principle fails in producing its natural and ordinary effect on the conduct, there must exist some defect in the rational or moral character, for which no other good qualities can sufficiently atone. "He that careth not for his own house is worse than an infidel." But if this be acknowledged with respect to the interest we take in the concerns of our connections after our own disappearance from the present scene, why judge so harshly of the desire of posthumous fame? Do not the two principles often coöperate in stimulating our active exertions to the very same ends, more especially in those cases (alas! too common) where the inheritance of a respectable name is all that a good man has it in his power to bequeathe to his family?

How very powerfully it operates appears, not only from the heroical sacrifices to which it has led in every age of the world, but from the conduct of the meanest and most worthless of mankind, who, when they are brought to the scaffold in consequence of the clearest and most decisive evidence of their guilt, frequently persevere to the last, with the terrors of futurity full in their view, in the most solemn protestations of their innocence; and *that* merely in the hope of leaving behind them, not a fair, but an equivocal or problematical reputation.

With respect to the other parts of Wollaston's reasoning, that it is only the letters which compose our names that we can transmit to posterity, it is worthy of observation, that, if the argument be good for any thing, it applies equally against the desire of esteem from our contemporaries, excepting in those cases in which we ourselves are personally known by those whose praise we covet, and of whose applause we happen ourselves to be ear-witnesses. And yet, undoubtedly, according to the common judgment of mankind, the love of praise is more peculiarly the mark of a liberal and elevated spirit in cases where the gratification it seeks has nothing to recommend it to those whose ruling passions are interest or the love of flattery.* It is precisely for the same reason that the love of posthumous fame is strongest in the noblest and most exalted characters. If self-love were really the *sole* motive in all our actions, Wollaston's reasoning would prove

---

* That the desire of esteem, if a fantastic principle of action in the one of these cases, is equally so in the other, is remarked by Pope; but, instead of availing himself of this consideration to justify the desire of posthumous renown, he employs it as an argument to expose the nothingness of fame in all cases whatsoever.

"What 's fame? a fancied life in others' breath,
A thing beyond us e'en before our death.
All that we feel of it begins and ends
In the small circle of our foes or friends;
To all beside, as much an empty shade
An Eugene living as a Cæsar dead."

Essay on Man, Epistle IV. 237.

clearly the absurdity of any concern about our mem ory. Such a concern, as Dr. Hutcheson observes, "no *selfish* being, who had the modelling of his own nature, would choose to implant in himself. But, since we have not this power, we must be contented to be thus *outwitted by nature into a public interest against our will.*" *

As to the fact on which Wollaston's argument proceeds, is it not more philosophical to consider it as affording an additional *stimulus* to the instinctive love of posthumous fame, by holding it up to the imagination as the noblest and proudest boast of human ambition, to be able to entail on the casual combination of letters which composes our name the respect of distant ages, and the blessings of generations yet unborn? Nor is it an unworthy object of the most rational benevolence to render these letters a sort of magical spell for kindling the emulation of the wise and good wherever they shall reach the human ear.

Nor is it only in this instance that nature has "thus outwitted us" for her own wise and salutary purposes. By a mode of reasoning analogous to that of Wollaston, it would be easy to turn most, if not all, our active principles into ridicule. But what should we gain by the attempt, but a ludicrous exposition of that moral constitution which it has pleased our Maker to give us, and which, the more we study it, will be found to abound the more with marks of wise and beneficent design?

It is fortunate, in such cases, that, although the reasonings of the metaphysician may puzzle the understanding, they produce very little effect on the conduct. He may tell us, for example, that the admiration of female beauty is absurd, because *beauty*, as well as *color*, is a quality not existing in the object, but in the mind of the spectator; or (which brings the case still nearer to that under our consideration) he may allege that the whole charm of the finest countenance would van-

* *Nature and Conduct of the Passions*, Sect. I. Art. IV.

ish if it were examined with the aid of a microscope. In all such cases, as well as in the instance referred to by Wollaston, we are determined very powerfully by nature; in a way, indeed, that our reason cannot explain, but which we never fail to find subservient to valuable ends. For I am far from thinking that it would be of advantage to mankind if Wollaston's views were generally adopted. That the love of glory has sometimes covered the earth with desolation and bloodshed I am ready to grant; but the actions to which it generally prompts are highly serviceable to the world. Indeed, it is only by such actions that an enviable fame is to be acquired.

A strong conviction of this truth has led Dr. Akenside to express himself in one of his odes with a warmth which passes, perhaps, the bounds of strict propriety, but for which a sufficient apology may be found in the poetical enthusiasm by which it was inspired. The ode is said to have been occasioned by a sermon against the love of glory.

" Come, then, tell me, sage divine,
Is it an offence to own
That our bosoms e'er incline
Towards immortal glory's throne?
For with me nor pomp nor pleasure,
Bourbon's might, Braganza's treasure,
So can fancy's dream rejoice,
So conciliate reason's choice,
As one approving word of her impartial voice.

"If to spurn at noble praise
Be the passport to thy heaven,
Follow thou these gloomy ways;
No such law to me was given:
Nor, I trust, shall I deplore me
Faring like my friends before me,
Nor a holier heaven desire
Than Timoleon's arms acquire,
And Tully's curule chair, and Milton's golden lyre."

Having mentioned the name of Milton, I cannot forbear to add, that *he too* has called the love of fame an *infirmity*, although he has qualified this implied censure by calling it the "*infirmity of a noble mind.*" He has distinctly acknowledged, at the same time, the heroic sacrifices of ease and pleasure to which it has prompted the most distinguished benefactors of the human race.

> "Fame is the spur that the clear spirit doth raise
> (The last infirmity of noble minds)
> To scorn delights and live laborious days."

IV. *Hume's Theory respecting its Origin.*] I must not dismiss this subject without taking some notice of a theory started by Mr. Hume with respect to the origin of the love of praise; a theory which applies to this passion even when it has for its object the praise of our contemporaries. "Of all opinions," he observes, "those which we form in our own favor, however lofty and presuming, are at bottom the frailest, and the most easily shaken by the contradiction and opposition of others. Our great concern in this case makes us soon alarmed, and keeps our passions upon the watch; our consciousness of partiality still makes us dread a mistake; and the very difficulty of judging concerning an object which is never set at a due distance from us, nor seen in a proper point of view, makes us hearken anxiously to the opinion of others who are better qualified to form opinions concerning us. Hence that strong love of fame with which all mankind are possessed. It is in order to fix and confirm their favorable opinion of themselves, *not from any original passion*, that they seek the applause of others." *

I think it cannot be doubted that the circumstance here mentioned by Mr. Hume adds greatly to the pleasure we derive from the possession of esteem; but it sufficiently appears from the facts already stated, particularly from the early period of life at which this principle makes its appearance, that there is a satisfaction arising from the possession of esteem perfectly unconnected with the cause referred to by this author. Mr. Hume has therefore mistaken a concomitant effect for the cause of the phenomenon in question.

---

* *Dissertation on the Passions*, Sect II. § 10.

In remarking, however, this concomitant effect, he must be allowed to have called our attention to a fact of some importance in the philosophy of the human mind, and which ought not to be overlooked in analyzing the compounded sentiment of satisfaction we derive from the good opinion of others. Nor is this the only accessory circumstance that enhances the pleasure resulting from the gratification of the original principle. If in those cases where we are somewhat doubtful of the propriety of our own conduct we are anxious to have in our favor the sanction of public opinion, so, on the other hand, when we are satisfied in our own minds that our conduct has been right, *part* of the pleasure we receive from esteem arises from observing the just views and candid dispositions of others. Nor is it less indisputable, on the contrary supposition, that when, in consequence of calumny and misrepresentation, we fail in obtaining that esteem to which we know ourselves to be entitled, our disappointment at missing our just reward is aggravated, to a wonderful degree, by our sorrow for the injustice and ingratitude of mankind. Still, however, it must be remembered that these are only *accessory* circumstances, and that there is a pleasure resulting from the possession of esteem which is not resolvable into either of them, and which appears to be an ultimate fact in the constitution of our nature.

V. *Incidental Benefits resulting from the Love of Fame.*] From the passage formerly quoted from Wollaston it appears that he apprehended the love of fame to be justifiable only in *two* cases. The one is, when we desire it as a confirmation of the rectitude of our own judgments; the other, when the possession of it can be attended with some real and solid good. But why, I must again repeat, offer any apology for our obeying a natural principle of our constitution, so long as we preserve it under due regulation?

It is not unworthy of remark, that this principle is one of those with which our fellow-creatures are most disposed to sympathize. With what indignation do we hear the slightest reflection cast on the memory of one who was dear to us, and how sacred do we feel the duty of coming forward in his defence! Nor is this sympathy confined to the circle of our acquaintance. It embraces the wise and good of the most remote ages, and prompts us irresistibly to protect their fame from the assaults of envy and detraction. Whatever theory philosophers may adopt as to the origin of this sympathy, its utility in preserving immaculate the reputation of those ornaments of humanity whom mankind look up to as models for imitation is equally indisputable.

I have already said that the desire of esteem is, on the whole, a useful principle of action; for, although there are many cases in which the public opinion is erroneous and corrupted, there are many more in which it is agreeable to reason, and favorable to the interests of virtue and of mankind. The habits, therefore, which this principle of action has a tendency to form are likely, in most instances, to coincide with those which are recommended by a sense of duty. In many men, accordingly, who are very little influenced by higher principles, a regard to the opinion of the world (or, as we commonly express it, a regard to character) produces a conduct honorable to themselves and beneficial to society.

To this observation it may be added, that the habits to which we are trained by the desire of esteem render the acquisition of *virtuous* habits more easy. The desire of esteem operates in children before they have a capacity to distinguish right from wrong; or at least the former principle of action is much more powerful *in their case* than the latter. Hence it furnishes a most useful and effectual engine in the business of education, more particularly by training us early to exertions of self-command and self-denial. It teaches us, for example, to restrain our appetites within those bounds which decency prescribes, and thus forms us to habits of moderation and temperance. And although our conduct cannot be denominated virtuous so long as a regard tc the opinion of others is our only motive, yet the habits we thus acquire in infancy and childhood render it more easy for us to subject our passions to the authority of reason and conscience as we advance to maturity. "In that young man," said Sylla, speaking of Cæsar, "who walks the streets with so little regard to modesty, I foresee many Mariuses." His idea probably was, that on a temper so completely divested of sympathy with the feelings of others society could lay little hold, and that whatever principle of action should happen to gain the ascendant in his mind was likely to sacrifice to its own gratification the restraints both of honor and of duty.

VI. *Adam Smith confounds Desire of Esteem with the Moral Motive.*] These, and some other considerations of the same kind, have struck Mr. Smith so forcibly, that he has been led to resolve our *sense of duty* into a regard to the good opinion, and a desire to obtain the *sympathy*, of our fellow-creatures. I shall afterwards have occasion to examine the principal arguments he alleges in support of his conclusions. At present I shall only remark, that, although his theory may account for the desire which all men, both good and bad, have to *assume the appearance of virtue*, it never can explain the origin of our notions of duty and of moral obligation. One striking proof of this is, that the love of fame can only be completely gratified by the *actual* possession of those qualities for which we wish to be esteemed; and that, when we receive praises which we know we do not deserve, we are conscious of a sort of fraud or imposition on the world.

> "All fame is foreign but of true desert, —
> Plays round the head, but comes not to the heart."

In further confirmation of the same doctrine it may be observed, that, although the desire of esteem is often a useful auxiliary to our sense of duty, and although, in most of our good actions, the two principles are perhaps more or less blended together, yet the merit of virtuous conduct is always enhanced, in the opinion of mankind, when it is discovered in the more private situations of life, where the individual cannot be suspected of any views to the applauses of the world. Even Cicero, in whose mind vanity had at least its due sway, has borne testimony to this truth: — "Mihi quidem laudabiliora videntur omnia, quæ sine venditatione et sine populo teste fiunt: non quo fugiendus sit (omnia enim benefacta in luce se collocari volunt) sed tamen nullum theatrum virtuti conscientiâ majus est."* So

---

* *Tusc. Disp.*, Lib. II. 26. "Besides, to me, indeed, every thing seems the more commendable, the less the people are courted, and the fewer eyes there are to see it. Not that observation is to be avoided, for every generous action loves the public view; still, there is no theatre for virtue like the witness of a good conscience." The same remark is made by Pliny in one of his epistles, Lib. III. Epist. XVI., where it is illustrated by one of the most beautiful anecdotes recorded in the annals of our species. Although no English version can possibly do justice to the conciseness and spirit of Pliny's own language, I shall, for the sake of my unlearned readers, quote the anecdote referred to above, in the admirable translation of Mr. Melmoth.

"I have frequently observed, that, amongst the noble actions and remarkable sayings of distinguished persons in either sex, those which have been most celebrated have not always been the most illustrious; and I am confirmed in this opinion by a conversation I had yesterday with Fannia. This lady is granddaughter to that celebrated Arria who animated her husband to meet death by her own glorious example. She informed me of several particulars relating to Arria, not less heroical than this famous action of hers, though less taken notice of, which, I am persuaded, will raise your admiration as much as they did mine. Her husband, Cæcinna Pætus, and his son, were both at the same time attacked with a dangerous illness, of which the son died. This youth, who had a most beautiful person and amiable behaviour, was not less endeared to his parents by his virtues than by the ties of affection. His mother managed his funeral so privately, that Pætus did not know of his death. Whenever she came to his bed-chamber she pretended her son was better; and, as often as he in quired after his health, would answer that he had rested well, or had eat with an appetite. When she found she could no longer restrain her grief, but her tears were gushing out, she would leave the room, and, having given vent to her passion, return again with dry eyes, as if she had dismissed every sentiment of sorrow at her entrance. The action was no doubt truly noble, when, drawing the dagger, she plunged it in her breast, and then presented it to her husband, with that ever memorable, I had atmost said divine expression, — '*Pætus, it is not painful.*' It must, however, be considered that, when she spoke and acted thus, she had the prospect of immortal glory before her eyes to encourage and support her. But was it not something much greater, without the view of such powerful motives, to hide her tears, to conceal her grief, and cheerfully seem the mother when she was so no more?"

far, therefore, are the desire of esteem and the sense of duty from being radically the same principle of action, that the former is only an *auxiliary* to the latter, and is always understood to diminish the merit of the agent in proportion to the influence it had over his determinations.

An additional proof of this may be derived from the miserable effects produced on the conduct by the desire of fame, when it is the *sole*, or even the *governing*, principle of our actions. In this case, indeed, it seldom fails to disappoint its own purposes, for a lasting fame is scarcely to be acquired without a steady and consistent conduct, and such a conduct can only arise from a conscientious regard to the suggestions of our own breasts. The pleasure, therefore, which a being capable of reflection derives from the possession of fame, so far from being the original motive to worthy actions, presupposes the existence of other and of nobler motives in the mind.

Nor is this all; when a competition happens between the desire of fame and a regard to duty, if we sacrifice the latter to the former we are filled with remorse and self-condemnation, and the applauses of the world afford us but an empty and unsatisfactory recompense; whereas a steady adherence to the right, even although it should accidentally expose us to calumny, never fails to be its own reward. Whether, therefore, we regard our lasting happiness or our lasting fame, the precept of Cicero is equally deserving of our attention.

"Neither make it your study to secure the applauses of the vulgar, nor rest your hopes of happiness on rewards which men can bestow. Let virtue, by her own native attractions, allure you in the paths of honor. What others may say of you is *their* concern, not *yours;* nor is it worth your while to be out of humor for the topics which your conduct may supply to their conversation." — "Neque sermonibus vulgi dederis te, nec in præmiis humanis spem posueris rerum tuarum; suis te oportet illecebris *ipsa virtus* trahat ad verum decus. Quid de te alii loquantur, ipsi videant: sed loquentur tamen." *

---

* *Somn. Scipionis.*

Section IV.

THE DESIRE OF POWER.

I. *Early Manifestations of this Principle.*] The manner in which the *idea of power* is at first introduced into the mind has been long a perplexing subject of speculation to metaphysicians, and has given rise to some of the most subtile disquisitions of the human understanding. But, although it be difficult to explain its origin, the idea itself is familiar to the most illiterate, even at the earliest period of life; and the desire of possessing the corresponding object seems to be one of the strongest principles of human conduct.

In general, it may be observed, that, whenever we are led to consider ourselves as the authors of any effect, we feel a sensible pride or exultation in the consciousness of *power*, and the pleasure is in general proportioned to the greatness of the effect, compared with the smallness of our exertion.

What s commonly called the pleasure of activity is in truth the pleasure of *power*. Mere exercise, which produces no sensible effect, is attended with no enjoyment, or a very slight one. The enjoyment, such as it is, is only corporeal.

The infant, while still on the breast, delights in exerting its little strength on every object it meets with, and is mortified when any accident convinces it of its own imbecility. The pastimes of the boy are, almost without exception, such as suggest to him the idea of his *power*. When he throws a stone, or shoots an arrow, he is pleased with being able to produce an effect at a distance from himself; and, while he measures with his eye the amplitude or range of his missile weapon, contemplates with satisfaction the extent to which his power has reached. It is on a similar principle that he loves to bring his strength into comparison with that of his fellows, and to enjoy the consciousness of superior prowess. Nor need we search in the *malevolent* dispositions of our nature for any other motive to the apparent acts of cruelty which he sometimes exercises over the inferior animals, — the sufferings of the animal, in such cases, either entirely escaping his notice, or being overlooked in that state of pleasurable triumph which the wanton abuse of *power* communicates to a weak and unreflecting judgment. The active sports of the youth captivate his fancy by suggesting similar ideas, — of strength of body, of force of mind, of contempt of hardship and of danger. And accordingly such are the occupations in which Virgil, with a characteristical propriety, employs his young Ascanius.

> "At puer Ascanius mediis in vallibus acri
> Gaudet equo; jamque hos cursu, jam præterit illos;
> Spumantemque dari pecora inter inertia votis
> Optat aprum, aut fulvum descendere monte leonem." *

II. *Increases our Desire of Knowledge in after Life.*] As we advance in years, and as our animal powers lose their activity and vigor, we gradually aim at extending our influence over others by the superiority of fortune and station, or by the still more flattering superiority of intellectual endowment, by the force of our understanding, by the extent of our information, by the arts of persuasion, or the accomplishments of address. What but the idea of power pleases the orator in managing the reins of an assembled multitude, when he silences the reason of others by superior ingenuity, bends to his purposes their desires and passions, and, without the aid of force or the splendor of rank, becomes the arbiter of the fate of nations!

To the same principle we may trace, in part, the pleasure arising from the discovery of general theorems

* *Æneid.*, Lib. IV. 156.

> "While there, exulting, to his utmost speed
> The young Ascanius spurs his fiery steed,
> Outstrips by turns the flying social train,
> And scorns the meaner triumphs of the plain:
> The hopes of glory all his soul inflame;
> Eager he longs to run at nobler game,
> And drench his youthful javelin in the gore
> Of the fierce lion, or the mountain boar.

in the sciences. Every such discovery puts us in possession of innumerable particular truths or particular facts, and gives us a ready command of a great stock of knowledge, of which we could not, with equal ease, avail ourselves before. It increases, in a word, our *intellectual power* in a way very analogous to that in which a machine or engine increases the mechanical power of the human body.

The discoveries we make in natural philosophy have, beside this effect, a tendency to enlarge the sphere of our power over the material universe; first, by enabling us to accommodate our conduct to the established course of physical events; and secondly, by enabling us to call to our aid many natural powers or agents as instruments for the accomplishment of our purposes.

In general, every discovery we make with respect to the laws of nature, either in the material or moral worlds, is an accession of power to the human mind, inasmuch as it lays the foundation of prudent and effectual conduct in circumstances where, without the same means of information, the success of our proceedings must have depended on chance alone. The *desire of power*, therefore, comes, in the progress of reason and experience, to act as an auxiliary to our instinctive *desire of knowledge;* and it is with a view to strengthen and confirm this alliance that Bacon so often repeats his favorite maxim, that *knowledge* and *power* are synonymous or identical terms.

III. *Other Passions resolvable, in part at least, into the Desire of Power.*] The idea of power is, *partly* at least, the foundation of our *attachment to property.* It is not enough for us to have the *use* of an object. We desire to have it completely at our own disposal, without being responsible to any person whatsoever for the purposes to which we may choose to turn it. "There is an unspeakable pleasure," says Addison, "in calling any thing one's own. A freehold, though it be but in ice and snow, will make the owner pleased in the possession and stout in the defence of it."

Avarice is a particular modification of the *desire of power*, arising from the various functions of *money* in a commercial country. Its influence as an active principle is greatly strengthened by habit and association, insomuch that the original desire of power is frequently lost in the acquired propensities to which it gives birth; the possession of *money* becoming, in process of time, an ultimate object of pursuit, and continuing to stimulate the activity of the mind after it has lost a relish for every other species of exertion.*

The *love of liberty* proceeds in part, if not wholly, from the same source; from a desire of being able to do whatever is agreeable to our own inclination. Slavery mortifies us, because it limits our power.

Even the love of tranquillity and retirement has been resolved by Cicero into the desire of power. "Multi autem et sunt et fuerunt, qui eam, quam dico, tranquillitatem expetentes, a negotiis publicis se removerint, ad otiumque perfugerint. . . . . . His idem propositum fuit quod regibus, ut ne quâ re egerent, ne cui parerent, libertate uterentur; cujus proprium est sic vivere ut velis. Quare, cum hoc commune sit potentiæ cupidorum cum iis quos dixi otiosis; alteri se adipisci id posse arbitrantur, si opes magnas habeant, alteri, si contenti sint et suo, et parvo." †

---

* Berkeley in his *Querist* has started the same idea.

"Whether the real end and aim of men be not *power?* and whether he who could have every thing else at his wish or will would value *money?*"

To this query the good Bishop has subjoined another, which one would hardly have expected from a writer so zealously attached to Tory and High-Church principles.

"Whether the public aim in every well-governed state be not, that each member, according to his just pretensions and industry, should have POWER?"

Naturam expellas furcâ, tamen usque recurret.

† *De Off.*, Lib. I. 20, 21. "Now there have been and are many who have withdrawn from public business, and sought in retirement the tranquillity of which I am speaking. These men have proposed to themselves the same end with kings; namely, that they may need nothing, be subject to no one, and enjoy freedom, the leading privilege of which is to live as you please. They, therefore, who aspire after power have this in common with those who court retirement, that the former think they are able to attain the same object by the possession of a vast fortune which the other look for in contentment with their present means, however humble."

The idea of power is also, *in some degree*, the foundation of *the pleasure of virtue.* We love to be at liberty to follow our own inclinations, without being subject to the control of a superior; but even this is not sufficient to our happiness. When we are led by vicious habits, or by the force of passion, to do what reason disapproves, we are sensible of a mortifying subjection to the inferior principles of our nature, and feel our own littleness and weakness. On the other hand, *he that ruleth his spirit* feels himself *greater than he that taketh a city.* "It is pleasant," says Dr. Tillotson, "to be virtuous and good, because *that* is to excel many others. It is pleasant to grow better, because *that* is to excel ourselves. It is pleasant to mortify and subdue our appetites, because *that* is victory. It is pleasant to command our passions, and keep them within the bounds of reason, because this is empire."

From the observations now made, it appears that the desire of power is subservient to important purposes in our constitution, and is one of the principal sources both of our intellectual and moral improvements. An examination of the effects which it produces on society would open views very strikingly illustrative of benevolent intention in the Author of our frame. I shall content myself, however, with remarking, that the general aspect of *the fact* affords a very favorable view of human nature. When we consider how much *more* every man has it in his power to *injure* others than to promote their interests, it must appear manifest that society could not possibly subsist unless the benevolent affections had a very decided predominance over those principles which give rise to competition and enmity. Whoever reflects duly on this consideration will, if I do not deceive myself, be inclined to form conclusions concerning the dispositions of his fellow-creatures very different from the representations of them to be found in the writings of some gloomy and misanthropical moralists.*

* On ambition see Lieber, *Political Ethics*, Book III. Chap. iv. — Ed.

Section V.

EMULATION, OR THE DESIRE OF SUPERIORITY.

I. *Not a Malevolent Affection.*] This principle of action is classed by Dr. Reid with the affections, and is considered by him as a *malevolent affection.** He tells us, however, that he does not mean by this epithet to insinuate that there is any thing *criminal* in emulation, any more than in resentment when excited by an injury; but he thinks that it involves a sentiment of ill-will to our rival, and makes use of the word *malevolent* to express this sentiment, as the language affords no softer epithet to convey the idea.

I own it appears to me tnat emulation, considered as a principle of action, ought to be classed with the *desires*, and not with the *affections.* It is, indeed, frequently accompanied with a *malevolent* affection; but it is the desire of *superiority* which is the *active* principle, and the affection is only a concomitant circumstance.

I do not even think that this malevolent affection is a *necessary* concomitant of the desire of superiority. It is possible, surely, to conceive (although the case may happen but rarely) that emulation may take place between men who are united by the most cordial friendship, and without a single sentiment of ill-will disturbing their harmony.

II. *Distinction between Emulation and Envy.*] When emulation is accompanied with malevolent affection, it assumes the name of *envy.* The distinction between these two principles of action is accurately stated by Dr. Butler. " Emulation is merely the desire of superiority over others, with whom we compare ourselves. To desire the attainment of this superiority by the particular means of others being brought down below our

---

* *Essays on the Active Powers*, Essay III. Part II. Chap. v.

own level is the distinct notion of *envy*. From whence it is easy to see, that the real end which the natural passion, emulation, and which the unlawful one, envy, aims at is exactly the same; and, consequently, that to do mischief is not the end of envy, but merely the means it makes use of to attain its end."* Dr. Reid himself seems to have clearly perceived the distinction, although in other parts of the same section he has lost sight of it again. "He who runs a race," says he, "feels uneasiness at seeing another outstrip him. This is uncorrupted nature, and the work of God within him. But this uneasiness may produce either of two very different effects. It may incite him to make more vigorous exertions, and to strain every nerve to get before his rival. This is fair and honest emulation. This is the effect it is intended to produce. But if he has not fairness and candor of heart, he will look with an evil eye on his competitor, and will endeavour to trip him, or to throw a stumbling-block in his way. This is pure envy, the most malignant passion that can lodge in the human breast, which devours, as its natural food, the fame and the happiness of those who are most deserving of our esteem."†

In quoting these passages, I would not be understood to represent this distinction between emulation

---

* Sermon I., *On Human Nature*.

† Reid, *On the Active Powers*, Essay III. Part II. Chap. v. Dr. Beattie, in his *Elements of Moral Science*, after stating very correctly the speculative distinction between emulation and envy, observes with great truth, that it is extremely difficult to preserve the former wholly unmixed with the latter, and that emulation, though entirely different from envy, is very apt, through the weakness of our nature, to degenerate into it. To this remark he subjoins the following very striking practical reflection. "Let the man," says he, "who thinks he is actuated by generous emulation only, and wishes to know whether there be any thing of envy in the case, examine his own heart, and ask himself whether his friends, on becoming, though in an honorable way, his competitors, have less of his affection than they had before; whether he be gratified by hearing them depreciated; whether he would wish their merit less, that he might the more easily equal or excel them; and whether he would have a more sincere regard for them if the world were to acknowledge him their superior. If his heart answer all or any of these questions in the affirmative, it is time to look out for a cure, for the symptoms of envy are but too apparent." Part I. Chap. ii. § 5.

and envy as a novelty in the science of ethics; for the very same distinction was long ago stated with admirable conciseness and justness by Aristotle; whose *definitions*, (I shall take this opportunity of remarking by the way,) however censurable they may frequently be when they relate to *physical* subjects, are, in most instances, peculiarly happy when they relate to *moral* ideas. "Æmulatio bonum quiddam est, et bonis viris convenit; at invidere improbum est, et hominum improborum; nam æmulans talem efficere se studet, ut ipsa bona quoque nanciscatur: at invidens studet efficere, ut ne alter boni quid habeat." *

Before leaving the subject, I think it of consequence again to repeat, that, notwithstanding the speculative distinction I have been endeavouring to make between emulation and envy, the former disposition is so seldom altogether unmixed with the latter, that men who are conscious of possessing original powers of thinking can scarcely be at too much pains to draw a veil over their claims to originality, if they wish to employ their talents to the best advantage in the service of mankind.

> "Men must be taught as if you taught them not,
> And things unknown proposed as things forgot." †

In the observations which I have hitherto made upon emulation, I have proceeded on the supposition, that the subject of competition is the personal qualities of the individual. These, however, are not the great objects of ambition with the bulk of mankind, nor perhaps do they occasion jealousies and enmities so fatal to our morals and our happiness, as those which are occasioned by the seemingly partial and unjust distribution of the goods of fortune. To see the natural rewards of industry and genius fall to the

---

* Aristot., *Rhetor.*, Lib. II. Cap. xi. The whole chapter is excellent. I have adopted in the text the Latin version of Buhle. "Emulation is a good thing, and belongs to good men; envy is bad, and belongs to bad men. What a man is emulous of he strives to attain, that he may really possess the desired object; the envious are satisfied if nobody has it."

† Pope's *Essay on Criticism*, l. 574.

share of the weak and the profligate can scarcely fail to excite a regret in the best regulated tempers; and to those who are disposed (as every man perhaps is in some degree) to overrate their own pretensions, and to undervalue those of their neighbours, this regret is a source of discontent and misery, which no measure of external prosperity is sufficient to remove. The feeling, when it does not lead to any act of injustice or dishonor, is so intimately connected with our sense of merit and demerit, that many allowances for it will be made by those who reflect candidly on the common infirmities of humanity; and much indulgence is due from the prosperous to their less fortunate rivals. So much, indeed, is this indulgence recommended to us by all the best principles of our nature, and so painful is the reflection that we are even the innocent cause of disquiet to others, that it may be doubted whether the constraint and embarrassment produced by great and sudden accessions of prosperity be not more than sufficient to counterbalance any solid addition they are likely to bring to our own happiness.*

---

* The following admirable passage is from Smith's *Theory of the Moral Sentiments*, Part I. Sect II. Chap. v.:—"The man who, by some sudden revolution of fortune, is lifted up all at once into a condition of life greatly above what he had formerly lived in, may be assured that the congratulations of his best friends are not all of them perfectly sincere. An *upstart*, though of the greatest merit, is generally disagreeable, and a sentiment of envy commonly prevents us from heartily sympathizing with his joy. If he has any judgment, he is sensible of this, and, instead of appearing to be elated with his good fortune, he endeavours, as much as he can, to smother his joy, and keep down that elevation of mind with which his new circumstances naturally inspire him. He affects the same plainness of dress, and the same modesty of behaviour, which became him in his former station. He redoubles his attentions to his old friends, and endeavours more than ever to be humble, assiduous, and complaisant. And this is the behaviour which in his situation we most approve of; because we expect, it seems, that he should have more sympathy with our envy and aversion to his happiness than we have to his happiness. It is seldom that, with all this, he succeeds. *We* suspect the sincerity of his humility, and *he* grows weary of this constraint. In a little time, therefore, he generally leaves all his old friends behind him, some of the meanest of them excepted, who may, perhaps, condescend to become his dependents: nor does he always acquire any new ones; the pride of his new connections is as much affronted at finding him their equal, as that of his old ones had been by his becoming their superior; and it requires the most obstinate and persevering modesty to atone for this mortification to either. He generally grows weary

III. *The Desire to excel a universal Passion.*] Among the lower animals we see many symptoms of emulation, but in *them* its effects are perfectly insignificant when compared with those it produces on human conduct. Their emulation is chiefly confined to swiftness,* strength, or favor with their females. I think, too, among *dogs* we may perceive something like jealousy or rivalship in courting the favor of man. In our own race emulation operates in an infinite variety of directions, and is one of the principal sources of human improvement.

Human life has been often likened to a race, and the parallel holds, not only in the general resemblance, but in many of the minuter circumstances. When the horses first start from the barrier, how easy and sportive are their sallies,—sometimes one taking the lead, sometimes another! If they happen to run abreast, their contiguity seems only the effect of the social instinct. In proportion, however, as they advance in their career, the spirit of emulation becomes gradually more apparent, till at length, as they draw near to the goal, every sinew and every nerve is strained to the utmost, and it is well if the competition closes without some suspicion of jostling and foul play on the part of the winner.

---

too soon, and is provoked, by the sullen and suspicious pride of the one, and by the saucy contempt of the other, to treat the first with neglect and the second with petulance, till at last he grows habitually insolent, and forfeits the esteem of all. If the chief part of human happiness arises from the consciousness of being beloved, as I believe it does, these sudden changes of fortune seldom contribute much to happiness. He is happiest who advances more gradually to greatness, whom the public destines to every step of his preferment long before he arrives at it, in whom, upon that account, when it comes, it can excite no extravagant joy, and with regard to whom it cannot reasonably create either any jealousy in those he overtakes, or any envy in those he leaves behind."

In Bacon's *Essays* there is an article on *Envy*, abounding with original, and, in the main, just reflections. Even those which are somewhat questionable may be useful in suggesting materials of thought to others.

* One of the most remarkable instances of this that I have read of is the emulation of the race-horses at Rome when run without riders. This emulation is even said to be inspirited by the concourse of spectators.—See *Observations made in a Tour to Italy*, by the celebrated M. de la Condamine.

5*

How exact and melancholy a picture of the race of ambition, of the insensible and almost inevitable effect of political rivalship in extinguishing early friendships, and of the increasing eagerness with which men continue to grasp at the palm of victory till the fatal moment arrives when it is to drop from their hands for ever!

Artificial Desires.] As we have artificial *appetites*, so we have also artificial *desires*. Whatever conduces to the attainment of any object of natural desire is itself desired on account of its subservience to this end, and frequently comes in process of time to be regarded as valuable in itself, independent of this subservience. It is thus (as was formerly observed) that wealth becomes with many an ultimate object of desire, although it is undoubtedly valued at first merely on account of its subservience to the attainment of other objects. In like manner we are led to desire dress, equipage, retinue, furniture, on account of the estimation in which they are supposed to be held by the public. Dr. Hutcheson calls such desires *secondary* desires, and accounts for their origin in the way I have now mentioned. "Since we are capable," says he, "of reflection, memory, observation, and reasoning about the distant tendencies of objects and actions, and not confined to things present, there must arise, in consequence of our original desires, *secondary* desires of every thing imagined to be useful to gratify any of the primary desires, and that with strength proportioned to the several original desires, and the imagined usefulness or necessity of the advantageous object." — "Thus," he continues, "as soon as we come to apprehend the use of wealth or power to gratify any of our original desires, we must also desire them. Hence arises the universality of the desires of *wealth and power*, since they are the means of gratifying all other desires."* The only

* *Nature and Conduct of the Passions*, Sect. I. Art. II.

thing exceptionable in the foregoing passage is, that the author classes the desire of power with that of wealth; whereas I apprehend it to be clear, according to Hutcheson's own definition, that the former is a primary desire, and the latter a secondary one. Avarice, indeed, (as I have already remarked,) is but a particular modification of the desire of power generated by the conventional value which attaches to money in the progress of society, in consequence of which it becomes the immediate and the habitual object of pursuit in all the various departments of professional industry.

The author, also, of the Preliminary Dissertation prefixed to King's *Origin of Evil* attempts to explain, by means of the association of ideas, the origin, not only of avarice, but of the desire of knowledge and of the desire of fame, both of which I have endeavoured to show, in the preceding pages, are justly entitled to rank with the primary and most simple elements of our active constitution. That they, as well as all the other original principles of our nature, are very powerfully influenced by association and habit, is a point about which there can be no dispute; and hence arises the plausibility of those theories which would represent them as wholly factitious.*

* Dr. Hartley's once celebrated work, entitled *Observations on Man*, in which he has pushed the theory of association to so extravagant a length, and which, not many years ago, found so many enthusiastic admirers in England, seems to have owed its existence to the dissertation here referred to.

"The work here offered to the public," he tells us himself in his preface, "consists of papers written at different times, but taking their rise from the following occasion.

"About eighteen years ago I was informed that the Rev. Mr. Gay, then living, asserted the possibility of deducing all our intellectual pleasures and pains from association. This put me upon considering the power of association. Mr. Gay published his sentiments on this matter, about the same time, in a *Dissertation on the Fundamental Principle of Virtue*, prefixed to Mr. Archdeacon Law's translation of Archbishop King's *Origin of Evil*."

[Mr. Stewart speaks with too much confidence of the waning influence of the "once celebrated work" of Hartley. Since he wrote this note, one of the ablest defences of the Hartleian view has appeared in the *Analysis of the Human Mind*, by James Mill.

Most writers, holding with Stewart to a plurality of elementary desires, differ from him in making the desire of property and the desire of self-preservation to be of this number. See Upham's *Mental Philosophy*, Vol.

CHAPTER III.

OF OUR AFFECTIONS.

Section I.

GENERAL OBSERVATIONS.

I. *What Principles included under this Head.*] Under this title are comprehended all those active principles whose direct and ultimate object is the communication either of enjoyment or of suffering to any of our fellow-creatures. According to this definition, which has been adopted by some eminent writers, and among others by Dr. Reid, resentment, revenge, hatred, belong to the class of our affections, as well as gratitude or pity. Hence a distinction of the affections into *benevolent* and *malevolent*. I shall afterwards mention some considerations which lead me to think that the distinction requires some limitations in the statement.

Our *benevolent* affections are various, and it would not perhaps be easy to enumerate them completely.

II. Part. I. Chap iv., and Whewell's *Elements of Morality*, Book I. Chap. ii. On the desire of property, consult Lieber's *Political Ethics*, Book II. Chap. ii., and *Illustrations of the Passions*, Vol. I. Chap. v. Also the phrenologists, and particularly Gall.

On the other hand, the author of the article *Désir* in the *Dictionnaire des Sciences Philosophiques* reduces them to three, curiosity, ambition, and sympathy. This writer observes: — "The mind always knows, more or less, that which it desires; reason illuminates what sensibility pursues. Malebranche gave the saying of the poet, *Ignoti nulla cupido*, under a philosophical form of expression, when he defined *desire* to be 'the idea of a good which a man possesses not, but hopes to possess.' Desire is distinguished by this from the blind tendency which urges every being towards its end, whether it knows it or not. It is a spontaneous movement of nature transformed by intelligence, and constitutes, therefore, a phenomenon which cannot take place except among intelligent beings. A stone has its *affinities;* a brute has its *instincts;* man alone has his *desires*, because he alone has received the gift of thought."

Consult, also, on the subjects treated of in this chapter and the following, Gibon, *Cours de Philosophie*, Tom. I. p. 226 *et seq.;* Bautain, *Philosophie Morale* Tom. I. Chap. iv.; Dr. Whewell's edition of Butler's *Three Sermons on Human Nature*: with a Preface and Notes.]

The *parental* and the *filial affections*, the *affections of kindred*, *love*, *friendship*, *patriotism*, *universal benevolence*, *gratitude*, *pity to the distressed*, are some of the most important. Besides these there are peculiar benevolent affections excited by those moral qualities in other men which render them either amiable or respectable, or objects of admiration.

In the foregoing enumeration, it is not to be understood that all the benevolent affections particularly specified are stated as original principles, or ultimate facts in our constitution. On the contrary, there can be little doubt that several of them may be analyzed into the same general principle, differently modified according to the circumstances in which it operates. This, however, (notwithstanding the stress which has been sometimes laid upon it,) is chiefly a question of arrangement. Whether we suppose these principles to be all ultimate facts, or some of them to be resolvable into other facts more general, they are equally to be regarded as *constituent parts of human nature*, and, upon either supposition, we have equal reason to admire the wisdom with which that nature is adapted to the situation in which it is placed. The laws which regulate the acquired perceptions of sight are surely as much a part of our frame as those which regulate any of our original perceptions; and although they require for their development a certain degree of experience and observation in the individual, the uniformity of the result shows that there is nothing arbitrary or accidental in their origin.

The question, indeed, concerning the origin of our different affections, leads to some curious disquisitions, but is of very subordinate importance to those inquiries which relate to their nature and laws and uses. In many philosophical systems, however, it seems to have been considered as the most interesting subject of discussion connected with this part of the human constitution.

II. *Two Circumstances in which all the Benevolent*

Affections agree.] Before we proceed to consider any of our benevolent affections in detail, I shall make a few observations on two circumstances in which they all agree. In the first place, they are all accompanied with an agreeable feeling; and, secondly, they imply a desire of happiness or of good to their respective objects.*

1. That the exercise of all our kind affections is accompanied with an agreeable feeling will not be questioned. Next to a good conscience it constitutes the principal part of human happiness. With what satisfaction do we submit to fatigue and danger in the service of those we love, and how many cares do even the most selfish voluntarily bring on themselves by their attachment to others! So much, indeed, of our happiness is derived from this source, that those authors whose object is to furnish *amusement* to the mind avail themselves of these affections as one of the chief vehicles of pleasure. Hence the principal charm of *tragedy*, and of every other species of pathetic composition. How far it is of use to separate in this manner "the *luxury of pity*" from the opportunities of active exertion may perhaps be doubted. My own opinion on this question I have stated at some length in the *Philosophy of the Human Mind.*†

Without entering, however, in this place into the argument I have there endeavoured to support, I shall only remark at present, that the pleasures of kind affection are by no means confined to the virtuous part of our species. They mingle also with our criminal indulgences, and often mislead the young and thoughtless by the charms they impart to vice and folly. It is, indeed, from this very quarter that the chief dangers to morals are to be apprehended in early life; and it is a melancholy consideration to add, that these dangers are not a little increased by the amiable and attractive qualities by which nature often distinguishes those unfortunate

* See Reid *On the Active Powers*, Essay III. Part II. Chap. iii.

† Part I. Chap. vii. Sect. v.

men who would seem, on a superficial view, to be her peculiar favorites.

Nor is it only when the kind affections meet with circumstances favorable to their operation that the exercise of them is a source of enjoyment. Contrary to the analogy of most, if not all, of our other active principles, there is a degree of pleasure mixed with the pain even in those cases in which they are disappointed in the attainment of their object. Nay, in such cases it often happens that the pleasure predominates so far over the pain as to produce a mixed emotion, on which a wounded heart loves to dwell. When death, for example, has deprived us of the society of a friend, we derive some consolation for our loss from the recollection of his virtues, which awakens in our mind all those kind affections which the sight of him used to inspire; and in such a situation the indulgence of these affections is preferred, not only to every lighter amusement, but to every other social pleasure. *Heu quanto minus est cum reliquis versari quam tui meminisse!* The final cause of the agreeable emotion connected with the exercise of benevolence in all its various modes was evidently to induce us to cultivate with peculiar care a class of our active principles so immediately subservient to the happiness of society.*

2. All our benevolent affections imply a desire of happiness to their respective objects. Indeed, it is from this circumstance they derive their name.

III. *Our Benevolent Affections not resolvable into Self-love.*] The philosophers who have endeavoured to resolve our appetites and desires into self-love have given a similar account of our benevolent affections.

* See Lucan's picturesque and pathetic description of the behaviour of Cornelia, when she retired to the hold of the ship, to indulge her grief in solitude and darkness, after the murder of Pompey.

"Caput ferali obduxit amictu,
Decrevitque pati tenebras, puppisque cavernis
Delituit; *sævumque arctè complexa dolorem*
Perfruitur lacrymis, et amat pro conjuge luctum," &c., &c.
Pharsalia, Lib. IX. 109.

It is evident that this amounts to a denial of their existence as a separate class of active principles; for when a thing is desired, not on its own account, but as instrumental to the attainment of something else, it is not the desire of the *means*, but that of the *end*, which is in this case the principle of action.

In the course of my observations on the different affections, when I come to consider them particularly, I shall endeavour to show that this account of their origin is extremely wide of the truth. In the mean time, it may be worth while to remark, in general, how strongly it is opposed by the analogy of the other active powers already examined. We have found that the preservation of the individual and the continuation of the species are not intrusted to self-love and reason alone, but that we are endowed with various appetites, which, without any reflection on our part, impel us to their respective objects. We have also found, with respect to the acquisition of knowledge, (on which the perfection of the individual and the improvement of the species essentially depend,) that it is not intrusted solely to self-love and benevolence, but that we are prompted to it by the implanted principle of curiosity. It further appeared, that, in addition to our sense of duty, another incentive to worthy conduct is provided in the desire of esteem, which is not only one of our most powerful principles of action, but continues to operate in full force to the last moment of our being. Now, as men were plainly intended to live in society, and as the social union could not subsist without a mutual interchange of good offices, would it not be reasonable to expect, agreeably to the analogy of our nature, that so important an end would not be intrusted solely to the slow deductions of reason, or to the metaphysical refinements of self-love, but that some provision would be made for it, in a particular class of active principles, which might operate, like our appetites and desires, independently of our reflection? To say this of parental affection or of pity is saying nothing more in their favor than what was affirmed of hunger and thirst, that they prompt us to particular objects without any reference to our own enjoyment.

I have not offered these objections to the selfish theory with any view of exalting our natural affections into *virtues;* for, in so far as they arise from original constitution, they confer no merit whatever on the individual, any more than his appetites or desires. At the same time, (as Dr. Reid has observed,) there is a manifest gradation in the sentiments of respect with which we regard these different constituents of character.

Our *desires*, (it was formerly observed,) although not virtuous in themselves, are manly and respectable, and plainly of greater dignity than our animal appetites. In like manner it may be remarked that our benevolent affections, although not *meritorious*, are highly *amiable*. A want of attention to the essential difference between the ideas expressed by these two words has given rise to much confusion in different systems of moral philosophy, more particularly in the systems of Shaftesbury and Hutcheson.

As it would lead me into too minute a detail to consider our different benevolent affections separately, I shall confine myself to a few detached remarks on some of the most important.

The first place is undoubtedly due to what we commonly call *natural affection*, including under the term the affections of parents and children, and those of other near relations.

Section II.

OF THE AFFECTIONS OF KINDRED.

I. *The Parental Affection common to Animals and Men.*] The parental affection is common to us with most of the brutes, although with them it is variously modified according to their respective natures, and according as the care of the parent is more or less necessary for the preservation and nurture of the young.

Cicero remarks that this is no more than might have been expected from that beneficent providence everywhere conspicuous in nature. "Hæc inter se congruere non possunt, ut natura et procreari vellet et diligi procreatos non curaret." * — "Commune animantium omnium est conjunctionis appetitus, et cura quædam eorum quæ procreata sunt." †

When I ascribe parental affection to our own species, I do not mean to insinuate that there is any foundation for those stories which poets have feigned, of particular discriminating feelings which have enabled parents and children, after a long absence, or when they have never met before, mutually to recognize each other. The parental affection takes its rise from a *knowledge* of the relation in which the parties stand, and it is very powerfully confirmed by *habit.* All that I assert is, that it results naturally from that knowledge, and from the habits superinduced by the relation which the parties bear to each other; in which sense it may be justly said, (to adopt a beautiful and philosophical expression of Dr. Ferguson's,) that "natural affection springs up in the soul as the milk springs in the breast of the mother." ‡ Accordingly, it operates, in a great measure, independently of reflection and of a sense of duty. Reason, indeed, might satisfy a man that his children are particularly intrusted to his care, and that it is his duty to rear and educate them, — as reason might have induced him to eat and drink without the appetites of hunger and thirst; but reason cannot create an affection any more than an appetite. And, considering how little the conduct of mankind is in general influenced by a sense of duty, there are good grounds for thinking, that, were not reason in this case aided by a very powerful implanted principle, a very

---

* *De Finibus*, III. 19. "Nature would have been inconsistent if she had intended men to procreate, without providing at the same time that they should love their offspring."

† *De Offic.*, I. 4. "The passion which unites the sexes, and a certain affection for their young, are common to all animals."

‡ *Principles of Moral and Political Science*, Vol. I. p. 31.

small proportion out of the whole number of children brought into the world would arrive at maturity.

How much this affection depends upon *habit* appears from this, that, when the care of a child is devolved upon one who is not its parent, the parental affection is, in a great measure, transferred along with it. This (as Dr. Reid observes) is plainly "the work of nature," and is an additional provision made by her for the continuation and preservation of the species.

The parental affection, as we have hitherto considered it, is common to both sexes; but it cannot, I think, be denied, that it is in the heart of the *mother* that it exists in the most perfect strength and beauty. Indeed, I do not think that those have gone too far who have pronounced "*the heart of a good mother to be the masterpiece of nature's works.*" * There is no form, certainly, in which humanity appears so lovely, or presents so fair a copy of the Divine image after which it was made.

II. *Affections of Kindred the Foundation of our Social and Political Virtues.*] Nor are these affections of parent and child useful solely for the preservation of the race. They form the heart in infancy for its more extensive social duties, and gradually prepare it for those affections which constitute the character of the good citizen; not to mention that, in every period of life, it is our private attachments which furnish the most powerful of all incentives to patriotism and heroic virtue. Nothing, therefore, could be more unphilosophical than the opinion of Plato, that the indulgence of the domestic charities unfitted men for the discharge of their political duties; an opinion which he carried so far as to propose, that, as soon as a child was born, it should be separated from its parents, and educated ever after at the expense of the public. It has been often observed that persons brought up in foundling hospitals have seldom turned out well in the world; and al-

* See Marmontel, *Leçons sur la Morale*, p. 132, et seq.

though I doubt not that various splendid exceptions to this proposition may be quoted, I am inclined to think, that, if the special accidents connected with these exceptions were fully known, they would be found, instead of invalidating, to confirm the general rule. One thing, at least, is obvious, that, in that best of all educations which nature has provided for us in the ordinary circumstances of our condition, it formed an important part of her plan to soften the heart betimes amid the scenes of domestic life; and, accordingly, it is under the shelter of these scenes that all the social virtues may be seen to shoot up with the greatest vigor and luxuriancy. Even the sterner qualities of fortitude and bravery, so far from being inconsistent with a warm and susceptible heart, are almost its inseparable attendants, insomuch that we always *expect* to find them united. How true, in this respect, to all the best feelings of our nature, is the beautiful story recorded of Epaminondas, that, after the battle of Leuctra, he thanked the gods that his parents still survived to enjoy his fame!

It is remarked by Dr. Beattie that Homer and Virgil, the most accurate of all observers, and the most faithful of all painters of human character, always unite the domestic attachments with the more splendid virtues of their heroes. The scene between Hector and Andromache, and the interview between Ulysses and his father after an absence of twenty years, are pronounced by the same excellent critic to be the finest passages in the Iliad and Odyssey. He observes further, that, in the portrait of Achilles, his love to his parents forms one of the most prominent and distinguishing features, and that "this single circumstance throws an amiable softness into the most terrific human personage that was ever described in poetry." How powerful a charm the Æneid derives from the same source it is needless to mention, as it is the chief groundwork of the interest inspired by the whole texture of the fable. In no instance is it more affecting than in the address of Euryalus to Nisus before they set out on their desperate expedition by night; and I believe few will deny that the pious concern which he expresses for his aged parent in that moment of approaching peril accords perfectly with the gallantry of his spirit, and interests us more than any thing else in his fortunes.

"Contra quem talia fatur
Euryalus: me nulla dies tam fortibus ausis
Dissimilem arguerit; tantùm fortuna secunda,
Haud adversa cadat: sed te super omnia dona,
Unum oro: genetrix Priami de gente vetustâ
Est mihi, quam miseram tenuit non Ilia tellus,
Mecum excedentem, non mœnia regis Acestæ:
Hanc ego nunc ignaram hujus quodcumque pericli est
Inque salutatam linquo nox, et tua testis
Dextera, quòd nequeam lacrymas perferre parentis.
At tu, oro, solare inopem, et succurre relictæ.
Hanc sine me spem ferre tui; audentior ibo
In casus omnes. Percussa mente dederunt
Dardanidæ lacrymas: ante omnes pulcher Iulus,
Atque animum patriæ strinxit pietatis imago." *

I shall conclude this section in the words of Lord Bacon: — "Unmarried men are best friends, best mas-

* *Æneid.*, Lib. IX. 280.

"'All of my life,' replies the youth, 'shall aim,
Like this one hour, at everlasting fame.
Though fortune only our attempt can bless,
Yet still my courage shall deserve success.
But one reward I ask, before I go, —
The greatest I can ask, or you bestow.
My mother, — tender, pious, fond, and good,
Sprung, like thy own, from Priam's royal blood, —
Such was her love, she left her native Troy,
And fair Trinacria, for her darling boy;
And such is mine, that I must keep unknown
From her the danger of so dear a son:
To spare her anguish, lo! I quit the place
Without one parting kiss, one last embrace!
By night, and that respected hand, I swear,
Her melting tears are more than I can bear!
For her, good prince, your pity I implore;
Support her, childless, and relieve her, poor;
O, let her, let her find, (when I am gone,)
In you, a friend, a guardian, and a son!
With that dear hope, emboldened shall I go,
Brave every danger, and defy the foe.'
"Charmed with his virtue all the Trojan peers,
But, more than all, Ascanius melts in tears,
To see the sorrows of a duteous son
And filial love, a love so like his own."

ters, best servants, but not always best subjects, for they are light to run away, and almost all fugitives are of that condition. For soldiers, I find that the generals in their hortatives commonly put men in mind of their wives and children; and I think the despising of marriage among the Turks maketh the vulgar soldier the more base. Certainly, wife and children are a kind of discipline of humanity; and single men, though they be many times more charitable, because their means are less exhaust, yet, on the other side, they are more cruel and hard-hearted, because their tenderness is not so often called upon." *

Section III.

OF FRIENDSHIP.

I. *Pleasures of Friendship.*] Friendship, like all the other benevolent affections, includes two things, an agreeable feeling, and a desire of happiness to its object.

Besides, however, the agreeable feeling common to all the exertions of benevolence, there are some peculiar to friendship. I before took notice of the pleasure we derive from communicating our thoughts and our feelings to others; but this communication prudence and propriety restrain us from making to strangers; and hence the satisfaction we enjoy in the society of one to whom we can communicate every circumstance in our situation, and can trust every secret of our heart.

There is also a wonderful pleasure arising from the sympathy of our fellow-creatures with our joys and with our sorrows, nay, even with our tastes and our humors; but, in the ordinary commerce of the world, we are often disappointed in our expectations of this enjoyment, — a disappointment which is peculiarly incident to men of genius and sensibility superior to the common, who frequently feel themselves "alone in the midst of a crowd," and reduced to the necessity of ac-

* Bacon's *Essays. Of Marriage and Single Life.*

commodating their own temper, and their own feelings, to a standard borrowed from those whom they cannot help thinking undeserving of such a sacrifice.

It is only in the society of a friend that this sympathy is at all times to be found; and the pleasing reflection, that we have it in our power to command so exquisite a gratification, constitutes, perhaps, the principal charm of this connection. "What we call affection," says Mr. Smith, "is nothing but an habitual sympathy." I will not go quite so far as to adopt this proposition in all its latitude, but I perfectly agree with this profound and amiable moralist in thinking, that the experience of this sympathy is the chief foundation of friendship, and one of the principal sources of the pleasures which it yields. Nor is it at all inconsistent with this observation to remark, that, where the groundwork of two characters in point of moral worth is the same, there is sometimes a contrast in the secondary qualities, of taste, of intellectual accomplishments, and even of animal spirits, which, instead of presenting obstacles to friendship, has a tendency to bind more strongly the knot of mutual attachment between the parties. Two very interesting and memorable examples of this may be found in Cuvier's account of the friendship between Buffon and Daubenton,* and in Playfair's account of the friendship between Black and Hutton.†

I do not mean here to enter into the consideration of the various topics relating to friendship which are commonly discussed by writers on that subject. *Most* of these, indeed I may say *all* of them, are beautifully illustrated by Cicero in the treatise *De Amicitia*, in which he has presented us with a summary of all that was most valuable on this article of ethics in the writings of preceding philosophers; and so comprehensive is the view of it which he has taken, that the modern authors who have treated of it have done little more than to repeat his observations.

---

* *Recueil des Eloges Historiques.* M. Daubenton.

† *Biographical Account of the late Dr. James Hutton.* *Works*, Vol. IV.

II. *Can Friendship subsist between more than Two Persons?*] One question concerning friendship much agitated in the ancient schools was, whether this connection can subsist in its full perfection between more than two persons; — and I believe it was the common decision of antiquity that it *cannot*. For my own part, I can see no foundation for this limitation, and I own it seems to me to have been suggested more by the dreams of romance, or the fables of ancient mythology, than by good sense or an accurate knowledge of mankind. The passion of love between the sexes is indeed of an exclusive nature; and the jealousy of the one party is roused the moment a suspicion arises that the attachment of the other is in any degree divided; (and, by the way, this circumstance, which I think is strongly characteristical of that connection, deserves to be added to the various other considerations which show that *monogamy* has a foundation in human nature.) But the feelings of friendship are of a perfectly different sort. If our friend is a man of discernment, we rejoice at every new acquisition he makes, as it affords us an opportunity of adding to our own list of worthy and amiable individuals, and we eagerly concur with him in promoting the interests of those who are dear to his heart. When we ourselves, on the other hand, have made a new discovery of worth and genius, how do we long to impart the same satisfaction to a friend, and to be instrumental in bringing together the various respectable and worthy men whom the accidents of life have thrown in our way!

I acknowledge, at the same time, that the number of our attached and confidential friends cannot be great, otherwise our attention would be too much distracted by the multiplicity of its objects, and the views for which this affection of the mind was probably implanted would be frustrated by its engaging us in exertions beyond the extent of our limited abilities; and, accordingly, nature has made a provision for preventing this inconvenience, by rendering friendship the fruit only of long and intimate acquaintance. It is strengthened by the acquaintance which the parties have, not only with each other's personal qualities, but with their histories, situations, and connections from infancy, and every particular of this sort which falls under their mutual knowledge forms to the fancy an additional relation by which they are united. Men who have a very wide circle of friends, without much discrimination or preference, are justly suspected of being incapable of genuine friendship, and indeed are generally men of cold and selfish characters, who are influenced chiefly by a cool and systematical regard to their own comfort, and who value the social intercourse of life only as it is subservient to their accommodation and amusement.

III. *How we are affected by the Distresses of our Friends.*] That the affection of friendship includes a desire of happiness to the beloved object, it is unnecessary to observe. There is, however, a certain limitation of the remark, which occurs among the *Maxims* of La Rochefoucauld, and which has been often repeated since by misanthropical moralists, "That, in the distresses of our best friends, there is always something which does not displease us." It may be proper to consider in what sense this is to be understood, and how far it has a foundation in truth. It is expressed in somewhat equivocal terms; and, I suspect, owes much of its plausibility to this very circumstance.

From the triumphant air with which the maxim in question has been generally quoted by the calumniators of human nature, it has evidently been supposed by them to imply that the misfortunes of our best friends give us more pleasure than pain.* But this La Rochefoucauld has not said, nor, indeed, could a proposition so obviously false and extravagant have escaped the pen

* It was plainly in this sense that Swift understood it when he prefixed it as a motto to the verses on his own death.

"As Rochefoucauld his maxims drew
From nature, I believe them true.
If what he says be not a joke,
We mortals are strange kind of folk."

of so acute a writer. What La Rochefoucauld has said amounts only to this, that, in the distresses of our best friends, the pain we feel is not altogether unmixed; — a proposition unquestionably true, wherever we have an opportunity of soothing their sorrows by the consolations of sympathy, or of evincing, by more substantial services, the sincerity and strength of our attachment. But the pleasure we experience in such cases, so far from indicating any thing selfish or malevolent in the heart, originates in principles of a directly opposite description, and will be always most pure and exquisite in the most disinterested and generous characters. The maxim, indeed, when thus interpreted, is not less true when applied to our own distresses than to those of our friends. In the bitterest cup that may fall to the lot of either, there are always mingled some cordial drops, — in the misfortunes of others, the consolation of *administering* relief, — in our own, that of *receiving* it from the sympathy of those we love.

Whether La Rochefoucauld, in the satirical humor which dictated the greater part of his maxims, did not wish, in the present instance, to convey by his words a little more than *meets the ear*, I do not presume to determine.

Section IV.

OF PATRIOTISM.

I. *Provision made for a Division of Mankind into distinct Communities.*] Notwithstanding the principles of union implanted by nature in the human breast, it was plainly *not* her intention that society should always go on increasing in numbers. A foundation is laid for a division of mankind into distinct communities, in those natural divisions on the surface of the globe that are formed by chains of mountains, impassable rivers, and the oceans which separate the larger continents; and the same end is further answered by those principles of enmity which, in the earlier stages of society, never fail to estrange neighbouring tribes from each other and which continue to operate with a very powerful effect even in periods of knowledge and refinement.

I shall not at present attempt to analyze particularly the origin of these principles of disunion among mankind. I shall only remark, that they do not imply any original malignity in the human heart; on the contrary, they seem to have their source in the social nature of man, — in those affections which attach him to the tribe he belongs to, and to the country which gave him birth. This remark has been so excellently illustrated by Lord Shaftesbury and by Dr. Ferguson, that it would be quite superfluous to enlarge upon it here. Contenting myself, therefore, with a reference to their works,* I shall proceed to some other views of the subject, where the field of observation does not seem to be so completely exhausted.

---

* See Shaftesbury's *Essay on the Freedom of Wit and Humor*, Part III. Sect. 2, and Ferguson's *Essay on the History of Civil Society*, Part I. Sect. 4. The former observes: — "It is strange to imagine that *war*, which of all things appears the most savage, should be the passion of the most heroic spirits. But it is in war that the knot of fellowship is closest drawn. It is in war that mutual succor is most given, mutual danger run, and common affection most exerted and employed. For heroism and philanthropy are almost one and the same. Yet, by a small misguidance of the affection, a lover of mankind becomes a ravager; a hero and deliverer becomes an oppressor and destroyer." "Vast empires are in many respects unnatural; but particularly in this, that, be they ever so well constituted, the affairs of many must in such governments turn upon a very few; and the relation be less sensible, and in a manner lost, between the magistrate and people, in a body so unwieldy in its limbs, and whose members lie so remote from one another, and distant from the head. It is in such bodies as these that strong factions are aptest to engender. The associating spirits, for want of exercise, form new movements, and seek a narrower sphere of activity, when they want action in a greater. Thus we have wheels within wheels. And in some national constitutions, (notwithstanding the absurdity in politics,) we have one empire within another. Nothing is so delightful as to incorporate." In the same strain Ferguson: — "The titles of *fellow-citizen* and *countryman*, unopposed by those of *alien* and *foreigner*, to which they refer, would fall into disuse, and lose their meaning. We love individuals on account of personal qualities; but we love our country, as it is a party in the divisions of mankind; and our zeal for its interests is a predilection in behalf of the side we maintain." "'My father,' said a Spanish peasant, 'would rise from his grave, if he could foresee a war with France' What interest had he, or the bones of his father, in the quarrels of princes?"

The foundation which nature has laid for a diversity of languages, of customs, of manners, and of institutions among mankind, adds force to the principles of division and repulsion already mentioned. These circumstances derive their effect, indeed, from the *ignorance* of men, which is apt to mistake a diversity of arbitrary signs and arbitrary ceremonies for a diversity of opinions and of moral sentiments; and accordingly, as society advances, and reason improves, the effect becomes gradually less and less sensible. As the effect, however, is universal among rude nations, and as it is the unavoidable result of the general laws of our constitution when placed in certain circumstances, we may consider it as a part of the plan of Providence with respect to our species; and we may presume that here, as in other instances, that plan tends ultimately to some wise and beneficent purpose, though by means which appear to us, at first view, to have a very unfavorable aspect. What these purposes are it is impossible for our limited faculties to trace completely; but even *we*, narrow and partial as our views at present are, may perceive *some* salutary consequences resulting from these apparent disorders of the moral world. I shall only mention the tendency which a constant state of hostility and alarm must have among barbarous tribes to bind and consolidate in each of them apart the political union; and, by strengthening the hands of government, to prepare the way for the progress of society. We may add, the exercise which it gives to many of our most important moral principles, and the powerful stimulus it applies to our intellectual capacities. The discipline is indeed rough, but it is perhaps the only one of which the mind of man, in a certain state of his progress, is susceptible.

II. *Tendency of Civilization to diminish the Causes of Disunion.*] If these observations are well founded, may we not presume to offer a conjecture, that, as this final cause ceases to exist in proportion as government advances to maturity, and as the moral causes of hostility among nations (arising from diversity of language and of manners) cease to operate upon men of enlightened and liberal minds, the tendency of civilized society is to diminish the dissensions among different communities, and to unite the human race in the bonds of amity? The just views of political economy which Mr. Smith and some other authors have lately opened, and which demonstrate the absurdity of commercial jealousies, all contribute to encourage the same pleasing prospect; but, alas! it is a prospect which the vices and prejudices of men allow us to indulge only in those moments of enthusiasm when our benevolent wishes for mankind, and our confidence in the wisdom and goodness of Providence, transport us from the calamities and atrocities of our own times, to anticipate the triumphs of reason and humanity in a more fortunate age.

In my *Philosophy of the Human Mind* I have remarked, that "there are many prejudices which are found to prevail universally among our species in certain periods of society, and which seem to be essentially necessary for maintaining its order in ages when men are unable to comprehend the purposes for which governments are instituted. As society advances, these prejudices gradually lose their influence on the higher classes, and would probably soon disappear altogether, if it were not supposed to be expedient to prolong their existence as a source of authority over the multitude. In an age, however, of universal and unrestrained discussion, it is impossible that they can long maintain their empire; nor ought we to regret their decline, if the important ends to which they have been subservient in the past experience of mankind are found to be accomplished by the growing light of philosophy. On this supposition, a history of human prejudices, in so far as they have supplied the place of more enlarged political views, may, at some future period, furnish to the philosopher a subject of speculation no less pleasing and instructive than that beneficent wisdom of nature which guides the operations of the lower animals, and which, even in our own species, takes upon itself the care of the individual in the infancy of human reason." *

The remarks which have been now made on the sources of disunion and hostility among mankind in the earlier periods of society, and on the final causes to which this constitution of things is subservient, afford one remarkable illustration of the conjecture which I have hazarded in the foregoing passage.

Before proceeding to consider the affection of patriotism, it was necessary to turn our attention for a moment to the principles of disunion in our species, as the idea of patriotism proceeds on the supposition, that mankind are divided into distinct communities, with separate, if not with rival and hostile interests.

III. *Exciting Causes of Patriotism.*] The exciting causes of patriotism (abstracted from all considerations of reason and duty) are many. We are formed with so strong a disposition to associate with and to love our own species, that the imagination lays hold with eagerness of every circumstance, how slight soever, that can form a bond of union; a common language, a common religion, common laws, even a common appellation, — not to mention the prudential considerations of common enemies and a common interest. The feelings which these uniting circumstances inspire attach us even to the *territory* which our fellow-citizens inhabit, by the same law of *association* that endears to us the spot where a friend was born, or the scene where we have enjoyed any social pleasure; and thus the imagination forms to itself a complex idea of *countrymen* and *country*, which impresses every susceptible heart with irresistible force. In perusing the history of either, how remote soever the period it describes may be, we feel an interest which no other narrative inspires. We sympathize with the fortunes of those who trod the same ground that we now tread, and we appropriate to ourselves a share of the glory they acquired by their

* Part I. Chap. iv. Sect. viii.

bravery and virtue. "When the late Mr. Anson (Lord Anson's brother) was on his travels in the East, he hired a vessel to visit the Isle of Tenedos. His pilot, an old Greek, as they were sailing along, said with some satisfaction, ''T was there our fleet lay.' Mr. Anson demanded, '*What fleet?*' '*What fleet!*' replied the old man, a little piqued at the question, 'why, our Grecian fleet at the siege of Troy.'" This anecdote, (which I borrow from the *Philological Inquiries* of Mr. Harris,*) naturally excites a smile; but it is, at the same time, so congenial to feelings inseparable from our constitution, that its effect seems to me to border on the pathetic, and I presume there are few who have read it without some emotion.

It is not a little remarkable, with respect to this natural attachment to the scenes of our infancy and youth, that it is commonly strongest among the inhabitants of barren and mountainous countries. This would appear to indicate that it is produced less by the recollection of agreeable physical impressions than of *moral* pleasures, — pleasures which probably derive an additional zest from the absence of those interesting or amusing objects which dissipate the attention by inviting the thoughts abroad. Where nature has been sparing in her external bounty, men become the more dependent for their happiness on internal enjoyment; it is thus that the storms and gloom of winter give a higher relish to the pleasures of society. Perhaps, too, the thin and scattered population of such countries may contribute something to the romantic enthusiasm of the domestic and private attachments, as it is certain that the opposite extreme of a crowded and busy population seldom fails to extinguish all the more ardent social affections. Among the inhabitants of Europe this attachment to home is said to be the most remarkable in the Swiss and the Laplanders, who, when removed to a distance from their native scenes, are subject to a particular species of despondency, to which medical writers

* Part III. Chap. v.

have given the name of *nostalgia*. It is thus described by Haller, who was himself a native of Switzerland, and who, in some of his poetical pieces, composed during the period of his academical studies in Holland, has sufficiently shown that his own heart was not proof against its influence.

"*Nostalgia* genus est mœroris subditis reipublicæ meæ familiaris, etiam civibus, a desiderio nati suorum. Is sensim consumit ægros et destruit, nonnunquam in rigorem et maniam abit, alias in febres lentas. Eum spes sanat. Etiam animalia consuetâ societate privata, nonnunquam depereunt, et ex pullis amissis etiam lutræ maris Kamtschadalensis. Sic ex amore frustrato lenta et insanabilis consumptio sequitur, quod Angli *cor ruptum* vocant." *

We are informed by another medical writer, (Sauvages,) that he has known this disorder in the son of a common beggar, who could scarcely be said to have any home but the streets and public roads.†

"Thus every good his native wilds impart
Imprints the patriot passion on his heart.
And even the ills that round his mansion rise
Enhance the bliss his scanty fund supplies.
Dear is that shed to which his soul conforms,
And dear that hill that lifts him to the storms.
And as a child, when scaring sounds molest,
Clings close and closer to its mother's breast,
So the loud tempest and the whirlwind's roar
But bind him to his native mountains more." ‡

The sources of patriotism hitherto mentioned arise chiefly from the *imagination* and from the *association of ideas*, and have little or no connection with our rational and moral powers. They presuppose, indeed, sensibility, social attachment, and force of mind, but they do not

* *Elem. Physiol.*, Lib. XVII. Sect. 2, § 5. "*Nostalgia* is a malady common among my countrymen, originating in a longing for home. It gradually consumes and wears out the patient, sometimes going off in chills and mania, sometimes in a slow fever. Hope cures it. Even animals, when deprived of their accustomed companions, will sometimes die; as is the case with the sea-otter of Kamtschatka when bereft of her young. So, likewise, a lingering and incurable consumption follows disappointed love, which the English call a *broken heart*."

† *Nosologia Methodica.*

‡ Goldsmith's *Traveller*.

necessarily imply *reflection* or a *sense of duty*. They are the natural result of our constitution when placed in certain circumstances; and hence, though not coeval with our birth, nor after their appearance unsusceptible of analysis, the affection they produce, in so far as it arises from *them* without the coöperation of any other motive, may be considered as a *blind impulse*, analogous in its operation to those desires and appetites which have been already mentioned. This affection may be called, for the sake of distinction, *instinctive patriotism*.

IV. *Patriotism in Small and in Large Countries.*] The circumstances which have been enumerated as the sources of instinctive patriotism operate with peculiar force in small communities, where the extent of the territory and the body of the people, falling under the habitual observation of every citizen, present more definite objects to the imagination, and affect the heart more deeply, than what is only conceived from description. *Here*, too, the individual feels his importance as an active member of the state, and the consciousness of what he is able to do for its prosperity contributes powerfully to promote his patriotic exertions.

In an extensive and populous country, the instinctive affection of patriotism is apt to grow languid among the mass of the people, and therefore it becomes the more necessary to impress on their minds those considerations of reason and duty which recommend public spirit as one of the principal branches of morality. What these considerations are, I shall afterwards endeavour to point out in treating of the duties we owe to our fellow-creatures. At present I shall only remark, that, as *instinctive* patriotism decays, so *rational* patriotism acquires force, in proportion to the extent of territory and to the multitude of fellow-citizens it embraces; in other words, in proportion to the magnitude of that sum of happiness which it aspires to secure and to augment.

Such considerations, however, can have weight only with men whose sense of duty is strong; and as, unfortunately, this is not the case with a great proportion of mankind, it is of the utmost consequence, in every state of society, to cherish as much as possible the instinctive affection of patriotism, and to counteract those causes that tend to extinguish it. For this purpose, nothing is more likely to be effectual than to diffuse a general taste for historical and geographical reading. A peasant who has never extended his thoughts beyond his own province, and who sees every thing flourishing and happy around him, is apt to consider the enjoyments he possesses as inseparable from the human race, and no more connected with any particular system of laws than the advantages he derives from the immediate bounty of nature. It is the study of history and geography alone that can remove this prejudice, by showing us, on the one hand, the narrow limits within which the political happiness of our species has hitherto been confined, and, on the other, the singular combination of accidental circumstances to which we are indebted for the blessings we enjoy. This effect of history, indeed, tends rather to cherish *rational* than *instinctive* patriotism; but it operates also wonderfully on the latter affection, by leading us to contrast our own country and countrymen with other lands and other nations, and thereby presenting a more definite and interesting object to the imagination and to the heart. When, from the transactions of past ages and of foreign lands, we return to what is near and familiar, we are affected somewhat in the same manner as if we met with a fellow-citizen in a distant country. Absence from home never fails to endear it to a mind possessed of any sensibility. The extent of our country, too, seems to diminish to our intellectual eye in proportion as the object recedes from us, and we feel a sensible relation to what we before regarded with complete indifference. The natives of the same country in Scotland feel towards each other a partial predilection when they meet in the metropolis of Great Britain; and the circumstance of being born in this island forms a tie of friendship between individuals in the other quarters of the globe. The study of history operates somewhat in the same manner, though not perhaps in the same degree. By transporting us in imagination over the surface of this planet, and by assembling before our view the myriads who have occupied it before us, it serves to define to our thoughts more distinctly the particular community to which we belong, and strengthens the bond of relationship that unites us to all its members.

I shall only add further on this subject, that, when the extent and population of a country are so *very* great as to give it a decided preëminence among neighbouring nations, it has a tendency to produce (partly by interesting the vanity, and partly by dazzling the imagination) an attachment to *national glory*, which operates both on the vulgar and on men of better education in a way extremely analogous to the instinctive patriotism felt by the member of a small community. A remarkable instance of this occurred in the national character of the French prior to the late revolution; nor does it seem to have altered in this respect since that event, if we may judge from the indignation with which the idea of a confederate republic has always been received. A feeling of the same kind may be traced in various expressions employed by Livy in the preface to his *Roman History*. "Utcunque erit, juvabit tamen rerum gestarum memoriæ principis terrarum populi, pro virili parte, et ipsum consuluisse; et si in tanta scriptorum turbâ mea fama in obscuro sit, nobilitate ac magnitudine eorum qui nomini officient meo me consoler. Res est præterea et immensi operis, ut quæ supra septingentesimum annum repetatur, et quæ ab exiguis profecta initiis eo creverit, ut jam magnitudine laboret sua: et legentium plerisque haud dubito, quin primæ origines proximaque originibus, minus præbitura voluptatis sint, festinantibus ad hæc nova, quibus jampridem prævalentis populi vires se ipsæ conficiunt." *

---

* "However that may be, I shall at all events derive no small satisfaction from the reflection that my best endeavours have been exerted in transmitting to posterity the achievements of the greatest people in the world; and if, amidst such a multitude of writers, my name should not emerge

The very danger which such an empire was exposed to from its enormous magnitude, and from the seeds of destruction which it carried in its bosom, seems to heighten the patriotic affection of the historian, by awakening an anxious solicitude for its impending fate. The contrast between this feeling of national pride, and a melancholy anticipation of those calamities to which national greatness leads, gives the principal charm to this exquisite composition.

Section V.

OF PITY TO THE DISTRESSED.

I. *Office and important Uses of Compassion.*] As the unfortunate chiefly stand in need of our assistance, so there is provided in every breast a most powerful advocate in their favor; an advocate, to whose solicitations it is impossible even for the most obdurate to turn always a deaf ear. The appropriation of the word *humanity* to this part of our constitution affords sufficient evidence of the common sentiments of mankind upon the subject.

"Mollissima corda
Humano generi dare se natura fatetur,
Quæ lacrymas dedit. Hæc nostri pars optima sensûs.
. . . . . . Separat hoc nos
A grege mutorum." *

---

from obscurity, I shall console myself by considering the distinguished reputation and eminent merit of those who stand in my way in the pursuit of fame. It may be further observed, that such a subject must require a work of immense extent, as our researches must be carried back through a space of more than seven hundred years; that the state has, from very small beginnings, gradually increased to such a magnitude that it is now distressed by its own bulk; and, besides, that there is every reason to apprehend that the generality of readers will receive but little pleasure from the accounts of its first origin, or of the times immediately succeeding, but will be impatient to arrive at these modern times, in which the powers of this overgrown state have been long employed in working their own destruction."

* Juv., *Sat.* XV. 131, 142.

"Nature, who gave us tears, by that alone
Proclaims she made the feeling heart our own;
And 't is our noblest sense. . . . . .
. . . . . This marks our birth;
Our great distinction from the beasts of earth."

The general principle of benevolence, or of good-will to our fellow-creatures, (of which I shall treat afterwards, when I come to consider our moral duties,) as it disposes us to promote the happiness of others, so it restrains us from doing them evil, and prompts us to relieve their distresses. The office of compassion or pity is more limited. It impels us to relieve distress; it serves as a check on resentment and selfishness, and the other principles which lead us to injure the interests of others; but it does not prompt us to the communication of positive happiness. Its object is to *relieve*, and sometimes to *prevent*, suffering; but not to augment the enjoyment of those who are already easy and comfortable. We are disposed to do this by the general spirit of benevolence, but not by the particular affection of pity.

The final cause of this constitution of our nature is very ingeniously and happily pointed out by Dr. Butler in his second sermon *On Compassion*. This profound philosopher observes, that, "supposing men to be capable of happiness and of misery in degrees equally intense, yet they are liable to the latter during longer periods of time than they are susceptible of the former. We frequently see men suffering the agonies of pain for days, weeks, and months together, without any intermission, except the short suspensions of sleep, — a stretch of misery to which no state of high enjoyment can approach in point of duration. Such, too, is our constitution, and that of the world around us, that the sources of our sufferings are placed much more within the power of other men than the sources of our pleasures, so that there is no individual (however incapable he may be to add to the happiness of his fellow-creatures) who has it not in his power to do them great and extensive mischief. To prevent the abuse of this power when we are under the influence of any of the angry passions, by means of a particular affection tending to check the excess of resentment, was, therefore, of more consequence to the comfort of human life than it would have been to superadd to the general principle of good-will a particular affection prompting to the communication of positive enjoyment. The power we have over the misery of our fellow-creatures being a more important trust than our power of promoting the happiness of those already comfortable, the former stood more in need of a *guard* to check its excesses than the latter of a *stimulus* to animate its exertions. But, further, as it is more in our power to *communicate* misery than happiness, so it is more in our power to *relieve* misery than to superadd enjoyment. Hence an additional reason for implanting in our constitution the affection of compassion, while there is none analogous to it urging us by an instinctive impulse to acts of general benevolence."

The final causes of compassion, then, are to prevent and to relieve misery, — to *prevent* misery by checking the violence of our own angry passions, and to *relieve* misery by calling our attention, and engaging our good offices, to every object of distress within our reach. The latter is the more common and the more important of its offices, at least in the present state of society. And it is this which I have chiefly in view in the following observations.

I have said that compassion calls or arrests our attention to the distressed objects within our reach. When we are immersed in the business of the world, or intoxicated with its pleasures, we are apt to overlook, and sometimes to withdraw from, scenes of misery. It is the office of compassion to plead the cause of the wretched, or rather to solicit us to take their case under our consideration; for so strong is the sense which all men have of the duty of beneficence, that, if they could only be brought to exercise their powers of reflection on the facts before them, they could scarcely ever fail to relieve distress, when, in consistency with other obligations, it was in their power to do so. One striking proof of this is, that the active zeal of humanity is (*cæteris paribus*) strongest in those men whose warm imaginations present to them lively pictures of the sufferings of others; and that there is scarcely any man, however callous and selfish, whose beneficence may not be called forth by a skilful and eloquent description of any scene of misery. General considerations with regard to our social duties will often have little weight; but if the attention can only be fixed to facts, nature, in most instances, accomplishes the rest. Hence the importance in our constitution of the affection of compassion, which, amidst the tumult of business or of pleasure, stops us suddenly in our career, and reminds us that we have social duties to fulfil; calls upon us to examine the claims of the helpless, and aggravates our guilt if we disregard its admonition.

II. *An Instinctive, and not, in itself, a Moral Principle.*] Compassion, according to the view now given of it, is an *instinctive impulse* prompting to a particular object, analogous in many respects to the animal appetites already considered. It is, indeed, one of the most amiable, and one of the most important parts of our constitution; but it is *not* an object of *moral* approbation. Our duty lies in the proper regulation of it, — in considering with attention the facts it recommends to our notice, and in acting with respect to them as reason and conscience prescribe. It is hardly necessary for me to add, that there are cases in which these inform us that we *ought not* to follow the impulse of compassion, and in which it is no less meritorious in us to resist its solicitations than to deny ourselves the unlawful gratification of a sensual appetite; and even in those instances in which our duty calls us to obey its impulse, our merit does not arise from the affection we feel, but from doing what our conscience approves of as *right*, on a deliberate consideration of the action we are to perform, when examined in all its bearings and consequences.

Notwithstanding, however, the unquestionable truth of this theoretical conclusion, it is nevertheless certain, that a strong and habitual tendency to indulge this affection affords no slight presumption in favor of the worth and benevolence of a character. Whoever reflects, on the one hand, upon its general coincidence with what a sense of duty prescribes, and, upon the other, on the nature of those circumstances by which its indulgence is checked and discouraged among men of the world, will, I apprehend, readily assent to the truth of this observation. The poet, perhaps, went a little too far when he stated, as a general and unqualified maxim, Ἀγαθοὶ ἀριδάκρυες ἄνδρες; * but, upon the whole, I am inclined to think that this maxim, with all the exceptions which may contradict it, will be found much nearer to the fact than they who have been trained in the schools of fashionable *persiflage* will be disposed to acknowledge.

III. *The Affection of Pity not a Modification of Self-love.*] The philosophers who attempt to resolve the whole of human conduct into self-love have adopted various theories to explain the affection of pity. Without stopping to examine these, I shall confine myself to a simple statement of the fact, which statement will at once show how far all of these are erroneous, and will point out the oversight in which they have originated. Whoever reflects carefully on the effect produced on his own mind by objects which excite his pity must be sensible that it is a compounded one; and therefore, unless we are at pains to analyze it carefully, we may be apt to mistake some one of the ingredients for the whole combination.

---

* "Good men are prone to shed tears." — "The poets," says Mr. Wollaston, "who of all writers undertake to imitate nature most, oft introduce even their heroes weeping. (See how Homer represents Ulysses, *Od.*, E 151 *et seq.*) The tears of men are in truth very different from the cries and ejulations of children. They are *silent streams*, and flow from other causes, commonly some tender, or perhaps philosophical reflection. It is easy to see how hard hearts and dry eyes come to be fashionable. But for all that, it is certain the *glandulæ lacrymales* are not made for nothing." *Religion of Nature Delineated*, Sect. VI. § xvii.

It is also remarked by Descartes, that the tears of children and of old men (in which both are apt to indulge) flow from different sources. "Senes sæpe lacrymantur ex amore et gaudio. . . . . . Infantes raro ex lætitia lacrymantur, sæpius ex tristitia, etiam quam amor non comitatur." (*De Passionibus*, Secunda Pars, Art. cxxxiii.) The important facts here described have seldom been remarked; and the statement of them does honor to Descartes, as an attentive and accurate observer of human nature in the beginning and towards the close of its history.

On the sight of distress we are distinctly conscious, I think, of three things: — 1st. A painful emotion in consequence of the distress we see. 2d. A selfish desire to remove the cause of this uneasiness. 3d. A disposition to relieve the distress from a *benevolent* and disinterested concern about the sufferer. If we had not this last disposition, and if it were not stronger than the former, the sight of a distressed object would invariably prompt us to fly from it, as we frequently see those men do in whom the second ingredient prevails over the third. In ordinary cases, the impulse of pity attaches us to the cause of our sufferings; and we cling to it, even although we are conscious that we can afford no relief but the consolation of sympathy; — a demonstrative proof that one at least of the ingredients of pity (and in most men the prevailing ingredient) is purely disinterested in its nature and origin.*

* There is a passage in Hazlitt's *Essays on the Principles of Human Action*, 2d ed., pp. 131 *et seq.*, which exposes a common fallacy on this subject. "It is absurd to say, that, in compassionating the distress of others, we are only affected by our own pain and uneasiness, since this very pain arises from our compassion. It is putting the effect before the cause. Before I can be affected by my own pain, I must be put in pain. If I am affected by, or feel pain and sorrow at, an idea existing in my mind, which idea is neither pain itself nor an idea of my own pain, in what sense can this be called the *love of myself?* Again, I am equally at a loss to conceive how, if the pain which this idea gives me does not impel me to get rid of it as it gives *me* pain, or as it actually affects myself as a distinct, momentary impression, but as it is connected with other ideas, that is, is supposed to affect *another*, — how, I say, this can be considered as the effect of self-love. The object, effort, or struggle of the mind is not to remove the idea or immediate feeling of pain from the [sympathizing] individual, or to put a stop to that feeling as it affects his temporary interest, but to produce a disconnection (whatever it may cost him) between certain ideas of other things existing in his mind, namely, the idea of pain and the idea of another person. Self, mere physical self, is entirely forgotten, both practically and consciously.

"'O, but,' it will be said, 'I cannot help feeling pain when I see another in actual pain, or get rid of the idea by any other means than by relieving the person, and knowing that it exists no longer.' But will this prove that my love of others is regulated by my love of myself, or that my self-love is subservient to my love of others? What hinders me from immediately removing the painful idea from my mind but that sympathy with others which stands in the way of it? That this independent attachment to the good of others is a *natural, unavoidable* feeling of the human mind is what I do not wish to deny. It is also, if you will, a mechanical feeling; but then it is neither a physical nor a selfish mechanism. I see

Although, however, this observation seems to me decisive against the theory in question, in whatever form it may be proposed, I cannot omit this opportunity of examining a new modification of the same hypothesis, which occurs in Mr. Smith's *Theory of Moral Sentiments.* The view of the subject which he has taken has the merit of entire originality, and, like all his other speculations and opinions, derives a strong recommendation from the splendid abilities and exemplary worth of the author. I hope, therefore, that the critical strictures upon it which I am now to offer will not be considered as a useless or unreasonable interruption of the discussions in which we are at present engaged.

Before entering on this argument, I shall just mention another hypothesis concerning the origin of compassion, which seems to me to approach more nearly to that of Mr Smith than any thing else I have met with in the works of his predecessors. I allude to the account of pity given by Hobbes, who defines it to be "the imagination or fiction of *future* calamity to *our-*

---

colors, hear sounds, feel heat and cold, and believe that two and two make four, by a certain mechanism, or from the necessary structure of the human mind; but it does not follow that all this has any thing to do with self-love. One half of the process, namely, the connecting the sense of pain with the idea of it, is evidently contrary to self-love; nor do I see any more reason for ascribing to that principle the uneasiness, *or active impulse which follows*, since my own good is neither thought of in it, nor follows from it except indirectly, slowly, and conditionally. The mechanical tendency to my own ease or gratification is so far from being the real spring o: natural motive of compassion, that it is constantly overruled and defeated by it.

"Lastly, should any desperate metaphysician persist in affirming that my love of others is still the love of myself, because the impression exciting my sympathy must exist in my mind and so be a part of myself, I should answer that this is using words without affixing any distinct meaning to them. The love or affection excited by any general idea existing in my mind can no more be said to be the love of myself, than the idea of another person is the idea of myself because it is I who perceive it. This method of reasoning, however, will not go a great way to prove the doctrine of an abstract principle of self-interest, for by the same rule it would follow that I *hate myself* in hating any other person."

From the preceding extract it will be seen that Hazlitt does not concede so much as Stewart to self-love. — Ed.

selves proceeding from the sense of *another* man's calamity."* In what respect this theory *coincides* with Mr. Smith's will appear from the remarks I am about to make. In the mean time, I shall only observe how completely the futility of Hobbes's definition is exposed by a single remark of Butler, that, if it were just, it would follow that the most fearful temper would be the most compassionate.† We may add, too, that our pity is more strongly excited by the distresses of an infant than by those of the aged, although the former are such as we cannot possibly be exposed to suffer a *second time*, and the *latter* such as we must expect to endure sooner or later, if the period of life should be prolonged to that term which the weakness of most individuals disposes them to wish for.

IV. *Adam Smith's Theory of Pity.*] The leading principles of Mr. Smith's theory, in as far as it applies to *pity* or *compassion*, are comprehended in the three following propositions:—

1st. That it is from our own experience alone we can form any idea of the sufferings of another person on any particular occasion.

2d. That the only manner in which we can form this idea is by supposing ourselves in the same circumstances with him, and then conceiving how we should be affected if we were so situated.

3d. That the uneasiness which we feel in consequence of the sufferings of another arises from our conceiving those sufferings to be our own.

The *first* of these propositions is unquestionable. Our notions of pain and of suffering are undoubtedly derived, *in the first instance*, from our own experience.

The *second* proposition is perhaps expressed with too great a degree of latitude. That, in order to under-

---

* *Human Nature*, Chap ix. § 10.

† See an excellent note on *Sermon* V. It contains an important hint about *sympathy*, which Mr. Smith has prosecuted with great ingenuity.

stand completely the sufferings of our neighbours in any particular instance, it is necessary for us to have been once placed in circumstances somewhat similar to his, I believe to be true, and there can be no doubt that it is frequently useful to us to direct our attention to the distresses of others, by conceiving their situation to be ours; but it does not appear to me that this process of the mind takes place in every case in which we are affected by the sight of misery. When we are once satisfied that a particular situation is a natural source of misery to the person placed in it, the bare perception of the situation is sufficient to excite an unpleasant emotion in the spectator, without any reference whatever to himself. This is easily explicable on the common doctrine of *the association of ideas.*

Nor is this all. The looks, the gestures, the tones of distress, speak in a moment from heart to heart, and affect us with an anguish more exquisitely piercing than any we are able to produce by all the various expedients we can employ to assist the imagination in conceiving the situation of the sufferer.

But, not to insist on these considerations, and granting the second proposition in all its extent, the third proposition is by no means a necessary consequence of it; for even in those cases in which we endeavour to awaken our compassion for the sufferings of our neighbour by conceiving ourselves placed in his situation, our compassion is not founded on a belief that the sufferings are *ours.* So long as we conceive ourselves in distress, we feel a certain degree of uneasiness; but this is not the uneasiness of compassion. In order to excite this, we must apply to our neighbour the result of what we have experienced in ourselves; or, in other words, having formed an idea of what he suffers by bringing his case home to ourselves, we must carry our attention back to *him* before he becomes the object of our pity. Nor is there any thing mysterious or wonderful in this process of the mind. That we are so formed as to expect that the operation of the same cause, in similar circumstances, will be attended with the same result, might be shown from a thousand instances. It is thus, that, having tried a physical experiment on certain substances, I take for granted that the result of a similar experiment on similar substances will be the same. It is thus that I conclude, with the most perfect confidence, that a wound given to my body in a particular organ would be instantly fatal; although it is worthy of remark, that in this case I have no direct evidence from experience that the internal structure of my body is similar to those of the bodies which anatomists have hitherto examined. Now, I apprehend, it is in the same manner, that, having once experienced the pain produced by an instrument of torture applied to myself, I take for granted that the effect will be the same when it is applied to another. In consequence of this application, the sentiment of compassion arises in my mind, during the continuance of which my attention is completely engrossed, not about myself, but about the real sufferer

And, indeed, if the case were otherwise, compassion would be ultimately resolvable into a selfish principle, and those men would be most ready to feel the distresses of others who are most impatient of their own. A remark similar to this, as I have already observed, is made by Dr. Butler, with respect to a theory of Hobbes, who defines pity to be the fiction of future calamity to ourselves from the sight of the present calamity of another. "Were this the case," says Butler, "the most fearful tempers would be the most compassionate." According to Mr. Smith, pity arises from the fiction, not of *future*, but of *present*, calamity to ourselves. The two theories approach very nearly to each other, and the same answer is applicable to both.*

* So far, indeed, is it from being true that those who are most impatient under their personal distresses are the most prone to commiserate the sorrows of others, that I apprehend the reverse of this supposition will be found agreeable to universal experience. The most unfeeling characters I have ever known have been men, not only tremblingly alive to the slightest evil which affected themselves, but whose whole attention seemed manifestly to be engrossed with their own comforts and luxuries. On the other hand, the nearest approaches I have happened to witness to stoical

In further proof that the distress produced by the sufferings of others arises from a conception that these distresses are our own, Mr. Smith mentions a variety of facts which he thinks establish his doctrine with demonstrative evidence. "When we see a stroke aimed and just ready to fall upon the leg or arm of another person, we naturally shrink and draw back our own leg, or our own arm, and when it does fall we feel it in some measure, and are hurt by it as well as the sufferer. The mob, when they are gazing at a dancer on the slack rope, naturally writhe and twist and balance their own bodies as they see him do, and as they feel that they must themselves do, if in his situation." In general, he observes, that, "as to be in pain or distress of any kind excites the most excessive sorrow, so to conceive or to imagine that we are in it excites some degree of the same emotion, in proportion to the vivacity or dulness of the conception." *

The facts here appealed to by Mr. Smith are indeed extremely curious, and I do not pretend to explain them. They are not, however, singular facts in our constitution, but belong to that class of phenomena which medical writers refer to what they call the *principle of imitation.*† Of this kind are the contagious effects of hysterics, of yawning, of laughter, of crying, &c. In these last cases Mr. Smith would suppose, if he were to apply the same reasoning he uses in analogous instances, that the effect arises from our conceiving ludicrous or sorrowful ideas similar to those by which these emotions are produced. But the primary

patience and fortitude under severe suffering have been invariably accompanied with a peculiarly strong disposition to social tenderness and sympathy. Gray alludes to this contrast in his *Ode on a Distant Prospect of Eton College:* —

"To each his sufferings; all are men
Condemned alike to groan;
The feeling, for another's pain,
The unfeeling, for his own."

* *Theory of Moral Sentiments*, Part I. Sect. I. Chap i.

† In my *Philosophy of the Human Mind*, Vol. III., I have distinguished this law of our nature by the more precise and unequivocal title of the Principle of *Sympathetic* Imitation.

effect seems to be produced on the body, and the secondary effect on the mind; somewhat in the same manner in which we can excite a sensible degree of the passion of anger in our own breast by imitating the looks and gestures which are expressive of rage. It does not appear to me that this bodily contagion of the expression of passion has any immediate connection with our fellow-feeling with distress. If it had, those would be most liable to it who felt the most deeply for the sorrows of others, — a conclusion which is certainly not agreeable to fact. During the madness of Belvidera, those who are the most powerfully affected by the representation are not the nervous ladies who catch from the actress something similar to a hysteric paroxysm; but they who, retaining their own reason, reflect on the train of misfortunes which have unhinged her mind, and who weep for her madness, not so much as a misfortune in itself, as an indication of that conflict of passions by which it was produced. The effect in the former case depends on a peculiar irritability and mobility of the bodily frame altogether unconnected with any of the moral sympathies or sensibilities of our nature.

Section VI.

OF RESENTMENT, AND THE VARIOUS OTHER ANGRY AFFECTIONS GRAFTED UPON IT, COMMONLY CONSIDERED BY ETHICAL WRITERS AS MALEVOLENT AFFECTIONS.

I. *Enumeration of the Malevolent Affections originating in Resentment.*] The names which are given to these affections in common discourse are various, *Hatred*, *Jealousy*, *Envy*, *Revenge*, *Misanthropy;* but it may be doubted if there be any principle of this kind implanted by nature in the mind, excepting the *Principle of Resentment*, the others being grafted on this stock by our erroneous opinions and criminal habits.

Emulation, indeed, (which is unquestionably an original principle of action,) is treated of by Dr. Reid under the title of the *Malevolent Affections.* But I formerly gave my reasons for classing this principle with the *desires*, and not with the *affections.* I acknowledged, indeed, that emulation is often accompanied with ill-will to our rival; but the malevolent affection is only a concomitant circumstance; and it is not the affection, but the desire of superiority, which can be justly regarded as the active principle.

Nor is this sentiment of ill-will a *necessary* concomitant of the desire of superiority; for there is unquestionably a solid distinction between emulation and envy, the latter of which is a corruption of the former, disgraceful to the character and ruinous to the happiness of whoever indulges it. In the case of envy, the malevolent affection arises, I believe, generally from some error of the judgment or some illusion of the imagination, leading us to refer the cause of our own want of success either to some injustice on the part of our rival, or to an unjust partiality in the world, which overrates his merits and undervalues ours. In both of these cases, the desire of superiority generates malevolent affections, by first leading us to apprehend *injustice*, and thus exciting the natural passion of resentment.

Before proceeding to consider this principle of action, it may be proper again to remark, that, when the epithet *malevolent* is applied to it, that word must not be understood to imply any thing criminal, at least so long as resentment is restrained within proper bounds, after having been originally excited by real injustice. The epithet *malevolent* is used only to express that temporary ill-will towards the author of the apprehended injustice with which resentment is necessarily accompanied till it begins to subside.

One of the first authors who examined with success this part of our constitution, and illustrated the important purposes to which it is subservient, was Bishop Butler, in an excellent discourse printed among his *Sermons.* The hints he has thrown out have evidently been of great use both to Lord Kames and Mr. Smith in their speculations concerning the principles of morals.

II. *Instinctive and Deliberate Resentment.*] To Butler we are indebted for the illustration of a very important distinction (which had been formerly hinted at by Hobbes) between *instinctive* and *deliberate* resentment Instinctive resentment operates in men exactly as in the lower animals, arising necessarily from any feeling of pain excited by external objects, and prompting us to a retaliation upon the cause of our suffering, without any exercise whatever of reflection and reason. It is thus that a child beats the ground after it has hurt itself by a fall, and that we sometimes see a passionate man wreak his vengeance on inanimate objects by dashing them to pieces. This species of resentment, however, subsides instantly, and we are ready next moment to smile at the absurdity of our conduct.

Deliberate resentment is excited only by intentional injury, and therefore implies a sense of justice, or of moral good or evil. It is plainly peculiar to a rational nature, though perhaps it is not very distinguishable from instinctive or animal resentment in the ruder state of our own species. It is observed by Dr. Robertson, that "the desire of vengeance which takes possession of the heart of savages resembles the instinctive rage of an animal rather than the passion of a man, and that it turns with undiscerning fury even against inanimate objects." He adds, "that, if struck with an arrow in battle, they will tear it from the wound, break and bite it with their teeth, and dash it on the ground."*

This distinction, too, is much insisted on by Lord Kames in various parts of his writings; and it is from him that I have borrowed the phrase of *instinctive resentment*, which he has substituted instead of *sudden resentment*, employed by Butler.

III. *The Final Cause of Instinctive Resentment.*] The final cause of instinctive resentment was plainly to defend us against sudden violence, (where reason would come too late to our assistance,) by rousing the powers

* *History of America*, Book IV. § 73.

both of mind and body to instant and vigorous exertion. A number of our other instincts are perfectly analogous to this. Such, for example, is the instinctive effort we make to recover ourselves when we are in danger of losing our balance,* and the instinctive de-

---

* Although I have followed Dr. Reid's language in calling this an *instinctive* effort, I am abundantly aware that the expression is not unexceptionable. On this head I perfectly agree (excepting in one single point) with the following remarks of Gravesande: —

"Il y a quelque chose d'admirable dans le moyen ordinaire dont les hommes se servent, pour s'empêcher de tomber: car dans le tems que, par quelque mouvement, le poids du corps s'augmente d'une coté, un autre mouvement rétablit l'equilibre dans l'instant. On attribue communément la chose à un *instinct naturel* quoiqu'il faille nécessairement l'attribuer à un art perfectionné par l'exercise.

"Les enfans ignorent absolument cet art dans les premières années de leur vie; ils l'apprennent peu à peu, et s'y perfectionnent, parce qu'ils ont continuellement occasion de s'y exercer; exercise qui, dans la suite, n'exige presque plus aucune attention de leur part; tout comme un musicién remue les doigts, suivant les règles de l'art, pendant qu'il apperçoit à peine qu'il y fasse le moindre attention." — *Œuvres Philosophiques* de M. S'Gravesande, p. 121, 2de Partie, Amsterdam, 1774.

The only thing I am disposed to object to in the foregoing passage is that clause where the author ascribes *the effort in question* to an *art*. Is it not manifestly as wide of the truth to refer it to *this* source as to a pure instinct?

The word *art* implies intelligence, — the perception of an *end*, and the choice of *means*. But where is there any appearance of either in an operation common to the whole species, (not excepting the idiot and the insané,) and which is practised as successfully by the brutes as by rational creatures?

Elephants (it is well known) were taught by the ancients to walk on the tight rope, on which occasions their trunk probably performed the office of a pole. Whoever has seen a peacock walk in a windy day along the branch of a tree must have observed the address with which he avails himself of his tail for the same purpose.

Nothing, however, can place in a stronger light the capacity of the brutes to acquire the nice management of the centre of gravity, than the mathematical exactness with which we may daily see horses in the *circus* adjusting the inclination of their bodies to the velocity of their circular speed. Here, indeed, a good deal is to be ascribed to the effects of human discipline, but by far the greater part of the groundwork is laid by nature in the instinctive dispositions of the animal. The acquisition seems to be almost as easy as that of the habits which constitute the acquired perceptions of sight.

In one of the last volumes of Dr. Clarke's *Travels* there is a figure of a goat, whom the author saw standing with its four feet collected together on the top of a cylindrical piece of wood of a few inches diameter. Nobody can doubt that the effects of discipline were greatly facilitated in this instance by the natural instincts of the goat, which probably accommodated themselves with very little instruction to the artificial circumstances in which they were forced to operate.

spatch with which we shut the eyelids when an object is made to pass rapidly before the face. In general it will be found, that, as nature has taken upon herself the care of our preservation during the infancy of our reason, so in every case in which our existence is threatened by dangers, against which reason is unable to supply a remedy *with sufficient promptitude*, she continues this guardian care through the whole of life.

The disposition which we sometimes feel, when under the influence of instinctive resentment, to wreak our vengeance upon inanimate objects, has suggested to Dr. Reid a very curious query, Whether, upon such an occasion, we may have a momentary belief that the object is alive? For my own part, I confess my inclination to answer this question in the affirmative. I agree with Dr. Reid in thinking, that, unless we had such a belief, our conduct could not possibly be what it frequently is, and that it is not till this momentary belief is at an end that our conduct appears to ourselves to be absurd and ludicrous. With respect to infants, there are many facts besides that now under consideration which render it probable that their first apprehensions lead them to believe all the objects around them to be animated, and that it is only in consequence of experience and reason that they come to form the notion of insentient substances. If this be the case, the illusion of imagination which leads us to ascribe life to things inanimate, when we are under the influence of instinctive resentment, may perhaps be owing to a momentary relapse into those apprehensions which were habitually familiar to us in the first years of our existence.

But whatever theory we adopt on the subject, there can be no doubt about the fact, that the final cause of this law of our nature was to secure and guard us against the sudden effects of external injuries in cases where there is not time for deliberation and judgment. With respect to the injuries we are liable to from our fellow-creatures, it secures us further by its effect in restraining *them* from acts of violence. "It is a kind of penal statute promulgated by nature, the execution of which is committed to the sufferer." *

IV. *Final Cause of Deliberate Resentment.*] In man the instinctive resentment subsides as soon as he is satisfied that no injury was intended; and it is only *intentional* injury that is the object of settled and deliberate resentment. The final cause of this species of resentment is analogous to that of the other, — to serve as a check on those men whose violent or malignant passions might lead them to disturb the happiness of their fellow-creatures.

In order to secure still more effectually so very important an end, we are so formed that the injustice offered to *others*, as well as to ourselves, awakens our resentment against the aggressor, and prompts us to take part in the redress of their grievances. In this case the emotion we feel is more properly denoted in our language by the word *indignation;* but (as Butler has remarked) our principle of action is in both cases fundamentally the same, — an aversion or displeasure at injustice and cruelty, which interests us in the punishment of those by whom they have been exhibited. Resentment, therefore, when restrained within due bounds, seems to be rather a sentiment of hatred against vice than an affection of ill-will against any of our fellow-creatures; and, on this account, I am somewhat doubtful (notwithstanding the apology I have already made for the title of this section) whether I have not followed Dr. Reid too closely in characterizing resentment, considered as an original part of the constitution of man, by the epithet of *malevolent.*

An additional confirmation of this doctrine arises from the following consideration: — that, in candid and generous minds, the whole object of resentment is to convince the person who has injured them that he has treated them unjustly, — to show him that he has formed an unfair estimate of their characters and of

* Reid, *On the Active Powers*, Essay III. Part II. Chap. v.

their talents, and to obtain such a superiority over him in point of *power* as to be able, by a generous forgiveness of his aggressions, to convert his malice into gratitude. In other words, in such minds the great object of resentment is to correct the faults of the delinquent, and to make a friend of an enemy.

This last observation points out, by the way, the final cause of a very remarkable circumstance accompanying the affection of resentment when excited by an injury offered to ourselves. We desire not only the punishment of the offender, but that we should have the power of inflicting the punishment with our own hand. It is probable that this originates partly in our love of power; but I believe it is chiefly owing to a secret wish of convincing our enemy, by the magnanimity of our conduct, how much he had mistaken the object of his hatred. In the mean and the malicious, the passion of revenge is gratified by any suffering inflicted on an enemy, whether by an indifferent person or by the hand of Heaven.

After all, however, that I have advanced in justification of this part of the human constitution, I must acknowledge that there is no principle of action which requires more pains, even in the best minds, to restrain it within the bounds of moderation. The imagination exaggerates the injuries that we ourselves have received; and mistaken views of human nature, concurring with low spirits or disappointed ambition, lead us to ascribe to our opponents worse motives than those from which they really have acted. We seldom, too, are sufficiently attentive to the situations and feelings of other men, and even where we do make an effort to place ourselves in their circumstances, it is not every man who is possessed of the degree of imagination requisite for that purpose. Our own sufferings, at the same time, are always present to our view, and force themselves on the notice of the most thoughtless without any effort on their part. And hence it is that an irritability to personal injury is often accompanied with a callousness to the feelings of others, and even with a disposition to put unfavorable constructions on their actions.

V. *How checked and restrained by Indignation in Others.*] In order to check the excesses to which this ungovernable passion is apt to lead us, nature has made a beautiful provision in that sentiment of indignation which the sight of injustice excites in the breast of the unconcerned spectator. This sentiment interests society in general in the cause of the oppressed, and serves to protect the weak against the wrongs of the powerful. As it is not, however, liable to the same excesses with the passion of resentment excited by a personal injury, it sympathizes only with the injured while his retaliations are restrained within the bounds of moderation. When resentment rises to cruel and relentless revenge, unconcerned spectators become disposed to abandon the cause they had espoused, and to transfer their protection to the original aggressor.

It does not follow from this observation that resentment and indignation are two distinct principles; for the whole difference between them may be accounted for from the different views we naturally take of our own wrongs and those of others. They are both founded in a sentiment of aversion and ill-will excited by injustice; but the one is more apt to pass the bounds of moderation than the other, in consequence of the facts being more strongly obtruded on our notice, and often exaggerated by the heightenings of imagination.

Mr. Smith has endeavoured, on the principles now stated, to account for the origin of our sense of justice. The passion of resentment, he thinks, when excited by a personal injury, would set no bounds to its gratification, but would lead us to sacrifice every thing to revenge. But, as we find that other men would not go along with us when our revenge ceases to bear any proportion to the original injury, we learn to adjust our retaliations, not to our own feelings, but to those of the impartial spectator. Hence the origin of our sense of justice, our regard for which arises from our desire of obtaining the sympathy and the support of society.

I shall afterwards state some objections to this theory, which appear to me unanswerable. In particular, I shall attempt to show, that, so far is our idea of justice from being posterior to the affections of resentment and indignation, and to a comparison between our own feelings and those of other men, that the very emotion of deliberate resentment presupposes the idea of justice, and of what is morally right and wrong. The fact, however, on which the theory proceeds is a most important one, and Mr. Smith has had great merit in illustrating it so fully. Lord Kames, in his *Historical Law Tracts*, has made a happy application of it to explain the origin and progress of criminal law. Which of these two authors first conceived the idea of applying it to *jurisprudence* does not appear to me to be perfectly certain. Both of them have evidently been much indebted, in their speculations concerning this part of human nature, to the *Sermons* of Bishop Butler.

VI. *All the Malevolent Affections attended by a Sense of Pain.*] I shall conclude this subject at present by remarking, that, as all the benevolent affections are accompanied with pleasant emotions, so all the malevolent affections are sources of pain and disquiet. This is true even of resentment, how justly soever it may be roused by the injurious conduct of others. Here, too, we may perceive a final cause perfectly analogous to that of which I formerly took notice in treating of the benevolent affections. As the pleasant emotion accompanying *these* seems evidently to have been intended as an incitement to us to cultivate and cherish them, so the painful feeling accompanying resentment, and every other affection which is hostile to our fellow-creatures, serves as a check on the habitual indulgence of them, and induces us, as soon as the first impulse of passion is over, and reason begins to reassume her empire, to obliterate every trace of them from the memory. Dr. Reid has expressed this last observation with great beauty, and has enforced it with uncommon felicity of illustration. "When we consider that, on the one hand, every benevolent affection is pleasant in its nature, is health to the soul and a cordial to the spirits; that nature has made even the outward expression of benevolent affections in the countenance pleasant to every beholder, and the chief ingredient of beauty in 'the human face divine'; that, on the other hand, every malevolent affection, not only in its faulty excesses, but in its moderate degrees, is vexation and disquiet to the mind, and even gives deformity to the countenance, it is evident that by these signals nature loudly admonishes us to use the former as our daily bread, both for health and pleasure, but to consider the latter as a nauseous medicine, which is never to be taken without necessity, and even then in no greater quantity than the necessity requires." *

After the clear, and, at the same time, cautious terms in which Butler, Kames, and Smith have expressed themselves concerning *resentment*, it is surprising to find some late writers of considerable name speaking of the *pleasure of revenge* as a natural gratification, of which every man is entitled to look forward to the enjoyment; and which, after the establishment of the political union, every man has a right to insist upon at the hands of the civil magistrate. Such, in particular, seems to be the opinion of Mr. Bentham, and of his very ingenious and eloquent commentator, M. Dumont: —

" Every species of satisfaction naturally brings in its train a punishment to the defendant, a pleasure of vengeance for the party injured. This pleasure is a gain: it recalls the riddle of Samson; it is the sweet which comes out of the strong; it is the honey gathered from the carcass of the lion. Produced without expense, net result of an operation necessary on other accounts, it is an enjoyment to be cultivated as well as any other; for the pleasure of vengeance, considered abstractly, is, like every other pleasure, only good in itself. It is innocent so long as it is confined within the limits

---

* *On the Active Powers*, Essay III. Part II. Chap. vi.

of the laws; it becomes criminal at the moment it breaks them. . . . . . Useful to the individual, this motive is also useful to the public, or, to speak more correctly, necessary. It is this vindictive satisfaction which often unties the tongue of the witness; it is this which generally animates the breast of the accuser, and engages him in the service of justice, notwithstanding the trouble, the expenses, the enmities, to which it exposes him; it is this which overcomes the public pity in the punishment of the guilty. . . . . .

"Some commonplace moralists, always the dupes of words, cannot understand this truth. 'The desire of vengeance is odious; all satisfaction drawn from this source is vicious; forgiveness of injuries is the noblest of virtues.' Doubtless, implacable characters, whom no satisfaction can soften, are hateful and ought to be so. The forgiveness of injuries is a virtue necessary to humanity; but it is only a virtue when justice has done its work, when it has furnished or refused a satisfaction. Before this, to forgive injuries is to invite their perpetration, — is to be, not the friend, but the enemy of society. What could wickedness desire more than an arrangement by which offences should be always followed by pardon?" *

The observations above quoted from Butler, Reid, and Smith will at once point out the limitations with which this passage must be understood, and will furnish a triumphant reply to it where it departs from the truth.†

---

* Bentham's *Principles of Penal Law*, Part I. Chap. xvi. The French translation by M. Dumont was published before the original, and was quoted by Mr. Stewart. I have taken the liberty to substitute the original, which has since appeared. — Ed.

† To the works already cited or referred to in this and the preceding chapters as illustrating what Mr. Stewart calls the Instinctive Principles of Action should be added Brown's *Philosophy of the Human Mind*, Lect. LXV.-LXXII.; Cogan's *Philosophical Treatise on the Passions*; Rauch's *Psychology*, Part II. Sect. II.; Damiron, *Psychologie*, Sect. II. Chap. ii. — Ed.

BOOK II.

OF OUR RATIONAL* AND GOVERNING PRINCIPLES OF ACTION.

CHAPTER I.

OF A PRUDENTIAL REGARD TO OUR OWN HAPPINESS, OR WHAT IS COMMONLY CALLED BY MORALISTS THE PRINCIPLE OF SELF-LOVE.

I. *Difference between the Animal and Rational Natures.*] The constitution of man, if it were composed merely of the *active principles* hitherto mentioned, would, in some important respects, be analogous to that of the brutes. His *reason*, however, renders his nature and condition, on the whole, essentially different from theirs; and, by elevating him to the rank of *a moral agent*, distinguishes him from the lower animals still more remarkably than by the superiority it imparts to his intellectual endowments.

Of this want of reason in the brutes, it is an obvious result, that they are incapable of looking forward to *consequences*, or of comparing together the different gratifications of which they are susceptible; and, accordingly, as far as we can perceive, they yield to every present impulse. Among the inhabitants of this globe

---

* To various active principles which have been already under our consideration, such, for instance, as the desire of knowledge, the desire of esteem, pity to the distressed, &c., &c., the epithet *rational* may undoubtedly be applied in one sense with propriety, as they exclusively belong to rational beings; but they are yet of a nature essentially different from those active principles of which we are now to treat, and which I have distinguished by the title of *Rational and Governing*. My reasons for using this language will appear in the sequel.

it is the exclusive prerogative of man, as an intelligent being, to take a comprehensive survey of his various principles of action, and to form plans of conduct for the attainment of his favorite objects. He is possessed, therefore, of the power of *self-government;* for how could a plan of conduct be conceived and carried into execution, without a power of refusing occasionally to particular active principles the gratification which they demand? This difference between the *animal* and the *rational* natures is well and concisely described by Seneca in the following words: — "*Animalibus pro ratione impetus; homini pro impetu ratio.*" *

According to the particular active principle which influences habitually a man's conduct, his character receives its denomination of *covetous*, *ambitious*, *studious*, or *voluptuous;* and his conduct is more or less systematical as he adheres to his general plan with steadiness or inconstancy.

II. *Importance of Self-control and of systematic and concentrated Action.*] It is hardly necessary for me to remark how much a man's success in his favorite pursuit depends on the systematical steadiness with which he keeps his object in view. That an uncommon measure of this quality often supplies, to a great degree, the place of genius, and that, where it is wanting, the most splendid endowments are of little value, are facts which have been often insisted on by philosophers, and which are confirmed to us by daily experience. The effects of this concentration of the attention to one particular end on the development and improvement of the intellectual powers in general have not been equally taken notice of. They are, however, extremely remarkable, as every person will readily acknowledge, who compares the sagacity and penetration of those individuals who have enjoyed its advantages with the weakness and incapacity and

* Seneca, *De Ira*, II. 16. "Animals have impulse for reason; man, reason for impulse."

dissipation of thought produced by an undecided choice among the various pursuits which human life presents to us. Even the systematical voluptuary, while he commands a much greater variety of sensual indulgences, and continues them to a much more advanced age, than the thoughtless profligate, seldom fails to give a certain degree of cultivation to his understanding, by employing his faculties habitually in one direction.

The only exception, perhaps, which can be mentioned to this last remark, occurs in the case of those men whose leading principle of action is *vanity*, and who, as their rule of conduct is borrowed from without, must, in consequence of this very circumstance, be perpetually wavering and inconsistent in their pursuits. Accordingly, it will be found that such men, although they have frequently performed splendid actions, have seldom risen to eminence in any one particular career, unless when, by a rare concurrence of accidental circumstances, this career has been steadily pointed out to them, through the whole of their lives, by public opinion.

"Alcibiades," says a French writer, "was a man not of ambition, but of vanity, — a man whose ruling passion was to make a noise, and to furnish matter of conversation to the Athenians. He possessed the *genius* of a great man, but his *soul*, the springs of which were too much slackened to urge him to constant application, could not elevate him, but by starts, to pursuits worthy of his powers. I can scarcely bring myself to believe that a man, whose versatility was such as to enable him when in Sparta to assume the severe manners of a Spartan, and when in Ionia to indulge in the refined voluptuousness of an Ionian, had received from nature the *stamina* of a great character." *

To what has been now observed in favor of syste-

* Quoted by Warburton in his note on Pope's character of the Duke of Wharton, *Moral Essays*, Ep. I. 190.

matical views in the conduct of life, it may be added, that they are incomparably more conducive to *happiness* than a course of action influenced merely by occasional inclination and appetite. Lord Shaftesbury goes so far as to assert, that even the man who is uniformly and systematically bad enjoys *more happiness* (perhaps he would have been nearer the truth if he had contented himself with saying that he suffers less misery) than one of a more mixed and more inconsistent character. "It is the thorough profligate knave alone, the complete unnatural villain, who can any way bid for happiness with the honest man. True interest is wholly on one side or on the other. All between is inconsistency, irresolution, remorse, vexation, and an ague fit, — from hot to cold, — from one passion to another quite contrary, — a perpetual discord of life, and an alternate disquiet and self-dislike. The only rest or repose must be through *one* determined considerate resolution, which, when once taken, must be courageously kept, and the passions and affections brought under obedience to it, — the temper steeled and hardened to the mind, — the disposition to the judgment. Both must agree, else all must be disturbance and confusion." *

To the same purpose Horace: —

> "Quanto constantior idem
> In vitiis, tanto levior miser, ac prior illo
> Qui jam contento, jam laxo fune laboret." †

III. *Examples of the Evils of Inconstancy.*] Of the state of a mind originally possessed of the most splendid endowments, but where every thing has been suffered to run into anarchy from the want of some controlling and steady principle of action, a masterly picture is drawn by Cicero in the following account of Catiline.

---

* *Essay on the Freedom of Wit and Humor*, Part IV. Sect. 1.

† Hor., *Sermo.*, Lib. II., Sat. VII. 18.

> "So constant was he to his darling vice,
> Yet less a wretch than he who now maintains
> A steady course, now drives with looser reins."

"Utebatur hominibus improbis multis, et quidem optimis se viris deditum esse simulabat; erant apud illum illecebræ libidinum multæ; erant etiam industriæ quidam stimuli ac laboris: flagrabant libidinis vitia apud illum; vigebant etiam studia rei militaris: neque ego unquam fuisse tale monstrum in terris ullum puto, tam ex contrariis diversisque inter se pugnantibus naturæ studiis cupiditatibusque conflatum. Quis clarioribus viris quodam tempore jucundior? quis turpioribus conjunctior? quis civis meliorum partium aliquando? quis tetrior hostis huic civitati? quis in voluptatibus inquinatior? quis in laboribus patientior? quis in rapacitate avarior? quis in largitione effusior?"*

In a person of this description, whatever indications of genius and ability he may discover, and whatever may be the great qualities he possesses, there is undoubtedly some tendency to insanity, which, if it were not the radical *source* of the evil, could hardly fail, sooner or later, to be the *effect* of a perpetual conflict between different and discordant passions. And, accordingly, this is the idea which Sallust seems to have formed of this extraordinary man. "His eyes," he observes, "had a disagreeable glare; his complexion was pale; his walk sometimes quick, sometimes slow; and his general appearance indicated a discomposure of mind approaching to madness."

I would not be understood to insinuate by this last observation, that, in every case in which we observe a conduct apparently inconsistent and irregular, we are entitled to conclude, all at once, that it proceeds from accidental humor, or from a disordered understanding.

---

* *Oratio pro M. Cœlio*, Sect. V. and VI "He was acquainted with a great number of wicked men, yet a pretended admirer of the virtuous. His house was furnished with a variety of temptations to lust and lewdness, yet with several incitements also to industry and labor: it was a scene of vicious pleasures, yet a school of martial exercises. There never was such a monster on earth, compounded of passions so contrary and opposite. Who was ever more agreeable at one time to the best citizens? who more intimate at another with the worst? who a man of better professions? who a fouler enemy to this city? who more intemperate in pleasure? who more patient in labor? who more rapacious in plundering? who more profuse in squandering?"

The knowledge of a man's ruling passion is often a key to what appeared, on a superficial view, to be perfectly inexplicable. Some excellent reflections on this subject are to be found in the first of Pope's *Moral Essays*, where they are most happily and forcibly illustrated by the character of the Duke of Wharton.

> "Search, then, the ruling passion: there alone
> The wild are constant, and the cunning known;
> The fool consistent, and the false sincere;
> Priests, princes, women, no dissemblers here.
> This clew, once found, unravels all the rest,
> The prospect clears, and Wharton stands confessed, —
> Wharton, the scorn and wonder of our days,
> Whose ruling passion was the lust of praise.
> Born with whate'er could win it from the wise,
> Women and fools must like him, or he dies.
>
> . . . . .
>
> Ask you why Wharton broke through every rule?
> 'T was all for fear the knaves should call him fool.
> Nature well known, no prodigies remain,
> Comets are regular and Wharton plain."

I have only to add to these observations of Pope, that I believe the inconsistencies he describes are chiefly to be found in the conduct of men whose ruling principle of action is *vanity*. I have already remarked, that while every other principle which gains an ascendant over the rest has a tendency to *systematize* our course of action, vanity has, on the contrary, a tendency to *disorganize* it, leading us always to look abroad for our rule of conduct, and thereby rendering it as wavering and inconsistent as the opinions and fashions of mankind. Where vanity, therefore, is the ruling passion of any individual, a want of system may be regarded as a necessary consequence of his general character.

IV. *Why the Desire of Happiness should be accounted a Rational, and not an Instinctive, Principle of Action.*] From the foregoing considerations it sufficiently appears how much the nature of man is discriminated from that of the brutes, in consequence of the comprehensive view which his reason enables him to take of his different principles of action, and of the deliberate choice he has it in his power to make of the genera. plan of conduct he is to pursue. There is another, however, and a very important respect, in which the rational nature differs from the animal,—that it is able to form the notion of *happiness*, or *what is good for it upon the whole*, and to deliberate about the most effectual means of attaining it. It is owing to this distinguishing prerogative of our species that we can avail ourselves of our past experience in avoiding those enjoyments which we know will be succeeded by suffering, and in submitting to lesser evils which we know are to be instrumental in procuring us a greater accession of good. "Sed inter hominem et belluam," says Cicero, "hoc maximè interest, quod hæc tantùm quantùm sensu movetur, ad id solum quod adest, quodque præsens est, se accommodat, paullulum admodum sentiens præteritum aut futurum. Homo autem, quoniam rationis est particeps, per quam consequentia cernit, causas rerum videt, earumque prægressus et antecessiones non ignorat; similitudines comparat, et rebus præsentibus adjungit atque annectit futuras; facile totius vitæ cursum videt, ad eamque degendam præparat res necessarias." *

It is implied in the very idea of *happiness* that it is a desirable object, and therefore self-love is an active principle very different from those which have been hitherto considered. These, for aught we know, may be the effect of arbitrary appointment, and they have accordingly been called *implanted* principles, or principles resulting from a positive accommodation of the constitution of man to the objects with which he is surrounded. The desire of happiness may be called a *rational* principle of action, being peculiar to a rational nature, and inseparably connected with it. It is im-

---

* *De Off.*, Lib. I. 4. "But between man and the lower animals there is in other respects the greatest difference. The latter, guided by the impulse of their senses alone, are confined to what is present, or near, with a very slight knowledge of the past or the future. Man, however, who partakes of reason, distinguishes the causes and the consequences of events, observes their progress, compares similar circumstances, connects the past with the future, surveys the whole course of life, and makes the necessary provision for its well-being."

possible to conceive a being capable of forming the notions of happiness and misery, to whom the one shall not be an object of desire, and the other of aversion.*

V. *Objections to the Term Self-love.*] In prefixing to this chapter the title of *Self-love*, the ordinary language of modern philosophy has been followed, as I am always anxious to avoid unnecessary innovations in the use of words. The expression, however, is exceptionable, for it suggests an analogy (where there is none in fact) between that regard which every rational being must necessarily have to his own happiness, and those benevolent affections which attach us to our fellow-creatures. There is surely nothing in the former of these principles analogous to the affection of *love*; and, therefore, to call it by the appellation of *self-love* is to suggest a *theory* with respect to its nature, and a theory which has no foundation in truth.

The word φιλαυτία was used among the Greeks nearly in the same sense, and introduced similar inaccuracies into their reasonings concerning the principle of morals. In our language, however, the impropriety does not stop here; for not only is the phrase *self-love* used as synonymous with the desire of happiness, but it is often confounded (in consequence of an unfortunate connection in their etymology) with the word *selfishness*, which certainly, in strict propriety, denotes a very different disposition of mind. In proof of this

* From this constitution of the human mind, as at once *sensitive* and *rational*, arise necessarily the emotions of hope and fear, joy and sorrow. The pleasurable emotion arising from good in expectation is called *hope*, the painful emotion arising from apprehended evil is called *fear*. The words *joy* and *sorrow* are more general, applicable alike to the emotions arising from the *experience* and from the *apprehension* of good and of evil The interest which our benevolent affections give us in the concerns of others inspires us (more particularly in the case of those to whom we are fondly attached) with emotions analogous to those which have a reference to our own condition.

The laws which regulate these emotions connected with the sensitive nature of man deserve a careful examination; but the subject does not fall under the present part of my plan.

it is sufficient to observe, that the word *selfishness* is always used in an unfavorable sense, whereas self-love, or the desire of happiness, is inseparable from our nature as rational and sensitive beings.

The mistaken notion that vice consists in an excessive self-love naturally arose from the application of the term *self-love*, or φιλαυτία, to express the desire of happiness. As benevolence, or the love of mankind, constitutes, in the opinion of many moralists, the whole of virtue, so it was not unnatural to conclude that the love of ourselves (which this mode of speaking seems to contrast with benevolence) was the radical source of all the vices. And, accordingly, this conclusion has been adopted by many writers, both ancient and modern. "If we scan," says Dr. Barrow, "the particular nature, and search into the original causes of the several kinds of naughty dispositions in our souls, and of miscarriages in our lives, we shall find inordinate self-love to be a main ingredient, and a common source of them all, so that a divine of great name had some reason to affirm that *original sin* (or that innate distemper from which men generally become so very prone to evil and averse to good) doth consist in self-love disposing us to all kinds of irregularity and excess."* In this passage, Dr. Barrow refers to the opinion of Zuinglius, who has expressly called self-love the original or radical sin in our nature. "Est ergo ista ad peccandum amore sui propensio, peccatum originale."

It is chiefly, however, from some of our English moralists that this notion concerning the nature of vice has derived its authority; and the plausibility of their reasonings on the subject has been much aided by that indiscriminate use of the words *self-love* and *selfishness* of which I have already taken notice.

I shall afterwards have occasion to show that vice does not consist in an excessive regard to our own happiness. At present I shall only remark, in addition

* Sermon, *On Self-Love in general.*

to what was said above with respect to the distinction between the meanings of the words *self-love* and *selfishness*, that the former is so far from expressing any thing blamable, that it denotes a principle of action which we never sacrifice to any of our implanted appetites, desires, or affections without incurring remorse and self-condemnation. When we see, for example, a man enslaved by his animal appetites, so far from considering him as under the influence of an excessive self-love, we pity and despise him for neglecting the higher enjoyments which are placed within his reach. Accordingly, those very authors who tell us that vice consists in an inordinate self-love are forced to confess that there are some senses of the word in which it expresses a worthy and commendable principle of action. "Reason," says Dr. Barrow, "dictateth and prescribeth to us, that we should have a sober regard to our true good and welfare; to our best interest and solid content; to that which (all things being rightly stated, considered, and computed) will in the end prove most beneficial and satisfactory to us; a self-love working in prosecution of such things, common sense cannot but allow and approve." * — "Τὸν μὲν ἀγαθὸν," says Aristotle, "δεῖ φίλαυτον εἶναι." And in another passage of the same chapter, "Δόξειε δ' ἂν ὁ τοιοῦτος μᾶλλον εἶναι φίλαυτος." †

As a further proof that selfishness is not synonymous with the desire of happiness, it may be observed, that, although we apply the epithet *selfish* to avarice and to low private sensuality, we never apply it to the desire of knowledge or to the pursuits of virtue, which are certainly sources of more exquisite pleasure than riches or sensuality can bestow.

> "Yet at the darkened eye, the withered face,
> The hoary head, I never will repine:
> But spare, O time! whate'er of mental grace,
> Of candor, love, or sympathy divine,
> Whate'er of fancy's ray, or friendship's flame, was mine."

---

* Sermon. *On Self-Love in general.*

† *Ethic. Nic*, Lib. IX. Cap. viii "A good man must be a lover of himself." "Such a man would seem to be the greatest of self-lovers."

Such a wish is surely dictated by the most rational view of our real interest; and yet no man will pretend that it contains any thing inconsistent with a generous and heroic mind. Had it been directed to wealth, to long life, or to the preservation of youthful beauty and vigor, it would have been universally condemned as selfish and contemptible.

VI. *Why some Pursuits are called Selfish, while others, though contributing still more to our own Good, are not.*] This restriction of the term *selfishness* to a particular class of human pursuits is taken notice of by Dr. Ferguson in his *Essay on Civil Society*, and seems to be considered by him as originating in a capricious, or rather in an inconsistent, use of language. "It is somewhat remarkable, that, notwithstanding men value themselves so much on qualities of the mind, on parts, learning, and wit, on courage, generosity, and honor, those men are still supposed to be in the highest degree selfish, or attentive to themselves, who are most careful about animal life, and who are least mindful of rendering that life an object worthy of care. It will be difficult, however, to tell why a good understanding, a resolute and generous mind, should not, by every man in his senses, be reckoned as much parts of himself as either his stomach or his palate, and much more than his estate or his dress. The epicure who consults his physician how he may restore his relish for food, and, by creating an appetite, renew his enjoyment, might at least, with an equal regard to himself, consult how he might strengthen his affection to a parent or a child, to his country or to mankind; and it is probable that an appetite of this sort would prove a source of enjoyment no less than the former." *

Of the difficulty here remarked by Dr. Ferguson, the solution appears to me to be this, that the word *selfishness*, when applied to a pursuit, has no reference to the *motive* from which the pursuit proceeds, but to the *effect*

* Part I. Sect. II.

it has on the conduct. Neither our animal appetites, nor avarice, nor curiosity, nor the desire of moral improvement, arise from self-love, but some of these active principles disconnect us with society more than others; and consequently, though they do not indicate a greater regard for our own happiness, they betray a greater unconcern about the happiness of our neighbours. The pursuits of the miser have no mixture whatever of the social affections; on the contrary, they continually lead him to state his own interest in opposition to that of other men. The enjoyments of the sensualist all expire within his own person; and, therefore, whoever is habitually occupied in the search of them must of necessity neglect the duties which he owes to mankind. It is otherwise with the desire of knowledge, which is always accompanied with a strong desire of social communication, and with the love of moral excellence, which, in its practical tendency, coincides so remarkably with benevolence, that many authors have attempted to resolve the one principle into the other. How far their conclusion, in this instance, is a necessary consequence of the premises from which it is deduced, will appear hereafter.

The foregoing observations coincide so remarkably with a passage in Aristotle's *Ethics*, that I am tempted to quote it at length in the excellent English translation of Dr. Gillies. After stating the same inconsistencies in our language about self-love which Dr. Ferguson has pointed out, Aristotle proceeds thus: —

"These contradictions cannot be reconciled but by distinguishing the *different senses* in which man is said *to love himself*. Those who reproach self-love as a vice consider it only as it appears in worldlings and voluptuaries, who arrogate to themselves more than their due share of wealth, power, or pleasure. Such things are to the multitude the objects of earnest concern and eager contention, because the multitude regards them as prizes of the highest value, and, in endeavouring to attain them, strives to gratify its passion at the expense of its reason. This kind of self-love, which belongs to the contemptible multitude, is doubtless obnoxious to blame, and in this acceptation the word is generally taken. But should a man assume a preëminence in exercising justice, temperance, and other virtues, though such a man has really more true self-love than the multitude, yet nobody would impute this affection to him as a crime. Yet he takes to himself the fairest and greatest of all goods, and those the most acceptable to the ruling principle in his nature, which is properly *himself*, in the same manner as the sovereignty in every community is that which most properly constitutes the state. He is said, also, to have, or not to have, the command of himself, just as this principle bears sway, or as it is subject to control; and those acts are considered as most voluntary which proceed from this legislative or sovereign power. Whoever cherishes and gratifies this ruling part of his nature is strictly and peculiarly a lover of himself, but in a quite different sense from that in which self-love is regarded as a matter of reproach; for all men approve and praise an affection calculated to produce the greatest private and the greatest public happiness; whereas they disapprove and blame the vulgar kind of self-love, as often hurtful to others, and always ruinous to those who indulge it." *

---

* Aristotle's *Ethics*, Book IX. Chap. viii.

Jouffroy accounts thus for the appearance of self-love (*égoisme*) in human nature: — "The faculties, as long as they are abandoned to the impulse of the passions, obey that passion which happens to be the strongest at the time, from which a twofold inconvenience ensues. In the first place, the passions are of all things the most unstable, the dominion of one being almost immediately supplanted by that of another, so that the faculties while under their exclusive control are incapable of continuous and connected effort, and consequently nothing of importance is effected. And, again, the good found in the satisfaction of the dominant passion at the moment often leads to serious evil, while, on the other hand, the evil of its not being satisfied often results in great and permanent good: from which it appears that nothing is less favorable to the attainment of our highest good than this exclusive dominion of the passions. Reason is not slow to discover this, or to conclude from it that, in order to obtain the highest possible good, our effective force must no longer be the prey of the mechanical impulse of the passions. It sees, on the contrary, how much better it would be, if, instead of being hurried away each instant by such impulse to the gratification of some new passion, it were freed from this constraint, and directed exclusively to the realization of the interest of all the

CHAPTER II.

OF THE MORAL FACULTY.

Section I.

THE MORAL FACULTY NOT RESOLVABLE INTO SELF-LOVE.

I. *Duty and Interest not the same.*] As some authors have supposed that vice consists in an excessive regard

passions taken together, — that is to say, the greatest good of our whole nature. Moreover, with the same degree of clearness that our reason conceives this course to be wise, it also conceives it to be practicable. We are certainly capable of judging what the highest good of our nature is; our reason enables us to do it. Equally certain is it that we can, if we please, take possession of our own faculties, and employ them to carry out this idea of our reason. That we have this power has been revealed even under the exclusive empire of passion; we have felt it in the spontaneous effort by which, in order to satisfy the dominant passion for the time being, we have concentrated all our forces on a single point. It is only necessary that we should do voluntarily what before we have done spontaneously, and *free will* appears. No sooner is this great revolution conceived, than it is accomplished. A new principle of action springs up within us, *interest well understood*, — a principle which is not a passion, but an idea; not a blind and instinctive prompting of our nature, but an intelligible, deliberate, and rational purpose; not an *impulse*, but a *motive*. Finding a point of support in this motive, the natural power we have over our faculties takes these faculties under its control, and in its effort to direct them according to this motive shakes off the bondage of the passions, and becomes itself more and more developed and free. From this time our active powers are delivered from the irregular, vacillating, and turbulent empire of the passions, and become submissive to the law of reason, which considers what will be for the greatest possible satisfaction of our tendencies, that is to say, the highest good of the individual, or self-interest well understood." — *Cours de Droit Naturel*, Leçon II. See the whole of this Lecture and the following one in the original, or in Mr. Channing's translation.

No writer has treated the subject of self-love with so much care and minuteness of discrimination as Jeremy Bentham, in the first volume of his *Introduction to the Principles of Morals and Legislation*. Here we have what has been called his Moral Arithmetic, by which he thinks to determine the relative value of different "lots of pleasure or pain"; and also what has been called his Moral Dynamics, or the doctrine of forces, motives, or sanctions, by which self-love, and through that the human will, is influenced and determined in all cases.

Paley, not content with making pleasure, considered as constituting human happiness, the only ultimate object of human pursuit, denies that the rational and moral pleasures, as such, are entitled to more regard than the rest. "In this inquiry," says he, "I will omit much usual declamation on

to our own happiness, so others have gone into the opposite extreme, by representing virtue as merely *a matter of prudence*, and a sense of duty but another name for *a rational self-love.* This view of the subject is far from being unnatural; for we find that these two principles lead in general to the same course of action; and we have every reason to believe, that, if our knowledge of the universe were more extensive, they would be found to do so in all instances whatever. Accordingly, by many of the best of the ancient moralists, our *sense of duty* was considered as resolvable into self-love, and the whole of *ethics* was reduced to this question, *What is the supreme good?* or, in other words, What is most conducive, on the whole, to our happiness? The same opinion, as will soon appear, has been adopted by various philosophers of the first eminence in England, and was long the prevailing system on the Continent.

That we have, however, a sense of duty, which is not resolvable into a regard to our happiness, appears from various considerations.

II. *First Argument. Expressed by distinct Terms in all Languages.*] There are, in all languages, words equivalent to *duty* and to *interest*, which men have constantly distinguished in their signification. They coincide in general in their applications, but they convey very different ideas. When I wish to persuade a man to a particular action, I address some of my arguments

---

the dignity and capacity of our nature; the superiority of the soul to the body, of the rational to the animal part of our constitution; upon the worthiness, refinement, and delicacy of some satisfactions, or the meanness, grossness, and sensuality of others; because I hold that pleasures differ in nothing but in continuance and intensity." — *Moral Philosophy*, Book I. Chap. vi. Dr. Whewell, in the Preface to his edition of Sir James Mackintosh's *Dissertation on the Progress of Ethical Philosophy*, says of this passage, — "If we could use such a term without an unbecoming disrespect towards a virtuous and useful writer, this opinion might properly be called *brutish*, since it recognizes no difference between the pleasures of man and those of the lowest animals."

For a very original and ingenious speculation respecting the nature of self-love and the natural disinterestedness of the human mind, see Hazlitt's *Essays on the Principles of Human Action*. Also his *Literary Remains*, Essay X., *On Self love.*

to a sense of duty, and others to the regard he has to his own interest. I endeavour to show him that it is not only his duty, but his interest, to act in the way that I recommend to him.

This distinction was expressed among the Roman moralists by the words *honestum* and *utile.* Of the former Cicero says, " Quod vere dicimus, etiamsi a nullo laudetur, natura esse laudabile." *

The τὸ καλόν among the Greeks corresponds, when applied to the conduct, to the *honestum* of the Romans. Dr. Reid remarks that the word καθῆκον (*officium*) extended both to the *honestum* and the *utile*, and comprehended every action performed either from a sense of duty, or from an enlightened regard to our true interest.† In English we use the word *reasonable* with the same latitude, and indeed almost exactly in the same sense in which Cicero defines *officium* : — " Id quod cur factum sit ratio probabilis reddi potest." ‡ In treating of such *offices*, Cicero, and Panœtius before him, first point out those that are recommended to us by our love of the *honestum*, and next those that are recommended by our regard to the *utile.*

This distinction between a sense of duty and a regard to interest is acknowledged even by men whose moral principles are not the purest, nor the most consistent. What unlimited confidence do we repose in the conduct of one whom we know to be *a man of honor*, even in those cases in which he acts out of the view of the world, and where the strongest temptations of worldly interest concur to lead him astray! We know that his heart would revolt at the idea of any thing base or unworthy. Dr. Reid observes that what we call *honor*, considered as a principle of conduct, " is

* *De Offic.*, Lib. I. 4. " Which, though none should praise it, we maintain with truth to be of itself praiseworthy."

† *Essays on the Active Powers*, Essay III. Part III. Chap. v.

‡ *De Offic.*, Lib. I. 3. " That, for the doing of which a reasonable motive can be assigned." But, as Sir W. Hamilton says in a note to the passage in Reid, ' this definition does not apply to καθῆκον or *officium* in general, but only to καθῆκον μέσον, *officium commune.*" — Ed.

only another name for a regard to duty, to rectitude, to propriety of conduct." This, I think, is going rather too far; for, although the two principles coincide *in general* in the direction they give to our conduct, they do not coincide always; the principle of *honor* being liable, from its nature and origin, to be most unhappily perverted in its applications by a bad education and the influence of fashion. At the same time, Dr. Reid's remark is perfectly in point, for the principle of honor is plainly grafted on a sense of duty, and necessarily presupposes its existence.

Dr. Paley, one of the most zealous advocates for the selfish system of morals, admits the fact on which the foregoing argument proceeds, but endeavours to evade the conclusion by means of a theory so extraordinary, that I shall state it in his own words. "There is always understood to be a difference between an act of *prudence* and an act of *duty*. Thus, if I distrusted a man who owed me a sum of money, I should reckon it an act of prudence to get another person bound with him; but I should hardly call it an act of duty. On the other hand, it would be thought a very unusual and loose kind of language to say, that, as I had made such a promise, it was *prudent* to perform it; or that, as my friend, when he went abroad, placed a box of jewels in my hands, it would be *prudent* in me to preserve it for him till he returned.

"Now, in what, you will ask, does the difference consist, inasmuch as, according to our account of the matter, both in the one case and the other, in acts of duty as well as acts of prudence, we consider solely what we ourselves shall gain or lose by the act.

"The difference, and the only difference, is this; that in the one case we consider what we shall gain or lose in the present world; in the other case, we consider also what we shall lose or gain in the world to come." *

* *Moral Philosophy*, Book II. Chap. iii. It is in view of passages like these that Dr. Brown expresses himself with indignant severity. "This form of the selfish system, which has been embraced by many theological writers of undoubted piety and purity, is notwithstanding, I cannot but

On this curious passage I have no comment to offer. A sufficient answer to it may, I trust, be derived from the following reasonings. In the mean time, it will be allowed to be at least one presumption of an essential distinction between the notions of duty and of interest, that there are different words to express these notions in all languages, and that the most illiterate of mankind are in no danger of confounding them together.

III. *Second Argument. Moral Emotions differ from all others in Kind.*] But, secondly, the emotions arising from the contemplation of what is right and wrong in conduct are different both in degree and *in kind* from those which are produced by a calm regard to our own happiness. Of this, I think, nobody can doubt, who considers with attention the operation of our moral principles in cases where their effects are not counteracted or modified by a combination with some other principles of our nature. In judging, for example, of *our own* conduct, our moral powers are warped by the influence of self-partiality and self-deceit; and, accordingly,

---

think, as degrading to the human character as any other form of the doctrine of absolute selfishness; or rather, it is in itself the most degrading of all the forms which the selfish system can assume: because, while the selfishness which it maintains is as absolute and unremitting as if the objects of personal gain were to be found in the wealth, or honors, or sensual pleasures of this earth, this very selfishness is rendered more offensive by the noble image of the Deity which is continually presented to our mind, and presented in all his benevolence, — not to be loved, but to be courted with a mockery of affection. The sensualist of the common system of selfishness, who never thinks of any higher object in the pursuit of the little pleasures which he is miserable enough to regard as happiness, seems to me, even in the brutal stupidity in which he is sunk, a being more worthy of esteem than *the selfish of another life;* to whose view God is ever present, but who view him always only to feel constantly in their heart that, in loving him who has been the dispenser of all these blessings which they have enjoyed, and who has revealed himself in the glorious character of the diffuser of an immortality of happiness, they love not the Giver himself, but only the gifts which they have received, or the gifts that are promised." — *Philosophy of the Human Mind*, Lect. LXXIX Wainewright endeavours to defend Paley against these and other charges. *Vindication of Dr. Paley's Theory of Morals*, Chap. iv., *et passim.*

The strict followers of Paley generally hold that we are indebted to the Christian revelation for our belief in a future retribution. If so, it would seem to follow from the passage in the text that none but Christians, or those who might be Christians, have any thing to do with "duties." — Ed.

we daily see men commit, without any remorse, actions, which, if performed by another person, they would have regarded with the liveliest sentiments of indignation and abhorrence. Even in this last case the experiment is not always perfectly fair; for where the actor has been previously known to us, our judgment is generally affected, in a greater or less degree, by our prepossessions or by our prejudices. In contemplating the characters exhibited in histories and in novels, the emotions we feel are the immediate and the genuine result of our moral constitution; and although they may be stronger in some men than in others, yet they are in all distinctly perceivable, even in those whose want of temper and of candor render them scarcely conscious of the distinction of right and wrong in the conduct of their neighbours and acquaintance. And hence, probably, (we may observe by the way,) the chief origin of the pleasure we experience in this sort of reading. The representations of the stage, however, afford the most favorable of all opportunities for studying the moral constitution of man. As the mind is here perfectly indifferent to the parties whose character and conduct are the subject of the fable, the judgments it forms can hardly fail to be impartial, and the feelings arising from these judgments are much more conspicuous in their external effects than if the play were perused in the closet; for every species of enthusiasm operates more forcibly when men are collected in a crowd. On such an occasion the slightest hint suggested by the poet raises to transport the passions of the audience, and forces involuntary tears from men of the greatest reserve and the most correct sense of propriety. The crowd does not *create* the feeling, nor even *alter its nature;* it only enables us to remark its operation *on a greater scale.* In these cases we have surely no time for reflection; and, indeed, the emotions of which we are conscious are such as no speculations about our own interest could possibly excite. It is in situations of this kind that we most completely forget ourselves as individuals, and feel the most sensibly the existence of those moral ties by which Heaven has been pleased to bind mankind together.

IV. *Third Argument. The Expediency of Virtue not obvious to common Experience.*] Although philosophers have shown that a sense of duty and an enlightened regard to our own happiness conspire in most instances to give the same direction to our conduct, so as to put it beyond a doubt that, even in this world, a virtuous life is true wisdom, yet this is a truth by no means obvious to the common sense of mankind, but deduced from an extensive view of human affairs, and an accurate investigation of the *remote consequences* of our different actions. It is from experience and reflection, therefore, we learn the connection between virtue and happiness; and, consequently, the great lessons of morality which are obvious to the capacity of all mankind could never have been suggested to them merely by a regard to their own interest. Indeed, this discovery which experience makes to us of the connection between virtue and happiness, both in the case of individuals and of political societies, furnishes one of the most pleasing subjects of speculation to the philosopher, as it places in a striking point of view the unity of design which takes place in our constitution, and opens encouraging and delightful prospects with respect to the moral government of the Deity.

It is a just and beautiful observation of Dr. Reid, that "although wise men have concluded that virtue is the only road to happiness, this conclusion is founded chiefly upon the natural respect men have for virtue, and the good and happiness that is intrinsic to it, and arises from the love of it. If we suppose a man altogether destitute of this principle, who considered virtue as only the means to another end, there is no reason to think that he would ever take it to be the road to happiness, but would wander for ever seeking this object where it is not to be found." *

* *Essays on the Active Powers*, Essay III. Part III. Chap. iv.

This observation leads me to remark further, that the man who is most successful in the pursuit of happiness is not he who proposes it to himself as the great object of his pursuit. To do so, and to be continually occupied with schemes on the subject, would fill the mind with anxious conjectures about futurity, and with perplexing calculations of the various chances of good and evil. Whereas the man whose ruling principle of action is a sense of duty conducts himself in the business of life with boldness, consistency, and dignity, and finds himself rewarded with that happiness which so often eludes the pursuit of those who exert every faculty of the mind in order to attain it.

Something very similar to this takes place with regard to nations. From the earliest accounts of mankind, politicians have been employed in devising schemes of national aggrandizement, and have proceeded on the supposition that the prosperity of their own country could only be advanced by depressing all others around them. It has now been shown, with irresistible evidence, that those views were founded on mistake, and that the prosperity of a country is intimately connected with that of its neighbours, insomuch that the enlightened statesman, instead of embarrassing himself with the care of a machine whose parts have become too complicated for any human comprehension, finds his labor reduced to the simple business of observing the rules of justice and humanity. It is remarkable, that, long before the date of these profound speculations in politics, for which we are indebted to Mr. Smith and to the French economists, Fénelon was led merely by the goodness of his heart, and by his speculative conviction of the intimate connection between virtue and happiness under the moral government of God, to recommend a free trade as an expedient measure in policy and to reprobate the mean ideas of national jealousy, as calculated to frustrate the very ends to which they are supposed to be subservient. Indeed, I am inclined to think that, as in conducting the affairs of private life, "the integrity of the upright man" is his surest guide, so, in managing the affairs of a great empire, a strong sense of justice, and an ardent zeal for the rights and for the happiness of mankind, will go further to form a great and successful statesman than the most perfect acquaintance with political details, unassisted by the direction of these inward monitors.

An author, too, in our own country, of sound judgment, and of very accurate commercial information, and who was one of the first in England who turned the attention of the public to those liberal notions concerning trade which are now become so prevalent, acknowledges that it was by a train of reasoning *a priori* that he was led to his conclusions. "Can we suppose," says he, "that Divine Providence has really constituted the order of things in such a sort, as to make the rule of natural self-preservation inconsistent with the fundamental principle of universal benevolence, and the doing as we would be done by? For my own part, I must confess, I never could conceive that an all-wise, just, and benevolent Being would contrive one part of his plan to be so contradictory to the other as here supposed, — that is, would lay us under one obligation as to morals, and another as to trade; or, in short, to make that to be our duty which is not, upon the whole, and generally speaking, (even without the consideration of a future state,) our interest likewise.

"Therefore I *concluded a priori* that there must be some flaw or other in the preceding arguments, plausible as they seem, and great as they are on the foot of human authority. For though the appearance of things at first sight makes for this conclusion, 'that poor countries must inevitably carry away the trade from rich ones, and consequently impoverish them,' the fact itself cannot be so." *

V. *Fourth Argument. Moral Judgments in Children precede the Calculations of Prudence.*] The same con-

---

* Tucker's *Four Tracts on Political and Commercial Subjects*, Tract I p. 20.

clusion is strongly confirmed by *the early period of life* at which our moral judgments make their appearance, long before children are able to form *the general notion of happiness*, and, indeed, in the very infancy of their reason. It is astonishing how powerfully a child of sensibility may be affected by any simple narration calculated to rouse the feelings of pity, of generosity, or of indignation, and how very early some minds formed in a happy mould are inspired with a consciousness of the dignity of their nature, and glow with the enthusiasm of virtue. Dr. Beattie has beautifully painted these openings of the moral character in the description he gives of the effect produced on his young Edwin by the fine old ballad of *The Babes in the Wood.*

"But when to horror his amazement rose,
A gentler strain the beldame would rehearse, —
A tale of rural life, a tale of woes,
The orphan babes and guardian uncle fierce.
O, cruel! will no pang of pity pierce
That heart by lust of lucre seared to stone?
For sure, if aught of virtue last, or verse,
To latest times shall tender souls bemoan
Those helpless orphan babes by thy fell arts undone.

"See where, with berries smeared, with brambles torn,
The babes now famished lay them down to die;
'Midst the wild howl of darksome woods forlorn,
Folded in one another's arms they lie.
Nor friend, nor stranger, hears their dying cry,
'For from the town the man returns no more.'
But thou who Heaven's just vengeance dar'st defy,
This deed with fruitless tears shall soon deplore,
When death lays waste thy house, and flames consume thy store.

"*A stifled smile of stern, vindictive joy*
Brightened one moment Edwin's starting tear; —
'But why should gold man's feeble mind decoy,
And innocence thus die by doom severe?'
O Edwin! while thy heart is yet sincere,
The assaults of discontent and doubt repel;
Dark even at noontide is our mortal sphere,
But let us hope, — to doubt is to rebel, —
Let us exult in hope that all shall yet be well." *

* *The Minstrel*, Book I. For a more extended statement of the proofs of man's moral nature, see Upham's *Mental Philosophy*, Vol. II. § 207 *et seq.* Also, Lieber's *Political Ethics*, Book I. Chap. II. — Ed.

Section II.

EXAMINATION OF HARTLEY'S THEORY OF THE FORMATION OF THE MORAL SENSE BY ASSOCIATION ALONE.

I. *This Theory eludes but in Part the foregoing Arguments.*] The reasonings already stated seem to me to furnish a sufficient refutation of the selfish theory of morals, as it is explained by the greater number of the philosophers who have adopted it; but, before leaving the subject, it is necessary for me to take notice of a doctrine fundamentally the same, though modified in such a manner as to elude *some* of the foregoing arguments, — a doctrine which has been maintained of late by various English writers of note, and which I suspect is at present the prevailing system in that part of the island. According to this doctrine, we do, indeed, in many cases, approve or disapprove of particular actions, without any reference to our own interest *at the time;* but it is asserted that it was views of self-interest which originally created these moral sentiments, and led us to *associate* agreeable or disagreeable emotions with human conduct. The origin of the moral faculty, in the opinion of these theorists, is precisely analogous to that of *avarice*, or of any of our other factitious principles of action. Money, it will not be disputed, is *at first* desired merely on account of its subservience to the gratification of our natural desires; but, in process of time, the association of ideas leads us to regard it as a desirable thing in itself, without any reference to this subservience or utility, and in many cases it continues to be coveted with an increasing passion, long after we have lost all relish for the enjoyments it enables us to purchase. In the same manner, a particular action which was at first approved or disapproved of, merely on account of its supposed tendency with respect to our own interest, comes, in process of time, to be approved or disapproved of the moment it is mentioned, and without any reflection on our part that we are able to recollect. Thus, without abandoning the old selfish principles, they contrive to evade the force of the arguments founded by Hutcheson and others on the *instantaneousness* with which our moral judgments are commonly pronounced. This, if I am not mistaken, is the theory of Dr. Law, of Dr. Hartley, of Dr. Priestley, of Dr. Paley, and of Dr. Paley's great oracle in philosophy, the author of *The Light of Nature Pursued.**

I am ready to acknowledge that this refinement on the old selfish system gives it a degree of plausibility which it did not originally possess, and obviates *one* of the objections to it formerly stated. But it must be remembered that this was not the *only* objection, and that there are several others which apply both to the old and new hypothesis with equal force.

Among these arguments, what I would lay the principal stress on is the degree of experience and reflection necessary for discovering the *tendency* of virtue to promote our happiness, compared with the very early period of life when the moral sentiments display themselves in their full vigor.

II. *Paley's Doctrine, that Moral Sentiments are generated by Imitation, unsatisfactory.*] In answer to this, it may perhaps be alleged, that, when once moral ideas have been formed by the process already described, they are caught by infants from their parents or preceptors, by a sort of imitation, and without any reflection on their part. "There is nothing," says Dr. Paley, "which children imitate, or apply more readily, than expressions of affection or aversion, of approbation, hatred, resentment, and the like; and when these passions and expressions are once connected, (which they

---

* Hartley, though he borrowed the hint and general idea from others, was chiefly instrumental in giving form and currency to this theory, and hence it commonly goes under his name. *Observations on Man*, Chap. IV. Sect. vi. It has found, perhaps, its ablest advocate in James Mill, *Analysis of the Human Mind*, Chap. XXIII. With both it is only part of a more general theory.—Ed.

will soon be by the same association which unites words with their ideas,) the passion will follow the expression, and attach upon the object to which the child has been accustomed to apply the epithet. In a word, when almost every thing else is learned by *imitation*, can we wonder to find the same cause concerned in the generation of our moral sentiments?" *

The plausibility of this reasoning arises entirely from the address with which the author introduces *indirectly* a most important fact with respect to the human mind; a fact which, by engrossing the attention of the reader, is apt to prevent his perceiving, on a superficial view, its inapplicability to the point in dispute, or at least its insufficiency to establish in its full extent the conclusion which is deduced from it. That imitation and the association of ideas have a great influence on our moral judgments and emotions, more particularly in our early years, every man must be sensible who has reflected at all on the subject; and it is a fact which deserves the serious consideration of all who have any concern in the education of youth. But does it therefore follow, that imitation and the association of ideas are sufficient to account for the *origin* of the power of moral perception, and for the *origin* of our notions of right and wrong? † On the contrary, the tendency we have in the infancy of our reason to follow in our moral judgments the example of those whom we love and reverence, and the influence of association, sometimes in guiding and sometimes in misleading us in what we praise or blame, *presuppose* the existence of the power of moral judg-

---

* *Moral Philosophy*, Book I. Chap. V.

† Mr. Stewart has said in another connection, *Philosophy of the Human Mind*, First Part, Chap. V. Part ii. Sect. ii.: — "The association of ideas can never account for the origin of a new notion, or of a pleasure essentially different from all the others which we know. It may, indeed, enable us to conceive how a thing indifferent in itself may become a source of pleasure, by being connected in the mind with something else which is naturally agreeable; but it *presupposes*, in every instance, the existence of those notions and those feelings which it is its province to combine." — ED.

ment, and of the general notions of right and wrong. The power of these adventitious causes over the mind is so great, that there is perhaps no *particular* practice which we may not be trained to approve of or to condemn; but wherever this happens, the operation of these causes supposes us to be already in possession of some faculty by which we are capable of bestowing approbation or blame. It is worthy, too, of remark, that it is only with respect to *particular* practices that education is capable of misleading us; for even when education perverts the judgment, it produces its effect by employing the instrumentality of our moral principles. In many cases it will be found that it operates by combining *a number* of principles against *one;* by associating, for example, a number of worthy dispositions and amiable affections with habits which, if divested of such an alliance, would be regarded as mean and contemptible.

To all this we may add, that our speculative judgments concerning *truth* and *falsehood*, as well as our judgments concerning *right* and *wrong*, are liable to be influenced by imitation and the association of ideas. Even in mathematics, when a pupil of a tender age enters first on the study of the elements, his judgment leans not a little on that of his teacher, and he feels his confidence in the truth of his conclusions sensibly confirmed by his faith in the superior understanding of those whom he looks up to with respect. It is only by degrees that he emancipates himself from this dependence, and comes at last to perceive the irresistible force of demonstrative evidence; and yet it will not be inferred from this that the *power of reasoning* is the result of *imitation* or of *habit.* The conclusion mentioned above with respect to the power of moral judgment is equally erroneous.

III. *Paley's Statement of the Question as to the Existence of a Moral Sense.*] The looseness and sophistry of Paley's reasonings on the subject of the moral faculty may be traced to the vague and indistinct conception he had formed of the point in question. In proof of this I shall transcribe his own words from his *Principles of Moral and Political Philosophy.* It is necessary to premise, that he introduces his argument against the existence of a moral sense by quoting a story from Valerius Maximus, which I shall present to my readers in Dr. Paley's version.

"The father of Caius Toranius had been proscribed by the Triumvirate. Caius Toranius, coming over to the interests of that party, discovered to the officers who were in pursuit of his father's life the place where he concealed himself, and gave them withal a description by which they might distinguish his person when they found him. The old man, more anxious for the safety and fortunes of his son than about the little that might remain of his own life, began immediately to inquire of the officers who seized him, whether his son was well, — whether he had done his duty to the satisfaction of his generals. 'That son,' replied one of the officers, 'so dear to thy affections, betrayed thee to us; by his information thou art apprehended and diest.' The officer with this struck a poniard to his heart, and the unhappy parent fell, not so much affected by his fate as by the means to which he owed it."

"Now," says Dr. Paley, "the question is, whether, if this story were related to the wild boy caught some years ago in the woods of Hanover, or to a savage without experience and without instruction, cut off in his infancy from all intercourse with his species, and consequently under no possible influence of example, authority, education, sympathy, or habit, — whether, I say, such a one would feel, upon the relation, any degree of that *sentiment of disapprobation of Toranius's conduct* which we feel, or not.

"They who maintain the existence of a moral sense, of innate maxims, of a natural conscience, that the love of virtue and hatred of vice are instinctive, or the perception of right and wrong intuitive, (all of which are only different ways of expressing the same opinion,) affirm that he would.

"They who deny the existence of a moral sense, &c., affirm that he would not.

"And upon this issue is joined."*

To those who are at all acquainted with the history of this dispute, it must appear evident that the question is here completely misstated; and that, in the whole of Dr. Paley's subsequent argument on the subject, he combats a phantom of his own imagination. The opinion which he ascribes to his antagonists has been loudly and repeatedly disavowed by all the most eminent moralists who have disputed Locke's reasonings against *innate practical principles;* and is, indeed, so very obviously absurd, that it never could have been for a moment entertained by any person in his senses.

Did it ever enter into the mind of the wildest theorist to imagine that the sense of seeing would enable a man, brought up from the moment of his birth in utter darkness, to form a conception of light and colors? But would it not be equally rash to conclude, from the extravagance of such a supposition, that the sense of seeing is not an original part of the human frame?

The above quotation from Paley forces me to remark further, that, in combating the supposition of a *moral sense*, he has confounded together, as *only different ways of expressing the same opinion*, a variety of systems, which are regarded by all our best philosophers, not only as essentially distinct, but as in some measure opposed to each other. The system of Hutcheson, for example, is identified with that of Cudworth, to which (as will afterwards appear) it stands in direct opposition. But although, in this instance, the author's logical discrimination does not appear to much advantage, the sweeping censure thus bestowed on so many of our most celebrated ethical theories has the merit of throwing a very strong light on that particular view of the subject which it is the aim of his reasonings to establish in contradiction to them all.†

---

* *Moral Philosophy*, Book I. Chap. V.

† On the subject of Paley's illustration cited in the text, Dr. Whewell

Section III.

THE MORAL CONSTITUTION OF HUMAN NATURE NOT DISPROVED BY THE DIVERSITY IN MEN'S MORAL JUDGMENTS.

I. *How far and in what Way our Moral Nature may be affected by Education.*] In the preceding observations I have endeavoured to prove that the moral faculty is an original principle of our constitution, which is

---

remarks: — "To expect to obtain moral axioms by referring the question to a jury of savages, or of men nearly approaching to savages in prejudice, ignorance, or passion, would certainly be a very wild expectation; and I hope it will not be considered a defect in any moral system to which we may be led, that it does not satisfy such an expectation as this. The notion, that an appeal to such a jury is the way to test moral axioms, is something like Paley's proposal of bringing the narration of an atrocious crime before Peter, the wild boy, who was bred up, or rather grew up, like a wild beast; and of doing this, in order to discern whether man has a natural abhorrence of crime. Paley himself points out the difficulty which makes such an experiment impossible: — 'If,' he says, 'he could be made to understand the story.' But it is evident that he *could not* be made to understand the story, except by growing up as a man among men, and *ceasing to be a wild boy*. And, in like manner, we must say of a supposed promiscuous jury of men, by whom you would test our moral axioms, If these men are so savage, and ignorant, and passionate, as to have in them the attributes of men *imperfectly unfolded*, they cannot tell you what moral truths are evident to man *as man*."

And again: — "Truths may be self-evident when we have made a certain progress in thinking, which are not self-evident when we begin to think. And this may be, not because the truths thus later discerned are dependent on the prerequisite truths by any logical tie, or can be inferred from them by argument; but because, by the train of thought by which we come to see those earlier gleams of truth, the mind is unfolded and instructed, so as to perceive the later and fuller light. This may be so, because in the process of thought thus previously gone through we have learnt to classify and distinguish the actions of men around us, or our own feelings and impulses within us. It may be that to groups and classes and relations of emotions and sentiments we have given names; and that through these names language has exercised its power of aiding thought, and has enabled us to see what, without such aid, we could not see. In these ways, and in others, moral truths may become evident to us, when we have made some little advance in the development of our moral nature, and in the power of apprehending such truth; although, so long as we were half imbruted by the absence of any calm and continued thought on such subjects, and by the scantiness of our acquaintance with those relations among men which are the materials for such thought, we were insensible to

not resolvable into any other principle or principles more general than itself; in particular, that it is not resolvable into self-love, or a prudential regard to our own interest. In order, however, completely to establish the existence of the moral faculty as an essential and universal part of human nature, it is necessary to examine with attention the objections which have been stated to this conclusion by some writers, who were either anxious to display their ingenuity by accounting in a different manner for the origin of our moral ideas, or who wished to favor the cause of skepticism by ex-

---

the evidence which now seems so glaring. It requires a *culture* of the human mind to make that evident which, nevertheless, is evident by the *nature* of the human mind.

"And, in truth, we cannot help asking why we should go to savages for the genuine voice of human nature. Why should it be supposed that men are more properly *men*, because in them some of the most important attributes of humanity remain *latent and undeveloped?* If cultured men see, as evident in morals, what savages do not see as evident, are not cultured men still *men?* And all that they know and think, in addition to what savages know and think, did they not come to know it by the use of their human faculties? The early Romans called every *stranger* an *enemy;* every *peregrinus* was *hostis*. The later Romans filled the theatre with thunders of applause, when the poet made the actor say,

'*Homo sum, humani nihil a me alienum puto.*'

Which of these two was the genuine voice of humanity? Was not the latter evidently the assent to the irresistible evidence of a moral truth? Was that earlier practical denial of this moral truth really the utterance of a moral conviction? Was it not an utterance which came from man, not as the utterance of *conviction*, but of uncontrolled fear and anger? not an articulate utterance in the name of humanity, but an inarticulate cry, borrowing part of its import from the ferine nature of the nation? It was a trace of the wolf's milk." — *Lectures on Systematic Morality*, Lect. II. pp. 34, 38. See also Lieber's *Political Ethics*, Book II. Chap. III, and Sedgwick's *Discourse on the Studies of the University*, pp. 57 *et seq.*, and Appendix (E).

"Peter the Wild Boy" made a great noise among scientific men in the early part of the last century. "Swift has immortalized him in his humorous production, *It cannot rain, but it pours; or, London strewed with Rarities.* Linnæus gave him a niche in the *Systema Naturæ*, under the denomination of *Juvenis Hanoveranus;* Buffon, De Paauw, and J. J. Rousseau have extolled him as the true child of nature, *the genuine unsophisticated man*. Monboddo is still more enthusiastic, declaring his appearance to be a much more important occurrence than the discovery of the planet Uranus." — Lawrence's *Natural History of Man*, Chap. II. He turned out to be an *idiotic* boy, who had been lost in the woods, or driven into them and abandoned, about a year before he was brought into such notice. — ED.

plaining away the reality and immutability of moral distinctions.

Among these objections, that which merits the most careful consideration, from the characters of those by whom it is maintained, is founded on the possibility of explaining the fact without increasing the number of original principles in our constitution. The rules of morality, it has been supposed, were, in the first instance, brought to light by the sagacity of philosophers and politicians; and it is only in consequence of the influence of education that they appear to form an original part of the human frame. The diversity of opinions among different nations with respect to the morality of particular actions has been considered as a strong confirmation of this doctrine.

But the power of education, although great, is confined within certain limits. It is, indeed, much more extensive than philosophers once believed, as sufficiently appears from those modern discoveries, with respect to the distant parts of the globe, which have so wonderfully enlarged our knowledge of human nature, and which show clearly that many sentiments and opinions, which had been formerly regarded as inseparable from the nature of man, are the results of accidental situation. If our forefathers, however, went into one extreme on this point, we seem to be at present in no small danger of going into the opposite one, by considering man as entirely a factitious being, that may be moulded into any form by education and fashion.

I have said that the power of education is confined within certain limits. The reason is obvious, for it is by coöperating with the natural principles of the mind that education produces its effects. Nay, this very susceptibility of education, which is acknowledged to belong universally to the race, presupposes the existence of certain principles which are common to all mankind.

The influence of education in diversifying the appearances which the moral constitution of man exhibits in different instances depends chiefly on that law of our constitution which was formerly called the association of ideas; and this law supposes, in every case, that there are opinions and feelings essential to the human frame, by a combination with which external circumstances lay hold of the mind, and adapt it to its accidental situation. What we daily see happen in the trifling article of dress may help us to conceive how the association of ideas operates in matters of more serious consequence. Fashion, it is well known, can reconcile us, in the course of a few weeks, to the most absurd and fantastical ornament; but does it follow from this that fashion could create our ideas of beauty and elegance? During the time we have seen this ornament worn, it has been confined, in a great measure, to those whom we consider as models of taste, and has been gradually associated with the impressions produced by the real elegance of their appearance and manner. When it pleases by itself, the effect is not to be ascribed to the thing considered abstractedly, nor to any change which our general notions of beauty have undergone, but to the impressions with which it has been generally connected, and which it naturally recalls to the mind. The case is nearly the same with our moral sentiments. A man of splendid virtues attracts some esteem also to his imperfections, and, if placed in a conspicuous situation, may corrupt the moral sentiments of the multitude in the same manner in which he may introduce an absurd or fantastical ornament by his whimsical taste in the articles of dress. The commanding influence of Cato's virtues seems to have produced somewhat of this effect on the minds of some of his admirers. He was accused, we are told, of intemperance in wine; nor do his apologists pretend altogether to deny the charge. "But," says one of them, "it would be much easier to prove that intemperance is a decent and respectable quality, than that Cato could be guilty of any vice." "Catoni ebrietas objecta est; et facilius efficiet, quisquis objecerit, hoc crimen honestum, quam turpem Catonem."

In general it may be remarked, that as education

may vary in particular cases the opinions of individuals with respect to the objects of taste, without being able to create our notions of beauty or deformity, of grandeur or meanness, so education may vary our sentiments with respect to particular actions, but could not create our notions of right and wrong, of merit and demerit.*

II. *Diversity in Men's Moral Judgments.*] With re-

* It is observed by Condorcet in his *Eloge* on Euler, "*That, if we except the common maxims of morality*, there is no one truth which can boast of having been so generally adopted, or through such a succession of ages, as certain ridiculous and pernicious errors." The assertion, although not without some foundation in fact, is manifestly expressed by this author in terms too strong and unqualified. I quote it here chiefly on account of the remarkable concession which it involves in favor of *the fundamental principles of morality*; — a subject on which it has been generally alleged, by skeptical writers, that our opinions are more liable than on most others to be warped by the influence of education and fashion.

[Sir James Mackintosh is a strenuous asserter of the general uniformity of men's moral judgments. "I do not speak of the theory of morals, but of the rule of life. First examine the fact, and see whether, from the earliest times, any improvement, or even any change, has been made in the practical rules of human conduct. Look at the code of Moses. I speak of it now as a mere human composition, without considering its sacred origin. Considering it merely in that light, it is the most ancient and the most curious memorial of the early history of mankind. More than three thousand years have elapsed since the composition of the Pentateuch; and let any man, if he is able, tell me in what important respects the *rule of life* has varied since that distant period. Let the Institutes of Menu be explored with the same view; we shall arrive at the same conclusion. Let the books of false religion be opened; it will be found that their moral system is, in all its grand features, the same. The impostors who composed them were compelled to pay this homage to the uniform moral sentiments of the world. Examine the codes of nations, those authentic depositories of the moral judgments of men; you everywhere find the same rules prescribed, the same duties imposed: even the boldest of those ingenious skeptics who have attacked every other opinion has spared the sacred and immutable simplicity of the rules of life. In our common duties, Bayle and Hume agree with Bossuet and Barrow. Such as the rule was at the first dawn of history, such it continues till the present day. Ages roll over mankind; mighty nations pass away like a shadow; virtue alone remains the same, immortal and unchangeable." — *Memoirs, by his Son*, Vol. I. Chap. III. p. 120.

Even should we think that the statement, as here made, needs further qualification, there can be no doubt that the common opinion errs still more on the other side. One reason why the points of difference in morals are thought to be more numerous than they really are is, that these alone are made the subject of frequent discussion; and properly so, because it is only in this way that they can be cleared up, and reconciled. — Ed.]

spect to the historical facts which have been quoted as proofs that the moral judgments of mankind are entirely factitious, we may venture to assert in general, that none of them justify so very extravagant a conclusion; that a great part of them are the effects of misrepresentation; and that others lead to a conclusion directly the reverse of what has been drawn from them. It would hardly be necessary, in the present times, to examine them seriously, were it not for the authority which, in the opinion of many, they still continue to derive from the sanction of Mr. Locke.

"Have there not been whole nations," says this eminent philosopher, "and those of the most civilized people, among whom the exposing their children, and leaving them in the fields to perish by want or wild beasts, has been the practice, as little condemned or scrupled as the begetting them? Do they not still, in some countries, put them into the same graves with their mothers, if they die in child-birth, or despatch them, if a pretended astrologer declares them to have unhappy stars? And are there not places where, at a certain age, they kill or expose their *parents* without any remorse at all? Where, then, are our innate ideas of justice, piety, gratitude; or where is that universal consent that assures us there are such inbred rules?" *

To this question of Locke's so satisfactory an answer has been given by various writers, that it would be superfluous to enlarge on the subject here. It is sufficient to refer, *on the origin of infanticide*, to Mr. Smith's *Theory of Moral Sentiments;* † and *on the alleged impiety among some rude tribes of children towards their parents*, to Charron *Sur la Sagesse*, ‡ and to an excellent note of Dr. Beattie's in his *Essay on Fable and Romance.* The reasonings of the last two

---

* Book I. Chap. III. § 9.

† Part V. Chap. II.

‡ Liv. II. Chap. VIII. Charron's argument is evidently pointed at certain passages in Montaigne's *Essays*, in which that ingenious writer has fallen into a train of thought very similar to that which is the groundwork of Locke's reasonings against *innate practical principles.*

writers are strongly confirmed by Mr. Ellis, in his *Voyage for the Discovery of a Northwest Passage*, and by Mr. Curtis (afterwards Sir Roger Curtis), in a paper containing *Some Particulars with Respect to the Country of Labradore*, published in the Philosophical Transactions for the year 1773.

In order to form a competent judgment on facts of this nature, it is necessary to attend to a variety of considerations which have been too frequently overlooked by philosophers; and, in particular, to make proper allowances for the three following: —

1. For the different situations in which mankind are placed, partly by the diversity in their physical circumstances, and partly by the unequal degrees of civilization which they have attained.

2. For the diversity of their speculative opinions, arising from their unequal measures of knowledge or of capacity; and,

3. For the different moral import of the same action under different systems of external behaviour.

III. *First Cause of Diversity in Men's Moral Judgments. Difference of Condition.* (1.) *As regards Property.*] In a part of the globe where the soil and climate are so favorable as to yield all the necessaries and many of the luxuries of life with little or no labor on the part of man, it may reasonably be expected that the ideas of men will be more loose concerning *the rights of property* than where nature has been less liberal in her gifts. As the right of property is founded, *in the first instance*, on the natural sentiment, that *the laborer is entitled to the fruits of his own labor*, it is not surprising that, where little or no labor is required for the gratification of our desires, theft should be regarded as a very venial offence. There is here no contradiction in the moral judgments of mankind. Men feel *there*, with respect to those articles which we appropriate with the most anxious care, as we, in this part of the world, feel with respect to *air*, *light*, and *water*. If a country could be found in which no injustice was apprehended in depriving an individual of an enjoyment which he had provided for himself by a long course of persevering industry, the fact would be something to the purpose. But *this*, we may venture to say, has not yet been found to be the case in any quarter of the globe. That the circumstance I have mentioned is the true explanation of the prevalence of theft in the South Sea Islands, and of the venial light in which it is there regarded, appears plainly from the accounts of our most intelligent navigators.

"There was another circumstance," says Captain Cook, speaking of the inhabitants of the Sandwich Islands, "in which the people perfectly resembled the other islanders we had visited. At first, on their entering the ship, they endeavoured to steal every thing they came near, or *rather to take it openly, as what we either should not resent, or not hinder.*" (January, 1778.)

In another place, talking of the same people:—"These islanders," says he, "merited our best commendations in their commercial intercourse, never once attempting to cheat us, either ashore or alongside the ships. Some of them, indeed, as already mentioned, *at first* betrayed a thievish disposition; or rather, they thought that they had *a right* to every thing they could lay their hands on; but they soon laid aside a conduct which we convinced them they could not persevere in with impunity."

In another part of the voyage, (April, 1778,) in which he gives an account of the American Indians near King George's Sound, he contrasts their notions on the subject of theft with those of the South Sea Islanders. "The inhabitants of the South Sea Islands, rather than be idle, would steal any thing they could lay their hands on, without ever considering whether it could be of use to them or no. The novelty of the object was with them a sufficient motive for endeavouring, by any indirect means, to get possession of it; which marked, that in such cases they were rather actuated by a childish curiosity than by a dishonest disposition, *regardless of the modes of supplying real wants.* The inhabitants of Nootka, who invaded our property, have not such an apology. They were *thieves* in the strictest sense of the word; for they pilfered nothing from us but what they knew could be converted to the purposes of private utility, and had a *real value*, according to their estimation of things." He adds, that he had "abundant proof that stealing is much practised among themselves"; — but it is evident, from the manner in which he expresses himself, that *theft* was not *here* considered in the same venial or indifferent light as in those parts of the globe where the bounty of nature deprives exclusive property of almost all its value.*

In general it will be found, that the ideas of rude nations on the subject of *property* are precise and decided, in proportion to *the degree of labor* to which they have been habituated in procuring the means of subsistence. Of one barbarous people, (the Greenlanders,) we are expressly told by a very authentic writer, (Crantz,) that their regard to property acquired by labor is not only strict, but approaches to superstition. "Not one of them," says he, "will appropriate to himself a sea-dog in which he finds one or more harpoons with untorn thongs; nor even carry away drift wood, or other things thrown up by the sea, *if they are covered with a stone*, because they consider this as an indication that they have already been appropriated by some other person." †

---

* See, also, Anderson's *Remarks*, February, 1777, and December, 1777.

† *History of Greenland*, Vol. I. p. 181. The following passage of Voltaire is perhaps liable to the charge of over-refinement; but it sufficiently shows that he saw clearly the general principle on which the lax opinions of some nations on the subject of theft are to be explained.

"On a beau nous dire, qu'à Lacedémone, le larcin étoit ordonné; ce n'est là qu'un abus des mots. La même chose que nous appellons *larcin*, n'etoit point commandée à Lacedémone; mais dans une ville, où tout etoit en commun, la permission qu'on donnoit de prendre habilement ce que des particuliers s'approprioient contre la loi, étoit une manière de punir l'esprit de propriété défendu chez ces peuples. *Le tien et le mien* étoit un crime, dont ce que nous appellons *larcin* étoit la punition." — Voltaire's *Account of Newton's Discoveries.* Some of his other remarks on Locke are very curious.

IV. (2.) *As regards the Uses of Money.*] Another very remarkable instance of an apparent diversity in the moral judgments of mankind occurs in the contradictory opinions entertained by different ages and nations on the moral lawfulness of exacting *interest* for the use of money. Aristotle, in the first book of his *Politics* (6th chap.), speaking of the various ways of getting money, considers agriculture and the rearing of cattle as honorable and natural, because the earth itself, and all animals, are by nature fruitful; "but to make money from money, which is barren and unfruitful," he pronounces "to be the worst of all modes of accumulation, and the utmost corruption of artificial degeneracy. By commerce," he observes, "money is perverted from the purpose of exchange to that of gain. Still, however, this gain is obtained by the mutual transfer of different objects; but usury, by transferring merely the same object from one hand to another, generates money from money; and the interest thus generated is therefore called 'offspring,' as being precisely of the same nature, and of the same specific substance, with that from which it proceeds." * — Similar sentiments with respect to *usury* (under which title was compre-

* Gillies's Translation. The argument of Aristotle is so extremely absurd and puerile, that it could never have led this most acute and profound philosopher to the conclusion it is employed to support, but may be justly numbered among the instances in which speculative men have exerted their ingenuity to defend, by sophistical reasonings, the established prejudices of the times in which they lived, and in which *the supposed evidence of the inference* has served, in their estimation, to compensate for the weakness of the premises. It is, however, worthy of remark, that the argument, such as it is, was manifestly suggested by the etymology of the word τόκος (interest), from the verb τίκτω, *pario, to breed* or *bring forth*; an etymology which seems to imply that the principal generates the interest. The same idea, too, occurs in the scene between Antonio and Shylock, in the *Merchant of Venice:* —

> "If thou wilt lend this money, lend it not
> As to thy friends; (for when did friendship take
> *A breed of barren metal from his friend?*)
> But lend it rather to thine enemy,
> Who, if he break, thou mayst with better face
> Exact the penalty."
>
> Act I. Scene III.

hended every *premium*, great or small, which was received by way of interest) occur in the Roman writers. "Concerning the arts," says Cicero, in his first book *De Officiis*, "and the means of acquiring wealth which are to be accounted liberal, and which mean, the following are the sentiments usually entertained. In the first place, those means of gain are in the *least* credit which incur the hatred of mankind, as those of tax-gatherers and usurers." The same author (in the second book of the same work) mentions an anecdote of old Cato, who, being asked what he thought of lending money upon interest, answered, "What do you think of the crime of murder?"

In the code of the Jewish legislator, the regulations concerning loans imply manifestly, that to exact a *premium* for the thing lent was an act of unkindness unsuitable to the fraternal relation in which the Israelites stood to one another. "Thou shalt not lend," it is said, "upon usury to thy brother: usury of money, usury of victuals, usury of any thing that is lent upon usury. Unto a stranger thou mayest lend upon usury; but unto thy brother thou shalt not lend upon usury; that the Lord thy God may bless thee in all that thou settest thine hand to, in the land whither thou goest to possess it." *

In consequence of this prohibition in the Mosaic law, the primitive Christians, conceiving that they ought to look on all men, both Jews and Gentiles, as *brethren*, inferred, (partly, perhaps, from the prohibition given by Moses, and partly from the general prejudices then prevalent against usury,) that it was against the Christian law to take interest from any man. And, accordingly, there is no crime against which the Fathers in their homilies declaim with more vehemence. The same abhorrence of usury of every kind appears in the canon law, insomuch that the penalty by that law is excommunication; nor is the usurer allowed burial until he has made restitution of what he got by usury, or security is given that restitution shall be made after his

* Deut. xxiii. 19, 20.

death. About the middle of the seventeenth century, we find the divines of the Church of England very often preaching against all interest for the use of money, even that which the law allowed, as a gross immorality. And not much earlier it was the general opinion, both of divines and lawyers, that, although law permitted a certain rate of interest to prevent greater evils, and in compliance with the general corruption of men, (as the law of Moses permitted polygamy, and authorized divorce for slight causes, among the Jews,) yet that the rules of morality did not sanction the taking *any interest* for money; at least, that it was a very doubtful point whether they did. The same opinion was maintained in the English House of Commons by some of the members who were lawyers, in the debate upon a bill brought in not much more than a hundred years ago.

I need not remark how completely the sentiments of mankind are now changed upon the subject; insomuch that a moralist or divine would expose himself to ridicule if he should seriously think it worth his while to use arguments to prove the lawfulness of a practice which was formerly held in universal abhorrence. The consistency of this practice (in cases where the debtor is able to pay the interest) with the strictest morality appears to us so manifest and indisputable, that it would be thought equally absurd to argue for it as against it.*

The diversity of judgments, however, on this particular question, instead of proving a diversity in the *moral*

---

* A learned gentleman, indeed, of the Middle Temple, Mr. Plowden, (a lawyer, I believe, of the Roman Catholic persuasion,) who published, about thirty years ago, a *Treatise upon the Law of Usury and Annuities*, has employed no less than fifty-nine pages of his work in considering the law of usury in a *spiritual view*. in order to establish the following conclusion: — "That it is not sinful, but lawful, for a British subject to receive legal interest for the money he may lend, whether he receive it in annual dividends from the public, or in interest from private individuals who may have borrowed it upon mortgage, bond, or otherwise." M. Necker, too, in the notes annexed to his *Eloge* on Colbert, thought it necessary for him to offer an apology to the Church of Rome for the freedom with which he ventured to write upon this critical subject. "Ce que je dis de interèt est sous un point de vue politique, et n'a point de rapport avec les respectables maximes de la religion sur ce point."

judgments of mankind, affords an illustration of the uniformity of their opinions concerning the fundamental rules of moral duty.

In a state where there is little or no commerce, the great motive for borrowing being necessity, the value of a loan cannot be ascertained by calculation, as it *may* be where money is borrowed for the purposes of trade. In such circumstances, therefore, every money-lender who accepts of interest will be regarded in the same odious light in which pawnbrokers are considered among *us;* and the man "who putteth out his money to usury" will naturally be classed (as he is in the words of Scripture) with him who "taketh reward against the innocent." †

These considerations, while they account for the origin of the opinions concerning the practice of taking interest for money among those nations of antiquity whose commercial transactions were few and insignificant, will be sufficient, at the same time, to establish its reasonableness and equity in countries where money is most commonly borrowed for the purposes of commercial profit, and where, of consequence, the use of it has a fixed and determinate value, depending (like that of any commodity in general request) on the circumstances of the market at the time. In such countries *both* parties are benefited by the transaction, and even the state is a gainer in the end. The *lenders* of money are frequently widows and orphans, who subsist on the interest of their slender funds, while the *borrowers* as frequently belong to the most opulent class of the community, who wish to enlarge their capital and extend their trade; and who, by doing so, are enabled to give further encouragement to industry, and to supply labor and bread to the indigent.

The prejudices, therefore, against usury among the ancient philosophers were the natural result of the state of society which fell under their observation.

---

† Ps. xv. 5.

The prohibition of usury among the Jews in their own mutual transactions, while they were permitted to take a *premium* for the money which they lent to strangers, was in perfect consistency with the other principles of their political code; commerce being interdicted, as tending to an intercourse with idolaters, and mortgages prevented by the indefeasible right which every man had to his lands.

V. (3.) *Want of an Efficient Police.*] I shall only mention one instance more to illustrate the effects of different states of society in modifying the moral judgments of mankind. It relates to the crime of assassination, which we now justly consider as the most dreadful of any; but which must necessarily have been viewed in a very different light when laws and magistrates were unknown, and when the only check on injustice was *the principle of resentment.* As it is the nature of this principle, not only to seek the punishment of the delinquent, but to prompt the injured person to inflict the punishment with his own hand, so in every country the criminal jurisdiction of the magistrate has been the last branch of his authority that was established. Where the police, therefore, is weak, murders must not only be more frequent, *but are really less criminal*, than in a society like ours, where the private rights of individuals are completely protected by law, and where there hardly occurs an instance, excepting in a case of self-defence, in which one man can be justified for shedding the blood of another. And even when, in a rude age, a murder is committed from unjustifiable motives of self-interest or jealousy, yet the frequency of the occurrence prevents the minds of men from revolting so strongly at the sight of blood as we do at present. It is on this very principle that Mr. Mitford accounts for the manners and ideas that prevailed in the heroic ages of Greece.

But it is unnecessary, on this head, to appeal to the history of early times, or of distant nations. In our own country of Scotland, about two centuries ago, what shocking murders were perpetrated, and seemingly without remorse, by men who were by no means wholly destitute of a sense of religion and morality! Dr. Robertson remarks, that "Buchanan relates the murder of Cardinal Beatoun and of Rizzio without expressing those feelings which are natural to a man, or that indignation which became an historian. Knox, whose mind was fiercer and more unpolished, talks of the death of Beatoun and of the Duke of Guise, not only without censure, but with the utmost exultation. On the other hand, the Bishop of Ross mentions the assassination of the Earl of Murray with some degree of applause. Blackwood dwells on it with the most indecent triumph; and ascribes it directly to the hand of God. Lord Ruthven, the principal actor in the conspiracy against Rizzio, wrote an account of it some time before his own death; and in all his long narrative there is not one expression of regret, or one symptom of compunction, for a crime no less dishonorable than barbarous. Morton, equally guilty of the same crime, entertained the same sentiments concerning it; and in his last moments, neither he himself, nor the ministers who attended him, seem to have considered it as an action which called for repentance. Even then he talks of 'David's slaughter' as coolly as if it had been an innocent or commendable deed."*

The reflections of Dr. Robertson on these assassinations, which were formerly so common in this country, are candid and judicious. "In consequence of the limit-

* *History of Scotland*, Book IV. The following lines, in which Sir David Lindsay reprobates the murder of his contemporary and enemy, Cardinal Beatoun, deserve to be added to the instances quoted by Dr. Robertson, as an illustration of the moral sentiments of our ancestors. They are expressed with a *naïveté* which places in a strong light both the moral and religious principles of that age.

"As for this Cardinal, I grant,
He was a man we well might want;
God will forgive it soon:
But of a sooth, the truth to say,
Altho' the loun be well away,
The act was foully done."

ed power of our princes, the administration of justice was extremely feeble and dilatory. An attempt to punish the crimes of a chieftain, or even of his vassals, often excited rebellions and civil wars. To nobles haughty and independent, among whom the causes of discord were many and unavoidable; who were quick in discerning an injury, and impatient to revenge it; who esteemed it infamous to submit to an enemy, and cowardly to forgive him; who considered the right of punishing those who had injured them as a privilege of their order, and a mark of independency; such slow proceedings were extremely unsatisfactory. The blood of their adversary was, in their opinion, the only thing that could wash away an affront. Where that was not shed, their revenge was disappointed; their courage became suspected, and a stain was left on their honor. That vengeance which the impotent hand of the magistrate could not inflict, their own could easily execute. Under a government so feeble, men assumed, *as in a state of nature*, the right of judging and redressing their own wrongs. And thus *assassination*, a crime of all others the most destructive to society, came not only to be allowed, but to be deemed honorable." In another passage he observes, that "mankind became thus habituated to blood, not only in times of war, but of peace; and from this, as well as other causes, contracted an amazing ferocity of temper and of manners."

VI. *Second Cause of Diversity in Men's Moral Judgments. Difference in Speculative Opinions.*] The second cause I mentioned of the apparent diversity among mankind in their moral judgments is the diversity in their speculative opinions.

The manner in which this cause operates will appear obvious, if it be considered that nature, by the suggestions of our moral principles, only recommends to us particular *ends*, but leaves it to our reason to ascertain the most effectual *means* by which these *ends* are to be attained. Thus nature points out to us our own happiness, and also the happiness of our fellow-creatures, as objects towards the attainment of which our best exertions ought to be directed; but she has left us to exercise our reason, both in ascertaining what the constituents of happiness are, and how they may be most completely secured. Hence, according to the different points of view in which these subjects of consideration may appear to different understandings, there must of necessity be a diversity of judgments with respect to the morality of the same actions. One man, for example, believes that the happiness of society is most effectually consulted by an implicit obedience *in all cases* to the will of the civil magistrate. Another, that the mischiefs to be apprehended from resistance and insurrection in cases of urgent necessity are trifling when compared with those which may result to ourselves and our posterity from an established despotism. The former will of course be an advocate for the duty of passive obedience; the latter for the *right*, and, in certain supposable cases, for the *obligation* of resistance. Both of these men, however, agree in the general principle, that it is our duty to promote to the utmost of our power the happiness of society; and they differ from each other only on a speculative question of expediency.

In like manner, there is a wide diversity between the moral systems of ancient and modern times on the subject of *suicide*. Both, however, agree in this, that it is the duty of man to obey the will of his Creator, and to consult every intimation of it that his reason can discover, as the supreme law of his conduct. They differed only in their *speculative doctrines* concerning the interpretation of the will of God, as manifested by the dispensations of his providence in the events of human life. The prejudices of the ancients on this subject were indeed founded in a very partial and erroneous view of circumstances (arising, however, not unnaturally, from the unsettled state of society in the ancient republics); but they only afford an additional instance of the numerous mistakes to which human *reason* is liable; not of a fluctuation in the judgments of mankind concerning the fundamental rules of moral duty.*

VII. *Third Cause of Diversity in Men's Moral Judgments. Different Systems of Behaviour.*] The different moral import, too, of the same material action, under different systems of external behaviour, deserves particular attention, in forming an estimate of the moral sentiments of different ages and nations.

This difference is chiefly owing to two causes: — First, to the different *conceptions of happiness and misery*, — of what is to be desired and shunned, — which men are led to form in different states of society. Secondly, to the *effect of accident*, which, as it leads men to speak different languages in different countries, so it leads them to express the same dispositions of the heart by different external observances.

1. Where the opinions of mankind vary concerning the external circumstances that constitute happiness, the external expressions of benevolence must vary of course. Thus, in the fact referred to by Locke concerning the Indians in the neighbourhood of Hudson's Bay, the wishes of the aged parent being different from what we are accustomed to observe in this part of the world, the marks of filial affection on the part of the child must vary also. "In some countries honor is associated with suffering, and it is reckoned a favor to be killed with circumstances of torture. Instances of this occur in the manners of some American nations, and in the pride which an Indian matron feels when placed on the funeral pile of her deceased husband." † In such cases an action may have to us all the external marks of extreme cruelty, while it proceeds from a disposition generous and affectionate.

---

* See Lieber's *Political Ethics*, Book I. Sect. xviii., where the conduct of the Thugs of India — a fanatical sect pursuing murder as a trade, and under the supposed sanction of religion — is reconciled with the moral constitution of human nature. — Ed.

† Ferguson's *Moral and Political Science*, Part II. Chap. II. Sect. iv. [For facts in confirmation of this doctrine, see *Historical Illustrations of the Passions*, particularly Vol. I. Chap. III. and IV.]

2. A difference in the moral import of the same action often arises from the same accidental causes which lead men, in different parts of the globe, to express the same ideas by different arbitrary signs.

What happens in the trifling forms and ceremonies of behaviour may serve to illustrate the operation of the same causes on more important occasions. "In the general principles of urbanity, politeness, or civility, we may venture to assert that the opinions of all nations are agreed; but in the expression of this disposition, we meet with endless varieties. In Europe, it is the form of respect to uncover the *head;* in Japan, the corresponding form is said to be to uncover the *foot* by dropping the slipper.* Persons unacquainted with any language but their own are apt to think the words they use natural and fixed expressions of things; while the words of a different language they consider as mere jargon, or the result of caprice. In the same manner, forms of behaviour different from their own appear offensive and irrational, or a perverse substitution of absurd for reasonable manners.

"Among the varieties of this sort, we find actions, gestures, and forms of expression, in their own nature indifferent, entered into the code of civil or religious duties, and enforced under the strongest sanctions of public censure or esteem; or under the strongest denunciations of the Divine indignation or favor.

"Numberless ceremonies and observances in the ritual of different sects are to be accounted for on the same principles which produce the diversity of names or signs for the same thing in the vocabulary of different languages. Thus, the generality of Christians when they pray take off their hats; the Jews when they pray put them on. Such acts, how strongly soever they may affect the imaginations of the multitude, may just-

* "Even here," Sir Joshua Reynolds ingeniously remarks, "we may perhaps observe a general idea running through all the varieties; to wit, the general idea of making the body less in token of respect, whether by bowing the body, kneeling, prostration, pulling off the upper part of the dress, or throwing aside the lower."

ly be considered as part of the arbitrary language of particular countries; implying no diversity whatever in the ideas or feelings of those among whom they are established." *

As a further proof of the impossibility of judging of the general character of a people from their opinions concerning the morality of *particular* actions, we may observe; that, in some of the writings of the ancient moralists, we meet with the most refined and sublime precepts blended promiscuously with dissuasives from the most shocking and detestable crimes; in one sentence, perhaps, a precept which may be read with advantage by the most enlightened of the present times; and in the next, a dissuasive from some crime which no one now could be supposed to perpetrate who had not arrived at the last stage of depravity.

I have dwelt very long on this subject, because, if it be painful to be staggered in our belief of the immutability of moral distinctions by the first aspect of the history of mankind, it affords a tenfold pleasure to those who feel themselves interested in the cause of morality, when they find, on an accurate examination, that those facts on which skeptics have laid the greatest stress are not only consistent with the moral constitution of man, but result necessarily from this constitution, diversified in its effects according to the different circumstances in which the individual is situated. To trace in this manner the essential principles of the human frame, amidst the various disguises it borrows from accidental causes, is one of the most interesting employments of philosophical curiosity; nor is there, perhaps, a more satisfactory gratification to a liberal mind, than when it recognizes, under the superstition, the ignorance, and the loathsome sensualities of savage life, the kindred features of humanity, and the indelible vestiges of that Divine image after which man was originally formed.

VIII. *Locke's Connection with this Controversy.*] The

* See Ferguson's *Moral and Political Science*, Part II. Chap. II. Sect. iv.

doctrines on this subject which I have hitherto been endeavouring to refute, (how erroneous soever in their principles, and dangerous in their consequences,) have been maintained by some writers who certainly were not unfriendly in their views to the interests of virtue and of mankind. In proof of this, I need only mention the name of Mr. Locke, who, in the course of a long and honorable life, distinguished himself no less by the exemplary worth of his private character, and by his ardent zeal for civil and religious liberty, than by the depth and originality of his philosophical speculations. His errors, however, ought not, on these accounts, to be treated with reverence; but, on the contrary, they require a more careful and severe examination, in consequence of the high authority they derive from his genius and his virtues. And accordingly, I have enlarged on such of his opinions as seemed to me favorable to skeptical views concerning the foundation of morals, at much greater length than the ingenuity or plausibility of his reasonings in support of them may appear to some to have merited.

To these opinions of Locke Lord Shaftesbury has alluded, in various parts of his works, with a good deal of indignation; and particularly in the following passage of his *Advice to an Author*. " One would imagine that our philosophical writers, who pretend to treat of morals, should far outdo our poets in recommending virtue, and representing what is *fair* and *amiable* in human actions. One would imagine, that, if they turned their eyes towards remote countries, (of which they affect so much to speak,) they should search for that simplicity of manners, and innocence of behaviour, which has been often known among mere savages, ere they were corrupted by our commerce, and, by sad example, instructed in all kinds of treachery and inhumanity. It would be of advantage to us to hear the cause of this strange corruption in ourselves, and be made to consider of our deviation from nature, and from that just purity of manners which might be expected, especially from a people so assisted and enlightened by religion

For who would not naturally expect more justice, fidelity, temperance, and honesty from Christians than from Mahometans or mere Pagans? But so far are our modern moralists from condemning any unnatural vices or corrupt manners, whether in our own or foreign climates, that they would have *vice* itself appear as natural as *virtue;* and, from the worst examples, would represent to us, 'that all actions are *naturally* indifferent; that they have no note or character of good or ill in *themselves*, but are distinguished by mere fashion, law, or *arbitrary* decree.' Wonderful philosophy! raised from the dregs of an illiterate, mean kind, which was ever despised among the great ancients, and rejected by all men of action or sound erudition; but, in these ages, imperfectly copied from the original, and, with much disadvantage, imitated and assumed in common, both by devout and indevout attempters in the moral kind." *

Besides these incidental remarks on Locke, which occur in different parts of Shaftesbury's writings, there is a letter of his addressed to a student at the university, which relates almost entirely to the opinion we have been considering, and contains some excellent observations on the subject.

In this letter Lord Shaftesbury observes, that "all those called *free writers* now-a-days have espoused those principles which Mr. Hobbes set afoot in this last age." "Mr. Locke," he continues, "as much as I honor him on account of other writings (viz. on government, policy, trade, coin, education, toleration, &c.), and as well as I knew him, and can answer for his sincerity, as a most zealous Christian and believer, did however go in the selfsame track, and is followed by the Tindals, and all the other ingenious free authors of our time.

"It was Mr. Locke that struck the home blow; for Mr. Hobbes's character and base, slavish principles of government took off the poison of his philosophy. It was Mr. Locke that struck at all fundamentals, threw

* Part III. Sect. iii.

all order and virtue out of the world, and made the very ideas of these (which are the same with those of God) unnatural, and without foundation in our minds *Innate* is a word he poorly plays upon; the right word, though less used, is *connatural*. For what has birth, or progress of the *fœtus* out of the womb, to do in this case? The question is not about the time the ideas entered, or the moment that one body came out of the other, but whether the constitution of man be such, that, being adult and grown up, at such or such a time, sooner or later, (no matter when,) the idea and sense of order, administration, and a God will not *infallibly, inevitably, necessarily, spring up in him?*" *

In this last remark, Lord Shaftesbury appears to me to place the question concerning *innate ideas* upon the right and only philosophical footing, and to afford a key to all the confusion which runs through Locke's argument on the subject. The observations which follow are not less just and valuable; but I must not indulge myself in any further extracts at present.†

These passages of Shaftesbury, in some of which the warmth of his temper has betrayed him into expressions disrespectful to Locke, have drawn on him a number of very severe animadversions, particularly from Warburton, in the preface to his *Divine Legation*

* *Letters to a Student at the University*, Let. VIII.

† Notwithstanding, however, the countenance which Locke's reasonings against *innate practical principles* have the appearance of giving to the philosophy of Hobbes, I have not a doubt that the difference of opinion between him and Lord Shaftesbury on this point was almost entirely verbal. Of this I have elsewhere produced ample proofs; but the following passage will suffice for my present purpose. "I would not be mistaken, as if, because I deny an innate law, I thought there were none but positive laws. There is a great deal of difference between an *innate law* and a *law of nature*, between something imprinted on our minds in their very original, and something that we, being ignorant of, may attain to the knowledge of, by the use and due application of our natural faculties. And I think they equally forsake the truth, who, running into the contrary extremes, either affirm an innate law, or deny that there is a law knowable by the light of nature, without the help of a positive revelation." — Locke's *Essay concerning Human Understanding*, Book I. Chap. III. § 13.

[See, however, Cousin, *Histoire de la Philosophie du XVIIIe Siècle*, Tom. II. Leçon XXe. Or Professor Henry's translation of the same, *Elements of Psychology*, Chap. V.]

of Moses. But although Shaftesbury's personal allusions to Locke cannot be justified, some allowance ought to be made for the indignation of a generous mind at a doctrine which (however well meant by the proposer) strikes at the very root of morality. In this instance, too, it is not improbable that the discussion of the general argument may have added to the asperity of his style, by reviving the memory of the private controversies which, it is presumable, had formerly been carried on between Locke and him on this important subject. It is well known that Shaftesbury was Locke's pupil, and also that their tempers and literary tastes were not suitable to each other. In this it is commonly supposed that the former was to blame; but, I presume, not *wholly.* Dr. Warton tells us, that Mr. Locke affected to despise poetry, and that he depreciated the ancients; "which circumstance," he adds, "as I am informed from undoubted authority, was the subject of perpetual discontent and dispute between him and his pupil, Lord Shaftesbury." * That Shaftesbury was not insensible to Locke's real merits appears sufficiently from a passage in the first of his *Letters to a Student at the University.* "However, I am not sorry that I lent you Locke's *Essay*, a book that may as well qualify men for business and the world as for the sciences and the university. No one has done more towards the recalling of philosophy from barbarity into use and practice of the world, and into the company of the better and politer sort, who might well be ashamed of it in its other dress. No one has opened a better and clearer way to reasoning."

Section IV.

LICENTIOUS SYSTEMS OF MORALS.

I. *Character of the Systems so named.*] The theories concerning the origin of our moral ideas which we

---

* *Essay on the Genius and Writings of Pope*, Sect. XII.

are now to consider, although they agree in many respects with that of Locke and his followers, have yet proceeded from very different views and intentions. They also involve some principles that are peculiar to themselves, and which, therefore, render a separate examination of them necessary for the complete illustration of this fundamental article of ethics. They have been distinguished by Mr. Smith by the name of the *Licentious Systems of Morals*, — a name which certainly cannot be censured as too harsh, when applied to those which maintain that the motives of all men are fundamentally the same, and that what we commonly call *virtue* is mere *hypocrisy.*

Among the licentious moralists of modern times, the most celebrated are the Duc de la Rochefoucauld, author of the *Maxims and Moral Reflections*, and Dr. Mandeville, author of the *Fable of the Bees.* By the generality of our English philosophers, these two writers are commonly coupled together as advocates for the same system, although their views and their characters were certainly extremely different. In the first editions of Mr. Smith's *Theory of Moral Sentiments*, he speaks of a licentious doctrine concerning morality, which, he says, " was first sketched by the delicate pencil of the Duc de la Rochefoucauld, and was afterwards enforced by the coarse but powerful eloquence of Dr. Mandeville." In the last edition of that work the name of La Rochefoucauld is omitted, from Mr. Smith's deliberate conviction that it was unjust to his memory to class him with an author whose writings tend directly to confound all our ideas of moral distinctions. On this point I speak from personal knowledge, having been requested by Mr. Smith, when I happened to be at Paris some years before his death, to express to the late excellent and unfortunate Duc de la Rochefoucauld his sincere regret for having introduced the name of his ancestor and that of Dr. Mandeville in the same sentence.

II. *La Rochefoucauld's Life and Personal Charac-*

ter.] The Duc de la Rochefoucauld, author of the *Maxims*, was born in 1613, and died in 1680. The early part of his education was neglected; but the disadvantages he labored under in consequence of this circumstance he in a great measure overcame by the force of his own talents. According to Madame de Maintenon, who knew him well, "he was possessed of a countenance prepossessing and interesting; of manners graceful and dignified; of much genius, and little acquired knowledge." The same excellent judge adds of him, that "he was intriguing, accommodating, and cautious; but that she had never known a friend more firm, more open, or whose counsels were of greater value. He loved raillery; and used to say, that personal bravery appeared to him nothing better than folly; and yet he himself was brave to an extreme. He preserved to the last the vivacity of his mind, which was always agreeable, though naturally serious."

In the share which he took in the political transactions of his times, he discovered a facility to engage in intrigues, without much steadiness in the pursuit of his object. This, at least, is a remark made on him by the Cardinal de Retz, who, in a portrait of him drawn with a masterly, though somewhat prejudiced hand, ascribes the apparent inconsistencies of his conduct to a natural want of resolution. A later writer,* more favorable to his memory, has attempted to account for them, with much plausibility, by that superiority of penetration, and that rigid integrity, which all his contemporaries allow to have been distinguishing features in his character; and which, though not sufficient to keep him wholly disengaged from intrigues in a court where every thing was put in motion by the spirit of party, rendered him soon disgusted with the pretended patriotism and the selfish politics of those with whom he acted. Accordingly, although he was induced by the force of early connections, and a natural facility of temper, to involve himself during a part of his life in

* M. Suard, in his edition of the *Maximes*, which appeared in 1778.

public affairs, and more particularly, to become a tool of the Duchess of Longueville in the cabals of the Fronde, his own taste seems to have attached him to a more private scene, where he could enjoy in freedom the society and friendship of a few chosen companions. Towards the end of his life he spent much of his time at the house of Madame de la Fayette, which appears, from the letters of her friend, Madame de Sévigné, to have been, at that period, the resort of all persons distinguished for wit and refinement. It was in the midst of this chosen society that he composed his *Memoirs of the Regency of Anne of Austria*, and also his *Moral Reflections and Maxims.*

III. *Influence of his Writings.*] Of these two works, the former is written with much elegance, and with a great appearance of sincerity; but the events which it records are uninteresting in the present age. Bayle, in his *Dictionary*, gives it the preference to the *Commentaries* of Cæsar; but the judgment of the public has not been equally favorable. "The *Memoirs* of the Duc de la Rochefoucauld," says Voltaire, in his account of the writers of the age of Louis XIV., "are *read;* but every one knows his *Maxims* by heart." In fact, it is almost entirely by these *maxims* (which, as Montesquieu observes, "have become the proverbs of men of wit") that the name of La Rochefoucauld is known; and it must be confessed that few performances have acquired to their authors a higher or more general reputation. "One of the works," says Voltaire, "which contributed most to form the taste of the nation to a justness and precision of thought and expression, was the small collection of maxims by Francis, Duc de la Rochefoucauld. Although there is but one idea in the book, that *self-love is the spring of all our actions*, yet this idea is presented in so great a variety of forms as to be always amusing. When it first appeared, it was read with avidity; and it contributed, more than any other performance since the revival of letters, to accustom writers to indulge themselves in an originality of thought, and to improve the vivacity, precision, and delicacy of French composition."*

That the tendency of these maxims is, upon the whole, unfavorable to morality, and that they always leave a disagreeable impression on the mind, must, I think, be granted.† At the same time, it may be fairly questioned if the motives of the author have in general been well understood, either by his admirers or by his opponents. In affirming that self-love is the spring of all our actions, there is no good reason for supposing that he meant to deny the reality of moral distinctions as a philosophical truth, — a supposition quite inconsistent with his own fine and deep remark, that *hypocrisy is itself a homage which vice renders to virtue.* He states it merely as a proposition, which, in the course of his experience as a man of the world, he had found very generally verified in the higher classes of society, and which he was induced to announce, without any qualification or restriction, in order to give more force and poignancy to his satire. In adopting this mode of writing, he has unconsciously conformed himself, like many other French authors, who have since followed his example, ‡ to a suggestion which

---

* *Siècle de Louis XIV.*, Chap. XXXII.

† Mr. Spence, in his *Anecdotes of Men and Books*, ascribes to Pope a remark on La Rochefoucauld which does no small honor to the poet's shrewdness and knowledge of human nature. I quote it in Spence's words. "As L'Esprit, La Rochefoucauld, and that sort of people, prove that all virtues are disguised vices, I would engage to prove all vices to be disguised virtues. Neither, indeed, is true; but this would be a more agreeable subject, and would overturn their whole scheme." — p. 11.

‡ Thus it has often been said by French writers, that "*no* man is a hero to his *valet de chambre*"; and the maxim, when properly understood, has some foundation in truth. It probably was meant by its original author to refer only to those petty circumstances of temper and behaviour which, without affecting the essentials of character, have a tendency to diminish, on a near approach, the theatrical effect of great men. It has, however, been frequently quoted as implying that there are none whose virtues will bear a close examination; in which acceptation, it is not more injurious to human nature than it is contrary to fact. How much more profound, as well as more pleasing, is the remark of Plutarch! "Real virtue is most loved where it is most nearly seen, and no respect which it commands from strangers can equal the never-ceasing admiration it excites in the daily intercourse of domestic life." — *Vit. Periclis.* It is indeed true, that

Aristotle has stated with admirable depth and acuteness in his *Rhetoric*. "Sentences or apothegms lend much aid to eloquence. One reason of this is, that they flatter the *pride* of the hearers, who are delighted when the speaker, making use of general language, touches upon opinions which they had before known to be true in part. Thus, a person who had the misfortune to live in a bad neighbourhood, or to have worthless children, would easily assent to the speaker who should affirm that *nothing* is more vexatious than to have any neighbours; *nothing* more irrational than to bring children into the world."* This observation of Aristotle, while it goes far to account for the imposing and dazzling effect of these rhetorical exaggerations, ought to guard us against the common and popular error of mistaking them for the serious and profound generalizations of science. As for La Rochefoucauld, we know, from the best authorities, that in private life he was a conspicuous example of all those moral qualities of which he seemed to deny the existence; and that he exhibited, in this respect, a striking contrast to the Cardinal de Retz, who has presumed to censure him for his want of faith in the reality of virtue.

In reading La Rochefoucauld, it should never be forgotten that it was within the vortex of a court he enjoyed his chief opportunities of studying the world, and that the narrow and exclusive circle in which he moved was not likely to afford him the most favorable specimens of human nature in general. Of the court of Louis XIV. in particular, we are told by a very nice and reflecting observer (Madame de la Fayette), that

---

some men, who are admired by the world, appear to most advantage when viewed at a distance; but, on the other hand, may it not be contended that many who are objects of general odium would be found, if examined more nearly, not to be destitute of estimable and amiable qualities? May we not even go further, and assert that the very worst of men have a mixture of good in their composition, and express a doubt whether human nature would gain or lose upon a thorough acquaintance with the conduct and motives of individuals?

* Lib. II. Cap. XXII.

"ambition and gallantry were the *soul*, actuating alike both men and women. So many contending interests, so many different cabals, were constantly at work, and in all of those women bore so important a part, that love was always mingled with business, and business with love. Nobody was tranquil or indifferent. Every one studied to advance himself by pleasing, serving, or ruining others. Idleness and languor were unknown, and nothing was thought of but intrigues or pleasures."

In the passage already quoted from Voltaire, he takes notice of the effect of La Rochefoucauld's maxims in improving the style of French composition. We may add to this remark, that their effect has not been less sensible in vitiating the tone and character of French philosophy, by bringing into vogue those false and degrading representations of human nature and of human life which have prevailed in that country more or less for a century past. Mr. Addison, in one of the papers of the *Tatler*, expresses his indignation at this general bias among the French writers of his age. "It is impossible," he observes, "to read a passage in Plato, or Tully, or a thousand other ancient moralists, without being a greater and better man for it. On the contrary, I could never read any of our modish French authors, or those of our own country who are the imitators and admirers of that nation, without being for some time out of humor with myself, and at every thing about me. Their business is to depreciate human nature, and to consider it under the worst appearances; they give mean interpretations and base motives to the worthiest of actions. In short, they endeavour to make no distinction between man and man, or between the species of man and that of the brutes."

IV. *Mandeville's Writings and Moral System.*] From the form in which La Rochefoucauld's maxims are published, it is impossible to attempt a particular examination of them; nor, indeed, do I apprehend that such an examination is necessary for any of the purposes which I have at present in view. So far as their tendency is unfavorable to the reality of moral distinctions, it is the same with that of Mandeville's system; and therefore the strictures I am now to offer on the latter writer may be applied with equal truth to the general conclusions which some have chosen to draw from the satirical observations of the former.

Dr. Mandeville was born in Holland, where he received his education both in medicine and in philosophy. He made his first appearance in England about the beginning of the last century, and soon attracted very general attention by the vivacity and licentiousness of his publications.

The work by which he is best known is a poem, first printed in 1714, with the title of *The Grumbling Hive, or Knaves turned Honest;* upon which he afterwards wrote *Remarks*, and published the whole at London in 1723, having for its title *The Fable of the Bees: or Private Vices, Public Benefits.* This book was presented by the grand jury of Middlesex the same year, and was severely animadverted on soon after by some very eminent writers, particularly by Dr. Berkeley, Bishop of Cloyne, and by Dr. Hutcheson of Glasgow in his various treatises on ethical subjects.

To the *Remarks on the Fable of the Bees*, the author has prefixed *An Inquiry into the Origin of Moral Virtue;* and it is to this inquiry that I propose to confine myself chiefly in the following strictures, as it exhibits his peculiar opinions concerning the principles of morals in a more systematical form than any of his other writings. In the course of the observations which I have to offer with respect to it, I shall perhaps be led to repeat one or two remarks which have been already suggested by the doctrines of Locke. But, for this repetition, I hope that the importance of the subject will be a sufficient apology.

The great object of Mandeville's inquiry into the origin of moral virtue is to show that all our moral sentiments are derived from education, and are the

14*

workmanship of politicians and lawgivers. "These," says he, "observing how selfish an animal man is, and how impossible, in consequence, it would be to retain numbers together in the same society without government, endeavoured to give his selfish principles a direction useful to the public. For this purpose they have labored in all ages to convince him that it is better to restrain than to indulge his appetites, and to consult the public interest than his own. The engine they employed in working upon him was flattery, which they addressed to vanity, one of the strongest principles of our nature. They contrasted *man* with the *lower animals*, and magnified the advantages he possesses over them. The human race they divided into two classes; the mean and contemptible, who, after the example of the brutes, gratify every animal propensity; and the generous and high-spirited, who, disdaining these low gratifications, bend their study to cultivate the nobler principles of our nature, and wage a continual war with themselves to promote the happiness of others. In the case of men possessed of an extraordinary degree of pride and resolution, these representations of politicians and moralists were able to effectuate a complete conquest of their natural appetites, and a complete contempt of their own *visible* interests; and even the feeble-minded and abject would be unwilling to rank themselves in the class to which they really belonged, and would strive to conceal their imperfections from the world, by their forwardness to swell the cry in praise of self-denial and of public spirit. Such," says Mandeville, "*was*, or at least *might have been*, the manner after which savage man was broke; and what we call the moral virtues are merely *the political offspring which flattery begot upon pride.*"

I shall not insist on the absurdity of supposing that *government* is an invention of political wisdom, and not the natural result of man's constitution, and of the circumstances in which he is placed. This, however improbable, is one of the least absurdities of Man deville's system. Its capital defect consists in supposing that the origin of our moral virtues may be accounted for from the power of *education*; a fundamental error, which is common to the system of Mandeville and that of Locke as commonly understood by his followers, and which I had formerly occasion to notice and refute. I shall not, therefore, enlarge upon it at present, but shall confine myself to those parts of Mandeville's philosophy which are peculiar to himself.

V. *His Erroneous Notions respecting Vanity and Pride.*] It appears from the passage just quoted, that the engine which Mandeville supposes politicians to employ for the purpose of creating the artificial distinction between virtue and vice is *vanity* or *pride*, which two words he uses as synonymous. He employs them, likewise, in a much more extensive sense than their common acceptation authorizes; to denote, not only an overweening conceit of our own character and attainments, or a weak and childish passion for the admiration of others, but that reasonable desire for the esteem of our fellow-creatures, which, so far from being a weakness, is a laudable and respectable principle.

The desire of esteem and the dread of contempt are undoubtedly among the strongest principles of our nature; but in good minds they are only subsidiary to the desire of excellence, nay, they cannot be effectually gratified if they are the first springs of our actions. To be pleased with the applause of others, it is not sufficient to possess the *appearance* of good qualities; we must possess the *reality*. A man of sense and delicacy is never more mortified than when he receives praise for qualities which he knows do not belong to him; and he is comforted, under the mistaken censures of the world, by the consciousness he does not deserve them. A desire of applause may, without detracting from our merit, mingle itself with the more worthy motives of our conduct; but if it is the *sole* motive, the attainment of the object will never communicate a lasting satisfaction.

"Falsus honor juvat, et mendax infamia terret,
Quem, nisi mendosum et mendacem?"*

Vanity, in propriety of speech, denotes a weakness arising from a perversion of the *desire of esteem.* A man is *vain* who values himself on what is unworthy of regard, as the external distinctions of equipage or dress. He, too, is *vain* who wishes to pass in the world for what he really *is not*, and boasts of qualities which he does not possess. We also give the name of *vanity* to that weakness which disposes a man to be pleased with flattery, and which leads him, not only to desire the esteem of others, but to place his happiness in public expressions of it. In every case, *vanity* denotes a weakness which is carefully to be distinguished from the love of true glory.

Mandeville uses the word to express every sentiment of regard that we feel for the good opinion of others; and, wherever this regard can be supposed to have had any influence on our conduct, he concludes that *vanity* was our principle of action.

From these observations, added to those formerly made on Locke, it follows, in the first place, that the whole of our moral sentiments cannot be accounted for from education. Secondly, that, by confounding together *vanity*, and a reasonable regard to the *esteem* of our fellow-creatures, Mandeville has expressed the fundamental proposition of his system in terms so vague and ambiguous as renders it impossible to form a distinct conception of his meaning. And, thirdly, that even this reasonable and laudable desire of esteem cannot be effectually gratified, if it be the sole principle of our conduct; and therefore cannot be *the only* source of our moral virtues.

From the principle of *vanity*, Mandeville endeavours to account for all the instances of self-denial that have occurred in the world. But he is not satisfied with ex-

* Hor., *Ep.* XVI. 39.

"False praise can charm, unreal shame control,
Whom, but a vicious or a sickly soul?"

plaining away in this manner the reality of moral distinctions. He endeavours to show that human life is nothing but a scene of hypocrisy, and that there is really little or none of that self-denial to be found that some men lay claim to. In his theory of moral virtue he seems to allow that education may not only teach a man to check his appetites in order to procure the esteem of others, but that it may teach him to consider such a conquest over the lower principles of his nature as noble in itself, and as elevating him still farther than nature had done above the level of the brutes. "Those men," says he, "who have labored to establish societies endeavoured, in the first place, to insinuate themselves into the hearts of men by flattery, extolling the excellences of our nature above other animals. They next began to instruct them in the notions of honor and shame, representing the one as the worst of all evils, and the other as the highest good to which mortals could aspire; — which being done, they laid before them how unbecoming it was the dignity of such sublime creatures to be solicitous about gratifying those appetites which they had in common with the brutes, and at the same time unmindful of those higher qualities that gave them the preëminence over all visible beings. They, indeed, confessed that these impulses of nature were very pressing; that it was troublesome to resist, and very difficult wholly to subdue them. But this they only used as an argument to demonstrate how glorious the conquest of them was on the one hand, and how scandalous on the other not to attempt it."

These arguments, it is evident, are addressed to *pride* rather than to *vanity;* and it is worthy of remark, that, though Mandeville never states the distinction between these two words, but, on the contrary, affects to consider them as synonymous, he plainly was aware of the import of both, and sometimes uses the one, and sometimes the other, as best suits his purpose. Thus, in the following passage, if the word *vanity* were substituted instead of *pride*, the impropriety could not escape the most careless reader. "Such men as, from no other motive but their love of *goodness*, perform a worthy action in silence, have, I confess, acquired more refined notions of virtue than those I have hitherto spoke of, yet even in these (with whom the world has never yet swarmed) we may discover no small symptoms of *pride;* and the humblest man alive must confess that the reward of a virtuous action, which is the satisfaction that ensues upon it, consists in a certain pleasure he procures to himself, by contemplating on his own worth; which pleasure, together with the occasion of it, are as certain signs of *pride* as looking pale and trembling at any imminent danger are the symptoms of fear."

From these passages, however, it is abundantly clear, that, in his theory of virtue, Mandeville admits the possibility of self-denial being exercised merely for the private gratification of the pride of the individual, without any regard to the opinions of other men. But in his commentary on the *Fable of the Bees*, he goes much farther, and attempts to show that there is really no self-denial in the world, and that what we call a conquest is only a concealed indulgence of our passions. To establish this point, he avails himself of the ambiguity of language. The passion of sex he, in every case, calls *lust;* every thing which exceeds what is necessary for the support of life he calls *luxury;* and thus confounding the innocent and reasonable gratifications of our passions with their vicious excesses, he pretends to show that there is really no virtue among men. "There are some of our passions," says Mr. Smith, "which have no other names except those which mark the disagreeable and offensive degree. The spectator is more apt to take notice of them in this degree than in any other. When they shock his own sentiments, when they give him some sort of antipathy and uneasiness, he is necessarily obliged to attend to them, and is from thence naturally led to give them a name. When they fall in with the natural state of his own mind, he is very apt to overlook them altogether, and either gives them no name at all, or, if he gives them any, it is one which marks rather the subjection and restraint of the passion than the degree which it is still allowed to subsist in after it is so subjected and restrained. Thus, the common names of the *love of pleasure* and of *the love of sex* denote a vicious and offensive degree of those passions. The words *temperance* and *chastity*, on the other hand, seem to mark rather the restraint and subjection in which they are kept under, than the degree which they are still allowed to subsist in. When he can show, therefore, that they still subsist in some degree, he imagines he has entirely demolished the reality of the virtues of temperance and chastity, and shown them to be mere impositions upon the inattention and simplicity of mankind. Those virtues, however, do not require an entire insensibility to the objects of the passions which they mean to govern. They only aim at restraining the violence of those passions so far as not to hurt the individual, and neither to disturb nor offend society.

"It is the great fallacy of Dr. Mandeville's book to represent every passion as *wholly* vicious, which is so in any degree, and in any direction. It is thus that he treats every thing as vanity which has any reference either to what are, or what ought to be, the sentiments of others; and it is by means of this sophistry that he establishes his favorite conclusion, that private vices are public benefits. If the love of magnificence, a taste for the elegant arts and improvements of human life, for whatever is agreeable in dress, furniture, or equipage, for architecture, statuary, painting, and music, is to be regarded as luxury, sensuality, and ostentation, even in those whose situation allows, without any inconveniency, the indulgence of those passions, it is certain that luxury, sensuality, and ostentation are public benefits, since, without the qualities upon which he thinks proper to bestow such opprobrious names, the arts of refinement could never find employment, and must languish for want of encouragement. Some popular ascetic doctrines which had been current before his time, and which placed virtue in the entire extirpation and annihilation of all our passions, were the real foundation of this licentious system. It was easy for Dr. Mandeville to prove, first, that this entire conquest never actually took place among men; and, secondly, that, if it was to take place universally, it would be pernicious to society, by putting an end to all commerce and industry, and, in a manner, to the whole business of human life. By the first of these propositions he seemed to prove that there was no real virtue, and that what pretended to be such was a mere cheat and imposition upon mankind; and by the second, that private vices were public benefits, since without them no society could prosper or flourish." *

VI. *On the General Impression and Practical Tendency of such Speculations.*] I shall not enter into a more particular examination of Mandeville's doctrines. I cannot, however, leave the subject without observing, that the *impression* which the author's writings produce on the mind affords a sufficient refutation of his principles. It was considered by Cicero as a strong presumption against the system of Epicurus, that "it breathed nothing generous or noble," *nihil magnificum, nihil generosum sapit;* and the same presumption will be found to apply, with tenfold force, to that theory which has been now under our discussion. If there be no real distinction between virtue and vice, — if the account given by Mandeville of the constitution of our nature be a just one, — why do his reasonings render us *dissatisfied* with our own characters, or inspire us with a detestation and contempt for mankind? Why do we turn with pleasure from the dark and uncomfortable prospects which *he* presents to us, to the delightful and elevating views of human nature which are exhibited in those philosophical systems which he attempts to explode? It will be said, perhaps, that all this arises from pride or vanity. When we read Mandeville, we

* *Theory of Moral Sentiments*, Part VII. Sect. II. Chap. IV.

are ashamed of the species to which we belong; while, on the contrary, our pride is gratified by those sublime but fallacious descriptions of disinterested virtue, with which the weakness or hypocrisy of some popular writers has flattered the moral enthusiasm of the multitude. But if Mandeville's account of our nature be just, whence is it that we come to have an idea of one class of qualities as more excellent and meritorious than another? Why do we consider pride or vanity as a less worthy motive for our conduct than disinterested patriotism or friendship, or a determined adherence to what we believe to be our duty? Why does human nature appear to us less amiable in *his* writings than in the writings of Addison? or whence the origin of those opposite sentiments which the very names of Addison and of Mandeville inspire? We shall admit the fact with respect to the *actual* depravity of man to be as he states it; but does not the impression his system leaves on the mind demonstrate that we are at least formed with the love and admiration of moral excellence, and that virtue was intended to be the law of our conduct? The question concerning the actual attainments of man must not be confounded with the question concerning the reality of moral distinctions. If Mandeville is successful in establishing his doctrine on the first of these points, the dissatisfaction his conclusions leave on the mind is sufficient to overturn his doctrine with respect to the latter. The remark of La Rochefoucauld, that "hypocrisy itself is a homage which vice renders to virtue," involves a satisfactory reply to all the arguments that have ever been drawn from the prevailing corruption of mankind against the moral constitution of human nature.

It is the capital defect of this system to confound together the two questions I have just stated, and to substitute a satire on vice and folly instead of a philosophical account of those moral principles which form an essential part of our frame. That there is a great deal of truth mixed with the sophistry it contains, I am ready to acknowledge; and if the author's remarks had been thrown into the form of satires, many of them might have been useful to the world, by the light they throw on human character, and by the assistance which individuals may derive from them in examining their own motives of action. Some apology might have been made, in this case, for the colorings which the author's facts have borrowed from his imagination. The object of the satirist is to reform; and for this purpose it may sometimes be of use to exaggerate the prevailing vices and follies of the time, in order to contrast more strongly what mankind *are* with what they *might* and *ought* to be. But the satirist who wishes well to his species, while he indulges his indignation against prevailing corruptions, will recollect, that, if his censures are just, they presuppose the reality of moral distinctions; and while he laments the depravity of the race, and chastises the follies and vices of individuals, he will reverence morality as the *Divine law*, and those essential principles of the human frame which bear the manifest signature of the Divine workmanship. To attempt to depreciate these can never answer a good purpose. On the contrary, it has a tendency to fill the minds of good men with a desponding skepticism, and to stifle every generous and active exertion; and if it does not actually increase the depravity of the world, it tends at least to strengthen the effrontery of vice, and to expose the wiser and better part of mankind to the impertinent raillery of fools and profligates.*

* As the *direct* influence of the writings of La Rochefoucauld and Mandeville has passed away for the most part, I have taken the liberty slightly to abridge what was said of them in the text, in order to make room for some account of a more distinguished moralist of the selfish school, Jeremy Bentham. What relates to Bentham himself is taken from Morell's *View of Speculative Philosophy in the Nineteenth Century*, Chap. IV.; what relates to his followers is taken from Mackintosh's *Progress of Ethical Philosophy*, Sect. VI. — Ed.

Appendix to Chapter II.

BENTHAM AND HIS FOLLOWERS.

I. *Bentham's Ethical Writings and Doctrines.*] Jeremy Bentham was born in London, in the year 1748, and at a very early age became a graduate of the University of Oxford. Whilst there, he directed his attention to the study of law and the cognate branch of ethics, and during the last year of his stay in that city became an ardent admirer and investigator of the principle of utility, chiefly from reading Dr. Priestley's *Essay upon Government.* In 1776 he published a *Fragment on Government,* and in 1789 appeared his grand work, entitled *Introduction to the Principles of Morals and Legislation.* The moral system which Bentham advocated in this latter work, and which he expanded more and more during a long and laborious life, at length came forth, in the year 1834, in its most complete, and at the same time most popular form, as a posthumous production, edited by Dr. Bowring, under the title of *Deontology; or the Science of Morality.*

The principles advocated under the name of *deontology* may be easily explained. The whole system takes its rise from the consideration that man is capable of pleasures and pains, and that, from the calculation of these, all moral action proceeds. On this theory, *good* is a word synonymous with *pleasure*, *evil* synonymous with *pain*, and all happiness consists in the possession of the one, and the absence of the other. Give me, says the utilitarian teacher, give me the human sensibilities,—joy and grief, pain and pleasure, and I will create a moral world. Pleasure and pain, then, the basis of our moral nature, are to be estimated according to their magnitude and extent; *magnitude*, referring to their intensity and duration; *extent*, depending on the number of persons who are affected by them. It is in the proper balancing of these, asserts Bentham, that all morality consists, and beyond this the words *virtue* and *vice* are emptiness and folly.

Pleasure or pain, however, may arise from two sources; it may arise from considerations affecting *ourselves*, or it may arise from the contemplation of *others*, the former being purely of a selfish nature, the latter being sympathetic. Hence originates a twofold division of virtue into *prudence* and *effective benevolence*, — both of them, however, alike having their ground in the pleasure we personally derive from their exercise. Prudence, again, is of two kinds, that which respects ourselves, which our author terms *self-regarding* prudence; and that which respects others, which he terms *extra-regarding* prudence. Effective benevolence, also, is twofold, *positive* and *negative;* the business of the former being to augment pleasure by voluntary exertion, that of the latter being to do the same by *abstaining* from action. Virtue, says Bentham, when separated from the pursuit of happiness, is absolutely nothing; and, accordingly, it is termed by him a fictitious entity. Inasmuch, also, as no one is supposed to have any motive for action different from the pursuit of pleasure or the avoidance of pain, we have the deontological doctrine educed, that every motive is abstractedly good, and that evil has to do with nothing but our actions or dispositions. In a word, we are to imagine, that man has originally no moral sentiment whatever, that he has no idea of one thing being right and another wrong, that all actions are to him in this respect absolutely alike, and that the conception of virtue, as well as the rules of morality, are all the product of experience, teaching us what actions produce happiness, and what suffering. Such is the moral system which is aptly enough termed the *greatest-happiness principle*, and such the virtue which is correctly expressed as the *art of maximizing our enjoyment.*

The style of the work from which I have made the above analysis is popular, witty, and somewhat amusing, but becomes at length tedious from repetition and tautology. It abounds in biting sarcasm against what is termed the dogmatism and "*ipse-dixitism*" of most other moralists; but, what is remarkable, is itself at the same time one of the most striking instances of reiterated *assertion* that is to be found among all the ethical writings of the present century.*

---

* A few selections will best illustrate Bentham's light and irreverent tone. Thus in Part I. Chap. II.: — "The talisman of arrogance, indolence, and ignorance is to be found in a single word, an authoritative imposture, which in these pages it will be frequently necessary to unveil. It is the word *ought*, — *ought* or *ought not*, as circumstances may be. In deciding 'You *ought* to do this, — You *ought not* to do it,' is not every question of morals set at rest? If the word be admissible at all, it 'ought' to be banished from the vocabulary of morals. There is another word which has a talismanic virtue, too, and which might be wielded to destroy many fatal and fallacious positions. 'You ought,' — 'You ought not,' says the dogmatist. '*Why?*' retorts the inquirer, — 'Why?' To say 'You ought' is easy in the extreme. To stand the searching penetration of a Why ' is not so easy. '*Why ought* I?' 'Because you ought,' is the not unfrequent reply; on which the Why? comes back again with the added advantage of having obtained a victory." A morality from the vocabulary of which the word "ought" is to be banished! It is hardly necessary to observe that the whole force of Bentham's "Why?" depends on his determination to accept no answer which is not satisfactory according to his theory of utilitarianism, — of course palpably illogical, as it begs the whole question.

Again in Chapter III.: — "The *summum bonum*, — the sovereign good, — what is it? The philosopher's stone that converts all metals into gold, — the balm Hygeian that cures all manner of diseases. It is this thing, and that thing, and the other thing; it is any thing but pleasure; it is the Irishman's apple-pie made of nothing but quinces." He then amuses himself by going a little more into detail with the various answers which philosophers and divines have made to the question proposed above. A single specimen will suffice. "But we are still at sea, and another set cry out, 'The habit of virtue'; the habit of virtue is the *summum bonum:* either this is the jewel itself, or the casket in which it is found. Lie all your life long in your bed with the rheumatism in your loins, the stone in your bladder, and the gout in your feet: have but the *habit of virtue*, and you have the *summum bonum*. *Much good may it do you*."

Once more, in Chapter IV.: — "The moral sense, say some, prompts to generosity; but does it determine what is generous? It prompts to justice; but does it determine what is just? It can decide no controversy; it can reconcile no difference. Introduce a modern partisan of the *moral sense*, and an ancient Greek, and ask each of them whether actions deemed blameless in ancient days, but respecting which opinions have now undergone great change, ought to be tolerated in a community. 'By no means,' says the modern; 'as my moral sense abhors them, therefore they ought not.' 'But mine,' says the ancient, 'approves of them; therefore they ought.' And there, if the modern keep his principles and his temper, the matter must end between them. Upon the ground of *moral sense* there is no going one jot further; and the result is, that the actions in question are at once laudable and detestable. The modern, then, as probably he will keep neither his principles nor his temper, says to the ancient, 'Your moral sense is nothing to the purpose; yours is corrupt, abominable, detestable; all nations cry out against you.' 'No such thing,' replies the ancient; 'and if they did, it would be nothing to the purpose; our business

II. *Objections to Bentham's System.*] In offering some remarks upon Bentham's philosophy, we must state distinctly, that we leave entirely out of the question his valuable labors in the department of jurisprudence, and refer simply to the principles of his moral theory. And here we would caution every ethical student against imagining, that he will find all the originality which is claimed for the deontologist by himself and his more ardent admirers. To speak of Bentham's "having found out the true psychological law of our nature, as Newton discovered that of the material universe," is not only metaphysically false, but, even allowing its philosophical accuracy, is *historically* untrue. To say nothing of the Epicureans of ancient times, and more recently of Hobbes, we might point out many writers who have given far more than passing allusions to the very same doctrine as that for which Bentham is so highly extolled, although they may not have expanded it so fully, or applied it so extensively, as was done in the case before us.* The professed supporters of utility, again, such as Hume and Paley, proceeded virtually upon the very same principle; and even if we pass over these, yet still we might refer to

---

was to inquire, not what people *think*, but what they *ought to think*.' Thereupon the modern kicks the ancient, or spits in his face; or, if he is strong enough, throws him behind the fire. One can think of no other method, that is at once natural and consistent, of continuing the debate."

It was Mr. Bentham's pleasure to persist in supposing that *all* his opponents, a few ascetics excepted, could be classed under the head of believers in a moral *sense*. A large proportion of them, as we shall soon see, hold that the moral faculty pertains to the *rational*, and not to the *sensitive*, element in human nature. That the moral faculty should make mistakes, and afterwards correct them, does not disprove its existence as a natural endowment of man, or its legitimate authority. If it did, we might disprove the existence and authority of the knowing or cognitive faculty in the same way; for that also makes mistakes, and afterwards corrects them. Because we say that children and savages have a conscience, we do not mean that they have one in the same stage of development, and consequently we do not mean that its decisions are as clear, or as correct, as in the case of the properly educated.— Ed.

* The only difference between Epicurus or Hobbes on the one side, and Bentham on the other, is, that the former drew their principles at once from human nature metaphysically considered,—while the latter gave no theory of man generally, but laid down his moral axioms as ultimate facts.

Gay's Preface to Archbishop King *On the Origin of Evil*, to the writings of Priestley, to the *Political Justice* of Godwin, and to many of the French moralists, for illustrations of the very same theory, which Bentham only somewhat more perseveringly elaborated. The greatest-happiness principle is, in fact, utilitarianism in one of its many different phases; and accordingly the objections which we have already urged against that doctrine apply with equal force to the one now before us. As the question, however, is of some importance, we shall specify a few other objections, which apply more directly to the utilitarian system, as held by the advocates of deontology; and,

1. There is in these writers a perpetual habit of confounding the *cause* of virtuous action with the *effect*. We have it reiterated again and again, as an unanswerable argument, that there must be a selfish pleasure experienced whenever we act on virtuous principles: for, if our action terminates in ourselves, it must arise from the prospect of our own happiness and advantage; if, on the other hand, we act for the welfare of others, still, we are told, it is only for the satisfaction of our own impulses that we seek to benefit them. Now, that there is pleasure attached to moral action, whether it be self-seeking or extra-seeking, we readily admit; but this is far from giving us a proof that such action *springs from any anticipation of the pleasure we hope to obtain.* It is a pleasure to a strong man to exercise his limbs; but this is no evidence that he cannot have any other motive than this for exercising them. To a man devoted to business, it is a pleasure to be perpetually absorbed in it; but still his activity may have many other grounds of excitement besides that one. Prove as you may, that pleasure actually accompanies, and even that we *expect* it to accompany, the practice of every virtue, the point is still far from being settled that there is no other spring of virtuous action in existence. The Deity, assuredly, may have given us a moral law, may have engraved it on our own minds, and placed it far beyond all the chances of human cal

culation; and yet may have attached pleasure to the obedience of it as a mark of his approval, and as a reward for our fidelity. The mere fact, therefore, that we always look for happiness to accompany virtuous action, does not at all prove that happiness is the ground of its moral excellence. This is confirmed when we consider,

2. That, upon investigating the moral phenonena of our minds, we find a class of affections which rise in their real worth just in proportion to their *disinterestedness.* If personal pleasure were the ground of virtue, then every affection ought to be esteemed higher in the scale of morality in proportion as it tends more directly to *self* as its object. Just the contrary is the case. The more our own individual interests are sacrificed in the pursuit of another's welfare, the higher rises the scale of virtue from which such conduct proceeds. If it be said that we sacrifice our own interests, because the pleasure of satisfying our benevolent feelings more than counterbalances the loss we sustain, we reply, that this only exhibits the vast strength of our purely disinterested affections, and affords no proof that, because they give us pleasure in their exercise, therefore they must be selfish in their origin. Only show in one single instance that the direct end of an action is for the sake of another to the sacrifice of ourselves, and the fact that we have a moral satisfaction in its performance does not in the slightest degree shake its purely unselfish character.

3. That there are certain *fixed* relations between man's moral sensibilities and outward actions is a fact resting upon the evidence of our consciousness; and it is to these eternal relations that we direct our inquiries, when we seek to lay the groundwork of a moral philosophy. Very different, however, is our employment when we are merely engaged in calculating for our future happiness, with pleasures and pains as our ciphers. What is a pleasure to one man is often a pain to another; that which offers to me satisfaction presents, perhaps, a prospect of naught but misery to you; so

that moral relations, on this principle, must be as uncertain and variable as are the temperaments or idiosyncrasies of individual minds. There needs to be, on the deontological system, a separate moral scale for every man; nay, we ought all to revise our own moral principles every year or two, to see whether that which was a pleasure to us some time ago may not now have become an object of dissatisfaction: whether, therefore, that which was virtue has not now become vice. Our reason, we contend, in opposition to this, forces us to form certain primary and fundamental moral judgments, just as much as it necessitates the existence of our primary beliefs with regard to the external world, or to the fact of an exertion of power in the production of every effect, or to the axioms which lie at the foundation of all mathematical reasoning. It is just as impossible for me practically to deny the obligation of justice, as it is to deny that the world exists, or that a whole is greater than a part. The one as well as the other rests upon the primary and undeniable facts of our own unchangeable consciousness, — facts which, though they may be disputed in theory, can never be denied in practice. That a philosophical dreamer may run his head against the wall on the score of his idealism, we do not dispute; nor do we doubt but that, in the case of moral obliquity, where the consequences of the folly are not so immediate, men may be found to reject the fundamental axioms of moral obligation; but in the healthy understandings of the mass of mankind, the one judgment is just as plainly developed as the other.

4. There is a secret *petitio principii* at the very foundation of all utilitarian reasoning like that of Bentham. Every man, it is affirmed, *ought* to seek the greatest happiness of the greatest number, as the fundamental principle of his actions in the world. But why *ought* he to do so? On what ground can it be shown, that I am bound to seek the welfare of myself or my fellow-creatures, if there is no such thing as moral obligation? If it *pleases* me more to inflict misery upon mankind, why am I not just as virtuous an agent in

doing so, as if I please myself by producing their happiness? The greatest-happiness principle itself must, in fact, rest upon the pedestal of moral obligation, otherwise there is no means of enforcing it as the true principle of action, either in our social or our political relations. Take away that firm resting-place which is afforded by the notion of duty, and expressed in the word *ought*, and we may sink from one position down to another, without ever reaching a solid basis on which we may plant our feet, and lay the first stone of a moral superstructure. That this is really the case is half acknowledged by the followers of Bentham, who are now visibly shrinking from the extreme view he has taken of utilitarianism, and seeking to *include* the idea of moral approbation, in order to give their doctrine some degree of strength and consistency.

5. Into the political consequences of this system we shall not allow ourselves to enter at any length. One thing, however, there is, of which we would remind those who hold up the excellence of Bentham's political writings as a proof of the soundness of his ethical system; we mean the fact that Hobbes, with a logic equally, if not more severe, deduced from the very same fundamental principles the propriety of all government being grounded on absolute despotism, as the form best suited to the wants of human nature. That Bentham was so successful on the subject of jurisprudence arose, we consider, from his giving up the strict view of the selfish system with which he started, and following the dictates of common sense and of a benevolence which were more consonant with his own disposition than they were with his moral theory.*

Moreover, there is a fundamental distinction between the principles of legislation and those of private morality, which should never be lost sight of. The former principles *suppose* the existence of the latter, and must

* Or rather, from his confounding the rule of *general* interest with that of *personal* interest; but this, as Jouffroy has shown, *Introduction to Ethics*, Lecture XIV., involves the abandonment of the principle on which his system is founded. — Ed.

proceed in strict accordance with them, whether it appear a matter of policy to do so or not. The object of the jurist is, simply to take men with their moral feelings as they are, already fixed and determined, and so to direct their actions as to bring about the greatest welfare of the community. Morality says, *Fiat justitia ruat cœlum;* jurisprudence points out *in what way* justice is to be done, so as to tend to the happiness of the whole nation. The one gives the absolute rule of action, the other only directs the details for social purposes. Moral law is immediately from God; political law, though springing from moral principles, is an adaptation of man; — the one is a code written upon the tablet of the human heart; the other, a code written in the statute-book of the empire, conformable, indeed, to moral law, but compiled for social utility. To morality, as a science, the utilitarian ground is entirely destructive, altering its universal and necessary aspect; in politics, utility, directed by moral precept, must be a chief element in every enactment. Bentham, looking at the subject with the eye of a jurist, by degrees became blind to every thing but the utilitarian element, — an error which, while only partially dangerous in legislation, is to the moralist fatal and deceptive from the very first step.

That Bentham was a great man, a courageous man, and in many respects a benevolent man, we believe all must be ready to admit; still, we cannot but think that he neither read enough to disabuse his mind of many a cherished notion, which a wider range of investigation would have exploded, nor ever cultivated enough that steady, reflective habit of mind which evolves truth from the observation of our inward consciousness, and reduces, by a close analysis, the admitted facts of human nature to their primary origin. With unexampled patience, he developed the influence of pleasure and pain upon human actions; but a deeper philosophy would have pointed out, that these are but the accompaniments of virtue, while the law and the imperative to its obedience come from a surer and a far more exalted source.

III. *General Objection to the Followers of Bentham.*] The followers of Mr. Bentham have carried to an unusual extent the prevalent fault of the more modern advocates of utility, who have dwelt so exclusively on the outward advantages of virtue as to have lost sight of the delight which is a part of virtuous feeling, and of the beneficial influence of good actions upon the frame of the mind.

"Benevolence towards others," says Mr. Mill, "produces a return of benevolence from them." * The fact is true, and ought to be stated. But how unimportant is it in comparison with that which is passed over in silence,—the pleasure of the affection itself, which, if it could become lasting and intense, would convert the heart into a heaven! No one who has ever felt kindness, if he could accurately recall his feelings, could hesitate about their infinite superiority. The cause of the general neglect of this consideration is, that it is only when a gratification is something distinct from a state of mind, that we can easily learn to consider it as a pleasure. Hence the great error respecting the affections, where the *inherent* delight is not duly estimated, on account of that very peculiarity of being a part of a state of mind, which renders it unspeakably more valuable as independent of every thing without. The social affections are the only principles of human nature which have no direct pains. To have any of these desires is to be in a state of happiness. The malevolent passions have properly no pleasures; for that attainment of their purpose which is improperly so called consists only in healing or assuaging the torture which

---

* *Analysis of the Human Mind*, Chap. XXIII.

The author of this work, James Mill, was born at Montrose, in Scotland, in 1773, and educated at Edinburgh, being destined for the church. He afterwards changed his views, established himself in London in 1800, and soon became acquainted with Bentham. He published his *History of British India* in 1818, which procured for him a place in the home establishment of the East India Company. He was also a large contributor to the *Supplement to the Encyclopædia Britannica*, (afterwards incorporated into the seventh edition of that work,) on subjects connected with politics and morals He died at Kensington in 1836. John Stuart Mill, a living writer of eminence, is his son.—ED.

envy, jealousy, and malice inflict on the malignant mind. It might with as much propriety be said that the toothache and the stone have pleasures, because their removal is followed by an agreeable feeling. These bodily disorders, indeed, are often cured by the process which removes the suffering; but the mental distempers of envy and revenge are nourished by every act of odious indulgence which for a moment suspends their pain.

The same observation is applicable to every virtuous disposition, though not so obviously as to the benevolent affections. That a brave man is, on the whole, far less exposed to danger than a coward, is not the chief advantage of a courageous temper. Great dangers are rare; but the constant absence of such painful and mortifying sensations as those of fear, and the steady consciousness of superiority to what subdues ordinary men, are a perpetual source of inward enjoyment. No man who has ever been visited by a gleam of magnanimity can place any outward advantage of fortitude in comparison with the feeling of being always able fearlessly to defend a righteous cause.* Even *humility*, in spite of first appearances, is a remarkable example. It has of late been unwarrantably used to signify that painful consciousness of inferiority which is the first stage of envy.† It is a term consecrated in Christian ethics to denote that disposition which, by inclining towards a modest estimate of our qualities, corrects the prevalent tendency of human nature to overvalue our merits and to overrate our claims. What can be a less doubtful or a much more considerable blessing than this constant sedative, which soothes and composes the irritable passions of vanity and pride?

* According to Cicero's definition of fortitude, "*Virtus pugnans pro æquitate.*" The remains of the original sense of *virtus*, *manhood*, give a beauty and force to these expressions, which cannot be preserved in our language. The Greek ἀρετή and the German *Tugend* originally denoted *strength*, afterwards *courage*, and at last *virtue*. But the happy derivation of *virtus* from *vir* gives an energy to the phrase of Cicero, which illustrates the use of etymology in the hands of a skilful writer.

† Mr. Mill's *Analysis of the Human Mind*, Chap. XXII. Sect. II.

What is more conducive to lasting peace of mind than the consciousness of proficiency in that most delicate species of equity which, in the secret tribunal of conscience, labors to be impartial in the comparison of ourselves with others? What can so perfectly assure us of the purity of our moral sense, as the habit of contemplating, not that excellence which we have reached, but that which is still to be pursued, — of not considering how far we may outrun others, but how far we are from the goal?

Those who have most inculcated the doctrine of utility have given another notable example of the very vulgar prejudice which treats the *unseen* as insignificant. Tucker is the only one of them who occasionally considers that most important effect of human conduct which consists in its action on the frame of the mind, by fitting its faculties and sensibilities for their appointed purpose. A razor or a penknife would well enough cut cloth or meat; but if they were often so used, they would be entirely spoiled. The same sort of observation is much more strongly applicable to habitual dispositions, which, if they be spoiled, we have no certain means of replacing or mending. Whatever act, therefore, discomposes the moral machinery of mind, is more injurious to the welfare of the agent than most disasters from without can be; for the latter are commonly limited and temporary; the evil of the former spreads through the whole of life. Health of mind, as well as of body, is not only productive in itself of a greater sum of enjoyment than arises from other sources, but is the only condition of our frame in which we are capable of receiving pleasure from without. Hence it appears how incredibly absurd it is to prefer, on grounds of calculation, a present interest to the preservation of those mental habits on which our well-being depends. When they are most moral, they may often prevent us from obtaining advantages. It would be as absurd to desire to lower them for that reason, as it would be to weaken the body lest its strength should render it more liable to contagious disorders of rare occurrence.

It is, on the other hand, impossible to combine the benefit of the general habit with the advantages of occasional deviation; for every such deviation either produces remorse, or weakens the habit, and prepares the way for its gradual destruction. He who obtains a fortune by the undetected forgery of a will, may indeed be honest in his other acts; but if he had such a scorn of fraud before as he must himself allow to be generally useful, he must suffer a severe punishment from contrition; and he will be haunted with the fears of one who has lost his own security for his good conduct. In all cases, if they be well examined, his loss by the distemper of his mental frame will outweigh the profits of his vice.

By repeating the like observation on similar occasions, it will be manifest that the infirmity of recollection, aggravated by the defects of language, gives an appearance of more selfishness to man than truly belongs to his nature; and that the effect of active agents upon the habitual state of mind, — one of the considerations to which the epithet "sentimental" has of late been applied in derision, — is really among the most serious and reasonable objects of moral philosophy. When the internal pleasures and pains which *accompany* good and bad feelings, or rather form a part of them, and the internal advantages and disadvantages which *follow* good and bad actions, are sufficiently considered, the comparative importance of *outward consequences* will be more and more narrowed; so that the Stoical philosopher may be thought almost excusable for rejecting it altogether, were it not an indispensably necessary consideration for those in whom right habits of feeling are not sufficiently strong. They alone are happy, or even truly virtuous, who have little need of it.

The later moralists who adopt the principle of utility have so *misplaced* it, that in their hands it has as great a tendency as any theoretical error can have to lessen the intrinsic pleasure of virtue, and to unfit our habitual feelings for being the most effectual inducements to good conduct. This is the natural tendency of a discipline which brings utility too closely and frequently into contact with action. By this habit, in its best state, an essentially weaker motive is gradually substituted for others which must always be of more force. The frequent appeal to utility as the standard of action tends to introduce an uncertainty with respect to the conduct of other men, which would render all intercourse insupportable. It affords, also, so fair a disguise for selfish and malignant passions, as often to hide their nature from him who is their prey. Some taint of these mean and evil principles will at least creep in, and by their venom give an animation not its own to the cold desire of utility. The moralists who take an active part in those affairs which often call out unamiable passions, ought to guard with peculiar watchfulness against self-delusions. The sin that must most easily beset them is that of sliding from general to particular consequences, — that of trying single actions, instead of dispositions, habits, and rules, by the standard of utility, — that of authorizing too great a latitude for discretion and policy in moral conduct, — that of readily allowing exceptions to the most important rules, — that of too lenient a censure of the use of doubtful means when the end seems to them good, — and that of believing unphilosophically, as well as dangerously, that there can be any measure or scheme so useful to the world as the existence of men who would not do a base thing for any public advantage. It was said of Andrew Fletcher, "He would lose his life to *serve* his country, but would not do a base thing to *save* it." Let those preachers of utility who suppose that such a man sacrifices *ends* to *means* consider whether the scorn of baseness be not akin to the contempt of danger, and whether a nation composed of such men would not be invincible. But theoretical principles are counteracted by a thousand causes, which confine their mischief as well as circumscribe their benefits. Men are never so good or so bad as their opinions. All that can be with reason apprehended is, that they may always produce some part of their natural evil, and that the mischief will be greatest among the many who seek excuses for these passions. Aristippus found in the Socratic representation of the union of virtue and happiness a pretext for sensuality; and many Epicureans became voluptuaries in spite of the example of their master, easily dropping by degrees the limitations by which he guarded his doctrines. In proportion as a man accustoms himself to be influenced by the utility of particular acts, without regard to rules, he approaches to the casuistry of the Jesuits and to the practical maxims of Cæsar Borgia.

IV. *Mr. Mill's Errors respecting Government and Education.*] Mr. Mill derives the whole theory of government* from the single fact, that every man pursues his interest when he knows it; which he assumes to be a sort of self-evident practical principle, if such a phrase be not contradictory. That a man's pursuing the interest of another, or indeed any other object in nature, is just as *conceivable* as that he should pursue his own interest, is a proposition which seems never to have occurred to this acute and ingenious writer. Nothing, however, can be more certain than its truth, if the term "interest" be employed in its proper sense of general well-being, which is the only acceptation in which it can serve the purpose of his arguments. If, indeed, the term be employed to denote the gratification of a predominant desire, his proposition is self-evident, but wholly unserviceable in his argument; for it is clear that individuals and multitudes often desire what they know to be most inconsistent with their general welfare. A nation, as much as an individual, and sometimes more, may not only mistake its interest, but, perceiving it clearly, may prefer the gratification of a strong passion to it. The whole fabric of his political reasoning seems to be overthrown by this single observation; and instead of attempting to explain the immense variety

* *Essay on Government*, in the *Encyclopædia Britannica*, seventh edition. His contributions to that work have also been collected in an octavo volume, and published separately. — Ed.

of political facts by the simple principle of a contest of interests, we are reduced to the necessity of once more referring them to that variety of passions, habits, opinions, and prejudices, which we discover only by experience.

Mr. Mill's *Essay on Education** affords another example of the inconvenience of leaping at once from the most general laws to a multiplicity of minute appearances. Having assumed, or at least inferred from insufficient premises, that the intellectual and moral character is entirely formed by circumstances, he proceeds, in the latter part of the essay, as if it were a necessary consequence of that doctrine, that we might easily acquire the power of combining and directing circumstances in such a manner as to produce the best possible character. Without disputing for the present the theoretical proposition, let us consider what would be the reasonableness of similar expectations in a more easily intelligible case. The general theory of the winds is pretty well understood; we know that they proceed from the rushing of air from those portions of the atmosphere which are more condensed into those which are more rarefied; but how great a chasm is there between that simple law and the great variety of facts which experience teaches us respecting winds! The constant winds between the tropics are large and regular enough to be in some measure capable of explanation; but who can tell why, in variable climates, the wind blows to-day from the east, to-morrow from the west? Who can foretell what its shiftings and variations are to be? Who can account for a tempest on one day, and a calm on another? Even if we could foretell the irregular and infinite variations, how far might we not still be from the power of combining and guiding their causes? No man but the lunatic in the story of Rasselas ever dreamt that he could command the weather. The difficulty plainly consists in the multiplicity and minuteness of the circumstances which

* In the *Encyclopædia Britannica*, seventh edition.

act on the atmosphere. Are those which influence the formation of the human character likely to be less minute and multiplied? *

---

* In reply to this criticism, and to other parts of the volume from which it is taken, Mr. Mill published anonymously, in 1835, an octavo volume, under the title of *A Fragment on Mackintosh*. On some points the defence is able and successful; but the effect of the whole is greatly impaired by the vituperation, not to say scurrility, in which it abounds.

After what has been said in the text, it is but justice to add, that the later followers or admirers of Bentham are not unable to see, or unwilling to acknowledge, his defects. A writer in the *Westminster Review*, for July, 1838, who begins by making the great hierophant of utilitarianism to be one of "the two great seminal minds of England in their age," expresses himself thus: — "Bentham's contempt of all other schools of thinkers, and his determination to create a philosophy wholly out of the materials furnished by his own mind, and by minds like his own, were his first disqualifications as a philosopher. His second was the incompleteness of his own mind as a representative of universal human nature. In many of the most natural and strongest feelings of human nature he had no sympathy; from many of its gravest experiences he was altogether cut off; and the faculty by which one mind understands a mind different from itself, and throws itself into the feelings of that other mind, was denied him by his deficiency of *imagination*.

"Bentham's knowledge of human nature is wholly empirical: and the empiricism of one who has had little experience. He had neither internal experience nor external; the quiet, even tenor of his life and his healthiness of mind conspired to exclude him from both. He never knew prosperity nor adversity, passion nor satiety; he never had even the experience which sickness gives, — he lived from childhood to the age of eighty-five in boyish health. He knew no dejection, no heaviness of heart. He never felt life a sore and a weary burden. He was a boy to the last. Self-consciousness, that demon of the men of genius of our time, from Wordsworth to Byron, from Goethe to Chateaubriand, and to which this age owes most both of its cheerful and its mournful wisdom, never was awakened in him. How much of human nature slumbered in him he knew not, neither can we know.

"This, then, is our idea of Bentham. He was a man both of remarkable endowments for philosophy and of remarkable deficiencies for it; fitted beyond almost any man for drawing from his premises conclusions not only correct, but sufficiently precise and specific to be practical, but whose general conception of human nature and life furnished him with an unusually slender stock of premises. It is obvious what would be likely to be achieved by such a man; what a thinker thus gifted and thus disqualified could be in philosophy. He could be a systematic and logical *half-man*, hunting *half-truths* to their consequences and practical application, on a scale both of greatness and minuteness not previously exemplified: and this is the character which posterity will probably assign to Bentham." — ED.

CHAPTER III.

ANALYSIS OF OUR MORAL PERCEPTIONS AND EMOTIONS.

I. *Butler's Proofs of Man's Moral Nature.*] Before proceeding to this extensive and difficult subject, I shall quote a passage from Dr. Butler, in which he has combined together, and compressed into the compass of a few paragraphs, all the most important arguments in proof of the existence of the moral faculty which have been hitherto under our review. While this quotation serves as a summary of what has already been stated, it will, I hope, prepare us for entering on the following discussions with greater interest and a more enlightened curiosity.

"That which renders beings capable of moral government is their having a moral nature, and moral faculties of perception and of action. Brute creatures are impressed and actuated by various instincts and propensities: so also are we. But, additional to this, we have a capacity for reflecting upon actions and characters, and making them an object to our thought; and on doing this we naturally and unavoidably approve some actions, under the peculiar view of their being virtuous and of good desert, and disapprove others as vicious and of ill desert. That we have this moral approving and disapproving faculty is certain from our experiencing it in ourselves, and recognizing it in each other. It appears from our exercising it unavoidably in the approbation and disapprobation even of feigned characters; from the words *right* and *wrong*, *odious* and *amiable*, *base* and *worthy*, with many others of like signification in all languages, applied to actions and characters; from the many written systems of morals which suppose it, since it cannot be imagined that all these authors, throughout all these treatises, had absolutely no meaning at all to their words, or a meaning merely chimerical; from our natural sense of gratitude, which implies a distinction between merely being the instrument of good and intending it; from the like distinction every one makes between injury and mere harm, which Hobbes says is peculiar to mankind, and between injury and just punishment, a distinction plainly natural, prior to the consideration of human laws. It is manifest great part of common language and of common behaviour over the world is formed upon supposition of such a moral faculty, whether called conscience, moral reason, moral sense, or Divine reason, — whether considered as a perception of the understanding, or as a sentiment of the heart, or, which seems the truth, as including both. Nor is it at all doubtful, in the general, what course of action this faculty, or practical discerning power within us, approves, and what it disapproves. For, as much as it has been disputed wherein virtue consists, or whatever ground for doubt there may be about particulars, yet in general there is in reality a universally acknowledged standard of it. It is that which all ages and all countries have made profession of in public, — it is that which every man you meet puts on the show of, — it is that which the primary and fundamental laws of all civil constitutions over the face of the earth make it their business and endeavour to enforce the practice of upon mankind, namely, justice, veracity, and regard to common good." *

Upon the various topics here suggested, a copious and instructive commentary might be written, but I think it better to leave them in the concise and impressive form in which they are proposed by the author.

II. *Theoretical and Practical Morals.*] The science of ethics has been divided by modern writers into two parts; the one comprehending the *theory of morals*, and the other its *practical doctrines.*

The questions about which the former is employed are chiefly the two following. *First*, by what *principle*

* *Dissertation on the Nature of Virtue.*

of our constitution are we led to form the notion of moral distinctions, — whether by that faculty which perceives the distinction between truth and falsehood in the other branches of human knowledge, or by a peculiar power of perception (called by some the moral sense) which is *pleased* with one set of qualities and *displeased* with another? *Secondly*, what is the *proper object of moral approbation?* or, in other words, what is the common quality or qualities belonging to all the different modes of virtue? Is it benevolence, or a rational self-love, or a disposition (resulting from the ascendant of reason over passion) to act suitably to the different relations in which we are placed? These two questions seem to exhaust the whole theory of morals. The scope of the one is to ascertain the origin of our moral ideas; that of the other to refer the phenomena of moral perception to their most simple and general laws.

The *practical doctrines* of morality comprehend all those rules of conduct which profess to point out the proper ends of human pursuit, and the most effectual means of attaining them; to which we may add, under the general title of *adminicles*, (if I may be allowed to borrow a technical word of Lord Bacon's,) all those literary compositions, whatever be their particular form, which have for their aim to fortify and animate our good dispositions by delineations of the beauty, of the dignity, or of the utility of virtue.

I shall not inquire at present into the justness of this division. I shall only observe that the words *theory* and *practice* are not in this instance employed in their usual acceptations. The theory of morals does not bear, for example, the same relation to the practice of morals that the theory of geometry bears to practical geometry. In this last science all the practical rules are founded on theoretical principles previously established. But in the former science the practical rules are obvious to the capacities of all mankind, while the theoretical principles form one of the most difficult subjects of discussion that has ever exercised the ingenuity of metaphysicians

Although, however, a complete acquaintance with the *practice* of our duty does not presuppose any knowledge of the theory of morals, it does not therefore follow that false theoretical notions upon this subject may not be attended with very pernicious consequences. On the contrary, nothing is more evident than this, that every system which calls in question the immutability of moral distinctions has a tendency to undermine the foundations of *all* the virtues, both private and public, and to dry up the best and purest sources of human happiness. When skeptical doubts have once been excited in the mind by the perusal of such systems, no exhortation to the practice of our duties can have any effect; and it is necessary for us, before we think of addressing the heart, or influencing the will, to begin with undeceiving and enlightening the understanding. It is for this reason, that, in such an age as the present, when skeptical doctrines have been so anxiously disseminated by writers of genius, it appears to me to be a still more essential object in academical instruction to vindicate the theory of morals against the cavils of licentious metaphysicians, than to indulge in the more interesting and popular disquisitions of practical ethics. On the former subject, much yet remains to be done. On the latter, although the field of inquiry is by no means as yet completely exhausted, the student may be safely trusted to his own serious reflections, guided by the precepts of those illustrious men who, in different ages and countries, have devoted their talents to the improvement and happiness of the human race.

In this department of literature, no country whatever has surpassed our own; whether we consider the labors of the great lights of the English Church, or the fugitive essays of those later writers who (after the example of Addison) have attempted to enlist in the cause of virtue and religion whatever aid fancy and wit and elegance could lend to the support of truth. It is scarcely necessary for me to mention the advantage which may be derived in the same study from the philosophical remains of ancient Greece and Rome, — due allowances being made for some unfortunate prejudices produced or encouraged by violent and oppressive systems of policy. Indeed, with the exception of a few such prejudices, it may with great truth be asserted, that they who have been most successful, in modern times, in inculcating the duties of life, have been the moralists who have trod the most closely in the footsteps of the Greek and Roman philosophers. The case is different with respect to the theory of morals, which, among the ancients, attracted comparatively but a small degree of attention, although one of the questions formerly mentioned (that concerning the *object* of moral approbation) was a favorite subject of discussion in their schools. The other question, however, (that concerning the *principle* of moral approbation,) with the exception of a few hints in the writings of Plato, may be considered as in a great measure peculiar to modern Europe, having been chiefly agitated since the writings of Cudworth in opposition to those of Hobbes; and it is this question, accordingly, (recommended at once by its novelty and difficulty to the curiosity of speculative men,) that has produced most of the theories which characterize and distinguish from each other the later systems of moral philosophy.

III. *Analysis of Moral Perceptions and Emotions.*] It appears to me that the diversity of these systems has arisen, in a great measure, from the partial views which different writers have taken of the same complicated subject; that these systems are by no means so exclusive of each other as has commonly been imagined; and that, in order to arrive at the truth, it is necessary for us, instead of attaching ourselves to any one, to avail ourselves of the lights which all of them have furnished. Our moral perceptions and emotions are, in fact, the result of different principles combined together. They involve a judgment of the understanding, and they involve also a feeling of the heart; and it is only by attending to both that we can form a just notion of our moral constitution. In confirmation of this remark, it will be necessary for us to analyze particularly the state of our minds, when we are spectators of any good or bad action performed by another person, or when we reflect on the actions performed by ourselves. On such occasions we are conscious of three different things: —

1. The perception of an action as right or wrong.
2. An emotion of pleasure or of pain, varying in its degree according to the acuteness of our moral sensibility.
3. A perception of the merit or demerit of the agent.

Section I.

OF THE PERCEPTION OF RIGHT AND WRONG.

I. *Views entertained by Hobbes.*] The controversy concerning the origin of our moral ideas took its rise in modern times, in consequence of the writings of Mr. Hobbes. According to him, we approve of virtuous actions, or of actions beneficial to society, from self-love, as we know that whatever promotes the interest of society has on that very account an indirect tendency to promote our own. He further taught, that, as it is to the institution of government we are indebted for all the comforts and the confidence of social life, the laws which the civil magistrate enjoins are the ultimate standards of morality.

Dangerous as these doctrines are, some apology may be made for the author from the unfortunate circumstances of the times in which he lived. He had been a witness of the disorders which took place in England at the time of the dissolution of the monarchy by the death of Charles the First; and, in consequence of his mistaken speculations on the politics of that period, he contracted a bias in favor of despotical government, and was led to consider it as the duty of a good citizen to strengthen, as much as possible, the hands of the civil magistrate, by inculcating the doctrines of passive obedience and non-resistance. It was with this view that he was led to maintain the philosophical principles which have been already mentioned. He seems likewise to have formed a very unfavorable idea of the clerical order, from the instances which his own experience afforded of their turbulence and ambition; and on that account he wished to subject the consciences of men immediately to the secular powers. In consequence of this, his system, although offensive in a very high degree to all sound moralists, provoked in a more peculiar manner the resentment of the clergy, and drew on the author a great deal of personal obloquy, which neither his character in private life, nor his intentions as a writer, appear to have merited.

II. *Reply of his Antagonists.*] Among the antagonists of Hobbes, the most eminent by far was Dr. Cudworth; and indeed modern times have not produced an author who is better qualified to do justice to the very important argument he undertook, by his ardent zeal for the best interests of mankind, by his singular vigor and comprehensiveness of thought, and by the astonishing treasures he had collected of ancient literature.

That our ideas of right and wrong are not derived from positive law, Cudworth concluded from the following argument: — "Suppose such a law to be established, it must either be right to obey it, and wrong to disobey it, or indifferent whether we obey or disobey it. But a law which it is indifferent whether we obey or not cannot, it is evident, be the source of moral distinctions; and, on the contrary supposition, if it is right to obey the law, and wrong to disobey it, these distinctions must have had an existence antecedent to the law." * In a word, it is from *natural* law that *positive* law derives all its force.

The same argument against Hobbes is thus stated by Lord Shaftesbury.

"It is ridiculous to say there is any obligation on

* Smith's *Theory of Moral Sentiments*, Part VII. Sect. III. Chap. II.

man to act sociably or honestly in a formed government, and not in that which is commonly called the state of nature. For, to speak in the fashionable language of our modern philosophy, society being founded on a compact, the surrender made of every man's private unlimited right into the hands of the majority, or such as the majority should appoint, was of free choice, and by a promise. Now the promise itself was made *in a state of nature*, and that which could make a *promise* obligatory in the state of nature must make *all other* acts of humanity as much our real duty and natural part. Thus faith, justice, honesty, and virtue must have been as early as the state of nature, or they could never have been at all. The civil union or confederacy could never make right or wrong if they subsisted not before. He who was free to any villany before his contract, will and ought to make as free with his contract when he sees fit. The natural knave has the same reason to be a civil one, and may dispense with his politic capacity as oft as he sees occasion; it is only his word stands in the way. A man is obliged to keep his word. Why? Because he has given his word to keep it. Is not this a notable account of the original of moral justice, and the rise of civil government and allegiance?" *

To these observations it may be added, that our notions of right and wrong are so far from owing their origin to positive institutions, that they afford us the chief standard to which we appeal, in comparing different positive institutions with each other. Were it not for this test, how could we pronounce one code to be more humane, more liberal, or more equitable than another? or how could we feel that, in our own municipal regulations, some are consonant and others repugnant to the principles of justice. "Let any one," says a learned and judicious civilian, "acquaint himself with the sanguinary system of Draco, and then view it as tempered with the philosophy of Solon, and

* *Freedom of Wit*, Part III. Sect. I.

the softer refinements of a better age; let him look with the eye of speculation upon an establishment that directs 'not to seethe a kid in its mother's milk'; nor to 'muzzle the ox when he treadeth out the corn'; when our brother's cattle go astray or fall down by the way, not to 'hide ourselves from them'; that acquits the betrothed damsel who was violated at a distance, and out of hearing, upon this compassionate suggestion, — 'For he found her in the field, and the betrothed damsel cried, and there was none to save her'; let him reflect, I say, on his own feelings when he considers these different enactments, and then judge how far they agree with the philosophy of Hobbes." *

Agreeably to this view of positive institutions, Demosthenes remarks, — "The laws of a country may be regarded as a *criterion* for estimating the morals of the state, and the prevailing character of the people." †

III. *Origin and History of Hobbes's Doctrine.*] It is justly observed by Cudworth, that the doctrines now under consideration are not peculiar to the system of Hobbes; and that similar opinions have been entertained in all ages by those writers who were either anxious to flatter the passions of tyrannical rulers, or who had a secret bias to atheistic and Epicurean principles.

In confirmation of this remark, he takes a review of

---

* Taylor *On the Civil Law*, p. 159.

† *Adv. Timocrat.* Taylor gives the passage from which this is taken in the version of the Latin translator: — "Illud igitur vobis est etiam considerandum, multos Græcorum sæpe decrevisse, vestris utendum esse legibus: id quod vobis laudi haud injuriâ ducitis. Nam verum illud mihi videtur, quod quendam apud vos dixisse ferunt: *omnes cordatos in ea esse sententia, ut leges nihil aliud esse putent quam mores civitates.* Danda igitur est opera, ut eæ quam optimæ esse videantur."

[A new interest has been awakened of late in Hobbes and his writings. See Cousin, *Cours d'Histoire de la Philosophie Morale au XVIIIe Siècle*, Première Partie: *Ecole Sensualiste*, Leçons VII.–IX. Jouffroy, *Introduction to Ethics*, Lectures XIII. and XIV. Damiron, *L'Histoire de la Philosophie au XVIIe Siècle*, Liv. III. Hazlitt's *Literary Remains*, Essay VI. Blakey's *History of Moral Science*, Chap. IV. Mackintosh's *Progress of Ethical Philosophy*, Sect. IV. *Fragment on Mackintosh*, Sect. II. Hallam's *Introduction to the Literature of Europe*, Vol. III. Chap. III. Sect. IV.]

the principal attempts that have been made to undermine the foundations of morals, both in ancient and modern times, and interweaves with this history many profound reflections of his own. The following paragraphs contain the substance of this part of his work, and I hope will furnish an interesting, as well as useful, introduction to the reasonings I am afterwards to offer in vindication of the reality and immutability of moral distinctions.

"As the vulgar generally look no higher for the original of moral good and evil, just and unjust, than the codes and pandects, the tables and laws, of their country and religion, so there have not wanted pretended philosophers *in all ages*, who have asserted nothing to be good and evil, just and unjust, *naturally and immutably*, φύσει καὶ ἀκινήτως; but that all these things were positive, arbitrary, and factitious only. Such Plato mentions, in his Tenth Book, *De Legibus*, who maintained, 'that nothing at all was *naturally* just, but men, changing their opinions concerning them perpetually, sometimes made one thing just, sometimes another; but whatever is decreed and constituted, that for the time is valid, being made so by acts and laws, but not by any nature of its own.' And Aristotle more than once takes notice of this opinion in his *Ethics*. 'Things honest and just, which politics are conversant about, have so great a variety and uncertainty in them, that they seem to be only by law and not by nature.' * And afterwards † — having divided τὸ δίκαιον πολιτικόν, 'that which is politically just,' into φυσικόν, i. e. 'natural,' 'which has everywhere the same force,' and νομικόν, i. e. 'legal,' 'which, before there be a law made, is indifferent, but, when once the law is made, is determined to be just or unjust' — he adds, 'Some there are that think there is no other just or unjust but what is made by law and men, because that which is natural is immutable, and hath everywhere the same force, whereas *jura* and *justa*, "rights" and "just things," are every-

* *Ethic. Nic.*, Lib. I. cap. I. † Lib. V. cap. X.

where different.' The latter, therefore, they conceive to be analogous to wine and wheat measures, whch vary from place to place, according to local customs; the former they compare to the properties of *fire*, which produce the same effects in Persia and Greece.

"After these succeeded Epicurus, the reviver of the Democritical philosophy, the frame of whose principles must needs lead him to deny justice and injustice to be natural things; and therefore he determines that they arise wholly from mutual pacts and covenants of men, made for their own convenience and utility. 'Those living creatures that could not make mutual covenants together not to hurt, nor to be hurt by, one another, could not, for this cause, have any such thing as just or unjust among them. And there is the same reason for those nations that either will not or cannot make such compacts: for there is no such thing as justice *by itself*, but only in the mutual congresses of men.' Or, (as the late compiler of the Epicurean system expresses the same meaning,) 'there are some who think that those things which are just are just according to their proper, unvaried nature, and that the laws do not make them just, but only prescribe according to that nature which they have: but *the thing is not so.*' *

"And since in this latter age the physiological hypotheses of Democritus and Epicurus have been revived, and successfully applied to the solving of some of the phenomena of the visible world, there have not wanted some that have endeavoured to vent also those other paradoxes of the same philosophers, viz. that there is no incorporeal substance, nor any natural difference between good and evil, just and unjust, and to recommend the same under a show of wisdom, as the

* It may be proper to mention that Cudworth alludes here to Gassendi, who was at much pains to revive the philosophy of Epicurus, both in physics and morals, rejecting, however, or palliating, those parts of it which are most exceptionable. With this philosopher, (who appears to have been a most amiable and exemplary man in private life, and who in learning was not surpassed by any of his contemporaries,) Hobbes lived in habits of very intimate friendship during his long residence in France. See Gassendi *Opera*, Tom. V. pp. 129 *et seq*.

deep and profound mysteries of the atomical and corpuscular philosophy, as if senseless matter and atoms were the original of all things, according to the song of old Silenus in Virgil. Of this sort is that late writer of ethics and politics, who asserts 'that there are no authentic doctrines concerning just and unjust, good and evil, except the laws which are established in every city; and that it concerns none to inquire whether an action be reputed just or unjust, good or evil, except such only whom the community have appointed to be the interpreters of their laws.' * 'In the state of nature,' according to him, 'nothing can be *unjust*, and the notions of right and wrong, justice and injustice, have there no place. Where there is no common power there is no law; where no law, no injustice.' † 'No law can be unjust.' ‡ Nay, temperance is no more *naturally* right, according to this philosopher, than justice. 'Sensuality, in the sense in which it is condemned, hath no place till there be laws.' §

"But whatsoever was the true meaning of these philosophers that affirm justice and injustice to be only by law, and not by nature, certain it is that diverse modern theologers do not only seriously, but zealously, contend, in like manner, that there is nothing absolutely, intrinsically, and naturally good and evil, just and unjust, *antecedently to any positive command or prohibition of God*; but that the arbitrary will and pleasure of God, (that is an Omnipotent Being, devoid of all essential and natural justice,) by its commands and prohibitions, is the first and only rule and measure thereof. Whence it follows unavoidably, that nothing can be imagined so grossly wicked, or so foully unjust or dishonest, but, if it were supposed to be commanded by this omnipotent Deity, must needs, upon that hypothesis, forthwith become holy, just, and righteous. For, though the ancient fathers of the Christian Church were very abhorrent from this doctrine, yet it crept up

---

* Hobbes, *De Cive*, Præfatio.

† *Leviathan*, Part I. Chap. XIII.

‡ Ibid., Part II. Chap. XXX.

§ Ibid., Part I. Chap. VI.

afterward in the scholastic age, Ockham being among the first that maintained 'that there is no act evil, but as it is prohibited by God, and which cannot be made good if it be commanded by him.' And herein Petrus Alliacus and Andreas de Novo Castro, with others, quickly followed him.

"Now the necessary and unavoidable consequences of this opinion are such as these:—'That to love God is *by nature* an indifferent thing, and is morally good only because it is enjoined by his command'; 'that holiness is not a conformity with the Divine nature and attributes'; 'that God hath no natural inclination to the good of the creatures, and might *justly* doom an innocent creature to eternal torment';—all which propositions, with others of the kind, are word for word asserted by some late authors. Though I think not fit to mention the names of any of them in this place, excepting only one, Joannes Szydlovius, who, in a book published at Franeker, hath professedly avowed and maintained the grossest of them. And yet neither he, nor the rest, are to be thought any more blameworthy herein than many others, that, holding the same premises, have either dissembled or disowned those conclusions which unavoidably follow therefrom, but rather to be commended for their openness, simplicity, and ingenuity in representing their opinion naked to the world such as indeed it is, without any veil or mask.

"Wherefore, since there are so many, both philosophers and theologians, that seemingly and verbally acknowledge such things as moral good and evil, just and unjust, yet contend, notwithstanding, that these are not *by nature* but *institution*, and that there is nothing naturally or immutably just or unjust, I shall from hence fetch the rise of this ethical discourse or inquiry concerning things good and evil, just and unjust, laudable and shameful, demonstrating, in the first place, that, if there be any thing at all good or evil, just or unjust, there must of necessity be something *naturally and immutably good and just.* And from thence I shall proceed afterward to show what this natural, immutable and eternal justice is, with the branches and species of it." *

IV. *Cudworth's Theory of Morals.*] The foregoing very long quotation, while it contains much valuable information with respect to the history of moral science, will be sufficient to convey a general idea of the scope of Cudworth's ethical inquiries, and of the prevailing opinions among philosophers upon this subject, at the time when he wrote. For the details of his argument I must refer to his work. It is sufficient for my present purpose to observe, that he seems plainly to have considered our notions of right and wrong as *incapable of analysis*, that is, (to use the language of more modern writers,) he considered them as *simple ideas* or *notions*, of which the names *do not admit of definition.* In this respect, also, his philosophy differs from that of Hobbes, who, as we have already remarked, ascribes our moral judgments, not to an immediate perception of the qualities of actions, but to a view of their *tendencies*, which we approve or disapprove according as they appear to be conducive or not to our own interest, or to that of society. Indeed, according to Hobbes, these two tendencies coincide, or rather are the same, for he apprehended that all our zeal for the public good originates in a selfish principle. "Man," he said, "is driven to society by necessity, and whatever promotes its interest is judged to have a remote tendency to promote his own." Thus he attempts to *account* for our approbation of virtue by resolving it into self-love, and of consequence, to resolve the notions expressed by the words *right* and *wrong* into other notions more simple and general. This theory I have already endeavoured to refute at some length, and I have only now to add to what was formerly remarked with respect to it, that, if it were agreeable to fact, the words *right* and *wrong*

* *Eternal and Immutable Morality*, Book I. Chap I. Here, as in some other cases, Mr. Stewart does not cite the whole of the passage continuously, as it stands in the original, but those parts only which are to his purpose, sometimes giving merely the substance. — Ed.

would be synonymous with *advantageous* and *disadvantageous;* and to say that those actions are right which are calculated to promote our own happiness would be an identical proposition.

Cudworth's opinion, on the contrary, led him to consider our perception of right and wrong as an ultimate fact in our nature. Indeed, to those whose judgments are not warped by preconceived theories, no fact with respect to the human mind can well appear more incontestable. We can define the words *right* and *wrong* only by synonymous words and phrases, or by the properties and necessary concomitants of what they denote. Thus, "we may say of the word *right*, that it expresses what we *ought to do*, what is *fair* and *honest*, what is *approvable*, what *every man professes to be the rule of his conduct*, what *all men praise*, and what *is in itself laudable, though no man praise it*." * In such definitions and explanations it is evident we only substitute a synonymous expression instead of the word defined, or we characterize the quality which the word denotes by some circumstance connected with it or resulting from it as a consequence; and therefore we may, with confidence, conclude that the word in question expresses a simple idea.

The two most important conclusions, then, which result from Cudworth's reasonings in opposition to Hobbes are these: — First, that the mind is able to form *antecedently to positive institution* the ideas of right and wrong; and secondly, that these words express *simple ideas, or ideas incapable of analysis.*

From these conclusions of Cudworth a further question naturally arose, — how the ideas of right and wrong were formed, and to what principle of our constitution they ought to be referred. This very interesting question did not escape the attention of Cudworth. And, in answer to it, he endeavoured to show that our notions of moral distinctions are formed by *reason*, or, in other words, by the power which distinguishes truth

* Reid, *On the Active Powers*, Essay III. Part III. Chap V.

from falsehood. And accordingly it became, for some time, the fashionable language among moralists, to say that virtue consisted, not in obedience to the law of a superior, but in *a conduct conformable to reason.*

At the time when Cudworth wrote, no accurate classification had been attempted of the principles of the human mind. His account of the office of reason, accordingly, in enabling us to perceive the distinction between right and wrong, passed without censure, and was understood merely to imply, that there is *an eternal and immutable distinction* between right and wrong, no less than between truth and falsehood; and that both these distinctions *are perceived by our rational powers*, or by those powers which raise us above the brutes.*

V. *Connection of Locke's Theory of the Origin of Ideas with this Inquiry.*] The publication of Locke's *Essay* introduced into this part of science a precision of expression unknown before, and taught philosophers to distinguish a variety of powers which had formerly been very generally confounded. With these great merits, however, his work has capital defects, and perhaps in no part of it are these defects more important than in the attempt he has made to deduce the origin of our knowledge entirely from *sensation* and *reflection.* To the former of these sources he refers the ideas we receive by our external senses, — of colors, sounds, hardness, &c. To the latter, the ideas we derive from consciousness of our own mental operations, — of memory, imagination, volition, pleasure, pain, &c. These, according to him, are the sources of *all* our simple ideas; and the only power that the mind possesses is to perform certain operations of analysis, combination, comparison, &c., on the materials with which it is thus supplied.

It was this system of Locke's which led him to those dangerous opinions that were formerly mentioned con-

---

* For some curious notices of Cudworth and the fate of his writings, see D'Israeli's *Amenities of Literature*, under the head of *The True Intellectual System of the Universe.* — Ed.

cerning the nature of moral distinctions, which he seems to have considered as *entirely the offspring of education and fashion.* Indeed, if the words *right* and *wrong* neither express simple ideas, nor relations discoverable by reason, it will not be found easy to avoid adopting this conclusion.

In order to reconcile Locke's account of the origin of our ideas with the immutability of moral distinctions, different theories were proposed concerning the nature of virtue. According to one,* for example, it was said to consist in a conduct conformable to *truth;* according to another,† in a conduct conformable to the *fitness of things.* The great object of all these theories may be considered as the same, to remove right and wrong from the class of simple ideas, and to resolve moral rectitude into a conformity with some relation perceived by reason or by the understanding.

VI. *Hutcheson's Theory of a Moral Sense.*] Dr. Hutcheson saw clearly the vanity of these attempts, and hence he was led, in compliance with the language of Locke's philosophy, to refer the origin of our moral ideas to a particular power of perception, to which he gave the name of the *moral sense.* "All the ideas," says he, "or the materials of our reasoning or judging, are received by some immediate powers of perception, internal or external, which we may call *senses.*" "Reasoning or intellect seems to raise no new species of ideas, but to discover or discern the relations of those received." ‡

According to this system, as it has been commonly explained, our perceptions of right and wrong are *impressions* which our minds are made to receive from particular actions, similar to the relishes and aversions

---

* Mr. Wollaston, in his *Religion of Nature Delineated.*

† Dr. Clarke, in his *Discourse concerning the Unchangeable Obligations of Natural Religion*, and in other works. [For the connection between Locke and the subsequent English ethical theories, see Jouffroy, Lectures XXI. and XXII.]

‡ *Nature and Conduct of the Passions*, Treatise II. Sect. I.

given us for particular objects of the external and internal senses.

That this was Dr. Hutcheson's own idea appears from the following passage, in which he endeavours to obviate some dangerous notions which were supposed to follow from this doctrine. "Let none imagine that calling the ideas of virtue and vice *perceptions of sense*, upon apprehending the actions and affections of another, does diminish their reality more than the like assertions concerning all pleasure and pain, happiness or misery. Our reason often corrects the report of our senses about the natural tendency of the external action, and corrects rash conclusions about the affections of the agent. But whether our moral sense be subject to such a disorder as to have different perceptions, from the same apprehended affections in an agent, at different times, as the eye may have of the colors of an unaltered object, it is not easy to determine; perhaps it will be hard to find any instance of such a change. What reason could correct if it fell into such a disorder, I know not, except suggesting to its remembrance its former approbations, and representing the general sense of mankind. But this does not prove ideas of virtue and vice to be previous to a sense, more than a like correction of the ideas of color in a person under the jaundice proves that colors are perceived by reason previously to sense." *

Mr. Hume, whose philosophy coincides in this respect with Dr. Hutcheson's, has expressed himself on this subject still more explicitly. "As virtue is an end, and is desirable on its own account, without fee or reward, merely for the immediate satisfaction which it conveys, it is requisite that there should be some sentiment which it touches, some internal taste or feeling, or whatever you please to call it, which distinguishes moral good and evil, and which embraces the one and rejects the other.

"Thus the distinct boundaries and offices of *reason*

---

* *Nature and Conduct of the Passions*, Treatise II. Sect. IV.

and of *taste* are easily ascertained. The former conveys the knowledge of truth and falsehood; the latter gives the sentiment of beauty and deformity, vice and virtue. The one discovers objects as they really stand in nature, without addition or diminution; the other has a productive faculty, and, gilding or staining all natural objects with the colors borrowed from internal sentiment, raises, in a manner, a new creation. Reason, being cool and disengaged, is no motive to action, and directs only the impulse received from appetite or inclination, by showing us the means of attaining happiness or avoiding misery. Taste, as it gives pleasure or pain, and thereby constitutes happiness or misery, becomes a motive to action, and is the first spring or impulse to desire and volition. From circumstances and relations, known or supposed, the former leads us to the discovery of the concealed and unknown. After all circumstances and relations are laid before us, the latter makes us feel from the whole a new sentiment of blame or approbation. The standard of the one, being founded on the nature of things, is eternal and inflexible, even by the will of the Supreme Being. The standard of the other, arising from the internal frame and constitution of animals, is ultimately derived from that Supreme Will which bestowed on each being its peculiar nature, and arranged the several classes and orders of existence." *

In the passage now quoted from Mr. Hume, a slight hint is given of his skepticism with respect to the immutability of moral distinctions; but, in some other parts of his writings, he has openly and avowedly expressed his opinions upon this important question. The words *right* and *wrong* (according to him) signify nothing *in the objects themselves* to which they are applied, any more than the words *sweet* and *bitter*, *pleasant* and *painful*, but only *certain effects in the mind of the spectator*. As it is improper, therefore, (according to the doctrines of some modern philosophers,) to say of an object of taste that it is sweet, or of heat that it

---

* *Principles of Morals*, Appendix I.

is in the fire, so it is equally improper to say of actions that they are right or wrong. It is absurd to speak of morality as a thing independent and unchangeable, inasmuch as it arises from *an arbitrary relation between our constitution and particular objects.* The distinction of moral good and evil is founded on the pleasure or pain which results from the view of any sentiment or character; and, as that pleasure or pain cannot be unknown to the person who feels it, it follows that there is just so much vice or virtue in any character as every one places in it; and that it is impossible in this particular we can ever be mistaken.*

Before we proceed to an examination of these conclusions, it may be worth while to remark, that they have not even the merit of originality; for we find from the *Theætetus* of Plato, as well as from other remains of antiquity, that the same skepticism prevailed among the Grecian sophists, and was supported by nearly the same arguments. Protagoras and his followers extended it to all truth, physical as well as moral, and maintained that every thing was relative to perception. The following maxims in particular have a wonderful coincidence with Hume's philosophy. "Nothing is true or false, any more than sweet or sour, *in itself*, but relatively to the perceiving mind." "Man is the measure of all things, and every thing is that, and no other, which to every one it *seems* to be, so that there can be nothing true, nothing existent, distinct from the mind's own perceptions."

With respect to this skeptical philosophy, as it is taught in the writings of Hume, it appears evidently, from what has been already said, to be founded entirely on the supposition, that our perception of the moral qualities of actions has some analogy to our perception of the sensible qualities of matter; and there-

* "Were I not afraid of appearing too philosophical, I should remind my reader of that famous doctrine, supposed to be fully proved in modern times, that tastes and colors, and all other sensible qualities, lie, not in the bodies, but merely in the senses. The case is the same with beauty and deformity, *virtue and vice.*" — Hume's *Essays, Moral, Political, and Literary*, Part I. Essay XVIII.

fore it becomes a very interesting inquiry for us to examine how far this supposition is agreeable to fact Indeed, this is the most important question that can be stated with respect to the theory of morals; and yet I confess it appears to me that the obscurity in which it is involved arises chiefly, if not wholly, from the use of indefinite and ambiguous terms.

That moral distinctions are perceived by a sense is implied in the definition of a sense already quoted from Dr. Hutcheson. "All the ideas, or the materials of our reasoning or judging, are received by some immediate powers of perception, internal or external, which we may call *senses.* Reasoning or intellect seems to raise no new species of ideas, but to discover or discern the relations of those received." If this definition be admitted, there cannot be a doubt that the origin of our moral ideas must be referred to *a sense;* at least there can be no doubt upon this point among those who hold, with Cudworth and with Price, that the words *right* and *wrong* express *simple ideas.* The latter of these authors, a most zealous opposer of a moral sense, (and although one of the driest and least engaging of our English moralists, yet certainly one of the most sound and judicious,) grants that the words *right* and *wrong* are incapable of a definition, and considers a want of attention to this circumstance as a principal source of the errors which have misled philosophers in treating of this part of moral science. "It is a very necessary previous observation," says he, "that *right* and *wrong* denote *simple ideas*, and are therefore to be ascribed to *some power of immediate perception* in the human mind. He that doubts need only try to enumerate the simple ideas they signify, or to give definitions of them when applied (suppose to *beneficence* or *cruelty*), which shall amount to more than synonymous expressions. From not attending to this, from giving definitions of these ideas, and attempting to derive them from *deduction* or *reasoning*, has proceeded most of that confusion in which the question concerning the foundation of morals has been involved. There are, undoubtedly, some actions that are *ultimately* approved, and for justifying which no reason can be assigned, as there are some ends which are *ultimately* desired, and for choosing which no reason can be given. Were not this true, there would be an infinite series or progression of reasons and ends subordinate to one another. There would be nothing at which to stop, and therefore nothing that could at all be approved or desired." *

It appears from the foregoing passage that Dr. Price, as well as Dr. Hutcheson, ascribes our ideas of moral distinctions to a power of immediate perception in the mind, and therefore the difference between them turns entirely on the propriety of the definition of a *sense* which Dr. Hutcheson has given.

It may be further observed, in justification of Dr. Hutcheson, that the skeptical consequences deduced from his supposition of a *moral sense* do not necessarily result from it. Unfortunately, most of his illustrations were taken from the *secondary* qualities of matter, which, since the time of Descartes, philosophers have been in general accustomed to refer to the mind, and not to the external object. But if we suppose our perception of right and wrong to be analogous to the perception of extension and figure, and other *primary* qualities, the reality and immutability of moral distinctions seem to be placed on a foundation sufficiently satisfactory to a candid inquirer. That our notions of primary qualities are necessarily accompanied with a conviction of their separate and independent existence was formerly shown; and, therefore, to compare our perception of right and wrong to our perception of extension and of figure, although it may not, perhaps, be very accurate or philosophical, does not imply any skepticism with respect to the immutability of moral distinctions; at least does not justify those skeptical inferences which Mr. Hume has endeavoured to deduce from Dr. Hutcheson's language.

* *Review of the Principal Questions in Morals*, Chap. I. Sect. III.

The definition, however, of a sense which Dr. Hutcheson has given is by far too general, and was plainly suggested to him by Locke's account of the origin of our ideas. The words *cause and effect*, *duration*, *number*, *equality*, *identity*, and many others, express simple ideas, as well as the words *right* and *wrong;* and yet it would surely be absurd to ascribe each of them to a particular power of perception, meaning thereby *a sense*. Notwithstanding this circumstance, as the expression *moral sense* has now the sanction of use, and as, when properly explained, it cannot lead to any bad consequences, it may be still retained without inconvenience in ethical disquisitions. It has been much in fashion among moralists since the time of Shaftesbury and Hutcheson, nor was it an innovation introduced by them; for the ancients often speak of a *sensus recti et honesti;* and, in our own language, *a sense of duty* is a phrase not only employed by philosophers, but habitually used in common discourse.*

VII. *Price's Theory of Intuitive Perception.*] To what part of our constitution, then, shall we ascribe the origin of the ideas of right and wrong? Dr. Price (returning to the antiquated phraseology of Cudworth) says, to the *understanding*, and endeavours to show, in opposition to Locke and his followers, that "the power which understands, or the faculty that discerns truth, is itself a source of new ideas."

This controversy turns solely on the meaning of words. The origin of our ideas of right and wrong is manifestly the same with that of the other simple ideas already mentioned; and, whether it be referred to the understanding or not, seems to me a matter of mere arrangement, provided it be granted that the words *right* and *wrong* express qualities of actions, and not merely

---

* For further notices of Hutcheson and the sentimental moralists generally, see Cousin, *Cours d'Histoire de la Philosophie Morale au XVIII*[e] *Siècle*, Seconde Partie: *Ecole Ecossaise;* — Jouffroy, *Introduction to Ethics*, Lectures XVI.-XX.; — and Alexander Smith's *Philosophy of Morals*, Part I. Chap. III. — Ed.

a power of exciting certain agreeable or disagreeable emotions in our minds.

It may perhaps obviate some objections against the language of Cudworth and Price to remark, that the word *reason* is used in senses which are extremely different: sometimes to express the whole of those powers which elevate man above the brutes, and constitute his rational nature, — more especially, perhaps, his intellectual powers; sometimes to express the power of deduction or argumentation. The former is the sense in which the word is used in common discourse; and it is in this sense that it seems to be employed by those writers who refer to it the origin of our moral ideas. Their antagonists, on the other hand, understand in general, by reason, the power of deduction or argumentation; a use of the word which is not unnatural, from the similarity between the words *reason* and *reasoning*, but which is not agreeable to its ordinary meaning. "No hypothesis," says Dr. Campbell, "hitherto invented has shown that, by means of the discursive faculty, without the aid of any other mental power, we could ever obtain a notion either of the beautiful or the good."* The remark is undoubtedly true; and it may be applied to all those systems which ascribe to *reason* the origin of our moral ideas, *if the expressions 'reason' and 'discursive faculty' be used as synonymous.* But if the word *reason* be used in a more general sense, to denote merely our rational and intellectual nature, there does not seem to be much impropriety in ascribing to it the origin of those simple notions which are not excited in the mind by the immediate operation of the senses, but which arise in consequence of the exercise of the intellectual powers upon their various objects.

A variety of intuitive judgments might be mentioned involving simple ideas, which it is impossible to trace to any origin but to the power which enables us to form these judgments. Thus it is surely an intuitive truth, that the sensations of which I am conscious, and

* *Philosophy of Rhetoric*, Book I. Chap. VII. Sect. IV.

all those I remember, belong to one and the same being, which I call *myself*. Here is an intuitive judgment involving the simple idea of *identity*. In like manner, the changes which I perceive in the universe impress me with a conviction, that some cause must have operated to produce them. Here is an intuitive judgment involving the simple idea of *causation*. When we consider the adjacent angles made by a straight line standing upon another, and perceive that their sum is equal to two right angles, the judgment we form involves the simple idea of *equality*. To say, therefore, that reason, or the understanding, is a source of new ideas, is not so exceptionable a mode of speaking as has sometimes been supposed. According to Locke, *sense* furnishes our ideas, and *reason* perceives their agreements or disagreements; whereas, in point of fact, these agreements or disagreements are in many instances simple ideas, of which no analysis can be given, and of which the origin must therefore be referred to reason, according to Locke's own doctrine.

In speaking of the hypothesis of a *moral sense*, I formerly observed that the expression was sanctioned by the example of the ancients. The same authority may be appealed to in justification of the language used by Cudworth and Price, whose ideas on the subject seem indeed to be still more conformable to the spirit of the Greek philosophy. The *leading principle of action*, τὸ ἡγεμονικόν, for example, so much insisted on by Plato and others, was plainly considered by them as the *faculty of reason;* τὸ φύσει δεσποτικὸν τουτέστι τὸ λογιστικόν, says Alcinoüs, *De Doctrina Platonis.** In Plato's *Theætetus*, too, Socrates observes, "that it cannot be any of the powers of sense that compares the perceptions of all the senses, and apprehends the general affections of things, and particularly *identity*, *number*, *similitude*, *dissimilitude*, *equality*, *inequality*, to which he adds καλὸν καὶ αἰσχρόν, *virtue and vice;* asserting that this power is

* Cap. XXVIII. "Sovereignty belongs by nature to the reasoning faculty."

reason, or the soul acting by itself separately from matter, and independently of any corporeal impressions and passions; and that, consequently, in opposition to Protagoras, knowledge is not to be sought for in sense, but in this superior part of the soul. It seems to me, that, for the perception of these things, a different organ or faculty is not appointed, but that the soul itself, and in virtue of its own power, observes these general affections of all things. So far we have advanced as to find that knowledge is by no means to be sought in sense, but in the power of the soul which it employs, when within itself it contemplates and searches out truth." *

---

* Plato could hardly have expressed himself with greater precision, had he been arguing against Hutcheson's doctrine of a moral sense. See on this subject Cudworth's *Immutable Morality*, Book III., and Price's *Review of the Principal Questions and Difficulties in Morals*, Chap. I. Sect. II.

[For the argument in the text, it is only necessary to mark the points of difference which distinguish the truths of the *pure* or *intuitive* reason from those of the *discursive* reason, or *reasoning*.

1. The former are simple and elementary judgments. They constitute a portion of what may be called the *data* of intelligence, resembling, in this respect, the *data* of sensation and consciousness. They result *immediately* from a law of our cognitive faculties, from our original constitution as rational beings, and therefore may be regarded, in this sense, as *primitive* or *innate*.

2. They are also recognized, assumed, or assented to, as soon as we have occasion to apply them, or as soon as the propositions containing them are understood. They are not *derived* truths, either by induction or deduction; they do not depend on testimony, or memory, or experience of any kind. All that experience does for them is to bring about the occasions, and the measure of development, on condition of which they spring up in the mind itself. They neither require nor admit of proof: reason *asserts* them as being *self-evident*; and, as such, they are acted on and assented to, in proportion as reason is unfolded, by all men. In this sense, therefore, they may be pronounced *universal*.

3. Again, reason not only affirms that these primitive and universal judgments are true, but, taking for granted the veracity of our cognitive faculties, that they cannot *not* be true. They relate to realities which cannot be made the objects of sense or consciousness, and consequently we cannot *imagine* what they are; nevertheless, the objects of sense and consciousness, as apprehended by the reason, *necessarily* presuppose these realities. These objects do not *contain* them, but reason sees that they *presuppose* them. In words we may deny that qualities presuppose a substance or *substratum*, in which they inhere, or that body presupposes space, which it measures and fills; but we are so far from being able actually to believe in the negative of these propositions, that we cannot bring ourselves by any effort to conceive of it as being *possible*. Hence, we conclude

VIII. *The Theory which we adopt must maintain the Reality and Immutability of Moral Distinctions.*] The opinion we form, however, on this point, is of little moment, provided it be granted that the words *right* and *wrong* express *qualities of actions.* When I say of an act of justice that it is *right*, do I mean merely that the act excites pleasure in my mind, as a particular color pleases my eye, in consequence of a relation which it bears to my organ? or do I mean to assert *a truth* which is as independent of my constitution as the equality of the three angles of a triangle to two right angles? Skepticism may be indulged in both cases, about mathematical and about moral truth, but in neither case does it admit of a refutation by argument.

For my own part, I can as easily conceive a rational being so formed as to believe the three angles of a triangle to be equal to *one* right angle, as to believe that, if he had it in his power, it would be *right* to sacrifice the happiness of other men to the gratification of his own animal appetites, or that there would be no *injustice* in depriving an industrious old man of the fruits of his own laborious acquisitions. The exercise of our reason in the two cases is very different; but in both cases we have a perception of *truth*, and are impressed with an irresistible conviction that the truth is immutable, and independent of the will of any being whatever.

In the passage which was formerly quoted from Dr. Cudworth, mention is made of various authors, par-

---

that the truths of the pure or intuitive reason are not only primitive and universal, but *necessary*.

Now the Rational School, of moralists, represented by such writers as Cudworth and Price, maintain that morality has its foundation in truths of this description, and not, as is held by the Sentimental School, represented by such writers as Hutcheson and Hume, in facts of sensibility, or in purely instinctive phenomena.

For more recent authorities on this subject, see Cousin, *Sur le Fondement des Idées Absolues du Vrai, du Beau, et du Bien.* Bouillier, *Theorie de la Raison Impersonnelle.* Coleridge's *Aids to Reflection;* particularly his comment on the eighth of the *Aphorisms on that which is indeed Spiritual Religion.* Whewell's *Philosophy of the Inductive Sciences*, Book I.

Jouffroy has given, *Introduction to Ethics*, Lectures XXI.-XXIII., an admirable criticism on Price, and other rational moralists of the same school, including Cudworth and Stewart. — ED.]

ticularly among the theologians of the scholastic ages, who were led to call in question the immutability of moral distinctions by the pious design of magnifying the perfections of the Deity. I am sorry to observe that these notions are not as yet completely exploded; and that, in our own age, they have misled the speculations of some writers of considerable genius, particularly those of Dr. Johnson, Soame Jenyns, and Dr. Paley. Such authors certainly do not recollect, that what they add to the Divine power and majesty they take away from his moral attributes; for if moral distinctions be not immutable and eternal, it is absurd to speak of the *goodness* or of the *justice* of God. "Whoever thinks," says Shaftesbury, "that there is a God, and pretends formally to believe that he is *just* and *good*, must suppose that there is independently such a thing as *justice* and *injustice*, *truth* and *falsehood*, *right* and *wrong*, according to which eternal and immutable standards he pronounces that God is *just*, *righteous*, and *true*. If the mere will, decree, or law of God be said absolutely to constitute *right* and *wrong*, then are these latter words of no signification at all [when applied to Him]." *

In justice, indeed, to one of the writers above mentioned, Dr. Paley, it is proper for me to observe, that the objection just now stated has not escaped his attention, and that he has even attempted an answer to it; but it is an answer in which he admits the justness of the inference which we have drawn from his premises; or, in other words, in which he admits, that, to speak of the moral attributes of God, or to say that he is *just*, *righteous*, and *true*, is to employ words which are altogether nugatory and unmeaning. That I may not be accused of misinterpreting the doctrine of this ingenious writer, who on many accounts deserves the popularity he enjoys, I shall quote his own statement of his opinion on this subject. "Since moral obligation depends, as we have seen, upon the will of God, *right*, which is correlative to it, must depend upon the same.

* *Inquiry concerning Virtue*, Part. III. Sect. II.

Right therefore signifies *consistency with the will of God.* But if the Divine will determine the distinction of right and wrong, what else is it but an identical proposition to say of God that he acts *right?* or how is it possible even to conceive that he should act *wrong?* Yet these assertions are intelligible and significant. The case is this: by virtue of the two principles, that God wills the happiness of his creatures, and that the will of God is the measure of right and wrong, we arrive at certain conclusions, which conclusions become rules; and we soon learn to pronounce actions right and wrong according as they agree or disagree with our rules, without looking further; and when the habit is once established of stopping at the rules, we can go back and compare with these rules even the Divine conduct itself; and yet it may be true, (only not observed by us at the time,) that the rules themselves are deduced from the Divine will." *

To this very extraordinary passage, (some parts of which I confess I do not completely comprehend, but which plainly gives up the *moral attributes of God* as a form of words that convey no meaning,) I have no particular answer to offer. That it was written with the purest intentions, and from the complete conviction of the author's own mind, I am perfectly satisfied from the general scope of his book, as well as from the strong testimony of the first names in England in favor of the worth of the writer; but it leads to consequences of the

---

* *Moral Philosophy,* Book II. Chap. IX. When Dr. Paley first appeared as an author, his reading on ethical subjects seems to me to have been extremely limited, and to have extended little farther than to the works of that ingenious and well-meaning, but fanciful and superficial writer, Abraham Tucker, author, under the fictitious name of Edward Search, Esq. of *The Light of Nature Pursued.* See the preface to the *Moral Philosophy.* The political part of Paley's book, although by no means unexceptionable displays talents so far superior to the moral, that one would scarcely suppose them to have proceeded from the same pen. [John Law, to whose father the book is dedicated, and who was himself a friend and fellow-tutor of Paley and afterwards Bishop of Elphin in Ireland, is said to have assisted in the composition of the work, and to have written the whole of the admirable chapter, *Of Reverencing the Deity.* Dyer's *Privileges of Cambridge,* Vol. II. p. 59.]

most alarming nature, coinciding in every material respect with the systems of those scholastic theologians whom Dr. Cudworth classes with the Epicurean philosophers of old, and whose errors that great and excellent writer has refuted with so splendid a display of learning, and such irresistible force of argument." *

Section II.

OF THE AGREEABLE AND DISAGREEABLE EMOTIONS ARISING FROM THE PERCEPTION OF WHAT IS RIGHT AND WRONG IN CONDUCT.

I. *Moral Beauty and Deformity.*] It is impossible to behold a good action without being conscious of a benevolent affection, either of love or of respect, towards the agent; and consequently, as all our benevolent affections include an agreeable feeling, every good action must be a source of pleasure to the spectator. Besides this, other agreeable feelings, of order, of utility, of peace of mind, &c., come, in process of time, to be associated with the general idea of virtuous conduct.

Those qualities in good actions which excite agreeable feelings in the mind of the spectator form what some moralists have called the *beauty of virtue.*

All this may be applied, *mutatis mutandis*, to explain what is meant by the *deformity of vice.*

This view of the moral faculty, which represents it as a species of *taste*, by which we are determined to the love of moral excellence, occurs very frequently in the works of the ancients. But I shall confine myself at present to one short quotation from Cicero. "Nec vero illa parva vis naturæ est rationisque, quòd unum hoc animal sentit quid sit ordo; quid sit, quod deceat; in factis dictisque qui modus. Itaque eorum ipsorum

* Even Wardlaw, though he rejects Butler's doctrine respecting a natural conscience in man, strenuously opposes those who make moral distinctions depend on the *will* of God. *Christian Ethics*, Lecture VI. See also Upham's *Mental Philosophy*, Vol. II. § 292 *et seq.* — Ed.

quæ adspectu sentiuntur, nullum aliud animal pulchritudinem, venustatem, convenientiam partium sentit; quam similitudinem natura ratioque *ab oculis ad animum transferens*, multo etiam magis pulchritudinem, constantiam, ordinem in consiliis factisque conservandum putat; cavetque ne quid indecorè, effeminatève faciat; tum in omnibus et opinionibus et factis, ne quid libidinosè aut faciat aut cogitet: quibus ex rebus conflatur et efficitur id, quod quærimus *honestum;* quod, etiam si nobilitatum non sit, tamen honestum sit; quodque verè dicimus, etiam, si à nullo laudetur, naturâ esse laudabile. Formam quidem ipsam, Marce fili, et tamquam faciem honesti vides; quæ *si oculis cerneretur*, mirabiles amores, ut ait Plato, excitaret sapientiæ." *

The same moralists who have applied to virtue and to vice the epithets I have now been endeavouring to define, have remarked, that, as in natural objects, so also in the conduct and characters of mankind, there are two different species of beauty; — the one what is properly called *beauty*, in the more limited and precise acceptation of the term; the other what is properly called *grandeur* or *sublimity*. The former naturally excites love toward the agent, the latter renders him an object of our admiration. To the former class belong the qualities of gentleness, candor, condescension, and humanity. To the latter, magnanimity, fortitude, inflexible justice, self-command, contempt of danger and contempt of death; those qualities which, as exhibited in the character of Cato, formed in the judgment of Sen-

---

* *De Off.*, Lib. I. 4, 5. "Nor is that power of nature and reason small which has given to man alone a perception of order and propriety, and a standard by which to regulate his speech and his actions. *Of the objects of sense*, no other animal is qualified to perceive the beauty, the grace, and the symmetry of parts. But reason enables man to make the same application of this perception of external nature *to the mind*, and to observe that a much higher beauty, harmony, and order ought to be preserved in designs and in actions, and that unbecoming opinions and dissolute conduct should be wholly avoided. From this constitution of nature arises that virtue we seek for, which, however little distinguished by the world, is still virtue, and which, though none approved, we justly affirm to be of itself praiseworthy. Such, my son Marcus, is the form and character of virtue, which, according to the opinion of Plato, '*if it could be distinguished by the eye*, would excite a wonderful love of wisdom.'"

cca a spectacle which Heaven itself might behold with pleasure. "Ecce spectaculum Deo dignum, ad quod respiciat Jupiter, suo operi intentus, vir fortis cum mala fortuna compositus." Illustrations of this kind abound in those writers who have adopted Shaftesbury's scheme of morals.

II. *Distinguishable from our Perceptions of Right and Wrong.*] Without deciding at present on the propriety of the expressions *moral beauty* and *moral deformity*, it is of consequence for us to remark, that our perception of the qualities which these words are employed to denote is plainly distinguishable from our perception of actions as *right* or *wrong*. The latter involves a judgment with respect to certain attributes of actions, which no more depend on our perception than the primary qualities of body depend on the informations we receive of them by our external senses, or than the distinction between mathematical truth and falsehood depends on the conclusions of our understanding. The words *beauty* and *deformity*, on the other hand, have always a reference to the feelings of the spectator, — to the delight or uneasiness which particular actions produce on the mind.

Nor are these perceptions distinguishable from each other merely in theory. The distinct operation of each in producing the moral sentiments of mankind is easily discernible by the most superficial observer; for, although they are always in some degree combined together, yet they are not always combined in the same relative proportions. There are some men who, with Marcus in the play, at the bare mention of successful iniquity, are "tortured even to madness"; while others, whose judgments with respect to morality are equally sound, possess that steady and dispassionate temper which

> "Can look on fraud, rebellion, guilt, and Cæsar,
> In the calm light of mild philosophy." *

* Addison's *Cato*, Act I. Scene I.

The rectitude, therefore, of our moral judgments is by no means to be estimated by the liveliness of the impressions which good or bad actions produce on the mind. Indeed, the same circumstances which contribute to the accuracy of the former have in some respects a tendency to weaken the latter. These, like all other passive impressions, are rendered more languid by custom;* whereas constant exercise and a proper application of our intellectual powers in general are absolutely necessary to guard us against the various errors by which the power of moral judgment is liable to be perverted. The liveliness, too, of our moral feelings depends much on accidental circumstances; — on constitutional temper, on education, on early associations, and, above all, on the culture which the power of imagination has received.

Notwithstanding, however, the reality and importance of this distinction, it has been but little attended to by the greater part of philosophers. The ancients had it in view when they spoke of the *honestum* and the *pulchrum*, the τὸ δίκαιον and the τὸ καλόν; but the moderns seem in general to have overlooked it almost entirely, some of them confining their attention exclusively to the one perception, and some to the other. Clarke, for example, and his followers, neglecting the consideration of our moral *feelings*, have treated of this part of our constitution as if it consisted wholly of a power of distinguishing between right and wrong; and hence their works, how satisfactory soever to the understanding, seldom engage the imagination, or interest the heart. Shaftesbury, on the other hand, and his numerous admirers, by dwelling exclusively on our perception of moral beauty and deformity, have been led into enthusiasm and declamation, and have furnished licentious moralists with a pretence for questioning the immutability of moral distinctions. Even Dr. Hutche-

* On further reflection, this proposition seems to me somewhat doubtful Perhaps it may be found that our moral impressions form a singular exception to this general law of our constitution.

son, one of the ablest and most judicious of his disciples, has contented himself with this partial view of our moral constitution. He everywhere describes virtue and vice by the *effects* accompanying the perception of them, and makes no distinction between the *rectitude* of an action, as approved by our *reason*, and its *gratefulness* to the *taste* of the observer, or its aptitude to excite his moral emotions.

III. *Errors resulting from an exclusive Regard to the Moral Emotions.*] Another erroneous conclusion of a very dangerous tendency has been suggested by the doctrines of Lord Shaftesbury's school. Accustomed to define *virtue* and *vice* by their agreeable or disagreeable effects on the mind of the spectator, his followers have been led to extend the meaning of these words far beyond their proper signification; and, as virtue forms always an agreeable and vice a disagreeable object of contemplation, they have concluded that the converse of the proposition is equally true, and that every thing that is agreeable or disagreeable in human character or conduct might be properly expressed by the words *virtue* and *vice*. Accordingly, Hume, proceeding on the same general principles with Hutcheson, has been led to adopt this very conclusion as a fundamental truth in ethics, and even to introduce it into the definition which he gives of *virtue*, — "virtue," according to his theory, "consisting in the possession of qualities which are useful or agreeable to ourselves or to others." * That this definition is erroneous is sufficiently evident; for nothing can be plainer than that the words *virtue* and *vice* are applicable only to those parts of our character and conduct which depend on our own voluntary exertions. Sensibility, gayety, liveliness, good-humor, natural affection, are a source of pleasure to every beholder, and wherever they are to be found entitle the possessor to the appellation of *amiable;* but in so far as they result from original constitution, or from external

* Hume's *Principles of Morals*, Sect. IX. Part I.

circumstances over which he had no control, they certainly do not render him an object of moral approbation.

A further inaccuracy in the philosophy of Shaftesbury and Hutcheson has arisen from the same source, the application of the epithets *virtuous* and *vicious* to the *affections of the mind.* In order to think with precision on this subject, it is necessary for us always to remember that the object of moral approbation is not *affections*, but *actions.* The efforts, indeed, we make to cultivate our amiable affections are in a high degree meritorious, because the object of the effort is to add to the happiness of those with whom we associate, and because the effort depends upon ourselves; but the merit in such cases does not consist in the affection, but in the efforts by which it has been cultivated.

The result of the remarks now made on the systems of Shaftesbury and Hutcheson amounts to this, that they do not draw the line sufficiently between constitutional good qualities, and those which are voluntary and meritorious. In common discourse, indeed, we frequently apply the word *virtue* to both, but it is the *last* alone which in strict propriety deserves the name: and, in our own case, it is of great consequence for us to attend to the distinction. In the case of others, as it is impossible for us to draw the line, and as the tendency of our nature is rather to think too unfavorably of our neighbours, it may be the safest rule to consider every action as meritorious which can be supposed, by any reasonable or plausible interpretation, to have probably, or even possibly, proceeded from a virtuous motive. The author of *The Man of Feeling*, among the many beautiful features in the character of Harley, has not failed to remark this candid and amiable disposition. "Her benevolence" — he is speaking of his heroine, Miss Walton — "was unbounded. Indeed, the natural tenderness of her heart might have been argued by the frigidity of a casuist as detracting from her virtue in this respect, for her humanity was a *feeling*, not a *principle.* But minds like Harley's are not very apt to make this distinction, and generally give our virtue credit for all that benevolence which is instinctive in our nature."

In offering these criticisms on the writings of Shaftesbury and Hutcheson, I would not be understood as detracting from their merits. I am fully sensible of the infinite service they have rendered to this branch of science, by rescuing it from the hands of monks and casuists, and restoring it to its ancient honors. The enthusiasm with which both of them have painted the charms of moral excellence, while it delights the imagination and exalts the taste, is admirably calculated to lay hold of the generous affections of youth, and to kindle in their breasts the glow of virtue. The *Rhapsody* of Shaftesbury in particular, whatever the blemishes in point of taste (and they are many) which a *critical* reader may find in it, will remain for ever a monument to the powers of his genius, as well as to the purity and elevation of his mind. It is in general free from the reprehensible sentiments which have given so much just offence in some of his earlier publications, and well merits the encomium which Thomson has bestowed on it in his enumeration of the illustrious names which have adorned the literary history of England.

> " The generous Ashley thine ! the friend of man,
> Who scanned his nature with a brother's eye,
> His weakness prompt to shade, — to raise his aim,
> To touch the finer movements of the mind,
> And with the moral beauty charm the heart."

Still, however, I must again repeat, that it is chiefly on account of their *practical tendency* that I would recommend these two eminent writers ; and that, in order to guard ourselves against the cavils of skeptics, it is necessary to look out for a more solid foundation to morality than their philosophy supplies.

IV. *Whether all Beauty depends on its being Significant or Suggestive of Mental Qualities.*] I must not leave this subject of *moral beauty*, without taking some notice of a speculation with respect to it, which formed one of the favorite doctrines of the Socratic school, and which Shaftesbury and some other modern writers have attempted to revive. In the observations I have hitherto made, I have proceeded on the supposition, that the words *beauty* and *sublimity* are applied to actions and characters metaphorically, or from an analogy between the emotions which certain moral qualities and certain material objects produce in the mind. This, which is certainly the more obvious and the more common doctrine, seems to have been adopted by Cicero in the passage which I have already quoted. And as the opinion we form concerning it has no connection with any of the inquiries in which we have just been engaged, I was unwilling to distract the attention by mentioning any other. The philosophers now referred to have adopted a conclusion directly opposite to this, and have maintained that the words *beauty* and *sublimity* express, in their *literal* signification, *qualities of mind;* and that material objects affect us in this way only by means of the moral ideas they suggest. For my own part, I am not prepared to say any thing very decided either on the one side or on the other; but I must confess that my present views rather incline to the last of these doctrines. The following considerations, in particular, seem to me to have great weight.

It is only in the case of our own minds that we have any direct or immediate knowledge either of intellectual or moral qualities. In the case of other men we know them only by their external effects; that is, either by the natural signs of intelligence and sentiment which we read in the countenance, or by the information we derive from artificial language, or by the inferences we draw from their conduct and behaviour. To all these external *effects*, but more particularly to the features of the countenance, we apply the epithet of *beautiful.* But I believe it will be found that this epithet is applicable to them *only*, or at least *chiefly*, in so far as they are *significant.* Into this question, however, when proposed in general terms, I shall not enter; nor shall I take upon me positively to say that there is no beauty in certain combinations of complexion and features, abstracted from any particular meaning. It is sufficient for my purpose, if it be granted that the beauty of the human face consists *chiefly* in its expression; and about this it is impossible there can be any controversy. The human face, therefore, it would appear, is beautiful *chiefly* as it presents to our conceptions the qualities of *mind.*

The same observation is applicable very nearly to the material universe in general. The pleasurable emotion it excites in the mind of the peasant or mechanic is extremely trifling; but to those whose understandings have received such a degree of cultivation as to be enabled to read in it the characters of power, wisdom, and goodness, how sublime, how beautiful, does it appear! Even in the case of particular objects, it may be doubted whether the beauty of order and uniformity does not arise *partly* from some obscure suggestion of design and intelligence. I say *partly*, because, independent of any such considerations, order and uniformity please from the aids they afford to our powers of comprehension and memory. If these observations are well founded, it will follow that it is *mind* alone that possesses *original and underived beauty;* and that what we call the beauty of the material world is chiefly, if not wholly, reflected from intellectual and moral qualities; as the *light* we admire on the disk of the moon and planets is, when traced to its original source, *the light of the sun.* The exclamation, therefore, of the poet in the following lines would appear, notwithstanding the enthusiasm which animates it, to be strictly and philosophically just.

"Mind, mind alone, — bear witness earth and Heaven! —
The living fountains in itself contains
Of beauteous and sublime. Here hand in hand
Sit paramount the graces. Here enthroned,
Celestial Venus, with divinest airs,
Invites the soul to never-fading joy." *

If with these doctrines of the Socratic school we combine the fine and philosophical speculations of Mr.

* Akenside, *Pleasures of Imagination*, Book I.

Alison with respect to the effect of *association*, they will be found to add greatly to the evidence of the general conclusion. Perhaps it may appear to some that the former speculations are resolvable into the latter. This, however, is not the case; for the former relate to *natural signs;* the latter to *arbitrary connections established in the mind by habit.* In the mind of the philosopher, for example, who traces in the universe the signatures of the Divine perfections, the beauties he contemplates cannot, with propriety, be referred to association, any more than the charms of a beautiful face the first time it is seen. But in a mind conversant with poetry, to which every object in nature recalls a thousand agreeable images, a great part of the pleasing effect must be referred to this source. Even here, however, *association* operates in a manner which illustrates and confirms the general theory, inasmuch as it produces its effect by making objects more *significant* than they were before; or, in other words, by rendering them the occasions of our conceiving intellectual and moral beauties, of which they are not naturally expressive.*

Whatever opinion we adopt on this speculative question, there can be no dispute about the fact, that good actions and virtuous characters form the most delightful of all objects to the human mind; and that there are no charms in the external universe so powerful as those which recommend to us the cultivation of the qualities that constitute the perfection and the happiness of our nature.

"Look, then, abroad through nature, to the range
Of planets, suns, and adamantine spheres,
Wheeling unshaken through the void immense,
And speak, O man! does this capacious scene,
With half that kindling majesty dilate
Thy strong conception, as when Brutus rose,
Refulgent from the stroke of Cæsar's fate,
Amid the crowd of patriots; and, his arm
Aloft extending, like eternal Jove
When guilt brings down the thunder, called aloud

* See the profound and eloquent reflections with which Mr. Alison concludes the first chapter of his admirable *Essays on the Nature and Principles of Taste.*

On Tully's name, and shook his crimson steel,
And bade the father of his country, Hail!
For, lo! the tyrant prostrate in the dust,
And Rome again is free? Is aught so fair,
In all the dewy landscapes of the spring,
In the bright eye of Hesper or the morn,
In nature's fairest forms, is aught so fair
As virtuous friendship? as the candid blush
Of him who strives with fortune to be just?
The graceful tear that streams for others' woes?
Or the mild majesty of private life,
Where peace with ever-blooming olive crowns
The gate, where honor's liberal hands effuse
Unenvied treasures, and the snowy wings
Of innocence and love protect the scene?" *

V. *Use to be made of this Connection between Natural and Moral Beauty.*] It is no less evident that these two kinds of *taste* (that for *natural* and that for *moral* beauty), if not ultimately resolvable into the same principle, are at least very nearly allied, or very closely connected; insomuch that every author who has treated professedly of the one has been insensibly led to illustrate his subject by frequent references to the other. Hence in poetry the natural and pleasing union of those pictures which recall to us the charms of external nature, and that *moral painting* which affects and delights the heart. The intentions of Nature, in thus associating the ideas of the *beautiful* and the *good*, cannot be mistaken. Much, I am persuaded, might be done by a judicious system of education, in following out the plan which Nature has herself, in this instance, so manifestly traced; as we find, indeed, *was* done to a very great degree in those ancient schools, who considered it as the most important of all objects to establish such a union between philosophy and the fine arts as might add to the natural beauty of Virtue every attraction which the imagination could give her.

It would be improper to bring this subject to a conclusion without mentioning the attempt which Mr. Hume has made to show that what we call the *beauty of virtue* is the *beauty of utility*. For a particular ex-

---

* Akenside, Book I.

amination and refutation of this opinion, I refer the reader to Mr. Smith's *Theory of Moral Sentiments.* Although, however, Mr. Smith differs from Mr. Hume in thinking that virtue pleases *because* we consider it to be *useful*, he agrees with him that all those qualities which we consider as amiable or agreeable are really useful either to ourselves or to others. In this respect their conclusions coincide with the doctrines of the Socratic school, and afford additional evidence of the beneficent solicitude with which Nature allures us to the practice of our duty. "Do you imagine," says Socrates to Aristippus, "that what is good is not beautiful? Have you not observed that these appearances always coincide? Virtue, for instance, in the same respect as to which we call it good, is ever acknowledged to be beautiful also. In the character we always join the two denominations together.* The beauty of human bodies corresponds, in like manner, with that economy of parts which constitutes them good; and in every circumstance of life the same object is constantly accounted both beautiful and good, inasmuch as it answers the purposes for which it is designed." †

Section III.

OF THE PERCEPTION OF MERIT AND DEMERIT.

I. *Origin and Use of Ideas of Merit and Demerit.*] The various actions performed by other men not only excite in our minds a benevolent affection towards them, or a disposition to promote their happiness, but impress us with a sense of the *merit* of the agents. We perceive them to be the proper objects of love and esteem, and that it is morally right that they should receive their *reward.* We feel ourselves called on to make their worth known to the world, in order to procure them the favor and respect they deserve; and if

---

* By the words καλοκάγαθός and καλοκάγαθία.

† Xenoph. *Memorab.*, Lib. III. c. 8. The translation is Akenside's.

we allow it to remain secret, we are conscious of injustice in suppressing the natural language of the heart.

On the other hand, when we are witnesses of an act of selfishness, of cruelty, or of oppression, *whether we ourselves are sufferers or not*, we are not only inspired with aversion and hatred towards the delinquent, but find it difficult to restrain our indignation from breaking loose against him. By this natural impulse of the mind a check is imposed on the bad passions of individuals, and a provision is made even before the establishment of positive laws for the good order of society.

In our own case, how delightful are our feelings when we are conscious of doing well? By a species of instinct we know ourselves to be the object of the esteem and attachment of our fellow-creatures, and we feel, with the evidence of a perception, that Heaven smiles on our labors, and that we enjoy the approbation and favor of the Invisible Witness of our conduct. Hence it is that we not only have a sense of *merit*, but an anticipation of *reward*, and look forward to the future with increased confidence and hope. Nor is this confidence weakened, provided we retain our integrity unshaken, by the strokes of adverse fortune, but, on the contrary, we feel it increase in proportion to the efforts that we have occasion to make; and even in the moment of danger and of death it exhorts us to persevere, and assures us that all will be finally well with us. Hence the additional heroism of the brave when they draw the sword in a worthy cause. They feel themselves animated with tenfold strength, relying on the succour of an invisible arm, and seeming to trust, while employed in promoting the beneficent purposes of Providence, "that guardian angels combat on their side." Although, however, this sense of merit which accompanies the performance of good actions convinces the philosopher of the connection which the Deity has established between virtue and happiness, he does not proceed on the supposition, that on particular occasions miraculous interpositions are to be made in his favor. That virtue is the most direct road to happiness he sees to be the case even in this world; but he knows that the Deity governs by general laws; and when he feels himself disappointed in the attainment of his wishes, he acquiesces in his lot, and looks forward with hope to futurity. It is an error of the vulgar to expect that good or bad fortune is, *even in this world*, to be the immediate consequence of good or bad actions, — a prejudice of which we may trace the influence in all ages and nations, but more particularly in times of superstition and ignorance. From this error arose the practices of *judicial combat*, and of *trial by ordeal*, both of which formerly prevailed in this part of the world, and of which the latter (as appears from the *Asiatic Researches*) kept its ground in Hindostan as late as 1784,* and probably keeps its ground at this day. Absurd as these ideas are, they show strongly how natural to the human mind are the sentiments now under consideration; for this belief of the connection between *virtue* and *good fortune* has plainly taken its rise from the natural connection between the ideas of *virtue* and *merit*, a connection which, we may rest assured, is agreeable to the general laws by which the universe is governed, but which the slightest reflection may satisfy us cannot always correspond with the order of events in such a world as we inhabit at present.

I am not certain but we may trace something of the same kind in the sports of children, who have all a notion that good fortune in their games of chance depends upon perfect *fairness* towards their adversaries, and that those are certain to lose who attempt to take secretly any undue advantage.

* "In the code of the Gentoo laws mention is made of the trial by ordeal, which was one of the first laws instituted by Moses among the Jews. See *Numbers*, Chap. V. Fire or water is usually employed; but in India the mode varies, and is often determined by the choice of the parties. I remember a letter from a man of rank, who was accused of corresponding in time of war with the enemy, in which he says, 'Let my accuser be produced; let me see him face to face; let the most venomous snakes be put into a pot; let us put our hands into it together; let it be covered for a certain time; and he who remaineth unhurt shall be innocent.'

"This trial is always accompanied with the solemnities of a religious ceremony" — Crawford's *Sketches of the Hindoos*, p. 298.

> "Pueri ludentes, Rex eris, aiunt,
> Si rectè facies." *

Indeed, the moral perceptions (although frequently misapplied in consequence of the weakness of reason and the want of experience) may be as distinctly traced in the mind at that time of life as ever afterwards, when surely it cannot be supposed that they are the result, as some authors have held, of a conviction, founded on actual observation, of the *utility* of virtue. †

---

* Horat. *Epist.*, Lib. I. Ep. 1. 59.

> "Let children sing
> Amid their sports, 'Do right and be a king.'"

† Cousin expresses clearly and forcibly his views of the connection between *merit* and *demerit* and the *rewards* and *punishments* rightfully inflicted by society. *Histoire de la Philosophie du XVIIIe Siècle*, Vingtième Leçon. We copy a single paragraph from Professor Henry's excellent translation, *Elements of Psychology*, Chap. V.: — "Without any doubt, it is useful to society to inflict contempt upon the violator of moral order; without doubt, it is useful to society to punish effectually the individual who attacks the foundations of social order. This consideration of utility is real; it is weighty; but I say that it is not the first, that it is only accessory, and that the immediate basis of all penalty is the idea of the essential *merit* and *demerit* of actions, — the general idea of order, which imperiously demands that the merit and demerit of actions, which is a law of reason and of order, should be realized in a society that pretends to be rational and well ordered. On this ground, and on this ground alone, *of realizing this law of reason and of order*, the two powers of society, opinion and government, appear faithful to their primary law. Then comes up utility, — the immediate utility of repressing evil, and the indirect utility of preventing it by example, that is, by fear. But this consideration has need of a basis superior to itself, in order to render it legitimate. Suppose, in fact, that there is nothing good or evil *in itself*, and consequently neither essential merit nor demerit, and consequently, again, no absolute right of blaming or punishing; *by what right*, then, I ask, do you blame or disgrace a man, or make him ascend the scaffold, or put him in irons for life, *for the advantage of others*, when the action of the man is neither good nor bad in itself, and *merits* in itself neither blame nor punishment? Suppose that it is not absolutely right, just in itself, to blame this man or to punish him, and the legitimacy and propriety of infamy and of glory, and of every species of reward and punishment, are at an end. Still further, I maintain if punishment has no other ground than utility, then even its *utility is destroyed;* for in order that a punishment may be useful, it is requisite, — 1st, that he upon whom it is inflicted, endowed as he is with the principle of merit and demerit, should regard himself as justly punished, and should accept his punishment with a suitable disposition; 2d, that the spectators, equally endowed with the principle of merit and demerit, should regard the culprit as justly punished according to the measure of his crime, and should apply to themselves by anticipation the same justice in case of crime, and should

II. *How to guard against Self-deceit.*] I shall conclude this subject by again recalling to the attention of the reader a very remarkable fact formerly stated, that our moral emotions seem to be stronger with respect to the conduct of others than our own. A man who can be guilty, apparently without remorse, of the most flagrant injustice, will yet feel the warmest indignation against a similar act of injustice in another; and the best of men know it to be in many cases a useful rule, before they determine on any particular conduct, to consider how they would judge of the conduct of another in the same circumstances. "Do to others as ye would that they should do unto you." This is owing to the influence of self-partiality and self-deceit. Mr. Smith has been so much struck with the difference of our moral judgments in our own case and in that of another, that he has concluded conscience to be *only* an application to ourselves of those rules which we have collected from observing our feelings in cases in which we are not personally concerned. I shall afterwards state some objections to which this opinion is liable.

Were it not for the influence of self-deceit, it could hardly happen that a man should habitually act in direct opposition to his moral principles. We know, however, that this is but too frequently the case. The most perfect conviction of the obligation of virtue, and the strongest moral feelings, will be of little use in reg-

---

be kept in harmony with the social order by the view of its legitimate penalties. Hence arises the utility of examples of punishments, whether moral or physical. But take away its foundation in justice, and you destroy the utility of punishment; you excite indignation and abhorrence, instead of awakening penitence in the victim, or teaching a salutary lesson to the public. You array courage, sympathy, every thing noble and elevated in human nature, on the side of the victim. You excite all energetic spirits against society and its artificial laws. Thus the utility of punishment is itself grounded in its justice, instead of justice being grounded in its utility. Punishment is the sanction of the law, and not its foundation. Moral order has its foundation not in punishment, but punishment has its foundation in moral order. The idea of right and wrong is grounded only on itself, on reason which reveals it. It is the condition of the idea of merit and demerit which is the condition of the idea of reward and punishment; and this latter is to the two former, but especially to the idea of right and wrong, in the relation of the consequence to the principle." — Ed.

ulating our conduct, unless we are at pains to attend constantly to the state of our own character, and to scrutinize with the most suspicious care the motives of our actions. Hence the importance of the precept so much recommended by the moralists of all ages, — "Know thyself."

These observations may convince us still more of the truth of what I have elsewhere remarked with respect to *sentimental reading*, and of its total insufficiency for forming a virtuous character without many other precautions.* Where its effects are corrected by habits of business, and every instance of conduct is *brought home* by the reader to himself, it may be a source of solid improvement; for although strong moral feelings do by no means alone constitute virtue, yet they add to the satisfaction we derive from the discharge of our duty, and they increase the interest we take in the prosperity of virtue in the world.

CHAPTER IV.

OF MORAL OBLIGATION.

I. *Ground of Obligation.*] According to some systems, moral obligation is founded entirely on our belief that virtue is enjoined by *the command of God.* But how, it may be asked, does this belief impose an obligation? Only one of two answers can be given. Either that there is a *moral fitness* that we should conform our will to that of the Author and the Governor of the universe; or that a *rational self-love* should induce us, from motives of prudence, to study every means of rendering ourselves acceptable to the Almighty Arbiter of happiness and misery.

On the first supposition, we reason in a circle. We

* *Philosophy of the Human Mind*, Part I. Chap. VIII. Sect. V.

resolve our sense of moral obligation into our sense of religion, and the sense of religion into that of moral obligation.

The other system, which makes virtue a mere *matter of prudence*, although not so obviously unsatisfactory, leads to consequences which sufficiently invalidate every argument in its favor. Among others, it leads us to conclude, — 1. That the disbelief of a future state absolves from all moral obligation, excepting in so far as we find virtue to be conducive to our present interest; 2. That a being independently and completely happy cannot have any moral perceptions or any moral attributes.

But, further, the notions of reward and punishment *presuppose* the notions of right and wrong. They are sanctions of virtue, or additional motives to the practice of it, but they suppose the existence of some previous obligation.

In the last place, if moral obligation be constituted by a regard to our situation in another life, how shall the existence of a future state be proved, or even rendered probable, by the light of nature? or how shall we discover what conduct is acceptable to the Deity? The truth is, that the strongest presumption for such a state is deduced from our natural notions of right and wrong, of merit and demerit, and from a comparison between these and the general course of human affairs.

It is absurd, therefore, to ask *why* we are bound to practise virtue. The very notion of virtue *implies* the notion of obligation. Every being who is conscious of the distinction between right and wrong carries about with him a law which he is bound to observe, notwithstanding he may be in total ignorance of a future state. "What renders obnoxious to punishment," as Dr. Butler has well remarked, "is not the foreknowledge of it, but merely the violating a known obligation." Or (as Plato has expressed the same idea), τὸ μὲν ὀρθὸν νόμος ἐστὶ βασιλικός.*

---

* *Minos.* "Right itself is a royal law."

From what has been stated, it follows that the moral faculty, considered as an active power of the mind, differs essentially from all the others hitherto enumerated. The least violation of its authority fills us with remorse. On the contrary, the greater the sacrifices we make in obedience to its suggestions, the greater are our satisfaction and triumph.

II. *Butler on the Supremacy of Conscience.*] The supreme authority of conscience, although beautifully described by many of the ancient moralists, was not sufficiently attended to by modern writers as a fundamental principle in the science of ethics till the time of Dr. Butler. Too little stress is laid on it by Lord Shaftesbury; and the omission is the chief defect in his system of morals. Shaftesbury's opinion, however, although he does not state it explicitly in his *Inquiry*, seems to have been precisely the same at bottom with that of Butler.*

With respect to Dr. Butler, I shall take this opportunity of remarking, that in his sermons *On Human Nature*, in the Preface to his *Sermons*, and in a short *Dissertation on Virtue* annexed to his *Analogy*, he has, in my humble opinion, gone farther towards a just explanation of our moral constitution than any other modern philosopher. Without aiming at the praise of novelty or of refinement, he has displayed singular penetration and sagacity in availing himself of what was sound in former systems, and in supplying their defects. He is commonly considered as an uninteresting and obscure writer: but, for my own part, I never could perceive the slightest foundation for such a charge; though I am ready to grant that he pays little attention to the graces of composition, and that the construction of his sentences is frequently unskilful and unharmonious. As to the charge of obscurity, which he himself anticipated from the nature of his subject, he has replied to it in the most satisfactory manner in the Preface al-

* See his *Advice to an Author*, Part I. Sect. II.

ready referred to. I think it proper to add, that I would by no means propose these sermons (which were originally preached before the learned Society of Lincoln's Inn) as models for the pulpit. I consider them merely in the light of philosophical essays. In the same volume with them, however, are to be found some practical and characteristical discourses, which are peculiarly interesting and impressive, particularly the sermons *On Self-deceit*, and *On the Character of Balaam;* both of which evince an intimate acquaintance with the springs of human action, rarely found in union with speculative and philosophical powers of so high an order. The chief merit, at the same time, of Butler as an ethical writer, undoubtedly lies in what he has written on *the supreme authority of conscience* as the governing principle of human conduct, — a doctrine which he has placed in the strongest and happiest lights, and which, before his time, had been very little attended to by the moderns. It is sometimes alluded to by Lord Shaftesbury, but so very slightly as almost to justify the censure which Butler bestows on this part of his writings.

The scope of Butler's own reasonings may be easily conceived from the passage of Scripture which he has chosen as the groundwork of his argument: — "For when the Gentiles, which have not the law, do by nature the things contained in the law, these, having not the law, are *a law unto themselves.*" *

---

* "Butler's writings," says Dr. Whewell, "have been of the greatest value in preserving and restoring among us true views of morality; but there are some expressions used by him, which, if not duly limited, may lead his followers into mistakes. Thus, he sometimes speaks, not only of the *authority*, but of the *supremacy*, of conscience. Now if by calling conscience *supreme*, it were meant that the principle so described is something possessing sovereign and original authority over men's other springs of action, this principle would necessarily be the proper ground of *rules of action;* and all such rules must be derived ultimately from this principle We should then, in order to frame rules of morality, or to decide any moral question, have to inquire how we can learn the decisions of conscience on such subjects. Conscience is our guide; where are we to learn what she says? Conscience, the law on the heart, is supreme over all laws; how are we to read this law? Conscience is the test of right and wrong; but *whose* conscience? for conscience belongs to a person. Butler's opponent

III. *Other Authorities for the same Doctrine.*] One of the clearest and most concise statements of this doctrine that I have met with is in a sermon *On the Nature and Obligation of Virtue*, by Dr. Adams of Oxford; the justness of whose ideas on this subject make

---

have constantly said, — 'You tell us that conscience is the proper guide of action; but whose conscience? ours, or yours? Our consciences point different ways; — can both be right? And if not both, how are we to know which?'

"These are familiar and popular arguments; but they appear to me to be decisive against all who ascribe to conscience a *supremacy*, in the proper sense of the term; — namely, a sovereign and ultimate authority over all other principles of action, so that, when a decision is pronounced by conscience, there is no further reason to be rendered for it, nor any higher decision to be sought. . . . . . But I think it is very plain that this was not Butler's view, — that he did not thus hold an original and independent faculty of conscience, whose decisions would form a permanent body of moral rules. I think that, with him, conscience was not a body of truths, but a process by which truth is to be obtained; — a faculty, if you choose, but a faculty which must be trained and exercised in order to be used, — which may be improved, instructed, and enlightened, — which may be blinded and perverted in individual men. Conscience is a faculty of man, as reason is a faculty; — a power by exercising which he may come to discern truths, not a repository of truths already collected in a visible shape. Conscience, indeed, *is* the *reason*, employed about questions of right and wrong, and accompanied with the *sentiments* of approbation and condemnation which, by the nature of man, cling inextricably to his apprehension of right and wrong. This is the view that we have been led to take of conscience. This is, as I conceive, Butler's view also. That by conscience he does not mean any special independent faculty, distinct from the reason with its accompanying moral sentiments, is, I think, evident from the whole current of his language. He does not confine himself to the single term *conscience*, in his account of the superior principle of our nature: on the contrary, he perpetually uses, for this term or with it, other terms, which give the same view of it which we have taken. He calls it 'reflection on conscience, an approbation of some principles or actions, and a disapprobation of others'; — and again, 'reflex approbation or disapprobation.' All the phrases which he employs manifestly point at a principle or faculty, not by which we necessarily *have*, but by which we may *get*, a true knowledge of the course which we ought to take under any given circumstances. We are, to use another of his phrases, 'to act suitably to our whole nature, and especially to the higher and better part of our nature'; the constitution of human nature being such that there is in it a higher and better part. This higher and better part tells us that injustice is worse than pain; but it does not tell us what acts are unjust, except through the process of reflection. The notion of injustice is necessarily the object of disapprobation to the conscience; but to unfold this notion of injustice into detail, so as to see what special acts are included in it, — this is the office of the reflection, that is, of the reason." *Lectures on Systematic Morality*, Lecture VI.

On the whole subject of conscience, see President Wayland's *Elements of Moral Science*, Book I. Chap. II. — Ed.

it the more surprising that his pupil and friend, Dr. Samuel Johnson, should have erred so very widely from the truth. "*Right*," says he, "implies *duty* in its idea. To perceive an action to be right is to see a reason for doing it in the action itself, abstracted from all other considerations whatever; and this perception, this acknowledged rectitude in the action, is the very essence of obligation, that which commands the approbation and choice, and binds the conscience, of every rational human being." — "Nothing can bring us under an obligation to do what appears to our moral judgment *wrong*. It may be supposed our interest to do this, but it cannot be supposed our duty. For, I ask, if some power, which we are unable to resist, should assume the command over us, and give us laws which are unrighteous and unjust, should we be under an obligation to obey him? Should we not rather be obliged to shake off the yoke, and to resist such usurpation, if it were in our power? However, then, we might be swayed by hope or fear, it is plain that we are under an obligation to *right*, which is antecedent, and in order and nature superior, to all other. Power may compel, interest may bribe, pleasure may persuade, but *reason* only can *oblige*. This is the only authority which rational beings can own, and to which they owe obedience."

Dr. Clarke has expressed himself nearly to the same purpose. "The judgment and conscience of a man's own mind concerning the reasonableness and fitness of the thing is the truest and formallest obligation; for whoever acts contrary to this sense and conscience of his own mind is necessarily *self-condemned;* and the greatest and strongest of all obligations is that which a man cannot break through without condemning himself. So far, therefore, as men are conscious of what is *right* and *wrong*, so far they are under an obligation to act accordingly." *

* *Discourse concerning the Unalterable Obligations of Natural Religion*, Proposition I. 3.

I would not have quoted so many passages in illustration of a point which appears to myself so very obvious, if I had not been anxious to counteract the authority of some eminent writers who have lately espoused a very different system, by showing how widely they have departed from the sound and philosophical views of their predecessors. I confess, too, I should have distrusted my own judgment, if, on a question so interesting to human happiness, and so open to examination, I had been led, by any theoretical refinements, to a conclusion which was not sanctioned by the concurrent sentiments of other impartial inquirers. The fact, however, is, that, as this view of human nature is the most simple, so it is the most ancient, which occurs in the history of moral science. It was the doctrine of the Pythagorean school, as appears from a fragment of Theages, a Pythagorean writer, published in Gale's *Opuscula Mythologica*. It is also explained by Plato in some of his Dialogues, in which he compared the soul to a commonwealth, and *reason* to the council of state, which governs and directs the whole.*

---

* "In Plato's Dialogues the question is repeatedly discussed, whether the rule of action for man be the pursuit of pleasure and gain, or the internal harmony of his nature. You will, many of you, recollect the lively and dramatic dialogue at the beginning of *The Republic*, in which the former of these opinions is asserted by one of the interlocutors, and the acute and decisive Socratic refutation which it encounters. You will recollect, too, the doctrine announced at the close of the fourth book, as the result of the previous discussion. 'Virtue, then, as we are thus led to see, is a health and beauty and well-being of the soul. Vice is a disease, and foulness, and infirmity.' And when the original question is, at this point of the argument, again asked, — whether it is better to be just or to be unjust, even if the injustice is to remain *unknown by all and to meet no punishment*, — the person to whom the argument is addressed, and who is, by this time, brought to a conviction of the truth of the doctrine which it is the object of the dialogue to inculcate, says, 'Nay, Socrates, this question is now ridiculously superfluous.' And in the ninth book, the discussion being really concluded, the speakers, playfully mimicking the practice of pronouncing, by the voice of a public crier, a solemn judgment upon the merit of a theatrical spectacle, agree to proclaim, — 'The son of Aristo gives his judgment that the most virtuous and just is also the most happy, and the wicked and unjust the most unhappy'; and further, 'that this is so, *even if their deeds are hidden from all, men and gods.*'" — Whewell's *Systematic Morality*, Lecture VI.

In the following passage from Cicero the same doctrine is enforced in a manner peculiarly sublime and expressive, or, as Lactantius says, *pœne divina voce.* " Est quidem vera *Lex*, recta ratio, naturæ congruens, diffusa in omnes, constans, sempiterna, quæ vocet ad officium jubendo, vetando a fraude deterreat, quæ tamen neque probos frustra jubet aut vetat, nec improbos jubendo aut vetando movet. Huic legi nec obrogari fas est, neque derogari ex hac aliquid licet, neque tota abrogari potest. Nec vero aut per senatum aut per populum solvi hac lege possumus: neque est quærendus explanator aut interpres ejus alius: nec erit alia Lex Romæ, alia Athenis, alia nunc, alia posthac; sed et omnes gentes, et omni tempore una lex et sempiterna et immutabilis continebit; unusque erit communis quasi magister et imperator omnium Deus. Ille legis hujus inventor, disceptator, lator. Cui qui non parebit, ipse se fugiet, ac, naturam hominis aspernatus, hoc ipso luet maximas pœnas, etiamsi cætera supplicia, quæ putantur, effugerit." *

It is very justly observed by Mr. Smith (and I consider the remark as of the highest importance), that, " if the distinction pointed out in the foregoing quotations between the moral faculty and our other active powers be acknowledged, *it is of the less consequence what particular theory we adopt concerning the origin of our moral ideas.*" And accordingly, though he resolves moral approbation ultimately into a *feeling of the mind*, he nevertheless represents the supremacy of conscience

---

* *De Repub.*, Lib. III. 22. " There is a true law, a right reason, congruous to nature, pervading all minds, constant, eternal; which calls to duty by its commands, and repels from wrong-doing by its prohibitions: and to the good does not command or forbid in vain, while the wicked are unmoved by its exhortations or its warnings. This law cannot be annulled, superseded, or overruled. No senate, no people, can loose us from it; no jurist, no interpreter, can explain it away. It is not one law at Rome, another at Athens; one at present, another at some future time; but one law, perpetual and immutable, it extends to all nations and all times, the universal sovereign. Of this law the author and giver is God. Whoever disobeys it flies from himself, and by the wrong thus done to his own nature, even though he should escape every other form of punishment, incurs the heaviest penalty."

as a principle which is equally essential to all the different systems that have been proposed on the subject. "Upon whatever we suppose our moral faculties to be founded," (I quote his own words,) "whether upon a certain modification of reason, upon an original instinct called a moral sense, or upon some other principle of our nature, it cannot be doubted that they are given us for the direction of our conduct in this life. They carry along with them the most evident badges of their authority, which denote that they were set up within us to be the supreme arbiters of all our actions; to superintend all our senses, passions, and appetites; and to judge how far each of them was to be either indulged or restrained. Our moral faculties are by no means, as some have pretended, upon a level in this respect with the other faculties and appetites of our nature, endowed with no more right to restrain these last than these last are to restrain them. No other faculty or principle of action judges of any other. Love does not judge of resentment, nor resentment of love. Those two passions may be opposite to one another, but cannot, with any propriety, be said to approve or disapprove of one another. But it is the peculiar office of those faculties now under consideration to judge, to bestow censure or applause upon all the other principles of our nature."

"Since these, therefore," continues Mr. Smith, "were plainly intended to be the *governing principles of human nature*, the rules which they prescribe are to be regarded as the commands and laws of the Deity promulgated by those vicegerents which he has thus set up within us. By acting according to their dictates we may be said, in some sense, to coöperate with the Deity, and to advance, as far as in our power, the plan of Providence. By acting otherwise, on the contrary, we seem to obstruct in some measure the scheme which the Author of Nature has established for the happiness and perfection of the world, and to declare ourselves in some measure the enemies of God. Hence we are naturally encouraged to hope for his extraordinary favor and reward in the one case, and to dread his vengeance and punishment in the other." *

I have only to add further on this subject, at present, that the supreme authority of conscience is felt and tacitly acknowledged by the worst no less than by the best of men; for even they who have thrown off all hypocrisy with the world are at pains to conceal their real character from their own eyes. No man ever, in a soliloquy or private meditation, avowed to himself that he was a villain; nor do I believe that such a character as Joseph, in *The School for Scandal*, (who is introduced as reflecting coolly on his own knavery and baseness, without any uneasiness but what arises from the dread of detection,) ever existed in the world. Such men probably impose on themselves fully as much as they do upon others. Hence the various artifices of self-deceit which Butler has so well described in his discourses on that subject.

It is said by St. Augustine, that at the delivery of that famous line of Terence, —

> "Homo sum, humani nihil a me alienum puto," —

"I am a man, and feel an interest in all mankind," — the whole Roman theatre resounded with applause.† We may venture to say that a similar sentiment, well pronounced by an actor, would at this day, in the most corrupt capital in Europe, be followed by a similar burst of sympathetic emotion.

> "Voyez à nos spectacles
> Quand on peint quelque trait de candeur, de bonté,
> Où brille en tout son jour la tendre humanité,
> Tous les cœurs sont remplis d'une volupté pure,
> Et c'est là qu'on entend *le cri de la nature*." ‡

"On such occasions," as a late writer remarks, "though we may think meanly of the genius of the poet, it is impossible not to think, and to be happy in thinking, highly of the people; — the people whose

* *Theory of Moral Sentiments*, Part III. Chap. V.

† See a note on this line in Coleman's translation of Terence's *Self-Tormentor*.

‡ Gresset, *Le Méchant*.

opinions may often be folly, whose *conduct* may sometimes be madness, but whose *sentiments* are almost always honorable and just; — the people whom an author may delight with bombast, may amuse with tinsel, may divert with indecency, but whom he cannot mislead in principle, nor harden into inhumanity. It is only the mob in the side boxes, who, in the coldness of self-interest, or the languor of outworn dissipation, can hear unmoved the sentiments of compassion, of generosity, or of virtue." *

CHAPTER V.

OF CERTAIN PRINCIPLES WHICH COÖPERATE WITH OUR MORAL POWERS IN THEIR INFLUENCE ON THE CONDUCT.

In order to secure still more completely the good order of society, and to facilitate the acquisition of virtuous habits, nature has superadded to our moral constitution a variety of auxiliary principles, which sometimes give rise to a conduct agreeable to the rules of morality and highly useful to mankind, where the merit of the individual, considered as a moral agent, is inconsiderable. Hence some of them have been confounded with our moral powers, or even supposed to be of themselves sufficient to account for the phenomena of moral perception, by authors whose views of human nature have not been sufficiently comprehensive. The most important principles of this description are, — 1st. A Regard to Character. 2d. Sympathy. 3d. The Sense of the Ridiculous. And 4th. Taste. The principle of Self-Love (which was treated of in a former section) coöperates very powerfully to the same purposes.

---

* Mackenzie's *Account of the German Theatre.* Transactions of the Royal Society of Edinburgh, Vol. II. Part II. p. 174.

Section I.

OF DECENCY, OR A REGARD TO CHARACTER.

Upon this subject I had formerly occasion to offer various remarks, in treating of the *desire of esteem*. But the view of it which I then took was extremely general, as I did not think it necessary for me to attend to the distinction between intellectual and moral qualities. There can be no doubt that a regard to the good opinion of our fellow-creatures has great influence in promoting our exertions to cultivate both the one and the other; but what we are more particularly concerned to remark at present is the effect which this principle has in strengthening our virtuous habits, and in restraining those passions which a sense of duty alone would not be sufficient to regulate.

I have before observed, that the desire of esteem operates in children before they have a capacity of distinguishing right from wrong; and that the former principle of action continues for a long time to be much more powerful than the latter. Hence it furnishes a most useful and effectual engine in the business of education, more particularly by training us early to exertions of self-command and self-denial. It teaches us, for example, to restrain our appetites within those bounds which *delicacy* prescribes, and thus forms us to habits of moderation and temperance. And although our conduct cannot be denominated virtuous so long as a regard to the opinion of others is our *sole* motive, yet the habits we thus acquire in infancy and childhood render it more easy for us to subject our passions to reason and conscience as we advance to maturity. The subject well deserves a more ample illustration; but at present it is sufficient to recall these remarks to the recollection of the reader.

Section II.

OF SYMPATHY.

I. *Nature and Functions of Sympathy.*] That there is an exquisite pleasure annexed by the constitution of our nature to the sympathy or fellow-feeling of other men with our joys and sorrows, and even with our opinions, tastes, and humors, is a fact obvious to vulgar observation. It is no less evident that we feel a disposition to accommodate the state of our own minds to that of our companions, wherever we feel a benevolent affection towards them, and that this accommodating temper is in proportion to the strength of our affection. In such cases sympathy would appear to be grafted on benevolence; and perhaps it might be found, on an accurate examination, that the greater part of the pleasure which sympathy yields is resolvable into that which arises from the exercise of kindness, and from the consciousness of being beloved.

II. *Adam Smith's Theory.*] The phenomena generally referred to sympathy have appeared to Mr. Smith so important, and so curiously connected, that he has been led to attempt an explanation from this single principle of all the phenomena of moral perception. In this attempt, however, (not to mention the vague use which he occasionally makes of the term,) he has plainly been misled, like many eminent philosophers before him, by an excessive love of simplicity; and has mistaken a very subordinate principle in our moral constitution (or rather a principle *superadded* to our moral constitution as an auxiliary to the sense of duty) for that faculty which distinguishes right from wrong, and which (by what name soever we may choose to call it) recurs to us constantly in all our ethical disquisitions, as an ultimate fact in the nature of man.

I shall take this opportunity of offering a few remarks on this most ingenious and beautiful theory, in the course of which I shall have occasion to state all that I think necessary to observe concerning the place which *sympathy* seems to me really to occupy in our moral constitution. In stating these remarks, I would be understood to express myself with all the respect and veneration due to the talents and virtues of a writer, whose friendship I regard as one of the most fortunate incidents of my life, but, at the same time, with that entire freedom which the importance of the subject demands, and which I know that his candid and liberal mind would have approved.

In addition to the incidental strictures which I have already hazarded on Mr. Smith's theory, I have yet to state two objections of a more general nature, to which it appears to me to be obviously liable. But before I proceed to these objections, it is necessary for me to premise (which I shall do in Mr. Smith's words) a remark which I have not hitherto had occasion to mention, and which may be justly regarded as one of the most characteristical principles of his system.

"Were it possible," says he, "that a human creature could grow up to manhood in some solitary place, without any communication with his own species, he could no more think of his own character, of the propriety or demerit of his own sentiments and conduct, of the beauty or deformity of his own mind, than of the beauty or deformity of his own face. All these are objects which he cannot easily see, which naturally he does not look at, and with regard to which he is provided with no mirror which can present them to his view. Bring him into society, and he is immediately provided with the mirror which he wanted before. It is placed in the countenance and behaviour of those he lives with, which always mark when they enter into and when they disapprove of his sentiments, and it is here that he first views the propriety and impropriety of his own passions, the beauty and deformity of his own mind." *

* *Theory of Moral Sentiments*, Part III. Chap. I.

III. *Two Objections to the Theory in general.*] To this account of the origin of our moral sentiments it may be objected, — 1st. That, granting the proposition to be true, "that a human creature, who should grow up to manhood without any communication with his own species, could no more think of the propriety or demerit of his own sentiments than of the beauty or deformity of his own face," it would by no means authorize the conclusion which is here deduced from it. The necessity of social intercourse, as an indispensable condition implied in the generation and growth of our moral sentiments, does not arise merely from its effect in holding up a mirror for the examination of our own character; but from the impossibility of finding, in a solitary state, any field for the exercise of our most important moral duties. In such a state the moral faculty would inevitably remain dormant and useless, for the same reason that the organ of sight would remain useless and unknown to a person who should pass his whole life in the darkness of a dungeon.

2d. It may be objected to Mr. Smith's theory, that it confounds the *means* or *expedients* by which nature enables us to correct our moral judgments, with the principles in our constitution to which our moral judgments owe their *origin*. These means or expedients he has indeed described with singular penetration and sagacity, and by doing so has thrown new and most important lights on *practical* morality; but, after all his reasonings on the subject, the metaphysical problem concerning the primary sources of our moral ideas and emotions will be found involved in the same obscurity as before. The intention of such expedients, it is perfectly obvious, is merely to obtain a just and fair view of circumstances; and after this view has been obtained, the question still remains, what constitutes the obligation upon me to act in a particular manner? In answer to this question it is said, that, from recollecting my own judgments in similar cases in which I have been concerned, I infer in what light my conduct will appear to society; that there is an exquisite satisfaction annexed to mutual sympathy; and that, in order to obtain this satisfaction, I accommodate my conduct, not to my own feelings, but to those of my fellow-creatures. Now I acknowledge that this may account for a man's assuming the *appearance* of virtue, and I believe that something of this sort is the real foundation of the rules of good breeding in polished society;* but in the important concerns of life I apprehend there is something more; for when I have once satisfied myself with respect to the conduct which an impartial judge would approve of, I feel that this conduct is *right* for me, and that I am under a moral obligation to put it in practice. If I had had recourse to no expedient for correcting my first judgment, I should nevertheless have formed some judgment or other of a particular conduct, as right, wrong, or indifferent, and the only difference would have been, that I should probably have decided improperly, from an erroneous or a partial view of the case.

From these observations I conclude that the words *right* and *wrong*, *ought* and *ought not*,† express simple ideas or notions, of which no explanation can be given. They are to be found in all languages, and it is impossible to carry on any ethical speculation without them. Of this Mr. Smith himself furnishes a remarkable proof in the statement of his theory, not only by the occasional use which he makes of these and other synonymous expressions, but by his explicit and repeated acknowledgments, that the propriety of actions cannot

---

* This remark I borrow from Dr. Beattie, who, in his *Essay on Truth*, observes, that the foundation of good breeding is "that kind of sensibility or sympathy by which we suppose ourselves in the situation of others, adopt their sentiments, and in a manner perceive their very thoughts." Part I. Chap. I. The observation well deserves to be prosecuted.

† Dr. Hutcheson, in his *Illustrations upon the Moral Sense*, calls *ought* a *confused word:* — "As to that confused word *ought*," &c. Sect. I. *ad fin.* But for this he seems to have had no better reason than the impossibility of defining it logically. And may not the same remark be applied to the words *time*, *space*, *motion?* Was there ever a language in which these words, together with those of *ought* and *ought not*, were not to be found? *Ought* corresponds with the δεῖ of the Greeks, and the *oportet* and *decet* of the Latins.

be always determined by the *actual* judgments of society, and that, in such cases, we must act according to the judgments which other men *ought* to have formed of our conduct. Is not this to admit that we have a standard of right and wrong in our own minds, of superior authority to any instinctive propensity we may feel to obtain the sympathy of our fellow-creatures?

It was in order to reconcile this acknowledgment with the general language of his system that Mr. Smith was forced to have recourse to the supposition of "*an abstract man* within the breast, the representative of mankind and substitute of the Deity, whom nature has constituted the supreme judge of all our actions." * Of this very ingenious fiction he has availed himself in various passages of the *first* editions of his book; but he has laid much greater stress upon it in the *last* edition, the sixth, published a short time before his death An idea somewhat similar occurs in Lord Shaftesbury's *Advice to an Author*, where he observes, with that quaintness of phraseology which so often deforms his otherwise beautiful style, that "when the wise ancients spoke of a demon, genius, or angel, to whom we are committed from the moment of our birth, they meant no more than enigmatically to declare, 'that we have each of us a patient in ourselves; that we are properly our own subjects of practice; and that we then become due practitioners, when, by virtue of an intimate recess, we can discover a certain duplicity of soul, and divide ourselves into two parties.'" He afterwards tells us, that, "according as this recess was deep and intimate, and the dual number practically formed in us, we were supposed by the ancients to advance in morals and true wisdom." †

By means of this fiction Mr. Smith has rendered his theory (contrary to what might have been expected from its first aspect) perfectly coincident in its practical tendency with that cardinal principle of the Stoical philosophy which exhorts us to search for the rules of

* Page 208, 5th edition.

† Part I. Sect. II.

life, not *without* ourselves, but *within*: — "Nec te quæsiveris extra." Indeed, Butler himself has not asserted the authority and supremacy of conscience in stronger terms than Mr. Smith, who represents this as a manifest and unquestionable principle, whatever particular theory we may adopt concerning the origin of our moral ideas. It is only to be regretted, that, instead of the metaphorical expression of "*the man within the breast*, to whose opinions and feelings we find it of more consequence to conform our conduct than to those of the whole world," he had not made use of the simpler and more familiar words *reason* and *conscience*. This mode of speaking was indeed suggested to him, or rather obtruded on him, by the theory of sympathy, and nothing can exceed the skill and taste with which he has availed himself of its assistance in perfecting his system; but it has the effect, with many readers, of keeping out of view the real state of the question, and (like Plato's commonwealth of the soul and council of state) to encourage among inferior writers a figurative or allegorical style in treating of subjects which, more than any other, require all the simplicity, precision, and logical consistency of which language is susceptible.

IV. *Particular Instances in which Smith lays too much Stress on Sympathy.*] A few slight observations on detached passages of Mr. Smith's theory will be useful in illustrating more fully certain phenomena referred by him, rather too exclusively, to the principle of sympathy or fellow-feeling.

In proof of the pleasure annexed to mutual sympathy, Mr. Smith remarks, that "a man is mortified when, after having endeavoured to divert the company, he looks around and sees that nobody laughs at his jest but himself." * It may be doubted, however, if in this case a disappointed sympathy be the chief cause of his uneasiness. Various other circumstances undoubtedly conspire, particularly the censure which the silence

* Part I. Sect. I. Chap. II.

of the company conveys of his taste and judgment, together with the proof it exhibits of their sullenness and want of good-humor.

The pleasure, too, which, according to Mr. Smith, we receive from reading to a stranger a poem whose effect on ourselves has been destroyed by repetition, may be explained, without any refinement about sympathy, by the satisfaction we always feel in communicating pleasure to another, combined with the flattering though indirect testimony paid to the justness of our taste by its coincidence with that of an individual whose judgment we respect. The *sympathy* of an acknowledged fool would certainly be in the same circumstances a source of mortification.

In mentioning these considerations, I do not mean to dispute that there is an exquisite pleasure arising from mutual sympathy; but only to suggest, that Mr. Smith has ascribed to this principle solely various phenomena, in accounting for which other causes appear to be no less deserving of attention.

The versatile and accommodating manners which Mr. Smith has so beautifully described in various passages of his *Theory* may be assumed from different motives, — in some men from a desire to promote the happiness of those around them; and where this is the case, it is unquestionably one of the most amiable and meritorious forms in which benevolence can appear, and contributes more by its daily and constant operation to increase the comfort of human life than those splendid exertions of virtue which we are so seldom called upon to make. In other men, in whom the benevolent affections are not so strong, it may proceed chiefly from a view to their own tranquillity and amusement, and may render them agreeable and harmless companions, without giving them any claim to the appellation of *virtuous*. In many it arises from views of self-interest and ambition; and in such men, whatever pleasure we may have derived from their society, these qualities never fail to inspire universal distrust and dislike, as soon as they are known to be the real motives of that pliancy and versatility with which we were at first captivated. It would appear, therefore, that the accommodating temper, where it is approved as morally *right*, is not approved on its own account, but as an expression of a *benevolent* disposition.

From the combined efforts of the actor and of the spectator towards a mutual sympathy, Mr. Smith endeavours to trace the origin of "two different sets of *virtues*." Upon the effort of the spectator to enter into the situation of the person principally concerned, and to raise his sympathetic emotions to a level with the emotions of the actor, are founded "the gentle, the amiable virtues, the virtues of candid condescension and indulgent humanity." Upon the effort of the person principally concerned to lower his own emotions, so as to correspond as nearly as possible with those of the spectator, are founded "the great, the awful, and respectable virtues, the virtues of self-denial, of self-government, of that command of the passions which subjects all movements of our nature to what our own dignity and honor, and the propriety of our own conduct, require." * If the word *qualities* were substituted for *virtues*, I agree in general with this doctrine. The mode of expression, however, certainly requires correction. "Candid condescension" and "indulgent humanity" are always amiable; and when they really proceed from a disposition habitually benevolent, are with great propriety called *virtues*. "Self-denial and self-government" are always *respectable*, and sometimes *awful* qualities, because they indicate a force of mind which few men possess; but it depends on the *motives* from which they are exercised, whether they indicate a virtuous or a vicious character.

As a further illustration of the foregoing doctrine, Mr. Smith considers particularly the degrees of the different passions which are consistent with propriety, and endeavours to show, that in every case it is decent or indecent to express a passion strongly, accord-

* Ibid., Chap V.

ing as mankind are disposed or not disposed to sympathize with it. It is unbecoming, for example, to express strongly any of those passions which arise from a certain condition of the body; because other men who are not in the same condition cannot be expected to sympathize with them. It is unbecoming to cry out with bodily pain, because the sympathy felt by the spectator bears no proportion to the acuteness of what is felt by the sufferer. The case is somewhat similar with those passions which take their origin from a particular turn or habit of the imagination.*

All violent expressions of such passions are undoubtedly offensive, and good breeding dictates that they should be restrained; but *not* because the spectator finds it difficult to enter into the situation of the person principally concerned; perhaps the opposite reason would be nearer the truth. To eat voraciously in the presence of a company who have already dined would be obviously indecent; but I apprehend, not so much so as to eat even moderately in presence of one whom we knew to be hungry, and who was not permitted to share in the repast. With respect to *bodily pain*, it appears to me that there is no calamity whatever which so completely interests the spectator, or with which his sympathy is so acute and lively. It is on this account that a steady composure under it, while it indicates the manly quality of self-command, has something in it peculiarly amiable, when we suppose that it proceeds in any degree from a tenderness for the feelings of others. In many surgical operations it is probable that the imagination of the pain exceeds the reality; and there cannot be a doubt, that, where the patient is the object of our love, the sufferings which *he* feels require less fortitude than ours.

Again, in the case of the unsocial passions of "hatred and resentment," the sympathy of the spectator "is divided" between the person who feels the passion and the person who is the object of it. "We are con-

* Ibid., Sect. II. Chap. I.

cerned for both, and our fear for what the one may suffer damps our resentment for what the other has suffered."* Hence the imperfect degree in which we sympathize with such passions, and the propriety, when under their influence, of moderating their expression to a much greater degree than in the case of any other emotions.

Abstraction made of all considerations of this kind, satisfactory reasons may be given for our listening with caution to the dictates of *resentment* when we ourselves are the sufferers. Experience must soon satisfy us how apt this passion is to blind the judgment, and to exaggerate in our estimation the injury we have received; and how certainly we lay in matter for future remorse for our cooler hours, if we obey its first suggestions. A wise man, therefore, learns to delay forming his resolutions till his passion has in some degree subsided; — *not* in order to obtain the sympathy of other men, but in order to secure the approbation of his own conscience. If he conceives to himself what conduct the impartial spectator will approve of, it is merely as an expedient to divest himself of the partialities of self-love; and when he acts agreeably to what he supposes to be, on this occasion, the unbiased judgment of spectators, his satisfaction arises, *not* from the possession of their sympathy, but from a consciousness that he has done his best to ascertain what was *right*, and has regulated his conduct accordingly.

"Where there is no envy in the case, our propensity to sympathize with joy is much stronger than our propensity to sympathize with sorrow."

"It is on account of this dull sensibility to the afflictions of others, that magnanimity amidst great distress always appears so divinely graceful."†

If this were true, would it not follow that the admiration of heroic magnanimity would be in proportion to the insensibility of the spectator?

"Finally, it is because mankind are more disposed

* Ibid., Chap. III.

† Ibid., Sect. III. Chap. I.

to court the favor, to comply with the humors, and to judge with indulgence the actions, of the prosperous than of the unfortunate, that we make parade of our riches, and conceal our poverty." — "It is the misfortunes of kings alone," Mr. Smith adds, "which afford the proper subjects for tragedy." *

Of this last proposition I confess I have some doubts, at least to the extent in which it is here stated; and I am inclined to think that, in those cases where it holds, it may be easily accounted for on more obvious principles. By far the greater number of tragedies are founded on historical facts; and history records only the transactions of men in elevated stations. But even in *these* tragedies the most interesting personages are frequently domestics or captives. The old shepherd in *Douglas* is surely a more interesting character than Lord Randolph. And for my own part I am not ashamed to confess that I have shed more tears at some *tragedies bourgeoises* and *comedies larmoyantes* of very inferior merit, than were ever extorted from me by the exquisite poetry of Corneille, Racine, or Voltaire.

The fortunes of the great, indeed, interest us more than those of men in inferior stations. But for this there are various causes, independent of that assigned by Mr. Smith. 1. Their destiny involves the fortunes of many, and frequently affects the public interest. 2. Their situation points them out to public attention, and renders them subjects of general and daily conversation; and, accordingly, we may remark a curiosity perfectly analogous to that which the history of the great excites with respect to the biography of all men who have been long and constantly in the view of the world. The trifling anecdotes in the life of Quin or Garrick find as many readers as the important events connected with the history of Frederic the Great.

V. *Historical Notices of the Doctrine.*] In my *Ac-*

* Ibid., Chap. II.

count of the Life and Writings of Mr Smith, I observed, that, according to the learned translator of Aristotle's *Ethics and Politics*, "the general idea which runs through Mr. Smith's *Theory of Moral Sentiments* was obviously borrowed from the following passage of Polybius. 'From the union of the two sexes, to which all are naturally inclined, children are born. When any of these, therefore, being arrived at perfect age, instead of yielding suitable returns of gratitude and assistance to those by whom they have been bred, on the contrary attempt to injure them by words or actions, it is manifest that those who behold the wrong, after having also seen the sufferings and the anxious cares that were sustained by the parents in the nourishment and education of their children, must be greatly offended and displeased at such proceeding. For man, who, among all the various kinds of animals, is alone endowed with the faculty of reason, cannot, like the rest, pass over such actions, but will make reflection on what he sees; and, comparing likewise the future with the present, will not fail to express his indignation at this injurious treatment; to which, as he foresees, he may also at some time be exposed. Thus again, when any one who has been succoured by another in the time of danger, instead of showing the like kindness to his benefactor, endeavours at any time to destroy or hurt him, it is certain that all men must be shocked by such ingratitude, through sympathy with the resentment of their neighbour, and from an apprehension also that the case may be their own. And from hence arises in the mind of every man a certain *notion* of the nature and force of duty, in which consists both the beginning and the end of justice. In like manner, the man who, in defence of others, is seen to throw himself the foremost into every danger, and even to sustain the fury of the fiercest animals, never fails to obtain the loudest acclamations of applause and veneration from all the multitude, while he who shows a different conduct is pursued with censure and reproach. And thus it is that the people begin to discern the nature of things honorable and base, and in what consists the difference between them; and to perceive that the former, on account of the advantage that attends them, are fit to be admired and imitated, and the latter to be detested and avoided.'" *

"The doctrine," says Dr. Gillies, "contained in this passage is expanded by Mr. Smith into a theory of moral sentiments. But he departs from *his author* in placing the perception of right and wrong in sentiment or feeling, ultimately and simply. Polybius, on the contrary, maintains, with Aristotle, that these notions arise from reason or intellect operating on affection or appetite; or, in other words, that the moral faculty is a compound, and may be resolved into two simpler principles of the mind." †

The only expression I object to in the preceding sentences is the phrase *his author*, which has the appearance of insinuating a charge of plagiarism against Mr. Smith; — a charge which, I am confident, he did not deserve, and to which the above extract does not, in my opinion, afford any plausible color. It exhibits, indeed, an instance of a curious coincidence between two philosophers in their views of the same subject, and as such I have no doubt that Mr. Smith himself would have remarked it, had it occurred to his memory when he was writing his book. Of such accidental coincidences between different minds, examples present themselves every day to those who, after having drawn from their internal resources all the lights they could supply on a particular question, have the curiosity to compare their own conclusions with those of their predecessors. And it is extremely worthy of observation, that, in proportion as any conclusion approaches to the truth, the number of previous approximations to it may be reasonably expected to be multiplied.

In the instance before us, however, the question about originality is of little or no moment, for the pe-

* Lib. VI. Cap. VI., Hampton's translation.

† Gillies's Aristot. *Ethics*, Book III. Chap. IV., note.

culiar merit of Mr. Smith's work does not lie in his general principle, but in the skilful use he has made of it to give a systematical arrangement to the most important discussions and doctrines of ethics. In this point of view, the *Theory of Moral Sentiments* may be justly regarded as one of the most original efforts of the human mind in that branch of science to which it relates; and even if we were to suppose that it was first suggested to the author by a remark of which the world had been in possession for two thousand years before, this very circumstance would only reflect a stronger lustre on the novelty of his design, and on the invention and taste displayed in its execution.

In the same work I have observed, that, "in studying the connection and filiation of successive theories, when we are at a loss in any instance for a link to complete the continuity of philosophical speculation, it seems much more reasonable to search for it in the systems of the immediately preceding period, and in the inquiries which *then* occupied the public attention, than in detached sentences, or accidental expressions gleaned from the relics of distant ages. It is thus only that we can hope to seize the precise point of view in which an author's subject first presented itself to his attention, and to account to our own satisfaction, from the particular aspect under which he saw it, for the subsequent direction which was given to his curiosity. In following such a plan, our object is not to detect plagiarisms, which we suppose men of genius to have intentionally concealed, but to fill up an apparent chasm in the history of science, by laying hold of the thread which insensibly guided the mind from one station to another." Upon these principles, our attention is naturally directed, on the present occasion, to the inquiries of Dr. Butler, in preference to those of any other author, ancient or modern. At the time when Mr. Smith began his literary career, Butler unquestionably stood highest among the ethical writers of England; and his works appear to have produced a still deeper and more lasting impression in Scotland than in the other part of the island. Of the esteem in which they were held by Lord Kames and Mr. Hume, satisfactory documents remain in their published letters; nor were his writings less likely to attract the notice of Mr. Smith, in consequence of the pointed and unanswerable objections which they contain to some of the favorite opinions of his predecessor, Dr. Hutcheson.

VI. *Butler's Views on this Subject.*] The probability of this conjecture is confirmed by the obvious and easy transition which connects the theory of sympathy with Butler's train of thinking in his Sermon *On Self-deceit.* In order to free the mind from the influence of its artifices, experience gradually teaches us (as Butler has excellently shown), either to recollect the judgments we have formerly passed in similar circumstances on the conduct of others, or to state cases to ourselves, in which we and all our personal concerns are left entirely out of the question. Hence it was not an unnatural inference, on the first aspect of the fact, that our only ideas of right and wrong, with respect to our own conduct, are derived from our sentiments with respect to the conduct of others. This, accordingly (as we have already seen), is the distinguishing principle of Mr. Smith's theory.

I have formerly referred to a note in Butler's fifth Sermon, in which he has exposed the futility of Hobbes's definition of pity. In the same note, it is remarked further by the very acute and profound author, that Hobbes's premises, if admitted to be sound, so far from establishing his favorite doctrine concerning the selfish nature of man, would afford an additional illustration of the provision made in his constitution for the establishment and maintenance of the social union. "If there be really any such thing as the fiction or imagination of danger to ourselves from sight of the miseries of others, which Hobbes speaks of, and which he has absurdly mistaken for the whole of compassion, — if there be any thing of this sort common to mankind distinct from the reflection of reason, it would be a most remarkable instance of what was farthest from his thoughts, namely, of a mutual sympathy between each particular of the species, — a fellow-feeling common to mankind. It would not, indeed, be an instance of our substituting others for ourselves, but it would be an example of our substituting ourselves for others." To those who are at all acquainted with Mr. Smith's book, it is unnecessary for me to observe how very precisely Butler has here touched on the general fact which is assumed as the basis of the *Theory of Moral Sentiments.*

In various other parts of Butler's writings there are manifest anticipations of Mr. Smith's ethical speculations. In his Sermon, for example, *On Forgiveness of Injuries*, he expresses himself thus: — " Without knowing particulars, I take upon me to assure all persons who think they have received indignities or injurious treatment, that they may depend upon it, as in a manner certain, that the offence is not so great as they themselves imagine. We are in such a peculiar situation, with respect to injuries done to ourselves, that we can scarce any more see them as they really are than our eye can see itself. If we could place ourselves at a due distance (that is, be really unprejudiced), we should frequently discern *that* to be in reality inadvertence and mistake in our enemy, which we now fancy we see to be malice or scorn. From this proper point of view we should likewise, in all probability, see something of these latter in ourselves, and most certainly a great deal of the former. Thus the indignity or injury would almost infinitely lessen, and perhaps at last come out to be nothing at all. Self-love is a medium of a peculiar kind; in these cases it magnifies every thing which is amiss in others, at the same time that it lessens every thing amiss in ourselves."

The following passage in Butler's Sermon *On Self-deceit* is still more explicit. " It would very much prevent our being misled by this self-partiality, to reduce that practical rule of our Saviour — *Whatsoever ye would that men should do to you, do ye even so to them*

— to our judgment or way of thinking. This rule, you see, consists of two parts. One is to substitute another for yourself when you take a survey of any part of your behaviour, or consider what is proper and fit and reasonable for you to do upon any occasion; the other part is, that you substitute yourself in the room of another, — consider yourself as the person affected by such a behaviour, or towards whom such an action is done, and then you would not only see, but likewise feel, the reasonableness or unreasonableness of such an action or behaviour." *

Section III.

OF THE SENSE OF THE RIDICULOUS.

I. *Objects of Ridicule.*] Another auxiliary principle to the moral faculty yet remains to be considered, — *the sense of ridicule*, and the anxiety which all men feel to avoid whatever is likely to render them the objects of it. The subject is extremely curious and interesting; but the time I have bestowed on the former article obliges me to confine myself to a very short explanation of the meaning of the word, and of the relation which the principle denoted by it bears to our nobler motives of action.

The natural and proper object of ridicule is those

---

* The same idea is stated with great clearness and conciseness by Hobbes. "There is an easy rule to know upon a sudden, whether the action I be to do be against the law of nature or not. And it is but this, — *That a man imagine himself in the place of the party with whom he hath to do, and reciprocally him in his.* Which is no more but changing (as it were) of the scales; for every man's passion weigheth heavy in his own scale, but not in the scale of his neighbour. And this rule is very well known and expressed in the old dictate, *Quod tibi fieri non vis, alteri ne feceris.*" — *De Corpore Politico*, Chap. IV.

It is observed by Gibbon that this golden rule of doing as we would be done by is to be found in a moral treatise of Isocrates. — *Decline and Fall of the Roman Empire*, Chap. LIV., note.

[For other critical notices of Adam Smith's theory, see Brown's *Philosophy of the Human Mind*, Lect. LXXX. and LXXXI. Cousin, *Philosophie Morale*, Seconde Partie: *Ecole Ecossaise*, Leçons IV.-VI. Jouffroy's *Introduction to Ethics*, Lectures XVI.-XVIII.]

smaller improprieties in character and manners which do not rouse our feelings of moral indignation, or impress us with a melancholy sense of human depravity. In the words of Aristotle, τὸ γέλοιον, or *the ridiculous*, may be defined to be τὸ αἶσχος ἀνώδυνον, *the deformed without hurt or mischief*, or (as he has explained his own meaning) "those smaller faults which are neither painful nor pernicious, but *unbeseeming*"; and "of which," he adds, "the proper correction is not *reproach*, but *laughter*."

In stating this as a general principle with respect to the ridiculous, I would not be understood to assert that every thing which is ridiculous implies *immorality*, in the strict acceptation of that word. Ignorance, absurdity in reasoning, even a want of acquaintance with the established ceremonial of behaviour, often provoke our laughter with irresistible force. What is ridiculous, however, always implies some imperfection, and exposes the individual to whom it attaches to a species of contempt, of which (how good-humored soever) no man would choose to be the object.

Perhaps, indeed, it might be found, on a more accurate analysis of this part of our constitution, that it is not, in such cases, merely the *intellectual* or *physical* defect which excites our ridicule, but the contrast between this and *some moral impropriety or imperfection*, which either conceals the defect from the individual himself, or induces him to attempt concealing it from others; and consequently, that the sentiment of ridicule always involves, more or less, a sentiment of moral disapprobation. One thing is certain, that intellectual and physical imperfections never appear *so* ridiculous as when accompanied with affectation, hypocrisy, vanity, pride, or an obvious incongruity between the pretensions of an individual and the education he has received, or the station in which he was originally placed.

Upon this question, however, I shall not at present presume to decide. It is sufficient for my purpose, if it be granted that nothing is ridiculous but what falls short, some way or other, of our ideas of excellence;

or (as Cicero expresses it), "Locus et regio quasi ridiculi, turpitudine et deformitate quadam continetur." *

II. *Final Cause of this Principle.*] Hence, I think, may be traced a beautiful *final cause* in this part of our frame. For while it enlarges the fund of our enjoyment, by rendering the more trifling imperfections of our fellow-creatures a source of amusement to us, it excites the exertions of every individual to correct those imperfections by which the ridicule of others is likely to be provoked. As our eagerness, too, to correct these imperfections may be presumed to be weak in proportion as we apprehend them to be, *in a moral view*, of trifling moment, we are so formed, that the painful feelings produced by ridicule are often more poignant than those arising from the consciousness of having rendered ourselves the objects of strong moral disapprobation. Even the consciousness of being *hated* by mankind is to the generality of men less intolerable than what the poet calls

> "The world's *dread laugh*,
> Which scarce the firm philosopher can scorn."

It furnishes no objection to these observations, that the sense of ridicule is not always favorable to virtuous conduct; and that it frequently tends very powerfully to mislead us from our duty. The same remark may be extended to *the desire of esteem*, and even to *the moral faculty*, — that they are liable to be perverted by education and fashion. But the great ends of our being are to be collected from the *general scope* of the principles of our constitution; not from the particular instances in which this scope is thwarted by adventitious circumstances; and nothing surely can be more evident than this, that the three principles just mentioned were all intended to coöperate together, and to lead to a conduct favorable to the improvement of the individual, and to the general interests of society.

---

* *De Oratore*, Lib. II. 58. "The place and, as it were, province of ridicule are confined to baseness and deformity."

The sense of ridicule, in particular, although it has a manifest reference to such a scene of imperfection as we are placed in at present, is, on the whole, a most important auxiliary to our sense of duty, and well deserves a careful examination in an analysis of the moral constitution of man. It is one of the most striking characteristics of the human constitution, as distinguished from that of the lower animals, and has an intimate connection with the highest and noblest principles of our nature. As Milton has observed, —

> "Smiles from *reason* flow,
> To brutes denied";

and it may be added, that they not only imply the power of *reason*, in the more limited acceptation of that word, as applicable to the perception of truth and falsehood, but the moral faculty, or that power by which we distinguish *right* from *wrong*. Indeed, they imply the power of *reason* (in both acceptations of the term) in a high state of cultivation.

In the education of youth, there is nothing which requires more serious attention than the proper regulation of the sense of ridicule; nor is there any instance in which the legislator has it more in his power to influence national manners, than by watching over those public exhibitions which avail themselves of this principle of human nature, as a vehicle of entertainment to the multitude.

Section IV.

OF TASTE, CONSIDERED IN ITS RELATION TO MORALS.

I. *Taste applicable to Morals.*] From the explanation formerly given of the import of the phrases *moral beauty* and *moral deformity*, it may be easily conceived in what manner the character and the conduct of our fellow-creatures may become subservient to the gratification of *taste*. The use which the poet makes of this class of our intellectual pleasures is entirely analogous to the resources which he borrows from the charms o external nature. By skilful selections and combinations, characters more exalted and more pleasing may be drawn than have ever fallen under our observation; and a series of events may be exhibited in perfect consonance to our moral feelings. Rewards and punishments may be distributed by the poet with an exact regard to the merits of individuals; and those irregularities in the distribution of happiness and misery, which furnish the subject of so many complaints in real life, may be corrected in the world created by his genius. Here, too, the poet borrows from nature the model after which he copies, not only as he accommodates his imaginary arrangements to his unperverted sense of justice, but as he accommodates them to the *general laws* by which the world is governed; for whatever exceptions may occur in particular cases, there can be no more doubt about the fact, that virtue is the direct road to happiness, and vice to misery, than that, in the material world, blemishes and defects are lost amid prevailing beauty and order.

The power of moral taste, like that which has for its object the beauty of material forms and the various productions of the fine arts, requires much exercise for its development and culture. The one species of taste, also, as well as the other, is susceptible of a *false* refinement, injurious to our own happiness, and to our usefulness as members of society.

II. *Dangers incident to a false Refinement of Moral Taste.*] With this false refinement of taste is sometimes connected the peculiar species of misanthropy which is grafted on a worthy and benevolent heart. When the standard of moral excellence we have been accustomed to dwell upon in imagination is greatly elevated above the common attainments of humanity, we are apt to become too difficult and fastidious (if I may use the expression) in our *moral taste;* or, in plainer language, to become unreasonably censorious of the follies and vices of our contemporaries. In such cases, it may happen that the native benevolence of the mind, by being habitually directed towards ideal characters, may prove a source of real dissatisfaction and dislike towards those with whom we associate. Such a disposition, when carried to an extreme, not only sours the temper, and dries up all the springs of innocent comfort which nature has so liberally provided for us in the common incidents of life, but, by withdrawing a man from active pursuits, renders all his talents and virtues useless to society. A character of this description has furnished to Molière the subject of the most finished of all his dramatic pieces, and to Marmontel, that of one of his most agreeable and useful tales. The former of these is universally known as the masterpiece of French comedy; but the latter possesses also an uncommon degree of merit by the hints it suggests for curing the weakness in which the character originates, and by the interesting contrast it exhibits between the *misanthrope* of Molière, and a man who unites inflexibility of principle with that accommodation of temper which is necessary for the practical exercise of virtue. The great nurse and cherisher of this species of misanthropy is solitary contemplation; and the only effect ual remedy is society and business, together with a habit of directing the attention rather to the correction of our own faults than to a jealous and suspicious examination of the motives which influence the conduct of our neighbours.

Considered as a principle of action, a cultivated moral taste, while it provides an effectual security against the grossness necessarily connected with many vices, cherishes a temper of mind friendly to all that is amiable, or generous, or elevated in our nature. When separated, however, as it sometimes is, from a strong sense of duty, it can scarcely fail to prove a fallacious guide; the influence of fashion, and of other casual associations, tending perpetually to lead it astray. This is more particularly remarkable in men to whom the gratifications of *taste in general* form the principal object of pursuit, and whose habits of life encourage them to look no higher for their rule of conduct than the way of the world.

The language employed by some of the Greek philosophers in their speculations concerning the nature of virtue seems, on a superficial view, to imply that they supposed the moral faculty to be wholly resolvable into a sense of the beautiful; and hence Lord Shaftesbury, Dr. Hutcheson, and others, have been led to adopt a phraseology which has the appearance of substituting taste, in contradistinction to reason and conscience, as the ultimate standard of right and wrong.

While on this subject, I cannot help taking notice of a highly exceptionable passage which occurs in one of Mr. Burke's later publications, — a passage in which, after contrasting the polished and courtly manners of the higher orders with the coarseness and vulgarity of the multitude, he remarks, that among the former "vice itself lost half its evil by losing all its grossness." * The fact, according to *my* view of things, is precisely the reverse; that the malignant contagiousness of vice is increased tenfold by every circumstance which draws a veil over or disguises its native deformity. On this argument volumes might be written, and I sincerely wish that a hand could be found equal to the task. At present, I must content myself with recommending it to the serious attention of moralists, as one of the most important topics of *practical ethics* which the actual circumstances of this part of the world point out as an object of philosophical discussion.

---

* At the close of the eloquent description of the queen, in his *Reflections on the Revolution in France.*

CHAPTER VI.

OF MAN'S FREE AGENCY.

SECTION I.

PRELIMINARY OBSERVATIONS.

I. *Man's Free Agency has been called in question by Speculative Minds.*] All the foregoing inquiries concerning the moral constitution of man proceed on the supposition, that he has a freedom of choice between good and evil, and that, when he deliberately performs an action which he knows to be wrong, he renders himself justly obnoxious to punishment. That this supposition is agreeable to the common apprehensions of mankind will not be disputed.

From very early times, indeed, the truth of the supposition has been called in question by a few speculative men, who have contended that the actions we perform are *the necessary result of the constitution of our minds, operated on by the circumstances of our external situation;* and that what we call moral delinquencies are as much a part of our destiny as the corporeal or intellectual qualities we have received from nature. The argument in support of this doctrine has been proposed in various forms, and has been frequently urged with the confidence of demonstration.*

This question about predestination and free-will has furnished, in all ages and countries, inexhaustible matter of contention, both to philosophers and divines. In the ancient schools of Greece it is well known how generally and how keenly it was agitated. Among the Mahometans it constitutes one of the principal

* The rest of this chapter was thrown by the author into an appendix In this edition it is inserted in its place, as being necessary to the discussion. Some retrenchments have been made in order to find room for the notes, which are intended to give some slight intimations of the present state of the controversy. — ED.

points of division between the followers of Omar and those of Ali; and among the ancient Jews it was the subject of endless dispute between the Pharisees and the Sadducees. It is scarcely necessary for me to add, what violent controversies it has produced, and still continues to produce, in the Christian world.

II. *Explanation of Terms used in this Controversy.*] As this controversy, like most others in metaphysics, has been involved in much unnecessary perplexity by the ambiguity of language, a few brief remarks on some equivocal terms connected with the question at issue may perhaps add something to the perspicuity and precision of the following reasonings.

1. The word *volition* is defined by Locke to be "an act of the mind, knowingly exerting that dominion it takes itself to have over any part of the man, by employing it in, or withholding it from, any particular action."* Dr. Reid defines it, more briefly, to be "the determination of the mind to do or not to do something which we conceive to be in our power." He remarks, at the same time, that "this definition is not strictly logical, inasmuch as *the determination of the mind* is only another term for volition. But it ought to be observed, that the most simple acts of the mind do not admit of being logically defined. The only way to form a precise notion of them is to reflect attentively upon them as we feel them in ourselves. Without this reflection, no definition can enable us to reason about them with correctness."†

2. It is necessary to form a distinct notion of what is meant by the word *volition*, in order to understand the import of the word *will;* for this last word properly expresses that *power* of the mind of which volition is the *act*, and it is only by attending to what we experience, while we are conscious of the act, that we can understand any thing concerning the nature of the power.

---

* *Essay concerning Human Understanding*, Book II. Chap. XXI. § 15.

† *Essays on the Active Powers*, Essay II. Chap. I.

The word *will*, however, is not always used in this its proper acceptation, but is frequently substituted for *volition;* as when I say that my hand moves in obedience to my *will*. This, indeed, happens to the names of most of the powers of the mind, — that the same word is employed to express the power and the act. Thus *imagination* signifies both the power and the act of imagining; *abstraction* signifies both the power and the act of abstracting; and so in other instances. But although the word *will* may, without departing from the usual forms of speech, be used indiscriminately for the power and the act, the word *volition* applies only to the latter; and it would undoubtedly contribute to the distinctness of our reasonings to restrict the signification of the word *will* entirely to the former.

It is not necessary, I apprehend, to enlarge any more on the meaning of these terms. It is to be learned only from careful reflection on what passes in our own minds, and to multiply words upon the subject would only involve it in obscurity.

3. There is, however, a state of the mind perfectly distinct both from the power and the act of willing, with which they have been frequently confounded, and of which it may therefore be proper to mention the characteristical marks. The state I refer to is properly called *desire*, the distinction between which and *will* was first clearly pointed out by Mr. Locke. "I find the *will*," says he, "often confounded with several of the affections, especially *desire*, and that by men who would not willingly be thought not to have had very distinct notions of things, and not to have writ very clearly about them." — "This," he justly adds, "has been no small occasion of obscurity and mistake in this matter, and therefore is, as much as may be, to be avoided." The substance of his remarks on the appropriate meaning of these two terms amounts to the two following propositions: — 1. That at the same moment a man may desire one thing and will another. 2. That at the same moment a man may have contrary desires, but cannot have contrary wills. The notions,

therefore, which ought to be annexed to the words *will* and *desire* are essentially different.

It will be proper, however, to state Mr. Locke's observations in his own words: — "He that shall turn his thoughts inwards upon what passes in his own mind when he *wills*, shall see that the will or power of volition is conversant about nothing but that particular determination of the mind whereby, barely by a thought, the mind endeavours to give rise, continuation, or stop to any action which it takes to be in its power. This, well considered, plainly shows, that the will is perfectly distinguished from desire, which, in the very same action, may have a quite contrary tendency from that which our wills set us upon. A man whom I cannot deny may oblige me to use persuasions to another, which, at the same time I am speaking, I may wish not to prevail on him. In this case, it is plain the will and desire run counter. I *will* the action that tends one way, whilst my desire tends another, and that the direct contrary. A man who, by a violent fit of gout in his limbs, finds a doziness in his head or a want of appetite in his stomach removed, desires to be eased too of the pain of his feet or hands (for wherever there is pain there is a desire to be rid of it); though yet, while he apprehends that the removal of the pain may translate the noxious humors to a more vital part, his *will* is never determined to any one action that may serve to remove this pain. Whence it is evident that desiring and willing are two distinct acts of the mind; and, consequently, that the will, which is but the power of volition, is much more distinct from desire." *

It is surprising how little this important passage has been attended to by Locke's successors.

Dr. Johnson on this, as on every other occasion where logical precision of ideas is called for in a definition, is strangely indistinct and inconsistent. *Will* he defines to be "that power by which we *desire* and purpose";

* *Essay concerning Human Understanding*, Book II. Chap. XXI. § 30.

and he gives as its *synonyme* the scholastic word *velleity.* On turning to the article *velleity*, we are told that "it is the school term used to signify *the lowest degree of desire*"; in illustration of which Dr. South is quoted, according to whom "the *wishing* of a thing is not properly the *willing* it, but it is that which is called by the schools an imperfect *velleity*, and imports no more than an idle, inoperative complacency in and *desire* of the end, without any consideration of the means."

4. Instead of speaking (according to common phraseology) of the *influence of motives on the will*, it would be much more correct to speak of the influence of motives on the *agent.* We are apt to forget what *the will* is, and to consider it as something inanimate and passive, the state of which can be altered only by the action of some external cause. The habitual use of the metaphorical word *motives*, to denote the *intentions* or *purposes* which accompany our voluntary actions, or, in other words, the *ends* which we have in view in the exercise of the power intrusted to us, has a strong tendency to confirm us in this error, by leading us to assimilate in fancy the *volition* of a mind to the *motion* of a body, and the circumstances which give rise to this volition to the *vis motrix* by which the motion is produced.

It was probably in order to facilitate the reception of his favorite scheme of necessity that Hobbes was led to substitute, instead of the old division of our faculties into the powers of the understanding and those of the will, a new division of his own, in which the name of *cognitive* powers was given to the former, and that of *motive* powers to the latter. To familiarize the ears of superficial readers to this phraseology was of itself one great step towards securing their suffrages against the supposition of man's free agency. To say that the will is determined by *motive* powers, is to employ a language which virtually implies a recognition of the very point in dispute. Accordingly, Mr. Belsham is at pains to keep the metaphorical origin of the word *motive* in the view of his readers, by prefixing to his argument in favor of the scheme of necessity the following definition: — "*Motive*, in this discussion, is to be understood in its most extensive sense. It expresses whatever MOVES or influences the mind in its choice." *

5. According to Mr. Locke, the ideas of *liberty* and of *power* are very nearly the same. "Every one," he observes, "finds in himself a power to begin or forbear, continue or put an end to, several actions in himself. From the consideration of the extent of this power of the mind over the actions of the man, which every one finds in himself, arise the ideas of liberty and necessity." And a few sentences afterwards: — "The idea of liberty is the idea of a power in any agent to do or forbear any particular action, according to the determination or thought of the mind, whereby either of them is preferred to the other. Where either of them is not in the power of the agent, to be produced by him according to his volition, there he is not at liberty, but under necessity." † That these definitions are not perfectly correct will appear hereafter. They approach, indeed, very nearly to the definitions of liberty and necessity given by Hobbes, Collins, and Edwards; whereas Locke, in order to do justice to his own decided opinion on the subject, ought to have included also in his idea of liberty a *power* over the determinations of his will.

It is owing in a great measure to this close connection between the ideas of *free will* and of *power*, and to the pleasure with which the consciousness of *power* is always accompanied, that we feel so painful a mortification in perusing those systems in which our free agency is called in question. Dr. Priestley himself, as well as his great oracle, Dr. Hartley, has acknowledged, that "he was not a ready convert to the doctrine of necessity, and that he gave up his liberty with great reluctance." ‡ But whence this reluctance to embrace

* *Elements of the Philosophy of the Mind*, Chap. IX. Sect. I.

† *Essay concerning Human Understanding*, Book II. Chap. XXI §§ 7, 8.

‡ *Doctrine of Philosophical Necessity Illustrated*, Preface.

a doctrine so "great and glorious," but from its repugnance to the natural feelings and natural wishes of the human mind?

Section II.

REVIEW OF THE ARGUMENT FOR NECESSITY.

I. *Concessions by the Advocates for Free Will.*] Before proceeding to an examination of this question, I shall premise a few principles in which both parties are agreed, or which at least appear *to me* to be concessions which the advocates for free will may safely make to their antagonists without any injury to their general argument.

1. Every action is performed with some view, or, in other words, is performed *from some motive.* Dr. Reid, indeed, denies this with zeal, but I am doubtful if he has strengthened his cause by doing so;* for he confesses that the actions which are performed without motives are perfectly trifling and insignificant, and not such as lead to any general conclusion concerning the merit or demerit of moral agents. I should therefore rather be disposed to yield this point than to dispute a proposition not materially connected with the question at issue. One thing is clear and indisputable, that it is only in so far as a man acts from motives or intentions, that he is entitled to the character of a rational being.

2. The merit of an action depends entirely on the motive from which it was performed. Dr. Reid remarks, that some necessitarians have triumphed in this principle as the very hinge of the controversy, whereas the truth is, that no reasonable advocate for free will ever called it in question.

II. *General Statement of the Argument for Necessity.*] So far, I think, we are justified in going. The great

* *Essays on the Active Powers*, Essay IV. Chap. IV.

question is, *How* do motives influence or determine the will? In answer to this question the necessitarians reason as follows:—

Every change in our nature, we are told, implies the operation of a *cause;* and this maxim, it is pretended, holds not only with respect to inanimate matter, but with respect to the changes which take place in the state of a mind. Every volition, therefore, must have been produced by a motive with which it is as necessarily connected as any other effect with its cause; and when different motives are presented to the mind at the same time, the will yields to the strongest, as necessarily as a body urged by two contrary forces moves in the direction of that which is most powerful.

The foregoing argument goes to prove, that all human actions are as necessarily produced by motives as the going of a clock is necessarily produced by the weights, and that no human action could have been otherwise than it really was. Nay, it applies also in full force to the Deity, and indeed to all intelligent beings whatever; for it is not founded on any thing peculiar to the *human* mind, but on the *impossibility of free agency;* and, of consequence, it leads to this general conclusion, that no *event* in the universe could have happened otherwise than it did.

Accordingly, Dr. Clarke has been at much pains to prove that the Deity *must be a free agent*, and therefore that free agency is not impossible; from which he infers that there must be some flaw in the reasonings just stated to prove that man is a necessary agent.* If this reasoning of Clarke's be admitted as conclusive, where is the absurdity, I would ask, of supposing that God may have been pleased to place man in a state of moral discipline, by imparting to him a freedom of choice between good and evil, in like manner as he has imparted to him various other faculties and powers essentially different from any thing we observe in the lower animals? Is not the contrary assertion a pre-

* *Demonstration of the Being and Attributes of God*, Prop. XII.

sumptuous attempt to set limits to the Divine Omnipotence?

Among the various forms which religious enthusiasm assumes, there is a certain prostration of the mind, which, under the specious disguise of a deep humility, aims at exalting the Divine perfections by annihilating all the powers which belong to human nature. "Nothing is more usual for fervent devotion," says Sir James Mackintosh, in speaking of some theories current among the Hindoos, "than to dwell so long and so warmly on the meanness and worthlessness of created things, and on the all-sufficiency of the Supreme Being, that it slides insensibly from comparative to absolute language, and, in the eagerness of its zeal to magnify the Deity, seems to annihilate every thing else."

This excellent observation may serve to account for the zeal displayed by many devout men in favor of the scheme of necessity. "We have nothing," they frequently and justly remind us, "but what we have *received*." But the question here is simply a matter of fact, whether we have or have not received from God the gift of free will; and the only argument, it must be remembered, which they have yet been able to advance for the negative proposition is, that this gift was impossible even for the power of God; — an argument, we may remark, which not only annihilates the power of man, but annihilates that of God also, and subjects him, as well as all his creatures, to the control of causes which he is unable to resist. So completely does this scheme defeat the pious views in which it has sometimes originated.

I say *sometimes;* for this very argument against the liberty of the will is employed by Spinoza, according to whom the free agency of man involves the absurd supposition of an *imperium in imperio* in the universe.* Voltaire, too, — who in his latter days, abandoning those principles for which he had before, when in the

* *Tractat. Polit.*, Cap. II. Sect. VI.

full vigor of his faculties, so zealously and eloquently contended, seems to have become a convert to the scheme of fatalism, — has on one occasion had recourse to an argument against man's free agency similar in substance to what is advanced by Spinoza in the passage now referred to. "En effet, il seroit bien *singulier* que toute la nature, tous les astres obeissent à des loix éternelles, et qu'il y eut un petit animal haut de cinq pieds, qui en mepris de ces lois pût agir toujours comme il lui plairoit au seul gré de son caprice." * "Singular!" exclaims Dr. Beattie, after quoting the preceding sentence; "ay, singular indeed, — but not a whit more singular than that this same animal of five feet should perceive, and think, and read, and write, and speak; attributes which no astronomer of my acquaintance has ever supposed to belong to the planets, notwithstanding their brilliant appearance and stupendous magnitude." † The reply is quite as good as the argument is entitled to.‡

---

* *Le Philosophe Ignorant*, XIII. "Indeed, it would be very singular that all nature, all the planets, should obey eternal laws, and that there should be a little animal, five feet high, who, in contempt of these laws, could act as he pleased, solely according to his caprice."

† *Essay on Truth*, Part II. Chap. II. Sect. III.

‡ In reply to the general argument for necessity founded on the theory of causation, I copy a few paragraphs from Tappan's *Review of Edwards's Inquiry into the Freedom of the Will.* — "Let us look at the connection of cause and phenomena a little more particularly. What is *cause?* It is that which is the ground of the possible and actual existence of phenomena. How is cause *known?* By the phenomena. Is cause *visible?* No; whatever is seen is phenomenal. We observe phenomena, and by the law of our intelligence we assign them to cause. But how do we *conceive* of cause as producing phenomena? By a *nisus*, an effort, or energy. Is this *nisus* itself a phenomenon? It is when it is *observed*. Is it always observed? It is not The *nisus* of gravitation we do not observe; we observe merely the facts of gravitation. The *nisus* of heat to consume we do not observe; we observe merely the facts of combustion. Where, then, do we observe this *nisus?* Only in will. Really, volition is the *nisus* or effort of that cause which we call *will*. When I wish to do any thing, I make an effort, a *nisus*, to do it; I make an effort to raise my arm, and I raise it. This effort is simply the volition. I make an effort to lift a weight with my hand; this effort is simply the volition to lift it, and immediately antecedent to this effort I recognize only my will, or really only myself. This effort, this *nisus*, this volition, — whatever we call it, — is in the will itself, and it becomes a phenomenon to us because *we* are causes that *know ourselves*. Every *nisus*, or effort, or volition, which we may make,

III. *Hobbes's Scheme of Necessity.*] According to the view of the subject that has now been taken, we are led to conclude that man possesses a power over the determinations of his will; — and this is precisely the scheme of what is commonly called *free will*, in opposition to that of *necessity*.

But this power over the determinations of the will has been represented by some philosophers as an absurdity and impossibility. Liberty, we are told, consists only in *a power to act as we will;* and it is impossible to conceive in any being a greater liberty than this. Hence it follows, that liberty does not extend to *the determinations of the will*, but only to *the actions consequent upon its determinations.* To say that we have

---

is in our consciousness: causes which are *not self-conscious*, of course, do not reveal this *nisus* to themselves; and they cannot reveal it to us because it is in the very bosom of the cause itself. What we observe in relation to all causes *not ourselves*, whether they be self-conscious or not, is not the *nisus*, but the sequents of the *nisus*. Thus in men we do not observe the volition or *nisus* in *their* wills, but the phenomena which form the sequents of the *nisus*. And in physical causes, we do not observe the *nisus* of these causes, but only the phenomena which form the sequents of this *nisus*. But when each one comes to *himself*, it is different. He penetrates himself, — knows himself. *He is himself the cause;* he himself *makes* the *nisus*, and is *conscious of it;* and this *nisus* to him becomes an effect, a *phenomenon*, — the first phenomenon by which he reveals himself, but a phenomenon by which he reveals himself only to himself. It is by the sequents of this *nisus*, the effects produced in the external visible world, that he reveals himself to others." — pp. 190 - 192.

That our particular volitions are the effects of the general power of willing, and not of external motives, is plain enough. But the determination of the general power of willing to put forth this or that particular volition, — is not this the effect of some cause? and if so, of what cause? Let us hear Mr. Tappan again: — "Does the objector allege, as a palpable absurdity, that there is, after all, nothing to account for the particular determination? I answer, that the particular determination is accounted for in the very quality or attribute of the cause. In the case of a physical cause, the particular determination is accounted for in the quality of the cause, which quality is to be necessarily correlated to the object. In the case of will, the particular determination is accounted for in the quality of the cause, which quality is to have the power to make the particular determination without being necessarily correlated to the object. A physical cause is a cause fixed, determined, and necessitated. The will is a cause contingent and free. A physical cause is a cause instrumental of a first cause; — the will is first cause itself. The Infinite Will is the first cause inhabiting eternity, filling immensity, and unlimited in its energy. The human will is first cause appearing in time, confined to place, and finite in its energy; but it is the same *in kind*, because made in the likeness of the

power to will such an action, is to say that we may will it if we will. This supposes the will to be determined by a prior will; and for the same reason, that will must be determined by a will prior to it, and so on in an infinite series of wills, which is absurd. To act freely, therefore, can mean nothing more than to act voluntarily; and this is all the liberty that can be conceived in man or in any other being.

Agreeably to this reasoning, Hobbes defines a free agent to be "he that can do if he will and forbear if he will." The same definition has been adopted by Leibnitz, by Collins, by Gravesande, by Edwards, by Bonnet, and by all later necessitarians.

Dr. Priestley ascribes this peculiar notion of free will to Hobbes as its author;* but it is in fact of much

---

Infinite Will. As first cause it is *self-moved;* it makes its *nisus* of itself, and of itself it forbears to make it; and within the sphere of its activity, and in relation to its objects, it has the power of selecting, by a mere arbitrary act, any particular object. It is a cause all whose acts, as well as any particular act, considered as phenomenon demanding a cause, are accounted for *in itself alone*." — pp. 222, 223.

"Acts of the will may be conceived of as analogous to intuitive or first truths. *First truths* require no demonstration; they admit of none; they form the basis of all demonstration. Acts of the will are *first movements* of *primary* causes, and as such neither require nor admit of *antecedent* causes, to explain their action. Will is the source and basis of all other cause. It explains all other cause, but in itself admits of no explanation. It presents the primary and all-comprehending *fact* of power. In God, will is infinite, primary cause, and uncreated: in man it is finite, primary cause, constituted by God's creative act, but not necessitated; for if necessitated it would not be will, — it would not be power after the likeness of the Divine power; it would be mere physical or secondary cause, and comprehended in the chain of natural antecedents and sequents." — p. 228.

Jouffroy says in reference to this point: — "The law, that every motive in material bodies is proportioned to the moving force which produced it, supposes a fact; namely, the *inertia* of matter. To apply this law to the relation which subsists between the resolutions of my will, and the motives which act upon it, is to suppose that my being, — that I, myself, am not a cause; for *a cause* is something which produces an act by its own proper power. That which is inert is not a cause; it may receive and transmit an impulse, but it cannot originate it. Are we, or are we not, *a cause?* Have we, or have we not, *a power in ourselves* of producing certain acts? It would seem necessary for us to decide this question, before we can rightly apply the law of external phenomena to internal operations." — *Introduction to Ethics*, Lecture IV. — Ed.

* "The doctrine of philosophical necessity is in reality a modern thing; not older, I believe, than Mr. Hobbes. Of the Calvinists, I believe Mr Jonathan Edwards to be the first. Others have followed his steps, espe-

older date, even among modern metaphysicians, coinciding exactly with the doctrine of those scholastic divines who contended for the *liberty of spontaneity*, in opposition to the *liberty of indifference*. It is, however, to Hobbes that the partisans of this opinion are indebted for the happiest and most popular illustration of it that has yet been given. "I conceive," says he, "liberty to be rightly defined, *the absence of all the impediments to action that are not contained in the nature and intrinsical quality of the agent*. As, for example, the water is said to descend *freely*, or to have *liberty* to descend by the channel of the river, because there is no impediment that way; but not across, because the banks are impediments. And though water cannot ascend, yet men never say it wants the *liberty* to ascend, but the *faculty* or *power*, because the impediment is in the nature of the water, and intrinsical. So also we say, he that is tied wants the *liberty* to go, because the impediment is not in him, but in his bands; whereas we say not so of him who is sick or lame, because the impediment is in himself." †

In order to judge how far the reasoning of Hobbes is in this instance satisfactory, it is necessary to attend to the various significations of the word *liberty;* for the sense in which Hobbes has defined it is only one of its acceptations, and by no means the sense in which it ought to be employed in this controversy.

1. Liberty is opposed to confinement of the body by superior force, as when a person is shut up in a prison. It is in this sense that Hobbes uses the word; for he tells us that liberty consists only in a power to act as

---

cially Mr. Toplady. But the inconsistency of his scheme with what is properly Calvinism appears by his dropping several of the essential parts of that system, and his silence with respect to others. And when the doctrine of necessity shall be thoroughly understood and well considered by Calvinists, it will be found to militate against almost all their peculiar tenets." — *Philosophical Necessity Illustrated*, Sect. XIII.

† See his treatise *Of Liberty and Necessity* under this head, *My Opinion about Liberty and Necessity*. Also, *Questions concerning Liberty, Necessity, and Chance clearly stated and debated between Dr. Bramhall and Thomas Hobbes*.

we will. And if the word had no other acceptation, the objection now stated would be a valid one; for as the will cannot be confined by any external force, neither can we with propriety ascribe to the will that species of liberty which is opposed to such confinement.*

2. Liberty is opposed to the restraints on human conduct arising from law and government; as when we say, that, by entering into a political society, a man gives up part of his natural liberty. In this sense liberty undoubtedly extends to the determinations of the will; and the very obligations which are opposed to it proceed on the supposition that the will is free. The establishment of law does not abridge this freedom, but, on the contrary, it takes for granted that we have

---

* "This is called the *liberty from co-action or violence*, the *liberty of spontaneity*, — *spontaneity*, τὸ ἑκούσιον. In the present question, this species of liberty ought to be thrown altogether out of account: it is admitted by all parties; is common equally to brutes and men; is not a peculiar quality of the will; and is, in fact, essential to it, for the will cannot possibly be forced. The *greatest spontaneity* is, in fact, the *greatest necessity*. Thus, a hungry horse, who turns of necessity to food, is said, on this definition of liberty, to do so with freedom, because he does so spontaneously; and, in general, the desire of happiness, which is the most necessary tendency, will, on this application of the term, be the most free.

"I may observe, that, among others, the definition of liberty given by the celebrated advocate of moral freedom, Dr. Samuel Clarke, is in reality only that of the liberty of spontaneity, viz.: — 'The power of self-motion or action, which, in all animate agents, is spontaneity, is, in moral or rational agents, what we properly call liberty.' *Fifth Reply to Leibnitz*, §§ 1-20, and *First Answer to the Gentleman of Cambridge*. This self-motion, absolutely considered, is itself necessary. . . . . . To *live* is to *act*, and as man is not free to live or not to live, so neither, absolutely speaking, is he free to act or not to act. As he lives, he is necessarily determined to act or energize, — to think and will; and all the liberty to which he can pretend is to choose between this mode of action and that. In scholastic language, man cannot have the liberty of *exercise*, though he may have the liberty of *specification*. The root of his freedom is thus necessity. Nay, we cannot conceive otherwise even of the Deity. As we must think him as necessarily existent, and necessarily living, so we must think him as necessarily active. Such are the conditions of human thought. It is thus sufficiently manifest that Dr. Clarke's inference of the fact of moral liberty, from the conditions of self-activity, is incompetent. And when he says, '*The true definition of liberty is the power to act*,' he should have recollected that this power is, on his own hypothesis, absolutely *fatal*, if it *cannot but act*. See his *Remarks on Collins*, pp. 15, 20, 27."

I copy the above from two notes of Sir W. Hamilton, in his edition of Reid's *Works*. *On the Active Powers*, Essay IV. Chap. I. and II. — Ed.

it in our power to obey or to transgress; proposing to us, on the one hand, the motives of duty and of interest, and setting before us, on the other, the consequences of wilful transgression.

3. Liberty is opposed to necessity; and it is in this sense the word is employed, when we say that man is a free and accountable being, and that the connection between motives and actions is not a necessary connection, like that between cause and effect. This species of liberty has been called by some *moral liberty.*

That there is nothing inconceivable in this idea appears, I hope, sufficiently from what has been already said. And indeed it is so far from being a metaphysical refinement or subtilty, that the common sense of mankind pronounces men to be accountable for their conduct only in so far as they are understood to be morally free. Whence is it that we consider the pain of the rack as an alleviation of the falsehoods extorted from the criminal? Plainly because the motives presented to him are supposed to be such as no ordinary degree of self-command is able to resist. And if we were only satisfied that these motives were *perfectly* irresistible, we would not ascribe to him any guilt at all.

As an additional confirmation of Hobbes's doctrine, it has been urged that human laws require no more to constitute a crime but that it be *voluntary;* and hence it has been inferred, that the criminality consists in the determination of the will, whether that determination be free or necessary.

The case just referred to affords a sufficient refutation of this argument. The confession of the criminal is surely *voluntary*, in the strict acceptation of that term; and yet we consider his guilt as alleviated in the same proportion in which we suppose his moral liberty to be abridged.

It is true that in most cases human laws require no more to constitute a crime than that it be voluntary; because, in general, motives are placed beyond the cognizance of earthly tribunals. But, *in a moral view*, merit and demerit suppose not only actions to be voluntary, but the agent to be possessed of moral liberty. And even earthly tribunals judge on the same principle, wherever it can be made to appear that the person accused was deprived of the power of self-government by insanity, or by some accidental paroxysm of passion.

I shall mention, in this connection, only one other argument in favor of the scheme of necessity; and I have reserved for it the last place, as it has been proposed with all the confidence of mathematical demonstration by a writer of no less note than Mr. Belsham. It is in the form of a *reductio ad absurdum;* and its more immediate object is to expose to ridicule the consequences which necessarily flow from the doctrine of free will.

The argument is this: — "According to the hypothesis of free will, the essence of virtue and vice consists in liberty; for example, benevolence without liberty is no virtue: malignity without liberty is no vice. Both are equally in a neutral state. Add a portion of liberty to both, benevolence instantly becomes an eminent virtue, and malignity an odious vice. That is, IF TO EQUALS YOU ADD EQUALS, THE WHOLES WILL BE UNEQUAL; than which nothing can be more absurd." *

On this reasoning, to which it would be unjust to deny the merit of complete originality, I have no comment to offer. I have quoted it chiefly as a specimen of the logical and mathematical skill of the present advocates for the doctrine of philosophical necessity. In this point of view, it forms an amusing contrast to the lofty pretensions of a sect which prides itself, not only on its superiority to vulgar prejudices, but on its sagacity in detecting a fraud so successfully practised on the rest of mankind by the Author of their moral constitution.

IV. *Argument of Leibnitz for Necessity.*] It is well

* *Elements of the Philosophy of the Human Mind,* Chap. IX. Sect. V.

known to all who have any acquaintance with the history of modern philosophy, that one of the fundamental principles of the Leibnitzian system is, that "nothing exists without a *sufficient reason* why it should be so, and not otherwise." Of this principle the following succinct account is given by Leibnitz himself, in his controversial correspondence with Dr. Clarke: — "The great foundation of mathematics is the principle of contradiction or identity; that is, that a proposition cannot be true and false at the same time. But in order to proceed from mathematics to natural philosophy, another principle is requisite (as I have observed in my *Theodicy*), I mean the principle of the *sufficient reason;* or, in other words, that nothing happens without a *reason* why it should be so rather than otherwise. And accordingly, Archimedes was obliged, in his book *De Æquilibrio*, to take for granted, that, if there be a balance in which every thing is alike on both sides, and if equal weights are hung on the two ends of that balance, the whole will be at rest. It is because no *reason* can be given why one side should weigh down rather than the other. Now by this single principle of the *sufficient reason* may be demonstrated the being of a God, and all the other parts of metaphysics or natural theology; and even in some measure those physical truths that are independent upon mathematics, such as the dynamical principles, or the principles of force." *

Some of the inferences deduced by Leibnitz from this almost gratuitous assumption are so paradoxical, that one cannot help wondering he was not staggered about its certainty. Not only was he led to conclude that the mind is necessarily determined in all its elections by the greatest apparent good, insomuch that it would be impossible for it to make a choice between two things perfectly alike; but he had the boldness to extend this conclusion to the Deity, and to assert, that

* *Collection of Papers which passed between Mr. Leibnitz and Dr. Clarke*, Leibnitz's Second Paper. For a full statement of Leibnitz's views on this and kindred questions, see his *Essais de Théodicée.*

two things perfectly alike could not have been produced even by Divine power. It was upon this ground that he rejected a *vacuum*, because all the parts of it would be perfectly like to each other; and that he also rejected the supposition of *atoms*, or similar particles of matter, and ascribed to each particle a *monad*, or active principle, by which it is discriminated from every other particle. The application of his principle, however, on which he evidently valued himself the most, was that to which I have already alluded, — the demonstrative evidence with which he conceived it to establish the impossibility of free agency, not only in man, but in any other intelligent being.

Let us examine, therefore, Leibnitz's principle as applicable to the determinations of the will, and consider what it implies, and how far it is agreeable to fact. And for this purpose it is necessary to attend to the various senses in which it may be understood.

1. When it is said, that for every voluntary action there must have been a sufficient reason, the proposition may be understood merely to imply, that every such action must have had a *cause*. And we may remark by the way, that this is the only interpretation of which the proposition admits, if the word *reason* be used in the same sense in which alone Leibnitz's maxim is applicable to inanimate matter. But in this sense of the proposition it does not at all affect the question about liberty and necessity; for it only implies that the action is an effect, which either proceeded from the free will of the agent (in which case *he* may justly be said to be the *cause* of the effect), or which did not proceed from his free will (in which case it must ultimately be referred to some *other* cause).

2. The principle of the *sufficient reason*, when applied to our voluntary actions, may be understood to imply, that the will is necessarily determined by *the greatest apparent good*. As this proposition is not peculiar to the system of Leibnitz, it may be proper to state it more fully.

The circumstances of our external situation, it has

been said, and the state of our appetites, desires, &c., at any particular time, evidently do not depend on us. Suppose, then, that I am under the influence of any two active principles which urge me in different directions, and that I deliberate which of them I am to obey. The conclusion my understanding forms on this subject does not depend on me, and this conclusion necessarily determines my will; for it is impossible for a man not to do what appears to him to be, on the whole, the best and most eligible thing at the moment. My will, therefore, in every case, depends as little on myself as the conclusion of my understanding when I give my assent to a mathematical demonstration.

The flaw of this reasoning, I apprehend, lies in that step in which it is affirmed that the will is necessarily determined by what appears to us to be *best* and most *eligible* at the moment;—and the only circumstance which gives the proposition the smallest degree of plausibility is the ambiguity of the language in which it is stated. For it may either imply that our volitions are necessarily agreeable to what we *will* at the time; in which case we only assert an identical proposition: or that the will is necessarily determined by what appears to us to be *morally* best and *really* most eligible at the time; in which case we assert what is contrary to fact.

3. The meaning of the proposition now under consideration may be understood to be this, — that for every action there must be a motive.

I have already said that in this sense I am disposed to admit the maxim. Dr. Reid, indeed, has very confidently maintained the negative; but I do not think (as I formerly observed), that by doing so he has strengthened his cause; for he confesses that the actions which are performed without motives are perfectly trifling and insignificant: nay, he acknowledges that the merit of an action depends entirely on the motive from which it is performed.

But although we grant this general proposition, it certainly does not follow from it that man is a necessary agent. The question is not concerning the *influ-*

ence of motives, but concerning the *nature* of that influence. The advocates for necessity represent it as the influence of a cause in producing its effect. The advocates for liberty acknowledge that the motive is the *occasion* of acting, or the *reason* for acting; but contend that it is so far from being the efficient cause of it, that it supposes the efficiency to exist elsewhere, namely, in the mind of the agent. Between these two opinions there is an essential distinction. The one represents man merely as a passive instrument. According to the other, he is really an *agent*, and the sole author of his own actions. He acts, indeed, from motives, but he has the power of choice among different ones. When he acts from a particular motive, it is not because this motive is *stronger* than others, but because he *willed* to act in this way. Indeed, it may be questioned if the word *strength* conveys any idea when applied to motives. It is obviously an analogical or metaphorical expression, borrowed from a class of phenomena essentially different.*

* "It is the strongest motive, say they, which determines the will. What is this strongest motive, I ask, and how do you measure the comparative force of motives? Is that the strongest motive, according to your idea, which determines the volition? If this is so, you are arguing in a circle; and instead of showing that it is the strongest motive which decides the will, you are merely saying that, as the determination of the will is in conformity with such or such a motive, therefore this motive is strongest.

"But, if we cannot judge from effect, we must find some *common measure* by which to decide. Let us inquire, then, what this measure can be.

"Of two impulses, manifestly unequal, it would be easy to determine the stronger; a vehement desire is distinguishable in our consciousness from one not so. And thus, merely from their vivacity and fervor, we may often recognize the stronger from the weaker passion. There is, then, if you choose to say so, a common measure between different impulses of our sensitive nature, which are peculiarly distinguished as *emotions*. On the other hand, of different courses of conduct which *reason* and *self-interest* bring into contrast, I may see that one is much more advantageous than another. There is, then, if you please, a means of comparing together different suggestions of self-interest: the suggestion which promises the most for my interest should have the most power over me. In the same way, among different *duties* which may present themselves to my judgment, there may be one which appears more obligatory than another; for there are duties of different degrees of importance, and in many cases I must sacrifice the less to the greater. I perceive, then, that, strictly

V. *Scheme of Necessity advocated by Collins and Edwards.*] The ablest defenders of free will have contended that the doctrine of necessity, when pushed to its logical consequences, must ultimately terminate in Spinozism. It seems to have been the great aim of Collins to vindicate his favorite scheme from this reproach, and to retaliate upon the partisans of free will the charge of favoring atheism and immorality. In proof of this, I have only to quote the account given by the author himself of the plan of his work.

"Too much care cannot be taken to prevent being misunderstood and prejudged in handling questions of such nice speculation as those of liberty and necessity; and therefore, though I might in justice expect to be read before any judgment be passed on me, I think it proper to premise the following observations: —

---

speaking, there is a possibility of comparing together the relative force of different motives originating from duty, and of different motives suggested by self-interest, or, finally, of different desires striving within me at a given moment. But between a *desire* on the one hand, and a conception of *interest* or of *duty* on the other, where, I ask, can you find a standard of comparison? If I assume *passion* as the measure, then, evidently, passion will appear the stronger motive; but if, on the other hand, I assume *interest* or *duty* as the measure, then desire becomes nothing, and duty or interest all in all. It depends, then, wholly upon the measure of comparison which I adopt, whether this or the other motive is strongest; which proves that there is no *common measure* of comparison to be applied at all times to these different kinds of motives, when we would estimate their relative force.

"Thus, in truth, in almost every case, to say that we yield to the strongest motive is to say what has no meaning; for in most cases it is impossible to determine the strongest motive. If I *will* to be prudent, I follow the motive of self-interest; if I *will* to be virtuous, I follow the motive of duty; if I *will* to be neither prudent nor virtuous, I follow passion; and in proportion as I yield to passion, to enlightened interest, or to duty, does the merit of my conduct vary. And here is a marvel for the advocate of necessity, and something which, in the sincerity of his conviction, he should ponder well. I, who am not free, — who, whatever resolution I have taken, have yet been fatally determined to take it by the strongest motive, — I feel that I am responsible for this resolution; and others, too, regard me as responsible; so that, according as I have been impelled to this or that act, do I believe myself to have merit or demerit, and pass sentence on myself as reasonable or unreasonable, prudent or foolish; and, in a word, apply to myself, though I have yielded necessarily to the strongest motive, certain expressions and names, all implying most decisively and forcibly that I was free to yield or resist, to take at my option this or that course, and, consequently, that this so-called strongest motive did not, after all, determine the act." — Jouffroy's *Introduction to Ethics*, Lect. IV.

"*First*, though I deny *liberty* in a certain meaning of that word, yet I contend for *liberty*, as it signifies a power in man to do as he wills or pleases.

"*Secondly*, when I affirm *necessity*, I contend only for *moral necessity*, meaning thereby that man, who is an intelligent and sensible being, is determined by his reason and his senses; and I deny man to be subject to such necessity as is in clocks, watches, and such other beings, which, for want of sensation and intelligence, are subject to an *absolute, physical*, or *mechanical necessity*.

"*Thirdly*, I have undertaken to show that the notions I advance are so far from being inconsistent with, that they are the sole foundations of, morality and laws, and of rewards and punishments in society; and that the notions I explode are subversive of them." *

In the prosecution of his argument on this question, Collins endeavours to show that man is a necessary agent: — 1. From experience. By *experience* he means our own consciousness that we *are* necessary agents. 2. From the impossibility of liberty. 3. From the consideration of the Divine prescience. 4. From the nature and use of rewards and punishments. And, 5. From the nature of morality.

In this view of the subject, and indeed in the very selection of his premises, it is remarkable how completely Collins has anticipated Dr. Jonathan Edwards, the most celebrated and indisputably the ablest champion, in later times, of the scheme of necessity. The coincidence is so perfect, that the outline given by the former of the plan of his work might have served with equal propriety as a preface to that of the latter. From the above-mentioned summary of the argument, and still more from the whole tenor of the *Philosophical Inquiry*, it is evident that Collins (one of the most obnoxious writers of his day to divines of all denominations) was not less solicitous than his successor, Edwards, to reconcile his metaphysical notions with man's account-

* *Philosophical Inquiry concerning Human Liberty*, Preface.

ableness and moral agency. The remarks, accordingly, of Clarke upon Collins's work are equally applicable to that of Edwards. It is to be regretted that they seem never to have fallen into the hands of this very acute and candid reasoner.* As for Collins, it is a re-

---

* *Remarks upon a Book entitled A Philosophical Inquiry concerning Human Liberty.* Voltaire, who in all probability never read either Clarke or Collins, has said that the former replied to the latter only by theological reasonings; — "Clarke n'a répondu à Collins qu'en théologien." (*Quest sur l'Encyc.*, Art. *Liberté.*) Nothing can be more remote from the truth. The argument of Clarke is wholly *metaphysical*, whereas his antagonist in various instances has attempted, though an avowed deist, to wrest to his own purposes the words of Scripture.

[For a full and elaborate answer to Edwards, see Mr. Tappan's *Review*, from which a long quotation has already been given, directed against one of his leading positions. We give another, on the distinction, so much insisted on by Edwards, and essential, indeed, to his scheme, between *moral* and *natural inability*.

"Man, they say, is morally unable to do good, and naturally able to do good, and therefore he can justly be made the subject of command, appeal, rebuke, and exhortation. Natural inability, as defined by this system, lies in the connection between the volition, considered as an antecedent, and the effect required. Thus I am naturally unable to walk, when, although I make the volition, my limbs, through weakness or disease, do not obey. Any defect in the powers or instrumentalities dependent for activity upon volition, or any impediment which volition cannot surmount, constitutes natural inability. According to this system, I am not held responsible for any thing which, through natural inability, cannot be accomplished, although the volition is made. But let us suppose that there is no defect in the powers or instrumentalities dependent for activity upon volition, and no impediment which volition cannot surmount, so that there need be only a volition in order to have the effect, and then the natural ability is complete: — I will to walk, and I walk. Now it is affirmed that a man is fairly responsible for the doing of any thing, and can be fairly urged to do it, when, as in this case, all that is necessary for the doing of it is a volition, although there may be a moral inability to the volition itself.

"Nothing, it seems to me, can be more absurd than this distinction. If it be granted to be absurd to urge men to do right when they are conceived to be totally unable to do right, it is equally so when they are conceived to have *only* a natural ability to do right; because this natural ability is of no avail without a corresponding moral ability. If the volition take place, there is, indeed, nothing to prevent the action; nay, 'the very willing is the doing of it': but then the volition, as an effect, cannot take place without a cause; and to acknowledge a moral inability is nothing less than to acknowledge that there is no cause to produce the required volition. The inability, under both representations, is a *total* inability. In the utter impossibility of a right volition is the utter impossibility of any good deed. When we have denied liberty in denying a self-determining power, these definitions, in order to make out a *quasi* liberty and ability, are nothing but ingenious folly and plausible deception.

"You tell the man, indeed, that *he can if he will;* and when he replies,

markable circumstance, that he attempted no reply to this tract of Clarke's, although he lived twelve years after its publication. The reasonings contained in it, together with those on the same subject in his correspondence with Leibnitz, and in his *Demonstration of the Being and Attributes of God*, form, in my humble opin-

---

that on your principles the required volition is impossible, you refer him to the common notions of mankind. According to these, you say, a man is guilty when he forbears to do right, since nothing is wanting to right-doing but a volition, and guilty when he does wrong, because he wills to do wrong. According to these common notions, too, a man may fairly be persuaded to do right, when nothing is wanting but a will to do right. But do we find *this distinction of natural and moral ability* in the common notions of men? When nothing is required to the performance of a deed but a volition, *do men conceive of any inability whatever?* Do they not feel that the volition has a metaphysical possibility, as well as that the sequent of the volition has a physical possibility?" — pp. 161 - 165.

We copy the following passage from Blakey's *History of the Philosophy of Mind*, Vol. IV. p. 515, as giving one of the latest European estimates of Dr. Edwards's merits as a philosopher: — "Dr. Edwards had a peculiarly constituted mind; — a mind capable of pursuing, with incomparable steadiness and clearness, the longest and most intricate chain of reasoning; but a mind, withal, by no means endowed with the loftiest powers of logical comprehension. He saw every link in a chain of reasoning with a microscopic eye, which, when its focal power was changed, made every thing at a distance appear hazy, clouded, and ill-defined. He could do one thing as no other man has ever been able to do it; he could reason from given or assumed premises with perspicuity, neatness, and power, and with an almost superhuman ease and correctness; but he could not embrace a philosophical system as a whole, and show its manifold bearings and relations to other branches of knowledge. He was an acute, but not a great, philosopher. His was a vivid and piercing light, but its illuminating rays, at a certain distance, became limited and scattered, and gave to all surrounding objects a disturbed and confused appearance. His ratiocination is so perfect of its kind, that it assumes the appearance of mechanism; and we feel a sort of secret dislike to have all the pegs and wires of an argument so minutely and obtrusively placed before us. Edwards has, in fact, been denominated a 'reasoning machine'; and the epithet is by no means misapplied or extravagant. But as a machine can only do its work *one way*, and we cannot humor it, or make its power more pliable, so in like manner do we find the intellectual mechanism of Edwards unyielding and unmanageable, except in its own peculiar fashion."

With an inconsistency by no means uncommon, Blakey, in his notice of Collins, quotes with approbation what Stewart says above of Collins as anticipating Edwards in every thing, and afterwards, in his notice of Edwards, says of the latter, that "he has stated and illustrated the principle of necessary connection in a manner altogether different from the way in which Collins, Priestley, Hume, and others have argued it."

See, also, an *Essay on the Genius and Writings of Edwards*, prefixed to the London edition of his works, 1834, by H. Rogers; and I. Taylor's Introduction to his edition of Edwards *On the Will*.]

ion, the most important, as well as powerful, of all his metaphysical arguments. The adversaries with whom he had to contend were both of them eminently distinguished by ingenuity and subtilty, and he seems to have put forth to the utmost his logical strength, in contending with such antagonists. "The liberty or moral agency of man," says his friend, Dr. Hoadly, "was a darling point to him. He excelled always, and showed a superiority to all, whenever it came into private discourse or public debate. But he never more excelled than when he was pressed with the strength Leibnitz was master of; which made him exert all his talents to set it once again in a clear light, to guard it against the evil of metaphysical obscurities, and to give the finishing stroke to a subject which must ever be the foundation of morality in man, and is the ground of the accountableness of intelligent creatures for all their actions."

To the arguments of Collins against man's free agency some of his followers have added the inconsistency of this doctrine with the known *effects of education* (under which phrase they comprehend also the moral effects of all the external circumstances in which men are involuntarily placed) in forming the characters of individuals.

The plausibility of this argument (on which so much stress has been laid by Priestley and others), arises entirely from the mixture of truth which it involves; or, to express myself more correctly, from the evidence and importance of *the fact* on which it proceeds, when that fact is stated with due limitations.

That the influence of *education*, in this comprehensive sense of the word, was greatly underrated by our ancestors is now universally acknowledged, and it is to Locke's writings, more than to any other single cause, that the change in public opinion on this head is to be ascribed. On various occasions he has expressed himself very strongly with respect to the *extent* of this influence, and has more than once intimated his belief, that the great majority of men continue through life what early education has made them. In making use, however, of this strong language, his object (as is evident from the opinions which he has avowed in other parts of his works) was only to arrest the attention of his readers to the practical lessons he was anxious to inculcate; and not to state a metaphysical *fact*, which was to be literally and rigorously interpreted in the controversy about liberty and necessity. The only sound and useful *moral* to be drawn from the *spirit* of his observation is the duty of gratitude to Heaven for all the blessings, in respect of education and of external situation, which have fallen to our own lot; the impossibility of ascertaining the involuntary misfortunes by which the seeming demerits of others may have been in part occasioned, and in the same proportion diminished; and the consequent obligation upon ourselves to think as charitably as possible of their conduct under the most unfavorable appearances. The truth of all this I conceive to be implied in these words of Scripture, — "To whom much is given, of them much will be required"; and, if possible, still more explicitly and impressively in the Parable of the Talents.

Is not the use which has been made by necessitarians of Locke's *Treatise on Education*, and other books of a similar tendency, only one instance more of that disposition, so common among metaphysical sciolists, to conceal from the world their incapacity to add to the stock of useful knowledge, by appropriating to themselves the conclusions of their wiser and more sober predecessors, under the startling and imposing disguise of universal maxims, admitting neither of exception nor restriction? It is thus that Locke's judicious and refined remarks on the association of ideas have been exaggerated to such an extreme by Hartley and Priestley, as to bring among cautious inquirers some degree of discredit on one of the most important doctrines of modern philosophy. Or, to take another case still more in point, it is thus that Locke's reflections on the effects of education in modifying the intellectual faculties, and (where skilfully conducted) in supplying their original defects, have been distorted into the puerile paradox of Helvetius, that the mental capacities of the whole human race are the same at the moment of birth. It is sufficient for me here to throw out these hints, which will be found to apply equally to a large proportion of other theories started by modern metaphysicians.

VI. *Ground taken by later Advocates of Necessity.*] It is needless to say, that neither Leibnitz nor Collins admitted the fairness of the inferences which Clarke conceived to follow from the scheme of necessity. But almost every page in the subsequent history of this controversy may be regarded as an additional illustration of the soundness of Clarke's reasonings, and of the sagacity with which he anticipated the fatal errors likely to ensue from the system which he opposed.

A very learned and pious disciple of Leibnitz, who made his first appearance as an author about thirty years after the death of his master, exclaims, — "Thus the same chain embraces the physical and moral worlds, binds the past to the present, the present to the future, the future to eternity.

"That wisdom which has ordained the existence of this chain has doubtless willed that of every link of which it is composed. A CALIGULA is one of those links, and this link is of iron. A MARCUS AURELIUS is another link, and this link is of gold. *Both* are necessary parts of one whole, which could not but exist. Shall God, then, be angry at the sight of the iron link? What absurdity! God esteems this link at its proper value: he sees it in its cause, and he approves this cause, for it is good. God beholds moral monsters as he beholds physical monsters. Happy is the link of gold! Still more happy if he know that he is *only fortunate*. [Heureux le chainon d'or! Plus *heureux* encore, s'il sait qu'il n'est qu'*heureux*.] He has attained the highest degree of moral perfection, and is nevertheless without pride, knowing that what he is is the necessary result of the place which he must occupy in the chain.

"The Gospel is the allegorical exposition of this system; the simile of the potter is its summary." *

In what essential respect does this system differ from that of Spinoza? Is it not even more dangerous in its practical tendency, in consequence of the high strain of mystical devotion by which it is exalted?

This objection, however, does not apply to the quotations which follow. They exhibit, without any coloring of imagination or of enthusiasm, the scheme of necessity pushed to the remotest and most alarming conclusions which it appeared to Clarke to involve; and, as they express the serious and avowed creed of two of our contemporaries (both of them men of distinguished talents), may be regarded as a proof that the zeal displayed by Clarke against the metaphysical principles which led ultimately to such results was not so unfounded as some worthy and able inquirers have supposed.

"All that is must be," says the Baron de Grimm, addressing himself to the Duke of Saxe Gotha, — "all that is must be, even because it is; this is the only sound philosophy; as long as we do not know this universe *a priori* (as they say in the schools), ALL IS NECESSITY. Liberty is a word without meaning, as you will see in the letter of M. Diderot."

The following passage is extracted from Diderot's letter here referred to.

"I am now, my dear friend, going to quit the tone of a preacher, to take, if I can, that of a philosopher. Examine it narrowly, and you will see that the word *liberty* is a word devoid of meaning; that there are not, and that there cannot be, free beings; that we are only what accords with the general order, with our organization, our education, and the chain of events. These dispose of us invincibly. We can no more conceive of a being acting without a motive, than we can of one of the arms of a balance acting without a weight. The motive is always exterior and foreign, fastened upon us

* Bonnet, *Principes Philosophiques*, Part VIII. Chap. VII.

by some cause distinct from ourselves. What deceives us is the prodigious variety of our actions, joined to the habit, which we catch at our birth, of confounding the *voluntary* and the *free.* We have been so often praised and blamed, and have so often praised and blamed others, that we contract an inveterate prejudice of believing that we and they *will and act freely.* But if there is no liberty, there is no action that merits either praise or blame; neither vice nor virtue; nothing that ought either to be rewarded or punished. What, then, is the distinction among men? The doing of good and the doing of ill! The doer of ill is one who must be destroyed or punished. The doer of good is lucky, not virtuous. But though neither the doer of good nor of ill be free, man is nevertheless a being to be modified; it is for this reason the doer of ill should be destroyed upon the scaffold. From thence the good effects of education, of pleasure, of grief, of grandeur, of poverty, &c.; from thence a philosophy full of pity, strongly attached to the good, nor more angry with the wicked than with the whirlwind which fills one's eyes with dust. Strictly speaking, there is but one sort of causes, that is, physical causes. *There is but one sort of necessity, which is the same for all beings.* This is what reconciles me to human kind; it is for this reason I exhort you to philanthropy. Adopt these principles if you think them good, or show me that they are bad. If you adopt them they will reconcile *you*, too, with others and with yourself; you will neither be pleased nor angry with yourself for being what you are. *Reproach others for nothing, and repent of nothing; this is the first step to wisdom.* Besides this, all is prejudice and false philosophy." *

Substantially the same doctrines have been recently introduced into this country, and I have no doubt with good intentions, by a very different class of philosophers, the greater part of whom have labored hard to

* *Correspondance Littéraire, Philosophique et Critique*, Tom. II. pp. 56, 60, *et seq.*

dispute the connection between the premises and some of the conclusions. Not so Mr. Belsham. "*Remorse*," says he, "is the exquisitely painful feeling which arises from the belief, that, in circumstances precisely the same, we might have chosen and acted differently. This *fallacious* feeling is superseded by the doctrine of necessity." And again, — "The doctrine of philosophical necessity supersedes *remorse*, so far as remorse is founded upon the belief, that, in the same previous circumstances, it was possible to have acted otherwise."

In another part of Mr. Belsham's work the following observation occurs: — "*Remorse* supposes free will. It arises from forgetfulness of the precise state of mind when the action was performed. It is of little or no use in moral discipline. In a degree it is even pernicious." As to our moral sentiments concerning the conduct and character of our fellow-creatures, Mr. Belsham is of opinion that the doctrine of necessity conciliates good-will to men. "By teaching us to look up to God *as the prime agent, and the proper cause of every thing that happens*, and to regard men as nothing more than instruments which he employs for accomplishing his good pleasure, it tends to suppress all resentment, malice, and revenge; while it induces us to regard our worst enemies with compassion rather than with hatred, and to return good for evil." *

From these extracts it appears that Mr. Belsham is not only himself convinced of the truth of the doctrine of necessity, considered as a philosophical dogma, but that he conceives it would be for the advantage of the world if all mankind were to become converts to his way of thinking. In this respect his system is certainly much more of a piece than that of Lord Kames, who, although he adopts zealously the doctrine of necessity, and represents the argument in support of it as

* *Elements of the Philosophy of the Mind*, pp. 284, 307, 316, 406. "The doctrine of necessity," says Dr. Hartley, "has a tendency to abate all resentment against men. Since all they do against us is by the appointment of God, it is rebellion against him to be offended with them." *Observations on Man*, Part I., Conclusion.

demonstrative, yet candidly acknowledges that our natural feelings are adverse to that doctrine; and even goes so far as to say, that, without such a feeling, the business of society could not be carried on. In this dilemma he attempts to reconcile the two opinions, by the supposition of *a deceitful sense of liberty.* We are so formed as to believe that we are free agents, when in truth we are mere machines, acting only so far as we are acted upon.

Perhaps no opinion on the subject of necessity was ever offered to the public which excited more general opposition than this hypothesis of a deceitful sense; and yet, if the argument for necessity be admitted, I do not see any other supposition which can possibly reconcile the conclusions of our reason with the feelings of which every man is conscious. Not that I would insinuate any apology for a doctrine, the absurdity of which is not only obvious, but ludicrous, inasmuch as it involves the supposition that the Deity *intended* that his creatures should believe themselves to be free agents; and that, while the great mass of mankind were thus deceived to their own advantage, a few minds of a superior order had the metaphysical sagacity *to detect the imposition.* Nor is this all. If the doctrine of necessity be just, it must one day or another become the universal and popular creed of mankind, as every doctrine which is true, and more especially every doctrine which is supported by demonstrative evidence, may be expected to become in the progress of human reason. What will *then* become of the great concerns of human life? Will man, as he improves in knowledge, be unfitted for the ends of his being, and exhibit an inconsistency between his reasoning faculties and his active principles, contrary to the invariable analogy of that systematical and harmonious design which is everywhere else so conspicuous in the works of nature? *

* This argument is very ably and forcibly stated in a small pamphlet on liberty and necessity, by the late learned and ingenious Mr. **Dawson,** of Sedbergh.

Lord Kames, who was a most sincere inquirer after truth, abandoned, in the last edition of his *Essays on Morality and Natural Religion*, the doctrine of a *deceitful sense of liberty;* and in so doing gave a rare example of candor and fairness as a reasoner. But I am very doubtful if the alterations which he made in his scheme did not impair the merits which in its original concoction it possessed in point of consistency. The first edition of this work appeared when the author was in the full vigor of his faculties; the last, when he was approaching to fourscore.*

* One of the ablest of the living asserters of necessity, John Stuart Mill, acknowledges, and endeavours to correct, the fatalistic implications and tendencies of that doctrine, as generally received. We will give his own words: —

"Though the doctrine of necessity, as stated by most who hold it, is very remote from fatalism, it is probable that most necessarians are fatalists, more or less, in their feelings. A fatalist believes, or half believes (for nobody is a consistent fatalist), not only that whatever is about to happen will be the infallible result of the causes which produce it (which is the true necessarian doctrine), but moreover that there is no use in struggling against it; that it will happen, however we may strive to prevent it. Now, a necessarian, believing that our actions follow from our characters, and that our characters follow from our organization, our education, and our circumstances, is apt to be, with more or less of consciousness on his part, a fatalist as to his own actions, and to believe that his nature is such, or that his education and circumstances have so moulded his character, that nothing can now prevent him from feeling and acting in a particular way, or at least that no effort of his own can hinder it. In the words of the sect [Robert Owen and his followers] which in our own day has so perseveringly inculcated, and so perversely misunderstood, this great doctrine, his character is formed *for* him, and not *by* him; therefore his wishing that it had been formed differently is of no use, — he has no power to alter it. But this is a grand error. He has, to a certain extent, a power to alter his character. Its being, in the ultimate resort, formed for him, is not inconsistent with its being, in part, formed *by* him as one of the intermediate agents His character is formed by his circumstances (including among these his particular organization); but his own desire to mould it in a particular way is one of those circumstances, and by no means one of the least influential. We cannot, indeed, directly will to be different from what we are. But did those who are supposed to have formed our characters directly will that we should be what we are? Their will had no direct power except over their own actions. They made us what they did make us, by willing, not the end, but the requisite means; and we, when our habits are not too inveterate, can, by similarly willing the requisite means, make ourselves different. If they could place us under the influence of certain circumstances, we, in like manner, can place ourselves under the influence of other circumstances. We are exactly

Section III.

IS THE EVIDENCE OF CONSCIOUSNESS IN FAVOR OF THE SCHEME OF FREE WILL, OR OF THAT OF NECESSITY?

I. *The Appeal to Consciousness.*] It has been lately said, by a very ingenious and acute writer, that, "in the

---

as capable of making our own character, *if we will,* as others are of making it for us.

"'Yes,' answers the Owenite, 'but these words, "if we will," surrender the whole point: since the will to alter our own character is given us, not by any efforts of ours, but by circumstances which we cannot help; it comes to us either from external causes, or not at all.' Most true: if the Owenite stops here, he is in a position from which nothing can expel him. Our character is formed by us, as well as for us; but the wish which induces us to attempt to form it is formed for us. And how? Not in general, by our organization or education, but by our experience, — experience of the painful consequences of the character we previously had; or by some strong feeling of admiration or aspiration, accidentally aroused. But to think that we *have* no power, and to think that we shall not *use* our power unless we have a motive, are very different things, and have a very different effect upon the mind. A person who does not wish to alter his character cannot be the person who is supposed to feel discouraged or paralyzed by thinking himself unable to do it. The depressing effect of the fatalist doctrine can only be felt where there *is* a wish to do what that doctrine represents as impossible. It is of no consequence what we think forms our character when we have no desire of our own about forming it; but it is of great consequence that we should not be prevented from forming such a desire by thinking the attainment impracticable, and that, if we have the desire, we should know that the work is not so irrevocably done as to be incapable of being altered. . . . . .

"The subject will never be generally understood, until that objectionable term [necessity] is dropped. The free-will doctrine, by keeping in view precisely that portion of the truth which the word *necessity* puts out of sight, — namely, the power of the mind to coöperate in the formation of its own character, — has given to its adherents a practical feeling much nearer to the truth than has generally, I believe, existed in the minds of necessarians. The latter may have had a stronger sense of the importance of what human beings can do to shape the characters of one another; but the free-will doctrine has, I believe, fostered, especially in the younger of its supporters, a much stronger spirit of self-culture." — *System of Logic,* Book VI. Chap. II. § 3.

The concessions contained in the last paragraph, considered as coming from a thorough-going necessitarian, are important. The modification in the understanding of the doctrine here proposed removes some of the purely psychological objections to it, but does not touch the moral objections. The doctrine is still as irreconcilable as ever with any intelligible acceptation of human accountability, or the moral government of God. And besides, when Mr. Mill asserts that "the feeling of moral freedom

controversy concerning liberty and necessity, the *only* question at issue between the disputants related to *a matter of fact*, on which they both appealed to the evidence of consciousness; namely, whether, all previous circumstances being the same, the choice of man be not also at all times the same." *

If the author of this observation had contented himself with saying that this question concerning *the matter of fact*, as ascertained by the evidence of consciousness, *ought* to have been considered as the *only* point at issue between the contending parties, I should most readily have subscribed to his proposition. Indeed, I have expressed myself very nearly to the same purpose in a former work.† But if it is to be understood as an historical statement of the manner in which the controversy has always, or even most frequently, been carried on, I must beg leave to dissent from it very widely. How many arguments against the freedom of the will have been in all ages drawn from the *prescience* of the Deity! How many still continue to be drawn by very eminent divines from the doctrines of predestination and of eternal decrees! Has not Mr. Locke himself acknowledged the impression which the former of these considerations made on his mind? "I own," says he, "freely to you the weakness of my understanding; that though it be unquestionable that there is omnipotence and omniscience in God our Maker, and though *I cannot have a clearer perception of any thing than that I am free*, yet I cannot make freedom in man consistent with omnipotence and omniscience in God, though I am as fully persuaded of both as of any truth I most firmly assent to; and therefore I have long since given off the consideration of that question, resolving all into this

---

which we are conscious of" is nothing but a "feeling of our being able to modify our own character *if we wish*," he asserts what the advocates of free will will not admit to be true. If what we do depends on our wishing to do it, and our wishing to do it does not depend on ourselves, then nothing depends on ourselves, — except to be the willing and active instruments of destiny. — Ed.

* *Edinburgh Review*, Vol. XXVII. p. 226. [By Sir James Mackintosh.]

† *Philosophy of the Human Mind*, Part II. Chap. I. Sect. II.

short conclusion, that if it be possible for God to make a free agent, then man is free, though I see not the way of it."

A still more recent exception to the general assertion, which has given occasion to this section, occurs in Lord Kames's hypothesis of a deceitful sense of liberty, noticed above, as maintained in the first edition of his *Essays on Morality and Natural Religion.* Here, upon the faith of some subtile metaphysical reasonings, the very ingenious author adopts the scheme of necessity in direct opposition to the evidence which he candidly confesses that consciousness affords of our free agency. Even the latest advocates for necessity, Priestley and Belsham, as well as their predecessor, Collins himself, while they appealed (in the very words of the learned critic) to the evidence of consciousness in proof of the fact, *that, all previous circumstances being the same, the choice of man is also at all times the same*; yet thought it worth their while to strengthen this conclusion by calling to their aid the theological doctrines already mentioned. I cannot, therefore, see with what color of plausibility it can be said that "this matter of fact has been the *only* question at issue between the disputants."

It may, however, be regarded as one great step gained in this controversy, if it may henceforth be assumed as a principle agreed on by both parties, that this is the *only* question which can be philosophically stated on the subject, and that all arguments drawn from the attributes of the Deity are entirely foreign to the discussion. I shall accordingly devote this section to an examination of *the fact*, agreeably to the representation of it given by our modern necessitarians.

In what I have hitherto said upon the subject, I have proceeded on the supposition, that the doctrine of free will is consistent with the common feelings and belief of mankind. That "all our actions do now, in experience, *seem* to us to be *free*, exactly in the same manner as they would do upon the supposition of our being really free agents," is remarked by Clarke in his reply to Collins. "And consequently," he adds, "though this alone does not amount to a strict demonstration of our being free, yet it leaves on the other side of the question nothing but a *bare possibility* of our being so framed by the Author of nature, as to be unavoidably deceived in this matter by every experience and every action we perform. The case is exactly the same," continues Dr. Clarke, "as in that notable question, *whether the world exists or no.* There is no demonstration of it from experience. There always remains *a bare possibility* that the Supreme Being may have so framed my mind as that I shall always necessarily be deceived in every one of my perceptions, as in a dream, though possibly there be *no material world*, nor any other creature whatsoever existing besides myself. Of this, I say, there always remains *a bare possibility*, and yet no man in his senses argues from thence that experience is no proof to us of *the existence of things.*" *

---

* *Remarks*, p. 19.

Cousin maintains liberty on the authority of consciousness. A free action is defined by him to be one "performed with the consciousness of power not to do it." He then proceeds to analyze a free action in order to ascertain precisely in what part it is free. According to him, the total action is resolvable into three elements, perfectly distinct: — "1. The *intellectual* element, which is composed of the knowledge of the motives for and against, of deliberation, of preference, of choice. 2. The *voluntary* element, which consists in an internal act, namely, the resolution, the determination to do it. 3. The *physical* element, or external action.

"The question now to be decided is, precisely in which of these three elements liberty is to be found, — that is, the power of doing with the consciousness of being able not to do. Does this power of doing, while conscious of the power not to do, belong to the *first* element, the intellectual element of the free action? It does not; for it is not at the will of a man to judge that such or such a motive is preferable to another; we are not master of our preferences; we judge in this respect according to our intellectual nature, which has its necessary laws, without having the consciousness of being able to judge otherwise, and even with the consciousness of not being able to judge otherwise, than we do. It is not, then, in this element that we are to look for liberty. Still less is it in the *third* element, in the physical action; for this action supposes an external world, an organization corresponding to it, and, in this organization, a muscular system sound and suitable, without which the physical action would be impossible. When we accomplish it, we are conscious of acting, but under the condition of a theatre of which we have not the disposal, and of instruments of which we have but an imperfect disposal, which we can neither replace if they escape us, — and they may do so every moment, — nor repair if they are out of order or unfaithful, as is often the case, and which are subject to laws peculiar to themselves, over which we have no power, and which we

II. *Consciousness vainly denied to be in Favor of Liberty.*] But this appeal to *consciousness* in proof of free agency proceeds altogether (according to some late writers) on a partial and superficial view of the subject; the evidence of *consciousness*, when all circumstances are taken into the account and duly weighed, being decidedly in favor of the scheme of necessity.

Dr. Hartley was, I believe, one of the first (if not the first) who denied that our consciousness is in favor of our free agency. "It is true," he observes, "that a man by internal feeling may prove his own free will, if by free will be meant the power of doing what a man wills or desires; or of resisting the motives of sensuality, ambition, &c., that is, free will in the popular and practical sense. Every person may easily recollect instances where he has done these several things, but these are entirely foreign to the present question. To prove that a man has free will in the sense opposite to mechanism, he ought to feel that he can do different things while the motives remain precisely the same. And here, I apprehend, the internal feelings are entirely against free will, where the motives are of a

---

scarcely even know. Whence it follows, that we do not act here with the consciousness of being able to do the contrary of what we do. Liberty, then, is no more to be found in the *third* than in the *first* element. It can then only be in the *second;* and there in fact we find it.

"Neglect the first and third elements, the judgment and the physical action, and let the second element, *the willing*, subsist by itself; analysis discovers in this single element two terms, namely, *a special act* of willing, and *the power* of willing, which is within us, and to which we refer the special act. That act is an effect in relation to the power of willing, which is its cause; and this cause, in order to producé its effect, has need of no other theatre, and no other instrument, than itself. It produces it directly, without any thing intermediate, and without condition; continues and consummates, or suspends and modifies; creates it, or annihilates it entirely; and at the moment it exerts itself in any special act, we are conscious that it might exert itself in a special act totally contrary, without any obstacle, without being thereby exhausted: so that, after having changed its acts a hundred times, the faculty remains integrally the same, inexhaustible and identical, amidst the perpetual variety of its applications, being always able to do what it does not do, and able not to do what it does. Here, then, in all its plentitude, is the characteristic of liberty." — Professor Henry's translation, *Elements of Psychology*, Chap. X. p. 319. See, also, Tappan's *Doctrine of the Will determined by an Appeal to Consciousness.* — ED.

sufficient magnitude to be evident: where they are not nothing can be proved." *

Mr. Belsham has enlarged still more fully on this subject. "When men," says he, "who have been guilty of a crime review the action in calmer moments, when the strength of passion has subsided, and the contrary motives appear in all their force, and perhaps magnified by the evil consequences of their vice and folly, they are ready to think that they might at the time have thought and acted as they now think and act; but this is a fallacious feeling, and arises from their not placing themselves in circumstances exactly similar." We are elsewhere told by Mr. Belsham, "that the popular opinion, that in many cases it was in the power of the agent to have chosen differently, the previous circumstances remaining exactly the same, arises either from a mistake of the question, from a *forgetfulness of the motives by which our choice was determined*, or from the extreme difficulty of placing ourselves in imagination in circumstances exactly similar to those in which the election was made." And still more explicitly and concisely in the following aphorism:— "The pretended consciousness of free will amounts to nothing more than forgetfulness of the motive." † To the same purpose Dr. Priestley has expressed himself. "A man, when he reproaches himself for any *particular action* in his past conduct, may fancy that, if he was in the same situation again, he would have acted differently. But this is a mere *deception;* and if he examines himself *strictly*, and takes in all circumstances, he may be satisfied that, with the *same inward disposition of mind*, and with precisely the *same views of things* that he had then, and exclusive of all others that he has acquired by reflection *since*, he could not have acted otherwise than he did." ‡

* *Observations on Man*, Part I., Conclusion.

† *Elements*, pp. 278, 279, 306.

‡ *Illustrations of Philosophical Necessity*, p. 99.

The very same view of the subject has been lately taken by Laplace, in his *Essai Philosophique sur les Probabilités.* "L'axiome connu sous le

If these statements be accurately examined, they will be found to resolve entirely into this identical proposition, that the *will* of the criminal, being supposed to remain in the same state as when the crime was committed, he could not have *willed* and acted otherwise. This proposition, it is obvious, does not at all touch the cardinal point in question, which is simply this: whether, all *other* circumstances remaining the same, the criminal had it not in his power to abstain from *willing* the commission of the crime. The vagueness of Priestley's language upon this occasion must not be overlooked; the words *inward disposition of mind* admitting of a variety of different meanings, and in this instance being plainly intended to include the act of the will, as well as every thing else connected with the criminal action.

In the preceding strictures, I have been partly anticipated by the following very acute remarks of Dr. Magee on the definitions of *volition* and of *philosophical liberty*, prefixed to Mr. Belsham's discussion of the doctrines now under our consideration. According to Mr. Belsham, "Volition is that state of mind which is immediately *previous* to actions which are called voluntary." "*Natural liberty*, or, as it is more properly called, *philosophical liberty*, or *liberty of choice*, is the power of doing an action or its contrary, *all the previous circumstances remaining the same*."* — "Now here," says Dr. Magee, "is the point of free will at once decided; for *volition* itself being included among the *previous circumstances*, it is a manifest contradiction to suppose the 'power of doing an action or its contrary, all the

---

nom de *principe de la raison suffisante* s'étend aux actions même que l'on juge indifférentes. La volonté la plus libre ne peut sans un motif déterminant leur donner naissance; car si, toutes les circonstances de deux positions étant exactement semblables, elle agissait dans l'une et s'abstenait d'agir dans l'autre, son choix serait un effet sans cause: elle serait alors, dit Leibnitz, le hasard aveugle des épicuriens. L'opinion contraire est une illusion de l'esprit qui perdant de vue les raisons fugitives du choix de la volonté dans les choses indifférentes, se persuade qu'elle s'est déterminée d'elle-même et sans motifs." — Under the head, *De la Probabilité*.

* *Elements*, p. 227.

previous circumstances remaining the same'; since that supposes the power to act *voluntarily against a volition.* After this," Dr. Magee justly and pertinently adds, "Mr. Belsham might surely have spared himself the trouble of the ninety-two pages which follow." *

And why have recourse, with Belsham and Priestley, in this argument, to the indistinct and imperfect recollection of the criminal at a *subsequent* period, with respect to the state of his feelings while he was perpetrating the crime? Why not make a direct appeal to his consciousness at the very moment when he was doing the deed? Will any person of candor deny, that, in the very act of transgressing an acknowledged duty, he is impressed with a conviction, as complete as that of his own existence, that his will is free, and that he is abusing, contrary to the suggestions of reason and conscience, his moral liberty? †

Sometimes, indeed, when we are under the influence of a violent appetite or passion, our judgment is apt to see things in a false light; and hence a wise man learns to distrust his own opinion when he is thus circumstanced, and to act, not according to his present judgment, but according to those general maxims of propriety of which his reason had previously approved in his cooler hours. All this, however, evidently proceeds on the supposition of his *free agency;* and, so far from implying any belief on *his* part of fatalism or of moral necessity, evinces in a manner peculiarly striking and satisfactory, the power which he feels himself to possess, not only over the *present*, but over the *future* determinations of his will. In some *other* instances, it happens that I believe *bonâ fide* an action to be right, at the moment I perform it, and afterwards discover that I judged improperly; — perhaps from want of sufficient information, or from a careless and partial view

* *Discourses and Dissertations on the Scriptural Doctrines of Atonement and Sacrifice*, Appendix, Vol. II. p. 180, note.

† "The free will of man," says Bolingbroke, "which no one can deny that he has, without *lying*, or renouncing his intuitive knowledge." — *Fragments*, No. XLII.

of the subject. In such a case, I may undoubtedly regret as a misfortune what has happened. I may blame myself for my carelessness in not having acquired the proper information before I acted; but I cannot consider myself as criminal in acting at that moment according to the views which I then entertained. On the contrary, if I had acted in opposition to these views, although my conduct might have been agreeable to the dictates of a more enlightened understanding than my own, yet, with respect to myself, the action would have been wrong.

If the doctrine of necessity were just, what possible foundation could there be for the distinction we always make between an accidental hurt and an intended *injury*, when received from another? or for the different sentiments of *regret* and of *remorse* that we experience, according as the misfortunes we suffer are the consequences of our own misconduct or not? What an alleviation of our sufferings when we are satisfied that we cannot consider ourselves as the authors of them! and what a cruel aggravation of our miseries, when we can trace them to something in which we have been obviously to blame! *

* Sir W. Hamilton accepts the fact of moral liberty on the evidence of consciousness; still he finds insuperable difficulties in *conceiving* of its possibility. In a note on Dr. Reid's definition of the liberty of a moral agent, he says: — "Moral liberty does not merely consist in the power of *doing what we will*, but in the power of *willing what we will*. For a power over the determinations of our will supposes an act of will that our will should determine so and so; for we can only freely exert power through a rational determination or volition. But then question upon question remains, and this *ad infinitum*. Have we a power (a will) over such anterior will? and until this question be definitively answered, which it never can be, we must be *unable to conceive the possibility of the fact of liberty*. But, though inconceivable, this fact is not therefore *false*. For there are many contradictories (and of contradictories, *one must*, and *one only can*, be true), of which we are equally unable to conceive the possibility of either. The philosophy, therefore, which I profess, annihilates the theoretical problem, — How is the scheme of liberty, or the scheme of necessity, to be rendered comprehensible? — by showing that both schemes are equally inconceivable; but it establishes liberty practically as a fact, by showing that it is either itself an immediate *datum*, or is involved in an immediate *datum* of consciousness.

Again he says: — "To conceive a *free act* is to conceive an act which, being a *cause*, is not in itself an *effect*; in other words, to conceive an ab-

Section IV.

OF THE SCHEMES OF FREE WILL, AND OF NECESSITY, CONSIDERED AS INFLUENCING PRACTICE.

I. *Tendency of the Scheme of Necessity to Pantheism and Atheism.*] Collins, in his inquiry concerning hu-

solute commencement. But is such by us conceivable?" According to him, in order to be a free agent it is not enough that a person is the cause of the determination of his own will; he must not be "determined to that determination." "But is the person," he asks, "an *original undetermined* cause of the determination of his will? If he be not, then he is not a *free* agent, and the scheme of necessity is admitted. If he be, in the first place, it is impossible to *conceive* the possibility of this; and, in the second, if the fact, though inconceivable, be allowed, it is impossible to see how a *cause undetermined by any motive* can be a *rational*, *moral*, *and accountable cause*. There is no conceivable medium between *fatalism* and *casuism*; and the contradictory schemes of liberty and necessity themselves are inconceivable. For as we cannot compass in thought an *undetermined cause*, — *an absolute commencement*, — the fundamental hypothesis of the one; so we can as little think *an infinite series of determined causes*, — *of relative commencements*, — the fundamental hypothesis of the other. The champions of the opposite doctrines are thus at once resistless in assault, and impotent in defence. Each is hewn down, and appears to die under the home-thrusts of his adversary; but each again recovers life from the very death of his antagonist, and, to borrow a simile, both are like the heroes in Valhalla, ready in a moment to amuse themselves anew in the bloodless and interminable conflict.

"The doctrine of moral liberty cannot be made conceivable, for we can only conceive the determined and the relative. As already stated, all that can be done is to show, — 1st. That, for the *fact* of liberty, we have, immediately or mediately, the evidence of consciousness; and, 2d. That there are, among the phenomena of mind, many facts which we *must* admit as actual, but of whose possibility we are wholly unable to form a notion. I may merely observe, that the fact of *motion* can be shown to be impossible, on grounds not less strong than those on which it is attempted to disprove the fact of *liberty*; to say nothing of many contradictories, neither of which can be *thought*, but one of which must, on the laws of contradiction and excluded middle, necessarily *be*. This philosophy — the *Philosophy of the Conditioned* — has not, however, either in itself, or in relation to its consequences, as yet been developed." — Hamilton's edition of Reid's Works, *Essays on the Active Powers*, Essay IV. Chap. I.

Kant comes to substantially the same conclusions. In his *Critic of Pure Reason*, under the head of "the antinomy of pure reason" in his "Transcendental Dialectic," he treats of liberty and necessity as constituting one of the "contradictions of transcendental ideas," both the "thesis" and the "antithesis" being demonstrable. Afterwards, in his *Critic of Practical Reason*, he maintains the *fact* of liberty as a corollary of the *fact* of moral obligation. — Ed.

man liberty, after endeavouring to show that "*liberty* can only be grounded on the 'absurd principles of Epicurean atheism,'" observes, that "the Epicurean atheists, who were the most popular and most numerous sect of the atheists of antiquity, were the great asserters of liberty;* as, on the other side, the Stoics, who were the most popular and numerous sect among the religionists of antiquity, were the great asserters of *fate* and *necessity*. The case was also the same among the Jews as among the heathens.† The Sadducees, who were esteemed an irreligious and atheistical sect, maintained the liberty of man. But the Pharisees, who were a religious sect, ascribed all things to fate or to God's appointment; and it was the first article of their creed, that *Fate and God do all;* and consequently, they could not assert a *true liberty*, when they asserted a *liberty* together with this fatality and necessity of all things." ‡

---

* In proof of this assertion, that the ancient Epicureans were advocates for man's free agency, Collins refers to Lucretius, Lib. II. v. 251 *et seq*. But it is to be observed that the liberty here ascribed to the will is nothing more than the *liberty of spontaneity*, which is conceded to it by Collins, and indeed by all necessitarians, without exception, since the time of Hobbes. Lucretius, indeed, speaks of this liberty as an exception to universal fatalism; but he nevertheless considers it as a *necessary effect of some cause*, to which he gives the name of *clinamen*, so as to render man as completely a piece of passive mechanism as he was supposed to be by Collins and Hobbes. The reason, too, which he gives for this is, that, if the case were otherwise, *there would be an effect without a cause*. — Ibid., v. 284.

† With respect to the opinions of the Sadducees and the Pharisees on man's free agency, see Cudworth's *Intellectual System*, with Mosheim's Notes and Dissertations, translated by Harrison, Book I Chap. I. § 4. According to Josephus, the Pharisees held "that some things, and not all, were the effects of fate, but some things were left in man's own power and liberty." — *Antiq. Jud.*, Lib. XIII. Cap. V. Sect. 9.

‡ In this passage, as in others, Collins plainly proceeds on the supposition, that all fatalists are of course necessitarians; and I agree with him in thinking, that this would be the case if they reasoned consequentially. It is certain, however, that a great proportion of those who have belonged to the first sect have disclaimed all connection with the second. The Stoics themselves, notwithstanding what is said above, furnish one very remarkable instance. I do not know any author by whom the liberty of the will is stated in stronger and more explicit terms than it is by Epictetus, in the first sentence of the *Enchiridion*. Indeed, the Stoics seem, with their usual passion for exaggeration, to have carried their ideas about the freedom of the will to an unphilosophical extreme.

To the same purpose Edwards attempts to show (and it is one of the weakest parts of his book) that the scheme of free will (by affording an exception to that dictate of common sense which leads us to refer every event to a cause) would destroy the proof *a posteriori* for the being of God. One thing is certain, that the two schemes of atheism and of necessity have been hitherto always connected together in the history of *modern* philosophy: not that I would, by any means, be understood to say, that every necessitarian must *ipso facto* be an atheist, or even that any presumption is afforded, by a man's attachment to the former sect, of his having the slightest bias in favor of the latter, but only that *every* modern atheist I have ever heard of has been a necessitarian. I cannot help adding, that by far the ablest necessitarians who have yet appeared have been those who followed out their principles till they ended in Spinozism; a doctrine which differs from atheism more in words than in reality.*

---

* "The following is Cousin's view of Spinoza's system. It apparently differs from what is said above, but really tends to the same conclusions. 'Instead of accusing Spinoza of atheism, he ought to be reproached for an error in the other direction. Spinoza starts from the *perfect and infinite being* of Descartes's system, and easily demonstrates that such a being is alone *being in itself*, but that a being finite, imperfect, and relative only participates of being, without possessing it in itself; — that being in itself is necessarily *one*; — that there is but *one substance*; — and that all that remains has only a *phenomenal* existence; — that to call phenomena finite *substances* is affirming and denying at the same time; for as there is but one substance which possesses being in itself, and the finite is that which participates of existence without possessing it in itself, a *substance finite* implies two contradictory notions. Thus, in the philosophy of Spinoza, *man* and *nature* are pure *phenomena*, *simple attributes* of that *one and absolute substance*, but attributes which are coeternal with their substance: for as phenomena cannot exist without a subject, the imperfect without the perfect, the finite without the infinite, and man and nature suppose God; so, likewise, the substance cannot exist without phenomena, the perfect without the imperfect, the infinite without the finite, and God on his part supposes man and nature. The error of his system lies in the predominance of the relation of phenomenon to being, of *attribute to substance*, over the relation of *effect to cause*. When man has been represented, not as a cause voluntary and free, but as necessary and uncontrollable desire, and as an imperfect and finite thought, God, or the supreme pattern of humanity, can be only a *substance*, and not a *cause*, — a being perfect, infinite, necessary, — the immutable *substance of the universe*, and *not its producing and creating cause*. In Cartesianism, the notion of substance figures more

II. *Moral and Political Tendencies of the Scheme of Necessity.*] In Bernier's *Abrégé de la Philosophie de Gassendi*, there are some very judicious observations on the practical tendency of the scheme of necessity; — a subject on which his opinion is entitled to great weight, not only from his long residence among the followers of Mahomet, but from those prepossessions in favor of this scheme which he may be presumed to have imbibed from his education under Gassendi. I shall quote a few of his concluding reflections.

---

conspicuously than that of cause; and this notion of substance, become altogether predominant, constitutes Spinozism.' — *Histoire de la Philosophie du XVIIIe Siècle*, Tome I. p. 465.

"The preponderance of the notion of substance and attribute over that of cause and effect, which Cousin here pronounces the vice of Spinoza's system, is indeed the vice of every system which contains the dogma of the necessary determination of will. The first consequence is pantheism; the second, atheism. I will endeavour to explain. When self-determination is denied to will, and it is resolved into mere desire, necessitated in all its acts from its preconstituted correlation with objects, then *will* really ceases to be *a cause*. It becomes an instrument of antecedent power, but is no power in itself, creative or productive. The reasoning employed in reference to the human will applies in all its force to the Divine will, as has been already abundantly shown. The Divine will therefore ceases to be a cause, and becomes a mere instrument of antecedent power. This antecedent power is the *infinite and necessary wisdom:* but infinite and necessary wisdom is eternal and unchangeable; what it is now, it always was; what tendencies or energies it has now, it always had; and therefore, whatever volitions it now necessarily produces, it always necessarily produced. If we conceive a volition to have been, in one direction, the immediate and necessary antecedent of creation; and, in another, the immediate and necessary sequent of infinite and eternal wisdom; then this volition *must have always existed*, and consequently *creation*, as the necessary effect of this volition, *must have always existed.* The eternal and infinite wisdom thus becomes *the substance*, because this is *existence in itself*, no antecedent being conceivable; and creation, that is to say, *man and nature*, imperfect and finite, participating only of existence, and not being existence in themselves, are *not* substances, but *phenomena*. But what is the relation of the phenomena to the substance? Not that of effect to cause; — this relation slides entirely out of view, the moment *will ceases to be a cause.* It is the relation simply of phenomena to being, considered as the necessary and inseparable manifestations of being; the relation of attributes to substance, considered as the necessary and inseparable properties of substance. We cannot conceive of substance without attributes or phenomena, nor of attributes or phenomena without substance: they are, therefore, coeternal in this relation. *Who*, then, is God? *Substance and its attributes; being and its phenomena.* In other words, the universe, as made up of substance and attributes, *is God.* This is pantheism; and it is the first and legitimate consequence of a necessitated will.

"De tout ceci jugez si j'ai sujet de croire cette doctrine si pernicieuse à la société humaine. Certainement à considerer que ce sont principalement les Mahométans qui s'en trouvent infectées, et que c'est principalement encore parmi elles presentement qu'elle est fomentée et entretenue, je douterois presque que ce fut l'invention de quelques uns de ces tyrans d'Asie, comme auroit peut-être un Mahomet, un Tamerlane, un Bajazet, ou quelqu'un de ces autres fléaux du monde qui pour assouvir leur ambition demandoit des soldats qui

"The second consequence is atheism. In the denial of will as a cause *per se*, — in resolving all its volitions into the necessary phenomena of the eternal substance, — we destroy *personality*: we have nothing remaining *but the universe*. Now we may call the universe *God*: but with equal propriety we call God *the universe*. This distinction of personality, this merging of God into necessary substance and attributes, is all that we mean by atheism. The conception is really the same, whether we name it *fate*, *pantheism*, or *atheism*.

"The arguments of many atheists might be referred to, to illustrate the connection between necessity and atheism. I shall here refer, however, to only one individual, remarkable both for his poetic genius and metaphysical acumen. I mean the late Percy Bysshe Shelley. He openly and unblushingly professed atheism. In his *Queen Mab* we find this line: 'There is no God.' In a note upon this line, he remarks, — 'This negation must be understood solely to affect a *creative* Deity. The hypothesis of a pervading spirit, *coeternal with the universe*, remains unshaken.' This last hypothesis is pantheism. Pantheism is really the negation of a creative Deity, — the identity, or at least necessary and eternal coexistence, of God and the universe. Shelley has expressed this clearly in another passage: —

> 'Spirit of nature! all-sufficing power,
> *Necessity! thou mother of the world!*'

"In a note upon this passage, Shelley has argued the doctrine of the necessary determination of will by motive with an acuteness and power scarcely inferior to Collins or Edwards. He makes, indeed, a different application of the doctrine, but a perfectly legitimate one. Collins and Edwards, and the whole race of necessitarian theologians, evidently toil under insurmountable difficulties, while attempting to base religion upon this doctrine, and effect their escape only under a fog of subtilties. But Shelley, in daring to be perfectly consistent, is perfectly clear. He fearlessly proceeds from necessity to pantheism, and thence to atheism and the destruction of all moral distinctions. 'We are taught,' he remarks, 'by the doctrine of necessity, that there is neither good nor evil in the universe, otherwise than as the events to which we apply these epithets have relation to our own peculiar mode of being. Still less than with the hypothesis of a God, will the doctrine of necessity accord with the belief of a future state of punishment.'" — Tappan's *Review of Edwards*, pp. 139, 145. For an exposition of Spinoza's theory, see Jouffroy's *Introduction to Ethics*, Lect. VI. and VII. — ED.

étant entêtés de predestination, s'abandonassent brutalement à tout, et se precipitassent même volontiers, aux occasions, la tête la première dans le fossé d'une ville assiégée pour servir du pont au reste de l'armée. Je sçais bien qu'on pourroit peut-être dire que cette opinion est mal prise et mal entendue par les Mahométans; mais quoi qu'il en soit, que doit on raisonablement penser d'une doctrine qui peut si aisément être mal-prise et qui peut, soit par erreur ou autrement, avoir si étranges suites?" *

The scheme of free will is not liable to any such objection, inasmuch as it seems quite impossible for the most ingenious sophistry to pervert it to any pernicious purpose. Indeed, its great object is to reconcile with the conclusions of our reason those moral feelings which are so essential, both to our own happiness and to the interests of society, that they have been regarded by some of the most acute as well as candid partisans of necessity as merciful illusions of the imagination, by which man is blinded to the melancholy fact of his real condition: "*Nervis alienis mobile lignum!*"

There is good reason to believe that the practical consequences produced by the scheme of necessity at the time of the Reformation alarmed the minds of some very able men by whom it was at first adopted.

---

* Tome VIII. p. 536 *et seq.* "Judge from what has been said whether I have not reason to think this doctrine pernicious to society. Indeed, when I consider that it is principally the Mahometans who are infected with it, that it is principally by them that it is still fomented and kept up, I almost suspect it to have been the invention of one of those Asiatic despots, of a Mahomet, a Tamerlane, a Bajazet, or some other scourge of the world, who, in order to glut his ambition, required soldiers besotted by a belief in predestination, and therefore ready to abandon themselves brutally to every thing, — to precipitate themselves headlong, if necessary, into the trenches of a besieged city to serve as a bridge for the rest of the army. Many will say, I am aware, that this doctrine is mistaken and misunderstood by the Mahometans; but, however this may be, what opinion can we reasonably entertain of a tenet which is so liable to be misapprehended, and is followed, either through mistake or otherwise, by such strange consequences?"

For a less unfavorable view of the practical tendency of a belief in necessity, see an article by Sir James Mackintosh, in the *Edinburgh Review*, Vol. XXVII. p. 180. — Ed.

"The Germans," says Dr. Burnet, "saw the ill effects of the doctrine of decrees. Luther changed his mind about it, and Melancthon wrote openly against it; and since that time the whole stream of the Lutheran churches has run the other way. But still Calvin and Bucer were both for maintaining the doctrine; only they warned the people not to think much about them, since they were secrets that men could not penetrate into. Hooper and many other good writers did often exhort the people from entering into these curiosities; and a *caveat* to the same purpose was put into the article about predestination." *

"Concerning the disputants themselves," says Dr. Jortin, "we may safely affirm, that the defenders of the liberty of man, and of the conditional decrees of God, have been, *beyond all comparison*, the more learned, judicious, and *moderate* men; and that severity and oppression have appeared most on the other side." †

Priestley has somewhere very justly remarked, that there are some men so happily born that no speculative theories are likely to mislead them from their duty; and of the truth of his observation I sincerely believe that his own private life afforded a very striking example. Little stress, therefore, is to be laid on *individual cases* as arguments for or against the practical tendency of any philosophical dogma. The case, however, is very different with respect to observations made on so great a scale as those above quoted from Bernier and Burnet. Let me add, that the practical influence of the scheme of necessity ought not to be judged of from the lives of its speculative partisans, but from those of persons who have been educated from their early years in the belief of it. In this point of view, it might be interesting to trace the history of the immediate descendants of some of the most zealous advocates for necessity. If the principles which they have advanced be just, particularly those they have laid

---

* *Burnet on the Reformation*, Part II. p. 113.

† *Six Dissertations*, Diss. I. p. 4.

down on the influence of education, the moral characters of their pupils should, or rather *must*, be exemplary in no common degree.

Section V.

ON THE ARGUMENT FOR NECESSITY DRAWN FROM THE PRESCIENCE OF THE DEITY.

I. *The Argument stated and answered.*] In reviewing the arguments that have been advanced on the opposite sides of this question, I have hitherto taken no notice of those which the necessitarians have founded on the *prescience of the Deity*, because I do not think them fairly applicable to the subject; inasmuch as they draw an inference from what is altogether placed beyond the reach of our faculties, against a fact for which every man has the evidence of his own consciousness. Some of the advocates, however, for liberty have ventured to meet their adversaries even on this ground; in particular, Dr. Clarke, in his *Demonstration of the Being and Attributes of God*, and Dr. Reid, in his *Essays on the Active Powers of Man.* Both of these writers have attempted to show, with much ingenuity and subtilty of reasoning, that, even although we should admit the prescience of God in the fullest extent in which it has ever been ascribed to him, it does not lead to any conclusion inconsistent with man's free agency. On their speculations on this point I have no commentary to offer.

The argument for necessity, drawn from the Divine prescience, is much insisted on both by Collins and Edwards; more especially by the latter, who, after insisting at great length on "God's certain foreknowledge of the volitions of moral agents," undertakes to show that "this *foreknowledge* infers a necessity of volition as much as an absolute decree."

Mr. Belsham, on this as on other occasions, rises above his predecessors in the boldness of his assertions. "The principal argument in favor of moral necessity and the insurmountable objection against the existence of philosophical liberty in any degree, or under any restrictions whatever, arises from the prescience of God. Liberty and prescience stand in direct hostility to each other. A philosopher, to be consistent, must give up one or the other." "Upon the whole, the advocates for philosophical liberty are reduced to the dilemma, either of denying the foreknowledge of God, *and thus robbing the Deity of one of his most glorious attributes*, or of admitting that God is the author of evil, in the same sense, and in the same degrees, in which this doctrine is charged upon the necessarians." *

On this argument I shall make but one remark, that, if it be conclusive, it only serves to identify still more the creed of the necessitarians with that of Spinoza. For if God certainly foresees all the future volitions of his creatures, he must, for the same reason, foresee all *his own* future volitions; and if this foreknowledge infers *a necessity* of volition in the one case, how is it possible to avoid the same inference in the other? Mr. Belsham seems to have been *not* unaware of this inference; but shows no disposition, on account of it, to shrink from his principles. "It is always to be remembered that the prescience of an *agent* necessarily includes predestination, though that of a *spectator* may not. It is nonsense to say that a being does not mean to bring an event to pass which he foresees to be the certain and inevitable consequence of his own previous voluntary action." †

I have already mentioned the attempt of Clarke and others to show that no valid argument against the scheme of free will can be deduced from the prescience of God, even supposing that prescience to extend to *all* the actions of voluntary beings. On this point I must decline offering any opinion of my own, because I conceive it as placed far beyond the reach of our faculties. It is sufficient for my purpose to observe, that, if it could be demonstrated (which, in my opinion, has not

* *Elements*, pp. 293, 302.

† *Elements*, p. 307.

yet been done) that the prescience of the volitions of moral agents is incompatible with the free agency of man, the logical inference would be, *not* in favor of the scheme of necessity, but that there are some events the foreknowledge of which implies an impossibility. Shall we venture to affirm that it exceeds the power of God to permit such a train of contingent events to take place, as his own foreknowledge shall not extend to? Does not such a proposition detract from the omnipotence of God, in the same proportion in which it aims to exalt his omniscience? *

---

* The strength of Edwards's argument to prove that "no future event can be certainly foreknown, whose existence is contingent, and without all necessity," may be summed up in the following syllogism: —

It is impossible for a thing to be certainly known to any intellect without evidence.

A contingent future event is without evidence.

Therefore, a contingent future event is a thing impossible to be certainly known.

Mr. Tappan says: — "I dispute both premises. That which is known by *evidence* or *proof* is *mediate* knowledge; — that is, we know it through something which is immediate, standing between the faculty of knowledge and the object of knowledge in question. That which is known *intuitively* is known *without proof;* and this is *immediate* knowledge. In this way all axioms or first truths, and *all facts of the senses*, are known. Indeed, evidence itself implies immediate knowledge, for the evidence by which any thing is known *is itself* immediate knowledge. To a Being, therefore, whose knowledge fills duration, future and past events may be as immediately known as present events. Indeed, can we conceive of God otherwise than as *immediately knowing* all things? An Infinite and Eternal Intelligence cannot be thought of under relations of time and space, or as arriving at knowledge through *media* of proof or demonstration. So much for the first premise. The second is equally untenable: — 'A contingent future event is without evidence.' We grant with Edwards that it is not self-evident, implying by that *the evidence arising from 'the necessity of its nature,'* as, for example, $2 \times 2 = 4$. What is self-evident [from being *immediately perceived*] does not require *any* [other] evidence or proof, but is *known immediately;* and a future contingent event may be self-evident [in this sense] as a fact lying before the Divine mind reaching into futurity, although it cannot be self-evident from 'the necessity of its nature.'" — *Review of Edwards*, p. 256.

The following remarks on the same subject are from Dr. Copleston's *Inquiry into the Doctrines of Necessity and Predestination*, p. 45, note. "Edwards, in his work on the *Freedom of the Will*, dwells much upon the distinction between *making* the event necessary, and *proving* it to be necessary. 'Whether prescience,' he says, 'be the thing that *makes* the event necessary or no, it alters not the case. Infallible foreknowledge may *prove* the necessity of the event foreknown, and yet not be the thing that *causes* the ne

II. *Source of the General Prevalence of Fatalism among Unenlightened Nations.*] It is a circumstance not a little curious in the history of the human mind, that, while men have been in all ages impressed with this irresistible conviction of their own free agency, they have nevertheless had a proneness, not only to admit the prescience of God in its fullest extent, but to suppose that there is a *fatal and irresistible destiny* attending every individual. Traces of this opinion occur in every country of the world of which we have received any account. We meet with it among the sages of Greece, and among the ignorant and unenlightened natives of St. Kilda. The following Arabian tale, which I quote from the late Mr. Harris, will place the import of the doctrine I now allude to in a more striking light than I could possibly do by any philosophical comment.

"The Arabians tell us," says this author, "that as Solomon (whom they supposed a magician from his superior wisdom) was one day walking with a person in Palestine, his companion said to him with horror, 'What hideous spectre is that which approaches us? I don't like his visage. Send me, I pray thee, to the remotest mountain of India.' Solomon complied,

---

cessity.' Part II. Sect. XII. But infallible foreknowledge, while it remains foreknowledge, *proves* nothing. When the being which possesses this foreknowledge *declares* that a thing will come to pass, that declaration indeed proves, or is a certain ground of assurance to us, that it *will* come to pass. Even then it does not prove the *event to be necessary*.

"If, however, the question be regarded as merely logical, namely, whether the very term *foreknowledge* does not imply a necessity in the thing foreknown, it must be decided by the established use of words. That such is not the received definition of the term may, I believe, be with confidence asserted; and the confusion, whenever it does prevail, seems to arise from the following cause. *We* may be unable to conceive how a thing not necessary in its nature can be foreknown; for *our* foreknowledge is in general limited by that circumstance, and is more or less perfect in proportion to the fixed or necessary nature of the things we contemplate, with which nature we become acquainted by experience, and are thus able to anticipate a great variety of events; but to subject the knowledge of God to any such limitation is surely absurd and unphilosophical, as well as impious; and, therefore, to mix up the idea of God's foreknowledge with any quality in the nature of the things foreknown is even less excusable than to be guilty of that confusion when speaking of ourselves." — Ed.

and the very moment he was sent off the spectre arrived, 'Solomon,' said the spectre, 'how came that fellow here? I was to have fetched him from the remotest mountain of India.' Solomon answered, 'Angel of Death, *thou wilt find him there*.'" *

The general prevalence of fatalism among unenlightened nations is the obvious effect of the insidious lessons inculcated by their religious instructors. The chief expedient employed by the priesthood in all rude countries for subjecting the minds of the people is to impress them with a belief that it is possible, by the study of auguries, of omens, or of judicial astrology, to gratify that misguided curiosity which disposes blind mortals anxiously to tear asunder the merciful veil drawn by Providence over futurity. "Wherever superstition," says Dr. Robertson, "is so established as to form a regular system, this desire of penetrating into the secrets of futurity is connected with it. Divination becomes a religious act; and priests, as the ministers of Heaven, pretend to deliver its oracles to man. They are the only soothsayers, augurs, and magicians who possess the sacred and important art of disclosing what is hid from other eyes." †

III. *No Dogma sufficient to efface the Consciousness of Moral Liberty.*] Between this creed and that of an inevitable fate or destiny the connection is necessary

---

* *Philosophical Inquiries*, Part III. Chap. VII. The following remark of M. Ancillon upon the difference between the Mahometan doctrine of destiny, and that which prevailed upon the same subject among the ancient Greeks, appears to me just and important. "Il y a une grande différence entre le destin des Orientaux, surtout depuis que Mahomet a fait, d'une doctrine généralement repandue avant lui, un article de foi, et le Polythéisme Grec. Le Grec lutte contre le destin, et tout en succombant sous sa force, il fait preuve de liberté: le Mahométan se résigne en aveugle avant l'événement; lors même qu'il agit, il agit en homme à qui l'action ne servira de rien. Le premier murmure contre ce pouvoir, et le supporte avec impatience; le second s'en félicite parce qu'il dispense de l'activité. Les Grecs plaçoient la force aveugle dans le destin; et la pensée qui lui résiste, et qui le combat, dans l'homme; chez les Mahométans la force aveugle est dans l'homme: cette force n'est qu'une force passive, et la pensée est dans le destin." — *Essais Philosophiques*, Tome I. pp. 150, 151.

† *History of America*, Book IV.

and obvious; and hence in every false religion the scheme of fatalism may be expected to form, not only an *essential*, but the *fundamental* article. The inconsiderable influence which this theological dogma (a dogma, too, peculiarly calculated to affect and even to overwhelm the imagination) has always had in stifling the sentiment of remorse on the commission of a crime, affords a demonstrative proof of the impotence of such scholastic refinements, when opposed to the feelings of nature, on a question concerning which these feelings form the only tribunal to which a legitimate appeal can be made. That a criminal, in order to alleviate the pang of remorse, may have sometimes sought for relief in this doctrine, is far from being improbable; but no man ever acted on this belief in the common concerns of human life; and, indeed, some of its most zealous partisans have acknowledged (particularly Lord Kames), that, were it to prevail universally as a practical principle, the business of the world could not possibly go on.

In the ancient Stoical system (as I have already observed), the doctrine of fatalism and that of man's free agency were both admitted as fundamental articles of belief. "By fate," says Mrs. Carter, "the Stoics seem to have understood a series of events appointed by the immutable councils of God, or that law of his providence by which he governs the world. It is evident by their writings that they meant it in no sense which interferes with the liberty of human actions." Of the truth of this remark the most satisfactory evidence is afforded by the very first sentence of the *Enchiridion* of Epictetus, in which it is explicitly stated, that "opinion, pursuit, desire, and aversion, and, in one word, whatever are our own actions, are in our own power." *

---

* That the doctrine of fatalism, however, led some of the Stoics to very impious and alarming consequences, appears from the following words, which Lucan puts into the mouth of Cato.

"Summum Brute nefas civilia bella fatemur,
Sed quo fata trahunt, virtus secura sequetur.
Crimen erit superis et me fecisse nocentem."

Phar. II. 254.

See, also, Lib. VII. 657. — Copleston, *Prælect. Acad.*, p. 277.

Such, too, is the philosophy of Virgil:—

> "Stat sua cuique dies, breve et irreparabile tempus
> Omnibus est vitæ; sed famam extendere factis
> Hoc virtutis opus." *

The doctrine, however, of fatalism, and of an inevitable destiny, must not be confounded with that of the *Divine prescience*, between which and the freedom of human actions some of our profoundest philosophers, as I have already observed (particularly Clarke and Reid), have labored to show that there is no inconsistency; while other writers of no less eminence have apprehended that there is no absurdity in supposing that the Deity may, for wise purposes, have chosen to open a source of contingency in the voluntary actions of his creatures, to which no prescience can possibly extend.

Whatever opinion we may adopt on this point, the conclusions formerly stated concerning man's free agency remain unshaken. Our own free will we know by our consciousness; and we can have no evidence for any other truth so irresistible as this. On the other hand, it would unquestionably be rash and impious in us, from the fact of our own free will, to deny that our actions may be foreseen by the Deity, or to measure the Divine attributes by a standard borrowed from our imperfect faculties. The conclusion of St. Augustine on this subject is equally pious and philosophical. "Wherefore we are nowise reduced to the necessity, either by admitting the prescience of God, to deny the freedom of the human will, or by admitting the freedom of the will to hazard the impious assertion, that the prescience

---

* *Æneid.*, Lib. X. 467.

> "To all that breathe is fixed the appointed date;
> Life is but short, and circumscribed by fate:
> 'T is virtue's work by fame to stretch the span,
> Whose scanty limit bounds the days of man."

The notions of Virgil, however, on this point, as is well observed by Servius, do not seem to have been quite consistent. How are the following lines, which he applies to Dido, to be reconciled with the above passage?

> "Nam quia nec fato, meritâ nec morte peribat;
> Sed misera ante diem."—*Idem*, Lib. IV. 695.

of God does not extend to all future contingencies: but, on the contrary, we are disposed to embrace *both* doctrines, and with sincerity to bear testimony to their truth, — the one that *our faith may be sound*, the other that *our lives may be good*." *

* The following passage in one of Gray's letters has a sufficient connection with what is said above to justify me in giving it a place here. Indeed, were the connection much slighter and less obvious than it is, little apology would be necessary for relieving the attention of the reader by quoting any thing relating to so important a subject from such a pen.

"I am as sorry as you seem to be, that our acquaintance harped so much on the subject of materialism when I saw him with you in town, because it was plain to which side of the long-debated question he inclined. That we are, indeed, mechanical and dependent beings, I need no other proof than my own feelings; and from the same feelings I learn with equal conviction, that we are not *merely* such. That there is a power within which struggles against the force and bias of that mechanism, commands its motion, and by frequent practice reduces it to that ready obedience we call *habit;* and all this in conformity to a preconceived opinion (no matter whether right or wrong), — to that least material of all agents, *a thought.* I have known many in his case, who, while they thought they were conquering an old prejudice, did not perceive that they were under the influence of one far more dangerous, — one that furnishes us with a ready apology for all our worst actions, and opens to us a full license for doing whatever we please; and yet these very people were not at all the more indulgent to other men (as they naturally should have been); their indignation at such as offended them, their desire of revenge on any body that hurt them, was nothing mitigated. In short, they wished to be persuaded of that opinion for the sake of its convenience, but were not so in their hearts; and they would have been glad (as they ought in common prudence) that nobody else should think the same, for fear of the mischief that might ensue to themselves. His French author I never saw, but have read fifty in the same strain, and shall read no more. *I can be wretched enough without them.*" — *Works*, by Mason, Letter XXXI.

I shall avail myself of this note to remark, that, on the subject of free will, though Locke has thrown out many important observations, he is on the whole more indistinct, undecided, and inconsistent than might have been expected from his powerful mind, when directed to so important a question. This was probably owing to his own strong feelings in favor of man's moral liberty, combined with the deep impression left on his philosophical creed by the writings of Hobbes, and by the habits of intimacy and friendship in which he lived with the acutest and ablest of all necessitarians, Anthony Collins. That Locke conceived himself to be an advocate for free will appears indisputably from many expressions in his chapter *On Power;* and yet in that very chapter he has made various concessions to his adversaries, in which he seems to yield all that was contended for by Hobbes and Collins; and accordingly, he is ranked, with some appearance of truth, by Priestley, with those who, while they opposed verbally the scheme of necessity, have adopted it substantially, without being aware of their mistake.

[To the multitude of works cited or referred to in this chapter may be added the following: — Crombie's *Essay on Philosophical Necessity;* Bray's *Philosophy of Necessity;* Cogan's *Ethical Questions*, Question IV.; Sir T. C. Morgan's *Sketches of the Philosophy of Morals*, Chap. II.; Bailey's *Essays on the Pursuit of Truth, &c.*, Essay III.; Gregory's *Essay in Defence of Philosophical Liberty;* Bockshammer *On the Freedom of the Human Will;* Charma, *Essai sur les Bases et les Développements de la Moralité*, Part. I. Sect. I., II.; Damiron, *Psychologie*, Liv. I. Sect. II. Chap. III.; Ballantyne's *Examination of the Human Mind*, Chap. III.; Gibon, *Cours de Philosophie*, Part. I. Chap. XIII.; Blakey's *Essay showing the Intimate Connection between our Notions of Moral Good and Evil and our Conceptions of the Freedom of the Divine and Human Wills;* Harvey's *Examination of the Pelagian and Arminian Theory of Moral Agency;* Day's *Inquiry respecting the Self-determining Power of the Will;* Day's *Examination of President Edwards's Inquiry on the Freedom of the Will.*]

BOOK III.

OF THE VARIOUS BRANCHES OF OUR DUTY.

The different theories which have been proposed concerning the nature and essence of virtue have arisen chiefly from attempts to trace all the branches of our duty to *one* principle of action; — such as a rational self-love, benevolence, justice, or a disposition to obey the will of God.

In order to avoid those partial views of the subject which naturally take their rise from an undue love of system, the following inquiries proceed on an arrangement which has, in all ages, recommended itself to the good sense of mankind. This arrangement is founded on the different objects to which our duties relate. 1st. The Deity. 2d. Our Fellow-Creatures. And, 3d. Ourselves.

CHAPTER I.

OF THE DUTIES WHICH RESPECT THE DEITY.

I. *The Duty of Religious Consideration.*] It is scarcely possible to conceive a man capable of reflection, who has not, at times, proposed to himself the following questions: — Whence am I? and whence the innumerable tribes of plants and of animals which I see, in constant succession, rising into existence? Whence the beautiful fabric of this universe? and by what wise and powerful Being were the principles of my constitution so wonderfully adapted to the various objects around me? To whom am I indebted for the distinguished rank which I hold in the creation, and for the numberless blessings which have fallen to my lot? And what return shall I make for this profusion of goodness? The only return I *can* make is by accommodating my conduct to the will of my Creator, and by fulfilling, as far as I am able, the purposes of my being.

But how are these purposes to be discovered? The analogy of the lower animals gives me here no information. They, too, as well as I, are endowed with various instincts and appetites; but their nature, on the whole, exhibits a striking contrast to mine. They are impelled by a blind determination towards their proper objects, and seem to obey the law of their nature in yielding to every principle which excites them to action. In my own species alone the case is different. Every individual *chooses* for himself the ends of his pursuit, and *chooses* the means which he is to employ for attaining them. Are all these elections equally *good?* and is there no *law* prescribed to man? I feel the reverse. I am able to distinguish what is right from what is wrong; what is honorable and becoming from what is unworthy and base; what is laudable and meritorious from what is shameful and criminal. *Here*, then, are plain indications of the conduct I *ought* to pursue. There is a law prescribed to man as well as to the brutes. The only difference is, that it depends on my own will whether I obey or disobey it. And shall I alone counteract the intentions of my Maker, by abusing that freedom of choice which he has been pleased to bestow on me, by raising me to the rank of a rational and moral being?

This is surely the language of *nature;* and which could not fail to occur to every man capable of serious thought, were not the understanding and the moral feelings in some instances miserably perverted by religious and political prejudices, and in others by the false refinements of metaphysical theories. How callous must be that heart which does not echo back the reflections which Milton puts into the mouth of our first parent?

"Thou sun, said I, fair light,
And thou, enlightened earth, so fresh and gay,
Ye hills and dales, ye rivers, woods, and plains,
And ye that live and move, fair creatures, tell,
Tell, if you saw, how came I thus, how here;
Not of myself; by some great maker then,
In goodness, as in power, preëminent;
Tell me how I may know him, how adore,
From whom I have, that thus I move and live,
And feel that I am happier than I know."

II. *The Duty of Piety.*] If the Deity be possessed of infinite moral excellence, we must feel towards him, in an infinite degree, all those affections of love, gratitude, and confidence, which are excited by the imperfect worth we observe among our fellow-creatures. Now it is only by conceiving all that is benevolent and amiable in man raised to the highest perfection, that we can form some faint notion of the Divine nature. To cultivate, therefore, an habitual love and reverence of the Supreme Being may be justly considered as the first great branch of morality; nor is the virtue of that man complete, or even consistent with itself, in whose mind those sentiments of piety are wanting.

Piety seems to be considered by Mr. Smith as founded in some degree on those principles of our nature which connect us with our fellow-creatures. The dejection of mind which accompanies a state of complete solitude; the disposition we have to impart to others our thoughts and feelings; the desire we have of other intelligent and moral natures to sympathize with our own, — all lead us, in the progress of reason and of moral perception, to establish gradually a mental intercourse with the Invisible Witness and Judge of our conduct. An habitual sense of the Divine presence comes at last to be formed. In every object or event that we see, we trace the hand of the Almighty, and in the suggestions of reason and conscience we listen to his inspirations. In this intercourse of the heart with God, (an intercourse which enlivens and gladdens the most desolate scenes, and which dignifies the duties of the meanest station,) the supreme felicity of our nature is to be found; and till it is firmly established, there remains a void in every breast which nothing earthly can supply; — a consideration which proves that religion has a foundation in the original principles of our constitution, while it affords us a presage of that immortal happiness which Providence has destined to be the reward of virtue.*

III. *Religion necessary as a Support to Public and Private Virtue.*] Although religion can with no propriety be considered as the *sole* foundation of morality, yet, when we are convinced that God is infinitely good, and that he is the friend and protector of virtue, this belief affords the most powerful inducements to the practice of every branch of our duty. It leads us to consider conscience as the vicegerent of God, and to attend to its suggestions as to the commands of that Being from whom we have received our existence, and the great object of whose government is to promote the happiness and the perfection of his whole creation.

These considerations not only are addressed to our gratitude, but awaken in the mind a sentiment of universal benevolence, and make us feel a relation to every part of the universe. In doing our duty, we conceive ourselves as fellow-workers with the Deity, and as willing instruments in his hands for promoting the benevolent purposes of his administration. This is that sublime sentiment of piety and benevolence which we meet with so often in the writings of the ancient Stoics. "Shall any one say," observes Antoninus, "'O beloved city of Cecrops!' and wilt not thou say, 'O beloved city of God'?"

In this manner it appears that a sense of religion is favorable to the practice of virtue in *two* respects; *first*, by leading us to consider every act of duty as an expression of gratitude to God; and, *secondly*, as leading us to regard ourselves as parts of that universal system

* For a further consideration of this important subject, see Butler's two Sermons *Upon Piety, or the Love of God.* Also, his *Analogy*, Part II. Chap. I. — Ed.

of which he is the Author and Governor. There is another respect in which it is calculated to influence our conduct very powerfully, as it is addressed to our *hopes* and *fears*. In this view religion is a species of authoritative *law*, enforced by the most awful sanctions, and of which it is impossible for us, by any art, to elude the penalties. In the case of the lower orders of men, who are incapable of abstract speculation, and whose moral feelings cannot be supposed to have received much cultivation, it is chiefly this view of religion, as addressed to their *hopes* and *fears*, that secures a faithful discharge of their duties as members of society. In vain would the civil magistrate attempt to preserve the order of society by annexing the penalty of death to heinous offences, if men in general apprehended that there was nothing to be feared beyond the grave. And it is of importance to remark, that this observation applies with peculiar force to the lower orders, who have commonly much less attachment to life than their superiors. Of this truth, all wise legislators, both ancient and modern, have been aware, and have seen the necessity of maintaining a sense of religion among their fellow-citizens, as the most powerful of all supports to the political order. "Ut aliqua in vita formido improbis esset posita, apud inferose jusmodi quædam illi antiqui supplicia impiis constituta esse voluerunt; quod videlicet intelligebant his remotis, non esse mortem ipsam pertimescendam."* They, on the other

* Cic. *Catil.* IV. "For it was on this account that the ancients invented those infernal punishments of the dead, to keep the wicked under some awe in this life, who, without them, would have no dread of death itself."

With these views, it is not surprising that some of the wisest of the heathen writers should have expressed themselves so very strongly concerning the guilt incurred by those who, by exposing to ridicule the fabulous mythology which formed the popular creed among their contemporaries, endangered the authority of those moral principles which were identified with it in the vulgar belief. There is good reason for thinking that the secret communicated to the initiated in the Eleusinian mysteries was *the unity of God;* a truth too sublime to be disclosed at once to the uninformed multitude, as it struck at the root of all those fables which were incorporated with their habits of thinking and feeling on the most important subjects. On this supposition we have a satisfactory explanation of a

hand, who have labored to loosen the bands of society, have found it necessary to begin with perverting or destroying the natural sentiments of the mind with respect to a future retribution. In ages when the religious principles of the multitude were too firmly riveted to be entirely eradicated, they have inculcated theological dogmas subversive of moral distinctions, as in the case of the antinomian teachers during our own civil wars. In other and more recent instances, they have avowedly attempted to establish a system of atheism. So true is the old observation, that the extremes of superstition and of infidelity unite in their tendency, and so completely verified are *now* the apprehensions which were expressed eighty years ago by Bishop Butler, that the spirit of irreligion (which, in his time, was beginning to grow fashionable among the higher ranks) might produce some time or other political disorders similar to those which arose from religious fanaticism in the preceding century. "Is there no danger that all this may raise somewhat like the levelling spirit upon atheistical principles, which, in the last age, prevailed upon enthusiastic ones, — not to speak of the possibility that different sorts of people may unite in it upon these contrary principles?" *

A prediction by a later writer of genius and discernment, and one well acquainted with the principles and manners of the world, is not unworthy of attention in the present times, in which we have seen it very remarkably verified in numberless instances. "I shall say nothing at present of the lower ranks of mankind. Though they have not yet got into the fashion of

---

noted passage in Horace, between which and the preceding lines it seems not easy at first to trace any connection.

Est et fideli tuta silentio
Merces. Vetabo, qui Cereris sacrum
Vulgarit arcanæ, sub ìsdem
Sit trabibus, fragilemve mecum
Solvat phaselum.

Carm. Lib. III. Ode II.

* *Sermon preached before the House of Lords*, January 30, 1740.

laughing at religion, and treating it with scorn and contempt, and I believe are too serious a set of creatures ever to come into it, yet we are not to imagine but that the contempt it is held in by those whose examples they are too apt to imitate will in time utterly shake their principles, and render them, if not as profane, at least as corrupt, as their betters. When this event happens, and we begin to feel the effects of it in our dealings with them, *those who have done the mischief* will find the necessity at last of turning religious in their own defence, and (for want of a better principle) to set an example of piety and good morals for their own interest and convenience." *

Nor is it merely in restraining men from grosser outrages, that a sense of religion operates as a compulsory law. Without a secret impression (of which it is impossible that the human mind can divest itself), that there is at all times an invisible witness of our thoughts, it is probable that the virtue of the best men would often yield to temptation. Even amidst the darkness of the heathen world, Xenophon had recourse to this impression to account for the inflexible integrity of Socrates, when he sat as one of the judges in the celebrated trial of the naval commanders. "Having taken," says Xenophon, "as was customary, the senatorial oath, by which he bound himself to act in all things conformably to the laws, and arriving in his turn to be president of the assembly of the people, he boldly refused to give his suffrage to the iniquitous sentence which condemned the nine captains, being neither intimidated by the menaces of the great, nor the fury of the people, but steadily preferring the sanctity of an oath to the safety of his person. For he was persuaded the gods watched over the affairs of men, in a way altogether different from what the vulgar imagined; for while *these* limited their knowledge to *some* particulars only, Socrates, on the contrary, extended it to all, firmly persuaded that they are everywhere present, and that

* Sterne's *Sermons*.

every word, every action, nay, even our most retired deliberations, were open to their view." *

In the last place, a sense of religion, where it is sincere, will necessarily be attended with a complete resignation of our own will to that of the Deity, as it teaches us to regard every event, even the most afflicting, as calculated to promote beneficent purposes, which we are unable to comprehend, and to promote, finally, the perfection and happiness of our own nature. This is the best, and, indeed, the only rational foundation of fortitude. Nay, it may be safely affirmed (as Socrates long ago observed in the *Phædo* of Plato), that whoever founds his fortitude on any thing else *is only valiant through fear*. In other words, he exposes himself to danger, merely from a regard to the opinion of others, and, of consequence, wants that internal principle of heroism which can alone arm the mind with patience under those misfortunes which it is condemned to bear in solitude, or under sorrows which prudence conceals from the public eye. But to the man who believes that every thing is ordered for the best, and that his existence and happiness are in the hands of a Being who watches over him with the care of a parent, the difficulties and dangers of life only serve to call forth the latent powers of the soul, by reminding him of the prize for which he combats, and of that beneficent Providence by which the conflict was appointed.

Safe in the hands of one disposing Power,
Or in the natal or the mortal hour.

IV. *Religion the First and Chief Branch of Mora Duty.*] The view which I have given of religion, a forming the first and chief branch of moral duty, an as contributing in its turn most powerfully to promot the practice of every virtue, is equally consonant to th spirit of the Sacred Writings, and to the most obviou dictates of reason and conscience; and accordingly i is sanctioned by the authority of all those philosophe

---

* *Memor.* Lib. I. Cap. I.

of antiquity who devoted their talents to the improvement and happiness of mankind. "It should never be thought," says Plato in one of his Dialogues, "that there is any branch of human virtue of greater importance than piety towards the Deity." The chief article of the *unwritten law* mentioned by Socrates is, "that the gods ought to be worshipped." "This," he says, "is acknowledged everywhere, and received by all men as the first command." * And to the same purpose Cicero, in the first book of his *Offices*, places in the first rank of duties those we owe to the immortal gods. "In ipsa communitate sunt gradus officiorum ex quibus, quid cuique præstet, intelligi possit: ut primà Diis immortalibus; secunda, patriæ; tertia, parentibus, deinceps gradatim reliquis debeantur." †

The elevation of mind which some of the most illustrious characters of antiquity derived from their religious principles, however imperfect and erroneous, and the weight which these principles gave them in their public and political capacity, are remarked by many ancient writers; and such, I apprehend, will always be found to be the case when the personal importance of the individual rests on the basis of public opinion. "But he," says Plutarch, "who was most conversant with Pericles, and most contributed to give him a grandeur of mind, and to make his high spirit for governing the popular assemblies more weighty and authoritative, — in a word, who exalted his ideas, and raised, at the same time, the dignity of his demeanour, — the person who did this was Anaxagoras the Clazomenian, whom the people of that age reverenced as the first who made *mind* or *intellect* (in opposition to *chance*) a principle in the formation and government of the universe." ‡

---

* Xen. *Memor.* Lib. IV. Cap. IV.

† Lib. I. Cap. ult. "In society itself our duties are of different degrees, in which the proper order of preference is readily understood: — first of all, our duties to the immortal gods; secondly, to our country; thirdly to our parents, and, after them, to other men in their several gradations."

‡ *Vit. Peric.*

The extraordinary respect which the Romans, during their period of greatest glory, entertained for religion, (false as their own system was in its mythological foundations, and erroneous in many of its practical tendencies,) has been often taken notice of as one of the principal sources of their private and public virtues. "The Spaniards," says Cicero, "exceed us in numbers; the Gauls in the glory of war; but we surpass all nations in that wisdom by which we have learned that all things are governed and directed by the immortal gods." *

In the latter periods of their history, this reverence for religion, together with the other virtues which gave them the empire of the world, was in a great measure lost; and we continually find their orators and historians drawing a melancholy contrast between the degeneracy of their manners and those of their ancestors. In the account which Livy has given of the consulate of Q. Cincinnatus, he mentions an attempt which the tribunes made to persuade the people that they were not bound by their military oath to follow the consul to the field, because they had taken that oath when he was a private man. But, however agreeable this doctrine might be to their inclinations, and however strongly recommended to them by the sanction of their own popular magistrates, we find that their reverence for the religion of an oath led them to treat the doctrine as nothing better than a cavil. Livy's reflection on this occasion is remarkable. "Nondum hæc, quæ nunc tenet seculum, negligentia Deûm venerat: nec interpretando sibi quisque jusjurandum leges aptas faciebat, sed suos potius mores ad ea accommodabat." †

* *Orat de Harusp. Respon.*, Cap. IX.

† Lib. III. Cap. XX. "But that disregard of the gods, which prevails in the present age, had not then taken place; nor did every one, by his own interpretations, accommodate oaths and the laws to his particular views, but rather adapted his practice to them."

CHAPTER II.

OF THE DUTIES WHICH RESPECT OUR FELLOW-CREATURES.

UNDER this title it is not proposed to give a complete enumeration of our social duties, but only to point out some of the most important, chiefly with a view to show the imperfections of those systems of morals which attempt to resolve the whole of virtue into one particular principle. Among these, that which resolves virtue into *benevolence* is undoubtedly the most amiable; but even this system will appear, from the following remarks, not only to be inconsistent with truth, but to lead to dangerous consequences.

SECTION I.

OF BENEVOLENCE.

I. *Hutcheson resolves all Virtue into Benevolence.*] Benevolence is so important a branch of virtue, that it has been supposed by some moralists to constitute the whole of it. According to these writers, good-will to mankind is the only *immediate* object of moral approbation; and the obligation of all our other moral duties arises entirely from their apprehended tendency to promote the happiness of society.

Among the most eminent partisans of this system in modern times, Mr. Smith mentions particularly Dr. Ralph Cudworth, Dr. Henry More, and Mr. John Smith of Cambridge; "but of all its patrons," he observes, "ancient or modern, Dr. Francis Hutcheson was undoubtedly beyond all comparison the most acute, the most distinct, the most philosophical, and, what is of the greatest consequence of all, the soberest and most judicious." *

* *Theory of Moral Sentiments*, Part VII. Sect. II. Chap. III.

In favor of this system, Mr. Smith acknowledges that there are many appearances in human nature which at first sight seem strongly to support it; and of some of these appearances Dr. Hutcheson avails himself with much acuteness and plausibility. First, whenever, in any action supposed to proceed from benevolent affections, some other motive is discovered, our sense of the merit of this action is just so far diminished as this motive is believed to have influenced it. Secondly, when those actions, on the contrary, which are commonly supposed to proceed from a selfish motive are discovered to have arisen from a benevolent one, it generally enhances our sense of their merit. Lastly, it was urged by Dr. Hutcheson, that, in all casuistical disputes concerning the rectitude of conduct, the ultimate appeal is uniformly made to utility. In the later debates, for example, about passive obedience and the right of resistance, the sole point in controversy among men of sense was, whether universal submission would probably be attended with greater evils than temporary insurrection when privileges were invaded. Whether what, upon the whole, tended most to the happiness of mankind was not also morally good, was never once made a question.

Since benevolence, therefore, was the only motive which could bestow upon any action the character of virtue, the greater the benevolence which was evidenced by any action, the greater the praise which must belong to it.

In directing all our actions to promote the greatest possible good, — in submitting all inferior affections to the desire of the general happiness of mankind, — in regarding one's self as but one of the many, whose prosperity was to be pursued no further than it was consistent with, or conducive to, that of the whole, — consisted the perfection of virtue.

Dr. Hutcheson held, further, that self-love was a principle which could never be virtuous in any degree or in any direction. This maxim he carried so far as to assert, that even a regard to the pleasure of self approbation, to the comfortable applauses of our own consciences, diminishes the merit of a benevolent action. "In the common judgments of mankind, however," says Mr. Smith, "this regard to the approbation of our own minds is so far from being considered as what can in any respect diminish the virtue of any action, that it is rather looked upon as the sole motive which deserves the appellation of virtuous."

Of the truth and correctness of these principles Dr. Hutcheson was so fully convinced, that, in conformity to them, he has offered some algebraical formulas for computing mathematically the morality of actions. Of this very extraordinary attempt, the following axioms, which he premises to his formulas, may serve as a sufficient specimen.

1. The *moral importance* of any agent, or the quantity of public good produced by him, is in a compound ratio of his benevolence and abilities, or M (moment of good) $= B \times A$.

2. In like manner, the moment of private good or interest produced by any person to himself is in a compound ratio of his self-love and ability, or $I = S \times A$.

3. When, in comparing the virtue of two agents, the abilities are equal, the moment of public good produced by them in like circumstances is as the benevolence, or $M = B \times 1$.

4. When benevolence in two agents is equal, and other circumstances alike, the moment of public good is as the abilities, or $M = A \times 1$.

5. The virtue, then, of agents, or their benevolence, is always directly as the moment of good produced in like circumstances, and inversely as their abilities, or $B = \frac{M}{A}$.*

II. *Objections to this Theory.*] As Dr. Hutcheson's example in the use of these formulas has not been fol-

* Hutcheson's *Inquiry into the Original of our Ideas of Beauty and Virtue*, Treatise II. Sect. III.

lowed by any of his successors, it is unnecessary to employ any arguments to expose the absurdity of this unsuccessful innovation in the usual language of ethics.* It is of more consequence to direct our attention to the substance of the doctrine which it was the great object of the ingenious author to establish.

And, in the first place, the necessary and obvious consequences to which this account of virtue leads seem to furnish a satisfactory proof of its unsoundness. For if the merit of an action depends on no other circumstance than the quantity of good intended by the agent, then the rectitude of an action can in no case be influenced by the mutual relations of the parties; — a conclusion contradicted by the universal judgment of mankind in favor of the paramount obligation of various other duties. It is sufficient to mention the obligations of gratitude, of veracity, and of justice.† Unless we admit these duties to be *immediately* obligatory, we must admit the maxim, that a good end may sanctify any means necessary for its attainment; or, in other words, that it would be lawful for us to dispense with the obligations of veracity and justice whenever, by doing so, we had a prospect of promoting any of the essential interests of society.

With respect to this maxim, I would only ask, Is it probable, *a priori*, that the wise and beneficent Author of the universe should have left the conduct of such a fallible and short-sighted creature as man to be regulated by no other principle than the private opinion of each individual with respect to the expediency of his actions? Or, in other words, by the conjectures which the individual might form on the good or evil resulting, *on the whole*, from an endless train of future contin-

* Dr. Hutcheson's attempt to introduce the language of mathematics into morals gave occasion to a valuable *Essay on Quantity*, by the late Dr. Reid. This essay may be found in the *Philosophical Transactions* of the Royal Society of London for the year 1748. [It is reprinted in Sir W. Hamilton's edition of Dr. Reid's Works.]

† See Butler's *Essay on the Nature of Virtue*, at the end of his *Analogy*.

gencies? Were this the case, the opinions of mankind concerning the rules of morality would be as various as their judgments concerning the probable issue of the most doubtful and difficult determination in politics. Numberless cases might be fancied, in which a person would not only *claim* merit to himself, but actually possess it, in consequence of actions which are generally regarded with indignation and abhorrence. Even men of the soundest judgment and most penetrating sagacity might frequently be led to the perpetration of enormities, if they had no other standard of right and wrong but what they derived from their own uncertain anticipations of futurity. And when we consider how small the number of such men is, in comparison with those whose understandings are perverted by the prejudices of education, and by their own selfish passions, it is easy to see what a scene of anarchy the world would become. Surely, if the Deity intended the happiness of his creatures, he would not build the *order* (I may say the *existence*) of society on so precarious a foundation. And here it deserves particularly to be mentioned, that one of the arguments commonly produced in support of the scheme is drawn from the benevolence of God. Benevolence, we are told, induced the Deity to call the universe into existence, and benevolence is the great law of his government; and as virtue in man must consist in conformity to the will of God, in imitating his moral perfections to the utmost of our power, it is concluded that virtue and benevolence are the same. But the premises here lead to a conclusion directly opposite; for if the happiness of mankind be the great end for which they are brought into being, it is presumable that the rules of their conduct are of such a nature as to be obvious to the capacities of all men of sincere and well-disposed minds. Accordingly, we find, (and the fact is in a peculiar degree worthy of attention,) that, while the theory of ethics involves some of the most abstruse questions which have ever employed the human faculties, the moral judgments and moral feelings of the most distant ages and nations, with respect to all the most essential duties of life, are one and the same.*

The reasonableness of the foregoing conclusion will be much confirmed, if we consider how much the happiness of mankind is often left to depend on the will of one or of a few individuals. The best men, in such circumstances, when invested with absolute power, might be rendered curses to the world by sanguine plans of beneficence; and the ambitious and designing would be supplied with specious pretences to justify the most cruel and tyrannical measures. In truth, it is this very plea of benevolent intention which has been employed to palliate, or rather to sanctify, the conduct of the greatest scourges of the human race. It is this very plea which, in former times, lighted up the fires of the Inquisition, and which, in our own age, has furnished a pretence for outrages against all the principles of justice and all the feelings of humanity.†

It may perhaps be urged, that the principle of benevolence, or a regard to utility, would lead to an *invariable* adherence to the rules of veracity, gratitude, and justice, because in this way more good is produced on the whole than could be obtained by any occasional deviations from them; that it is this idea of utility which first leads us to approve of these virtues; and that afterwards habit, or the association of ideas, makes us observe their rules without thinking of consequences. But is not this to adopt that mode of reasoning which Hutcheson censures so severely in the selfish philosophers? According to them, we labor to promote the public prosperity, because we believe our own to be intimately connected with it. They acknowledge, at the same time, that we often make a

---

* "Si quid rectissimum sit quærimus, perspicuum est. Si quid maximè expediat, obscurum." — Cic. *Ep. ad Fam.*, IV. 2.

† See the remarks on Paley's scheme of morals in Gisborne's *Principles of Moral Philosophy*, where these arguments are urged with great force [They are replied to by Wainewright, in his *Vindication of Dr. Paley's Theory of Morals*, Chap. II.]

real sacrifice of private to public advantage, and that we often exert ourselves in the public service without once thinking of our own interest. But all this they explain by habits and associations, which operate in this case as they do in the case of the miser, who, although his attachment to money was originally founded on the consideration of its uses, yet continues to accumulate wealth without once thinking of the ends to which it is subservient, and indeed long after he is able to enjoy those comforts which it can purchase.

Now, as I have said, the fallaciousness of this mode of reasoning has been pointed out by Dr. Hutcheson with great clearness and force; and the arguments he employs against it may with great justice be turned against himself. In general, the safest rule we can follow in our inquiries concerning the principles of human conduct is to acquiesce, in the first instance, in the plain and obvious appearance of facts; and if these conclusions are inaccurate, to correct them gradually, in proportion as a more attentive examination of our subject discovers to us the prejudices which education and accidental associations have blended with the truth. It is at least a presumption in favor of any system concerning the mind, that it falls in with the natural apprehensions of mankind in all countries and ages; — and I believe it will commonly be found that these are the systems which, in the progress of human reason, are justified by the most profound and enlightened philosophy. I state this observation with the greater confidence, as it coincides with the following admirable remark of Mr. Hume, — an author who had certainly no interest in inculcating such a doctrine, as he seems to have paid very little attention to it in the course of his own speculations.

" The case is not the same in moral philosophy as in physics. Many an hypothesis in nature, contrary to first appearances, has been found, on more accurate scrutiny, solid and satisfactory. Instances of this kind are so frequent, that a judicious as well as witty phi losopher* has ventured to affirm, if there be more than one way in which a phenomenon may be produced, that there is a general presumption for its arising from the causes which are the least obvious and familiar But the presumption always lies on the other side in all inquiries concerning the origin of our passions, and of the internal operations of the human mind. The simplest and most obvious cause which can there be assigned for any phenomenon is probably the true one. When a philosopher, in the explication of his system, is obliged to have recourse to some very intricate and refined reflections, and to suppose them essential to the production of any passion or emotion, we have reason to be extremely on our guard against so fallacious an hypothesis. The affections are not susceptible of any impression from the refinements of reason or imagination; and it is always found, that a vigorous exertion of the latter faculty necessarily, from the limited capacity of the human mind, destroys all activity in the former. Our predominant motive or interest is indeed frequently concealed from ourselves when it is mingled and confounded with other motives, which the mind, from vanity and self-conceit, is desirous of supposing more prevalent; but there is no instance that a concealment of this nature has ever arisen from the abstruseness and intricacy of the motive. A man that has lost a friend and patron may flatter himself that all his grief arises from generous sentiments, without any mixture of narrow or interested considerations; but a man that grieves for a valuable friend who needed his patronage and protection, how can we suppose that his passionate tenderness arises from some metaphysical regards to a self-interest which has no foundation in reality? We may as well imagine that minute wheels and springs, like those of a watch, give motion to a wagon, as account for the origin of passion from such abstruse reflections." †

* Fontenelle.
† *Inquiry concerning the Principles of Morals*, Appendix II.

III. *The same Objections applicable to the Doctrine of Utility, as held by Hume, Godwin, and Paley.*] The remarks which I have now made with respect to Dr. Hutcheson's philosophy are applicable, with some slight alterations, to a considerable variety of moral systems which have been offered to the world under very different forms, but which agree with him and with each other in deriving the practical rules of virtuous conduct from considerations of *utility*. All of these systems are but modifications of the old doctrine which resolves the whole of virtue into benevolence.

This theory of utility (which is of a very ancient date, and which in modern times has derived much celebrity from the genius of Mr. Hume) has been revived more recently by Mr. Godwin, and by the late Dr. Paley. Widely as these two writers differ in the *source* whence they derive their rule of conduct, and the *sanctions* by which they enforce its observance, they are perfectly agreed about its paramount authority over every other principle of action. "Whatever is *expedient*," says Dr. Paley, "is *right*. It is the utility of any moral rule alone which constitutes the obligation of it." * "But then it must be expedient *on the whole*, at the long run, in all its effects, collateral and remote, as well as those which are immediate and direct, as it is obvious that, in computing consequences, it makes no difference in what way or at what distance they ensue." †

* *Principles of Moral and Political Philosophy*. Book II. Chap. VI.

† Ibid. Chap. VIII. In another part of this work, Book VI. Chap. XII., Dr. Paley explicitly asserts that *every* moral rule is liable to be superseded in particular cases on the ground of expediency. "Moral Philosophy cannot pronounce that any rule of morality is so rigid as to bend to no exceptions; nor, on the other hand, can she comprise these exceptions within any previous description. She confesses that the obligation of every law depends upon its ultimate utility; that, this utility having a finite and determinate value, situations may be feigned, and consequently may possibly arise, in which the general tendency is outweighed by the enormity of the particular mischief." In such an event, ultimate utility would render it as much an act of duty to break the rule as it is on other occasions to observe it.

[Some have contended that Paley's *criterion* of right is not liable to the same objections with that of other selfish systems, because he does not make it turn on a calculation of the probable consequences of the *particular* action in hand, but on what is called "the doctrine of general conse

Mr. Godwin has nowhere expressed himself on this fundamental question of practical ethics in terms more decided and unqualified.

Of this theory of utility, so strongly recommended to some by the powerful talents of Hume, and to others by the well-merited popularity of Paley, the most satisfactory of all refutations is to be found in the work of Mr. Godwin. It is unnecessary to inquire how far the practical lessons he has inculcated are logically inferred from his fundamental principle; for although I appre-

---

quences." "The general consequence of any action may be estimated," he says, "by asking what *would be* the consequence if the *same sort* of actions were *generally* permitted." — *Moral Philosophy*, Book II. Chap. VIII But to this Coleridge, in *The Friend*, Vol. II. Essay XI., replies: —

1. "Here, as in all other calculations, the result depends on that faculty of the soul in the degrees of which men most vary from each other, and which is itself most affected by accidental advantages or disadvantages of education, natural talent, and acquired knowledge, — the faculty, I mean, of foresight and systematic comprehension. But surely morality, which is of equal importance to all men, ought to be grounded, if possible, in that part of our nature which in all men may and ought to be the same: in the conscience and the common sense."

2. "This criterion confounds morality with law; and when the author adds, that in all probability the Divine justice will be regulated in the final judgment by a similar rule, he draws away the attention from the *will*, that is, from the inward motives and impulses which constitute the essence of *morality*, to the outward act, and thus changes the virtue commanded by the Gospel into the mere legality which was to be enlivened by it. One of the most persuasive, if not one of the strongest, arguments for a future state rests on the belief, that, although by the necessity of things our outward and temporal welfare must be regulated by our outward actions, which alone can be the objects and guides of human law, there must yet needs come a juster and more appropriate sentence hereafter, in which our *intentions* will be considered, and our happiness and misery made to accord with the grounds of our actions. Our fellow-creatures can only judge what we *are* by what we *do;* but in the eye of our Maker what we *do* is of no worth, except as it flows from what we *are*."

3. "The criterion is also nugatory. The individual is to *imagine* what the general consequences *would* be, all other things remaining the same, *if* all men were to act as he is about to act. I scarcely need remind the reader what a source of self-delusion and sophistry is here opened to a mind in a state of temptation. Will it not say to itself, 'I know that all men will *not* act so; and the immediate good consequences, which I shall obtain, are *real*, while the bad consequences are imaginary and improbable'? When the foundations of morality have once been laid in the outward consequences, it will be in vain to recall to the mind what the consequences would be were all men to reason in the same way; for the very excuse of this mind to itself is, that neither its action nor its reasoning is likely to have any consequences at all, its immediate object excepted."

hend much might be objected to these, even on his own hypothesis, yet if such be the conclusions to which, in the judgment of so acute a reasoner, it *appeared* to lead with demonstrative evidence, nothing further is requisite to illustrate the practical tendency of a system which, absolving men from the obligations imposed on them with so commanding an authority by the moral constitution of human nature, abandons every individual to the guidance of his own narrow views concerning the complicated interests of political society.

---

4. " But suppose the mind in its sanest state. How can it possibly form a notion of the nature of an action considered as indefinitely multiplied, unless it has previously a distinct notion of the nature of the single action itself which is the multiplicand? If I conceive a crown multiplied a hundredfold, the simple crown enables me to understand what a hundred crowns are; but how can the notion *hundred* teach me what a crown is?"

5. "I confess myself unable to divine any possible use, or even meaning, in this doctrine of general consequences, unless it be that in all our actions we are bound to consider the effect of our example, and to guard as much as possible against the hazard of their being misunderstood. I will not slaughter a lamb, or drown a litter of kittens, in the presence of my child of four years old, because the child cannot understand my action, but will understand that his father has inflicted pain, and taken away life from beings that had never offended him. All this is true, and no man in his senses ever thought otherwise. But methinks it is strange to state that as a criterion of morality which is no more than an accessory aggravation of an action bad in its own nature, or a ground of caution as to the mode and time in which we are to do or suspend what is in itself good and innocent."

6. "The duty of setting a good *example* is no doubt a most important duty; but the example is good or bad, necessary or unnecessary, according as the action may be which has a chance of being imitated. I once knew a small, but (in outward circumstances at least) respectable congregation, four fifths of whom professed that they went to church *entirely* for the example's sake; in other words, to cheat each other and act a common lie! These rational Christians had not considered that example may *increase* the good or evil of an action, but can never *constitute* either."

7. "To the objection, that the doctrine of general consequences was stated as the criterion of the *action*, not of the *agent*, I might answer, that the author himself had in some measure justified me in not noticing this distinction, by holding forth the probability, that the Supreme Judge will proceed by the same rule. The agent may then safely be included in the action, if both here and hereafter the action only and its general consequences will be attended to. But my main ground of justification is, that the distinction itself is merely logical, — not real and vital. The *character* of the *agent* is determined by his view of the action; and that system of morality is alone true and suited to human nature, which unites the intention and the motive, the warmth and the light, in one and the same act of mind."]

Among the practical consequences which Dr. Paley deduces from the same principle, there are some which to my mind are not less revolting than those of Mr. Godwin. Such, for example, is the argument by which he controverts the received maxim of criminal jurisprudence, that *it is better for ten guilty persons to escape than for one innocent man to suffer.* But on this subject I need not enlarge. The sophistry, and, I am sorry to add, the reckless inhumanity displayed in this part of Paley's work, have been triumphantly exposed by that great and good man, Sir Samuel Romilly; — a man whom, long before his talents and worth were known to the public, I admired and loved, and whose memory I shall never cease to revere.*

---

* *Observations on the Criminal Law of England.* See, in particular, Note D.

[For some account of the writings and influence of Godwin, see the thirty-sixth Lecture of Professor Smyth, *On the French Revolution.* He begins his notice by observing, with reference to the time of the first French Revolution, — "I would wish to afford you some general notion of the sort of mental intoxication which then prevailed among those who should have been the guides and instructors of mankind. And looking round for this purpose, I shall select from the rest, as a memorable specimen of the whole, the once celebrated work of Mr. Godwin. The influence of the work I can myself remember. In any ordinary state of the world, it must have fallen lifeless from the press: highly metaphysical, continually running into general abstractions, into disquisitions never ending, still beginning, nothing was ever less fitted to attract a reader than the repulsive *Inquiry concerning Political Justice;* and if the state had not been out of joint, most assuredly scarce a reader would have been found. Some years after, when the success of the work had been established, Mr. Burke was asked whether he had seen it. 'Why, yes, I have seen it,' was the answer, 'and a mighty stupid-looking book it is.' No two words could better have described it. The late excellent Sir Samuel Romilly, who had then leisure to read every thing, told a friend who had never heard of it, that there had just appeared a book by far the most absurd that had ever come within his knowledge; this was the work of Godwin. Mrs. Barbauld, also, who at length by the progress of its doctrines was compelled to look at it, declared that what was good in the book was chiefly taken from Hume; that it was 'borrowed sense and original nonsense.' The work, however, prospered; this 'original nonsense' was then in great request, and at a high premium. Mr. Godwin had his admirers, had his school; there were Godwinians in those days, as well as Whigs and Tories, more particularly in the Inns of Court, and among the young lawyers; and this borrower of sense and retailer of nonsense, this dreamer of dreams and seer of visions, was suddenly transformed from a Dissenting clergyman, dissatisfied with his profession, and unknowing and unknown, into a person pointed at, as

That the practice of veracity and justice, and of all our other duties, is *useful* to mankind, is acknowledged

---

he walked in the metropolis of England, as a disturber of empires and a reformer of the world."

According to Mr. Godwin, every thing is to be referred to *justice*. General utility is the criterion of justice, and one of his extravagances consists in maintaining that all private affections and personal obligations are to be sacrificed to it. Professor Smyth goes on: —

"'But justice,' says Mr. Godwin, 'is no respecter of persons'; — very well. The illustrious Bishop of Cambray, for instance, was of more worth than his valet, and there are few of us, says Mr. Godwin, that would hesitate to pronounce, if the Bishop's palace were in flames, which of the two should be preserved. But again: —

"'Suppose I had been myself the valet,' says Mr. Godwin; 'I ought to have chosen to die, rather than Fénelon should have died. To have done otherwise would have been a breach of justice.' Somewhat alarming this, but let it pass; — very well. Again: — 'Suppose,' says Mr. Godwin, 'the valet had been my brother, or my father, or my benefactor; — this would not alter the truth of the proposition: the life of Fénelon would still be more valuable than that of the valet; and justice, pure, unadulterated justice, would still have preferred that which was most valuable; justice would have taught me to save the life of Fénelon at the expense of the other. What magic is there in the pronoun *my* to overturn the decision of impartial truth? My brother, or my father, may be a fool or a profligate, malicious, lying, or dishonest. If they be, of what consequence is it that they are *mine?*'

"This, then, was the result that was wanted, — filial duty at an end. The poor father was to see his son helping another person out of the flames, and be left himself to perish; — all upon the principle of justice, the foundation of all morality. Mathematicians, when their reasonings conduct them to some unnatural position, — that the greater is equal to the less, or the less to the greater, — immediately stop short, produce their phrase *quod est absurdum*, and think it high time to begin again."

The logic by which Godwin reasons away the obligation that exists between parent and child reminds Professor Smyth of the following passage in *Tristram Shandy:* —

"In that most entertaining performance, the lawyers are supposed discussing a law question before Yorick and my Uncle Toby. 'In the reign of Edward VI.,' says one of them, 'in the famous case, commonly known by the name of the Duke of Suffolk's case, as it was a great cause, and much depending upon its issue, and as many causes of great property were likely to be decided in times to come by the precedent to be then made, the most learned, as well in the laws of this realm as in the civil law, were consulted together; and not only the temporal lawyers, but the church lawyers, the jurisconsulti, the jurisprudentes, the civilians, the advocates, the commissaries, the judges of the consistory and prerogative courts of Canterbury and York, with the Master of the Faculties, were all unanimously of opinion, that the mother, the Duchess of Suffolk, was not of kin to her child.'

"'And what said the Duchess of Suffolk to it?' said my Uncle Toby. This was an unexpected question, it seems; and as nothing could be made of it, the lawyers voted the order of the day, and went on with

by moralists of all descriptions; and there is good reason for believing, that, if a person saw all the consequences of his actions, he would perceive that an adherence to their rules is useful and advantageous on the whole, even in those cases in which his limited views incline him to think otherwise. The same observation may be applied to *self-interest*, that the most effectual way of promoting it is to observe religiously the obligations of morality; and these are both very striking instances of that unity of design which is conspicuous alike in the moral and natural world. This makes it an easy matter for a philosopher to give a plausible explanation of all our duties from one principle, because the *general tendency* of all of them is to determine us to the same course of life. That benevolence *may be* the sole principle of action in the Deity is possible (although when we affirm that *it is so* we go beyond our depth); but the case is obviously very different with mankind. If the hypothesis be just with respect to the Deity, we must suppose that he enjoined the duties of veracity and justice, not on account of their intrinsic rectitude, but of their utility. But still, with respect to man they are indispensable laws, for he has an immediate perception of their rectitude. And indeed, if he had not, but were left to deduce their rectitude from the consequences which they have a tendency to produce, we may venture to affirm that there would not be enough of virtue left in the world to hold society together.

It is remarked by Mr. Smith, in a passage which

---

their law argument: this, when they had finished it, left the Duchess, as before, not of kin to her own child.

"'Let the learned say what they will, there must certainly,' quoth my Uncle Toby, 'be some manner of consanguinity between the Duchess of Suffolk and her son.'

"'The vulgar are of the same opinion to this hour,' quoth Yorick."

There is a remarkable coincidence in some of the definitions and speculations of Edwards and the Hopkinsian divines in this country, and those of Godwin. For references, see Ely's *Contrast between Calvinism and Hopkinsianism*, Chap. XI. See likewise Robert Hall's celebrated sermon *Modern Infidelity considered with respect to its Influence on Society*; and Dr Parr's *Spital Sermon*, especially the Notes. — ED.]

cannot be too frequently recalled to the reader's attention, that "although, in accounting for the operations of bodies, we never fail to distinguish the efficient from the final cause, in accounting for those of the mind we are very apt to confound these two different things with one another. When by natural principles we are led to advance those ends which a refined and enlightened reason would recommend to us, we are very apt to impute to that reason, as to their efficient cause, the sentiments and actions by which we advance those ends, and to imagine that to be the wisdom of man which in reality is the wisdom of God. Upon a superficial view, this cause seems sufficient to produce the effects which are ascribed to it, and the system of human nature seems to be more simple and agreeable when all its different operations are in this manner deduced from a single principle."

IV. *Reasons which have induced some Writers to resolve all Virtue into Benevolence.*] To the strictures already offered on Hutcheson's writings I have only to add, that he seems to consider virtue as a quality of our *affections*, whereas it is really a quality of our *actions;* or (perhaps in strict propriety) of those *dispositions* from which our actions immediately proceed. Our benevolent affections are always *amiable*, but, in so far as they are constitutional, they are certainly in no respect *meritorious.* Indeed, some of them are common to us with the brutes. When they are possessed in *an eminent degree*, we may perhaps consider them as a ground of moral esteem, because they indicate the pains which has been bestowed on their cultivation, and a course of active virtue in which they have been exercised and strengthened. On the contrary, a person who wants them is always an object of horror; chiefly because we know they are only to be eradicated by long habits of profligacy, and partly in consequence of the uneasiness we feel when we see the ordinary course of nature violated, as in a monstrous animal production. It is from these two facts that the plausibility of

Dr. Hutcheson's language on this subject in a great measure arises; but if the facts be accurately examined, they will be found perfectly consistent with the doctrine already laid down, that nothing is an object of moral praise or blame, but what depends on our own voluntary exertions; and of consequence, that these terms are not applicable to our benevolent or malevolent affections, so far as we suppose them to result necessarily from our constitutional frame.

In order to think with accuracy on this very important point of morals, it is also necessary to distinguish those benevolent affections which urge us to their respective objects by a blind impulse, from that rational and enlightened benevolence which interests us in the happiness of all mankind, and indeed of all the orders of sensitive being. This divine principle of action appears but little in the bulk of our species; for, although the seeds of it are sown in every breast, it requires long and careful cultivation to rear them to maturity, choked as they are by envy, by jealousy, by selfishness, and by those contracted views which originate in unenlightened schemes of human policy. Clear away these noxious weeds, and the genuine benevolence of the human heart will appear in all its beauty. No wonder, then, that we should regard with such peculiar sentiments of veneration the character of one whom we consider as the sincere and unwearied friend of humanity; for such a character implies the existence of *all the other virtues;* more particularly, candid and just dispositions towards our fellow-creatures, and a long course of persevering exertion in combating prejudice, and in eradicating narrow and malignant passions. The gratitude, besides, which all men must feel towards one in whose benevolent wishes they know themselves to be comprehended, contributes to enliven the former sentiment of moral esteem; and both together throw so peculiar a lustre on this branch of duty, as goes far to account for the origin of those systems which represent it as the only direct object of moral approbation.

It may be worth while to add, before leaving the subject, that, when a rational and habitual benevolence forms part of a character, it will *render the conduct perfectly uniform*, and will exclude the possibility of those inconsistencies that are frequently observable in individuals who give themselves up to the guidance of particular affections, either private or public. How often, for example, do we meet with individuals, who have great pretensions to public spirit, and even to humanity, on important occasions, who affect an habitual rudeness in the common intercourse of society! The public spirit of such men cannot possibly arise from genuine benevolence, otherwise the same principle of action would extend to every different part of the conduct by which the comfort of other men is affected; and in the case of most individuals, the addition they are able to make to human happiness, by the constant exercise of courtesy and gentleness to all who are within the sphere of their influence, is of far greater amount than all that can result from the more splendid and heroic exertions of their beneficence. A similar remark may be applied to such as are possessed of strong private attachments and of humanity to objects in distress, while they have no idea of public spirit; and also to those who lay claim to a more than common portion of patriotic zeal, while they avow a contempt for the general interests of humanity. In truth, all those offices, whether apparently trifling or important, which contribute to augment the happiness of our fellow-creatures, — civility, gentleness, kindness, humanity, patriotism, universal benevolence, — are only diversified expressions of the same disposition, according to the circumstances in which it operates, and the relation which the agent bears to others.

Section II.

OF JUSTICE.

I. *Definition and Origin of the Sense of Justice.*] The word *justice*, in its most extensive signification, denotes that disposition which leads us, in cases where our own temper, or passions, or interests are concerned, to determine and to act without being biased by partial considerations.

I had occasion formerly to observe, that a desire of our own happiness is inseparable from our nature as sensitive and rational beings; or, in other words, that it is impossible to conceive of a being capable of forming the ideas of happiness and misery, to whom the one shall not be an object of desire and the other of aversion. On the other hand, it is no less evident that this desire is a principle belonging to such beings *exclusively;* inasmuch as the very idea of *happiness*, or of *what is good for man on the whole*, presupposes the exercise of *reason* in the mind which is able to perform it, and as it is only a being possessed of the power of *self-government* which can pursue steadily this abstract conception, in opposition to the solicitations of present appetite and passion. This *rational self-love* (or, in other words, this regard to what is good for us on the whole) is analogous, in some important respects, to that *calm benevolence* which has been already illustrated. They are both characteristical endowments of a rational nature, and they both exert an influence over the conduct, in proportion as reason gains an ascendant over prejudice and error, and over those appetites which are common to us and to the brutes.

The inferior principles of action in our nature have all a manifest reference to one or other of these rational principles; for, although they operate without any reflection on our part, they all lead to ends beneficial to the individual or to society. Of this kind are hunger, thirst, the desire of knowledge, the desire of esteem, pity to the distressed, natural affection, and a variety of others. Upon the whole, these two great principles of action, *self-love* and *benevolence*, coincide wonderfully in recommending one and the same course of conduct; and we have great reason to believe, that, if we were acquainted with all the remote consequences of our actions, they would be found to coincide entirely. There are, however, cases in which there *seems* to be an interference between them; and, in such cases, the generality of mankind are apt to be influenced more than they ought to be by self-love, and the principles which are subsidiary to it. These sometimes lead them to act in direct opposition to their sense of duty; but much more frequently they influence the conduct by suggesting to the judgment partial and erroneous views of circumstances, and by persuading men that the line of their duty coincides with that which is prescribed by interest and inclination. Of all this every man capable of reflection must soon be convinced from experience, and he will study to correct his judgment in cases in which he himself is a party, either by recollecting the judgments he has formerly passed in similar circumstances on the conduct of others, or by stating cases to himself, in which his own interest and predilections are perfectly left out of the question. Now I use the word *justice* to express that disposition of mind which leads a man, where his own interest or passions are concerned, to determine and to act according to those judgments which he would have formed of the conduct of another placed in a similar situation.

But although I believe that expedients of this sort are necessary to the best of men for *correcting* their moral judgments in cases in which they themselves are parties, it will not therefore follow, (as I have before observed,*) that our ideas of right and wrong with respect to our own conduct are originally derived from our sentiments with respect to the conduct of others. If I had had recourse to no such expedient for correcting

* See p. 248.

my first judgment, I should still have formed some judgment or other of a particular conduct, as right, wrong, or indifferent, and the only difference would have been, that I should probably have decided improperly, from a false or a partial view of the case.

It is observed by Mr. Smith, as an argument against the existence of a *moral sense* or *moral faculty*, that these words are of very recent origin, and that it must appear very strange that a principle, which Providence undoubtedly intended to be the governing one of human nature, should hitherto have been so little taken notice of, as not to have got a name in any language. If this observation is levelled merely at these two expressions, I do not take upon me to defend their propriety. I use them because they are commonly employed by ethical writers of late, and because I do not think them liable to misinterpretation after the explanation of them I formerly gave. I certainly do not consider them as expressing an implanted relish for certain qualities of action analogous to our relish for certain tastes and smells. All I contend for is, that the words *right* and *wrong*, *ought* and *ought not*, express *simple ideas;* that our perception of these qualities in certain actions is *an ultimate fact of our nature;* and that this perception always *implies the idea of moral obligation.* When I speak of a moral sense or a moral faculty, I mean merely to express *the power we have of forming these ideas;* but I do not suppose that this bears any more analogy to our external senses than the power we have of forming the simple ideas of *number*, of *time*, or of *causation*, all which arise in the mind, we cannot tell how, when certain objects or certain events are perceived by the understanding. If those ideas were as important as those of right and wrong, or had been as much under the review of philosophers, we might perhaps have had *a sense of time*, *a sense of number*, and *a sense of causation.* And, in fact, something very like this language occurs in the writings of Lord Kames.

But if Mr. Smith meant to be understood as implying that the words *right* and *wrong*, *ought* and *ought not*, do not express simple ideas, I must take the liberty of remarking, in opposition to it, that, although the words *moral sense* and *moral faculty*, considered as indicating their source, are of late origin, this is by no means the case with the word *conscience*. It is indeed said, that conscience "does not immediately denote any moral faculty, by which we approve or disapprove, — that it supposes, indeed, the existence of some such faculty, but that it properly signifies our consciousness of having acted agreeably or contrary to its directions." * But the truth I take to be this, that the word *conscience* coincides exactly with the moral faculty, with this difference only, that the former refers to our own conduct alone, whereas the latter is meant to express also the power by which we approve or disapprove of the conduct of others. Now if this be granted, and if it be allowed that the former word is to be found in all languages, and that the latter is only a modern invention, is it not a natural inference, that our judgments, with respect to our own conduct, are not merely applications to ourselves of those we have previously formed with respect to the conduct of our fellow-creatures?

II. *The Duty of Candor; or Justice in our Appreciation of other Men.*] It would be endless to attempt to point out all the various forms in which the disposition formerly defined will display itself in life. I must content myself with mentioning one or two of its more remarkable effects, merely as examples of the influence it is likely to have on the conduct. One of the more important of these is that temper of mind we express by the word *candor*, which prevents our judgments with respect to other men from being improperly biased by our passions and prejudices. This, although at bottom the disposition is the same, may be considered in three lights: — 1st. As it is displayed in appreciating

* Smith's *Theory of Moral Sentiments*, Part VII. Sect. III. Chap. III.

the talents of others. 2d. In judging of their intentions. 3d. In controversy.

1. There is no principle more deeply implanted in the mind than the love of fame and of distinction, and there is none which, when properly regulated, is subservient to more valuable purposes. It is, at the same time, a principle which it is perhaps as difficult to restrain within the bounds of moderation as any other. In some ungoverned minds, it seems to get the better of every other principle of action, and must be a source to the possessor of perpetual mortification and disgust, by leading him to aspire at eminence in every different line of ambition, and to repine if in any one of them he is surpassed by others. In the midst of the astonishing projects which employed the sublime genius of Richelieu, his peace of mind was completely ruined by the success of the *Cid* of Corneille. The first appearance of this tragedy (according to Fontenelle) alarmed the Cardinal as much as if he had seen the Spaniards at the gates of Paris; and the most acceptable flattery which his minions could offer was to advise him to eclipse the fame of Corneille by a tragedy of his own. Nor did he aim merely at adding the fame of a poet to that of a statesman. Mortified to think that any one path of ambition was shut against him, he is said, when on his death-bed, to have held some conversations with his confessor about the possibility of his being canonized as a saint.

In order to restrain this violent and insatiable desire within certain bounds, there are many checks appointed in our constitution. In the first place, it can be *completely* gratified only by the actual possession of those qualities for which we wish to be esteemed, and of those advantages which are the proper grounds of distinction. A good man is never more mortified than when he is praised for qualities he does not possess, or for advantages in which he is conscious he has no merit. Secondly, although the gratification of this principle consists in a certain superiority over other men, we feel that we are not entitled to take undue advantages of them. We may exert ourselves to the utmost in the race of glory, but we are not entitled to obstruct the progress of others, or to detract from their reputation in order to advance our own. All this will be readily granted in general; and yet in practice there is surely nothing more difficult than to draw the line between emulation and envy, or to check that self-partiality which, while it leads us to dwell on our own advantages, and to magnify them in our own estimation, prevents us either from attending sufficiently to the merits of others, or from viewing them in the most favorable light. Of this difficulty a wise and good man will soon be satisfied from his own experience, and he will endeavour to guard against it as far as he is able, by judging of the merits of a rival, or even of an enemy, as he would have done if there had been no interference between them. He will endeavour, in short, to do *justice* to their merits, not merely in words, but in sincerity, and bring himself, if possible, to love and to honor that genius and ability which have eclipsed his own. Nor will he retire in disgust from the race because he has been outstripped by others, but will redouble all his exertions in the service of mankind; recollecting, that, if Nature has been more partial to others in her intellectual gifts than to him, she has left open to all the theatre of virtue, where the merits of individuals are determined, not by their actual attainments, but by the use and improvement they make of those advantages which their situation has afforded them.

2. Candor in judging of the intentions of others. I have before mentioned several considerations which render it highly probable that there is much less vice or criminal intention in the world than is commonly imagined, and that the greater part of the disputes among mankind arise from mutual mistake and misapprehension. Every man must recollect many instances in which his own motives have been grossly misapprehended by the world; and it is but reasonable for him to conclude, that the case may have been the same with

other men. It is but an instance, then, of that justice we owe to others, to make the most candid allowances for their apparent deviations, and to give every action the most favorable construction it can possibly admit of. Such a temper, while it renders a man respectable and amiable in society, contributes perhaps more than any other circumstance to his private happiness. "When you would cheer your heart," says Marcus Antoninus, "consider the excellences and abilities of your several acquaintance; the activity of one, the high sense of honor and modesty of another, the liberality of a third, and in other persons some other virtue. There is nothing so delightful as virtue appearing in the conduct of your contemporaries as frequently as possible. Such thoughts we should still retain with us." *

3. Perhaps there is no temper which so completely disqualifies us for the search of truth, as that which we experience when provoked by controversy or dispute. Some men undoubtedly are more misled by it than others; but I apprehend there is no one, however modest and unassuming, who will not own that, upon such occasions, he has almost always felt his judgment warped, and a desire of victory mingle itself, in spite of all his efforts, with his love of truth. Hence the aversion which all such men feel for controversy, — convinced from experience how likely it would be to betray themselves into error, and unwilling to afford an opportunity for displaying the envious and malignant passions of others. This amiable disposition has been often mentioned by the friends of Sir Isaac Newton as one of the most marked features in his character; and we are even told that it led him to suppress, for a course of years, some of his most important discoveries, which he knew from their nature were likely to provoke opposition. "He was indeed," says one of his biographers, "of so meek and gentle a disposition, and so great a lover of peace, that he would have rather chosen to remain in obscurity than to have the calm of life

* Book VI. c. 48.

ruffled by those storms and disputes which genius and learning always draw upon those who are most eminent for them. From his love of peace arose, no doubt, that unusual kind of horror which he felt for all disputes. Steady, unbroken attention, free from those frequent recoilings incident to others, was his peculiar felicity. He knew it, and he knew the value of it. When some objections, hastily made to his discoveries concerning light and colors, induced him to lay aside the design he had taken of publishing his Optical Lectures, we find him reflecting on that dispute, into which he had unavoidably been drawn, in these terms:—'I blamed my own imprudence for parting with so real a blessing as my quiet, to run after a shadow.' In the same temper, after he had sent the manuscript to the Royal Society, with his consent to the printing of it, upon Hooke's injuriously insisting that he had himself solved Kepler's problem before our author, he determined, rather than be involved again in a controversy, to suppress the third book; and he was very hardly prevailed on to alter that resolution." *

I shall only add further on this head, that a love of controversy indicates, not only an overweening vanity and a disregard for truth, but in general, perhaps always, it indicates a *mediocrity of genius;* for it arises from those feelings of envy and jealousy which provoke little minds to depreciate the merit of useful discoveries. He who is conscious of his own inventive powers, and whose great object is to add to the stock of human knowledge, will reject unwillingly any plausible doctrine till after the most severe examination, and will separate, with patience and temper, the truths it contains from the errors that are blended with them. No opinion can be more groundless than that a captious and disputatious temper is a mark of acuteness. On the contrary, a sound and manly understanding is in no instance more strongly displayed than in a quick perception of important truth, when imperfectly stated and

* Hutton's *Mathematical Dictionary*, Art. *Newton* (*Sir Isaac*).

blended with error;—a perception which may not be sufficient to satisfy the judgment completely at the time, or at least to obviate the difficulties of others, but which is sufficient to prevent it from a hasty rejection of the whole, from the obvious defects of some of the parts. Hence the important hints which an author of genius collects among the rubbish of his predecessors; and which, so far from detracting from his own originality, place it in the strongest possible light, by showing that an idea which was already current in the world, and which had hitherto remained barren and useless, may, in the mind of a philosopher, become the germ of an extensive system.

I cannot help taking this opportunity of remarking (although the observation is not much connected with the subject in which we are engaged), that something similar to this may be applied to our critical judgments in the fine arts. It is easy to perceive blemishes, but it is the province of genius alone to have a quick perception of beauties, and to be eager to applaud them. And it is owing to this, that, of all critics, a dunce is the severest, and a man of genuine taste the most indulgent.

III. *The Duty of Honesty; or Justice in respect to the Interests and Rights of other Men.*] The foregoing illustrations are stated at some length, in order to correct those partial definitions of justice which restrict its province to a rigorous observance of the rules of integrity or honesty in our dealings with our fellow-creatures. So far as this last disposition proceeds from a sense of duty, uninfluenced by human laws, it coincides exactly with that branch of virtue which has been now described under the title of *candor*.

In the instances hitherto mentioned, the disposition of justice has been supposed to operate in restraining the partialities of the temper and passions. There are, however, no instances in which its influence is more necessary than where our *interest* is concerned; or, to express myself more explicitly, where there is an apparent interference between our *rights* and those of other men. In such cases, a disposition to observe the rules of justice is called *integrity* or *honesty*, — which is so important a branch of justice that it has, in a great measure, appropriated the name to itself. The observations made by Mr. Hume and Mr. Smith, on the differences between justice and the other virtues, apply only to this last branch of it; and it is this branch which properly forms the subject of that part of ethics which is called *natural jurisprudence*.* In what remains of this chapter, when the word *justice* occurs, it is to be understood in the limited sense now mentioned.

The circumstances which distinguish this kind of justice from the other virtues are chiefly two. In the first place, its rules may be laid down with a degree of accuracy of which moral precepts do not in any other instance admit. Secondly, its rules may be enforced, inasmuch as every breach of them violates the rights of some other person, and entitles him to employ force for his defence or security.

Another distinction between justice and the other virtues is much insisted on by Mr. Hume. It is, according to him, an *artificial* and not a *natural* virtue, and derives all its obligations from the political union, and from considerations of utility. The principal argument alleged in support of this proposition is, that there is no implanted principle, prompting us by a blind impulse to the exercise of justice, similar to those affections which conspire with and strengthen our benevolent dispositions. But, granting the fact upon which this argument proceeds, nothing can be inferred from it that makes an essential distinction between the obligations of justice and of beneficence; for, so far as we act merely from the blind impulse of an affection, our conduct cannot be considered as virtuous. Our affections were given us to arrest our attention to particular objects, whose happiness is connected with our exertions, and to excite and support the activity of the

* *Theory of Moral Sentiments*, Part VII. Sect. VI.

mind, when a sense of duty might be insufficient for the purpose; but the propriety or impropriety of our conduct depends, in no instance, on the strength or weakness of the affection, but on our obeying or disobeying the dictates of reason and of conscience. These inform us, in language which it is impossible to mistake, that it is sometimes a duty to check the most amiable and pleasing emotions of the heart; — to withdraw, for example, from the sight of those distresses which stronger claims forbid us to relieve, and to deny ourselves that exquisite luxury which arises from the exercise of humanity. So far, therefore, as benevolence is a virtue, it is precisely on the same footing with justice; that is, we approve of it, not because it is agreeable to us, but because we feel it to be a duty.

It may be further remarked, that there are very strong implanted principles which serve as checks on *injustice;* the principles, to wit, of resentment and of indignation, which are surely as much a part of the human constitution as pity or parental affection. These principles imply a sense of injustice, and consequently of justice.

In the case of justice, also, there is always a *right* on one hand corresponding to an *obligation* on the other. If I am under an obligation, for example, to abstain from violating the property of my neighbour, he has a right to defend by force his property when invaded. It therefore appears that the rules of justice may be laid down in two different forms, either as a system of *duties* or as a system of *rights.* The former view of the subject belongs properly to the moralist, the latter to the lawyer. It is in this last form, accordingly, that the principles of justice have been stated by the writers on natural jurisprudence.

So far, there is nothing to be reprehended in the plan they have followed. On the contrary, a considerable advantage was gained in point of method by adopting that very comprehensive and accurate division of our rights which the civilians had introduced. As the whole object of law is to protect men in all that they may lawfully *do*, or *possess*, or *demand*, civilians have defined the word *jus*, or *right*, to be *facultas aliquid agendi, vel possidendi, vel ab alio consequendi*, — a lawful claim to do any thing, to possess any thing, or to demand something from some other person. The first of these may be called *the right of liberty*, or the right of employing the powers we have received from nature in every case in which we do not injure the rights of others; the second, *the right of property;* the third, *the rights arising from contract.* The last two were further distinguished from each other by calling the former (to wit, the right of property) a *real* right, and the latter (to wit, the rights arising from contract) *personal* rights, because they respect some particular person or persons from whom the fulfilment of the contract may be required.

This division of our rights appears to be comprehensive and philosophical, and it affords a convenient arrangement for exhibiting an indirect view of the different duties which justice prescribes. "What I have a right to do it is the duty of my fellow-creatures to allow me to do, without molestation. What is my property no man ought to take from me, or to disturb me in the enjoyment of it. And what I have a right to demand of any man it is his duty to perform." * Such a system, therefore, with respect to our rights, exhibits (though in a manner somewhat indirect and artificial) a system of the rules of justice.

Section III.

OF THE RIGHT OF PROPERTY.

I. *The Right of Property.*] The following observations on the *right of property* are introduced here chiefly with a view to show that men possess rights antecedent to the establishment of the political union.

It cannot, I apprehend, be doubted, that, according to the notions to which we, in the present state of so-

---

* Reid, *On the Active Powers*, Essay V. Chap. III.

ciety, are habituated from our infancy, the three following things are included in the idea of property.

1. A right of exclusive enjoyment.

2. A right of inquiry after our property, when taken away without our consent, and of reclaiming it wherever found.

3. A right of transference.

We do not consider our property in any object to be complete, unless we can exercise all these three rights with respect to it.

Lord Kames endeavours to show that these ideas are not agreeable to the apprehensions of the human mind in the ruder periods of society, but imply a refinement and abstraction of thought which are the result of improvement in law and government. The relation (in particular) of property, independent of possession, he thinks of too metaphysical a nature for the mind of a savage. "It appears to me," says he, "to be highly probable, that among savages, involved in objects of sense, and strangers to abstract speculation, property, and the rights or moral powers arising from it, never are with accuracy distinguished from the natural powers that must be exerted upon the subject to make it profitable to the possessor. The man who kills and eats, who sows and reaps, at his own pleasure, independent of another's will, is naturally deemed proprietor. The grossest savages understand power without right, of which they are made sensible by daily acts of violence; but property without possession is a conception too abstract for a savage, or for any person who has not studied the principles of law." *

With this remark I cannot agree; because I think the right of property is founded on a natural sentiment, which must be felt in full force in the lowest state of society. The sentiment I allude to is that of a moral connection between labor and a right of exclusive enjoyment to the fruits of it. This connection it will be proper to illustrate more particularly.

---

* *Historical Law Tracts*, Tract III.

Let us suppose, then, a country so fertile as to produce all the necessaries and accommodations of life without any exertions of human industry; it is manifest, that, in such a state of things, no man would think of appropriating to himself any of these necessaries or accommodations, any more than we in this part of the globe think of appropriating air or water. As this, however, is not, in any part of the earth, the condition of man, doomed as he is, by the circumstances of his birth, to eat his bread in the sweat of his brow, it would be reasonable to expect, *a priori*, that Nature would make some provision for securing to individuals the fruits of their industry. In fact, she *has* made such a provision in the natural sentiments of mankind, which lead them to consider industry as entitled to reward, and, in particular, the laborer as entitled to the fruit of his own labor. These, I think, may be fairly stated as *moral axioms*, to which the mind yields its assent as immediately and necessarily as it does to any axiom in mathematics or metaphysics.

How cruel is the mortification we feel when we see an industrious man reduced by some unforeseen misfortune to beggary in old age! We can scarcely help complaining of the precarious condition of humanity, and that man should be thus doomed to be the sport of accident; and we feel ourselves called on, as far as we are able, to repair, by our own liberality, this unjust distribution of the goods of fortune. On the other hand, it is difficult to avoid some degree of dissatisfaction when we see the natural and deserved reward of industry acquired all at once by a prize in the lottery or by gaming, although in this instance the uneasiness (as might be expected from the natural benevolence to the human mind) is trifling in comparison to what it is in the other case. Our dissatisfaction in particular instances is much greater when we see the laborer deprived by accident of the *immediate* fruit of his own labor; — when, for example, he has nearly completed a complicated machine, and some delicate part of it gives way, and renders all his toil useless.

If another person interferes with the fruit of his industry, our dissatisfaction and indignation are still more increased. We feel here a variety of sentiments. 1. A dissatisfaction that the laborer does not enjoy that reward to which his industry entitled him. 2. A dissatisfaction that another person, who did not labor, should acquire the possession of an object of value. And 3. An indignation against the man who deprived the laborer of his just reward.

This sentiment, that " the laborer deserves the fruit of his own labor," is the *chief*, or rather (abstracting positive institution) the *only*, foundation of the sense of property. An attempt to deprive him of it is a species of *injustice* which rouses the indignation of every impartial spectator; and so deeply are these principles implanted in our nature, that we cannot help feeling some degree of remorse when we deprive even a hive of bees of that provision which they had industriously collected for their own use.

The writers, indeed, on natural law ascribe in general the origin of property to *priority of occupancy*, and have puzzled themselves in attempting to explain how this act should appropriate to an individual what was formerly in common. Grotius and Puffendorf insist that this right of occupancy is founded upon a tacit but understood assent of all mankind, that the first occupant should become the owner. And Barbeyrac, Locke, and others, that the very act of occupancy alone, being a degree of bodily labor, is, from a principle of natural justice, without any compact, a sufficient foundation of property. Blackstone, although he thinks that the dispute about the manner in which occupancy conveys a right of property savors too much of scholastic refinement, expresses no doubt about its having this effect independent of positive institutions.*

Some later philosophers have founded the right of property on the general sympathy of mankind with

* See his *Commentaries*, Book II. Chap. I.

the *reasonable* expectation which the occupant has formed of enjoying unmolested the object he has got possession of, or of which he was the first discoverer; and on the indignation felt by the impartial spectator when he sees this reasonable expectation disappointed. This theory (which I have been assured from the best authority was adopted by Mr. Smith in his lectures on jurisprudence) seems to have been suggested by a passage in Dr. Hutcheson's *Moral Philosophy*, in which he says, that "it is immoral, when we can support ourselves otherwise, to defeat any innocent design of another; and that on this immorality is founded the regard we owe to the claims of the first occupant." In this theory, too, it is taken for granted that priority of occupancy founds a right of property, and that such a right may even be acquired by having accidentally *seen* a valuable object before it was observed by any other person.

In order to think with accuracy on this subject, it is necessary to distinguish carefully the *complete* right of property which is founded on *labor*, from the *transient* right of possession which is acquired by mere *priority of occupancy*. Thus, before the appropriation of land, if any individual had occupied a particular spot for repose or shade, it would have been *unjust* to deprive him of the possession of it. This, however, was only a transient right. The spot of ground would again become *common* the moment the occupier had left it; that is, the *right* of possession would remain no longer than the *act* of possession. Cicero illustrates this happily by the similitude of a theatre. "Quemadmodum theatrum, cum commune sit, recte tamen dici potest ejus esse eum locum quem quisque occuparit." *

The general conclusions which I deduce from the foregoing observations are these: —

1. That, in every state of society, *labor*, wherever it is exerted, is understood to found a right of property.

---

* *De Finibus*, Lib. III. 20. "As in a theatre the seats are all for common use, yet every man's place is his own when he has taken it."

2. That, according to natural law, (in the sense at least in which that phrase is commonly employed by writers on jurisprudence,) labor is the *only* original way of acquiring property.

3. That, according to natural law, mere *occupancy* founds only *a right of possession;* and that, wherever it founds a complete *right of property,* it owes its force to *positive institutions.*

II. *Origin and History of Property.*] An attention to these conclusions, in particular to the distinction between the *transient right of possession* founded on *occupancy,* and the *permanent right of property* founded on *labor,* will, if I mistake not, clear up some of the difficulties which involve the first steps in the history of property, according to the view of the subject given by Lord Kames; and it was with this view I was led to premise these general principles to the slight historical sketch I am now to offer.

With respect to that system which refers the origin of property to the political union and to considerations of utility, it seems sufficient to observe, that, so far is government from *creating* this *right,* its necessary effect is to subject it to certain limitations. Abstraction made of political confederation, every man's property is solely at his own disposal. He is supreme judge in his own cause, and may defend what he conceives to be his right as far as his power reaches. In the state of civil society his property is regulated by positive laws, and he must acquiesce in the judgment of his superiors with respect to his rights, even in those cases where he feels it to be unjust.

From the passage already quoted from Kames, it appears that he conceived the idea of property without possession to be of too abstract and metaphysical a nature to be apprehended by a savage; and he has collected a variety of facts to prove, that, according to the common notions of mankind, in the infancy of jurisprudence, the right of property is understood to cease the moment that possession is at an end. But on a more attentive examination of the subject, I apprehend it will be found that the ideas of savages, with respect to property, are the same with ours; that mere occupancy without labor founds only a right of possession; and that labor, wherever it is employed, founds an exclusive and permanent right to the fruits of it. Lord Kames's theory has obviously been suggested by the common doctrine with respect to the right of property being founded in priority of occupancy, compared with the acknowledged fact, that among rude nations occupancy does not establish a permanent right. The other arguments which he has alleged in support of his opinion will be found to be equally inconclusive.

Before I proceed to the consideration of these, it may be proper to observe, that we must not always form an idea of the sentiments of men from the *defects* of their laws. The existence, indeed, of a law is a proof of the sentiments which men felt when the law was made; but the defects of a law are not always proofs that men did not feel that there *were* disorders in the state of society which required correction. The laws of a country may not make provision for reparation to the original proprietor in the case of theft; but it will not follow from this that men do not apprehend the original proprietor to have any *right* when his property has been stolen from him. The application of this general remark to some of the arguments I am now to consider will, I hope, be so obvious, as to render it unnecessary for me to point it out particularly.

Among these arguments, one of the most plausible is founded on a general principle, which appears, from a variety of facts quoted by Kames, to run through most rude systems of jurisprudence, that, in the case of stolen goods, the claim of the *bonâ fide* purchaser is preferable to that of the original proprietor. This he accounts for from the imperfect notions they have of the metaphysical nature of property when separated from possession. But if this were the case, the same laws should support the claim of the *thief* against the original proprietor: or rather, indeed, neither the original proprietor, nor any one else, could conceive that he had any connection with the object stolen the moment after it was out of his possession. The fact is, that this respect paid to the *bonâ fide* purchaser is a proof, not of any misapprehension with respect to the idea of property, but of a weak government and an imperfect police. Where thefts are easily committed, and where no public fairs or markets are established, it would put a complete end to all transferences of property, if the *bonâ fide* purchaser were left exposed to the claims of former proprietors. Such a practice would be attended with still greater inconveniences than arise from the casual violations of property by theft; not to mention that the regard shown to the *bonâ fide* purchaser must have a tendency to repress theft, by redoubling the attention of individuals to preserve the actual possession of their property. That these or some other views of utility were the real foundation of the laws quoted by Kames is confirmed by an old regulation in our own country, prohibiting buying and selling, except in open market, — a regulation which had obviously been suggested by the experience of the inconveniences arising from the latent claims of former proprietors against *bonâ fide* purchasers.

Another argument mentioned by Kames in support of his theory is founded on the shortness of the term which completes prescription among rude nations; a single year, for example, in the case of movables, by the oldest law of the Romans. This law, he says, testifies that property, independent of possession, was considered to be a *right of the slenderest kind.* It is evident, that, upon his own principles, it should not in that state of society have been considered as a right at all. If it was conceived to subsist a single day after the possession was at an end, the metaphysical difficulty which he magnifies so much was obviously surmounted. In every society, it will be found expedient to fix some term for prescription, and the particular length of it must be determined by the circumstances of the society at the time. In general, as law improves, and government becomes more effectual, a greater attention to the stability of property, and consequently a longer term for prescription, may be expected.

The community of goods, which is said to take place among some rude nations, will be found, on examination, to be perfectly consistent with the account I have given of their ideas on the subject of property. Where the game is taken by a common effort, the natural sense of justice dictates that it should be enjoyed in common. And indeed, abstracting all considerations of justice, the experience of the precarious fortune of the chase would soon suggest to the common sense of mankind the expediency of such an arrangement. This, however, does not indicate any imperfection in their idea of property; for even in this state of society there are always some articles which are understood to be the exclusive property of the individual, such as his bow and arrows, and the instruments he employs in fishing.

I am confirmed in these conclusions by the account given by Dr. Robertson of the American Indians; and the more so, as the facts he mentions, and even his reasonings, stand in opposition to his own preconceived opinion. "*Nations*," he says expressly, "*which depend upon hunting are strangers to the idea of property*"; and yet, when he comes to explain himself, it appears that, even in the present age of metaphysical refinement, if our physical circumstances were the same, we should feel and judge exactly as they do. "As the animals," he continues, in the passage immediately following the last sentence I have quoted, "on which the hunter feeds are not bred under his inspection, nor nourished by his care, he can claim no right to them while they run wild in the forest. Where game is so plentiful that it can be caught with little trouble, men never dream of appropriating what is of small value, or of easy acquisition. Where it is so rare that the labor or danger of the chase requires the united efforts of a tribe or village, what is killed is a common stock, be longing equally to all who, by their skill or their courage, have contributed to the success of the excursion. The forest or hunting-grounds are deemed the property of the tribe, from which it has a title to exclude every rival nation. But no individual arrogates a right to any district of these in preference to his fellow-citizens. They belong equally to all, and thither, as to a general and undivided store, all repair in quest of sustenance. The same principles by which they regulate their chief occupation extend to that which is subordinate. Even agriculture has not introduced among them a complete idea of property. As the men hunt, the women labor together, and after they have shared the toils of the seed-time, they enjoy the harvest in common." *

In the notes and illustrations at the end of his History, Dr. Robertson seems to have been aware that he had expressed himself somewhat too strongly on this subject, and he has even gone so far as to intimate his suspicions that the common facts are not very accurately stated. "I strongly suspect that a community of goods, and an undivided store, are known only among the rudest tribes of hunters, and that, as soon as any species of agriculture or regular industry is known, the idea of an exclusive right of property to the fruits of them is introduced."

In support of this opinion, Dr. Robertson refers to accounts which he had received concerning the state of property among the Indians in very different regions of America. "The idea of the natives of Brazil," says the Chevalier de Pinto, who writes on this subject from personal observation, "concerning property is, that, if any person cultivate a field, he alone ought to enjoy the produce of it, and no other has a title to pretend to it. If an individual or a family go a hunting or fishing, what is caught belongs to the individual or family, and they communicate no part of it but to their Cazique, and such of their kindred as happen to be indisposed.

* *History of America*, Book IV. § 66.

"If any person in the village come to their hut, he may sit down freely and eat without asking liberty. But this is the consequence of their general principle of hospitality; for I never observed any partition of the increase of their fields, or the produce of the chase, which I could consider as the result of any idea concerning the community of goods. On the contrary, they are so much attached to what they deem to be their property, that it would be extremely dangerous to encroach on it. As far as I have seen or can learn, there is not one tribe of Indians in South America among whom that community of goods, which has been so highly extolled, is known. The circumstance in the government of the Jesuits most irksome to the Indians of Paraguay was the community of goods which those fathers introduced. This was repugnant to the original ideas of the Indians. They were acquainted with the rights of private exclusive property, and they submitted with impatience to the regulations which destroyed them."

"Actual possession," says a missionary who resided several years among the Indians of the Five Nations, "gives a right to the soil; but, whenever a possessor sees fit to quit it, another has as good a right to take it as he who left it. This law or custom respects not only the particular spot on which he erects his house, but also his planting ground. If a man has prepared a particular spot of ground, on which he proposes in future to build or plant, no man has a right to incommode him, much less to the fruit of his labors, until it appears that he voluntarily gives up his views. But I never heard of any formal conveyance from one Indian to another in their natural state. The limits of every canton are circumscribed, that is, they are allowed to hunt as far as such a river on this hand, and such a mountain on the other. This area is occupied and improved by individuals and their families. Individuals, not the community, have the use and profit of their own labors, or success in hunting."

III. *Property when rightfully created or recognized by Positive Laws not less Sacred.*] It must not, however, be inferred from what has been said, that in a civilized society there is any thing in that species of property which is acquired by labor to which individuals owe a more sacred regard than they do to every other species of property created or recognized by positive laws. Among these last there are *many* which have derived their origin from a principle no less obligatory than our natural sense of *justice*, a clear perception in the mind of the legislator (sanctioned perhaps by the concurrent experience of different ages and nations) of *general utility;* and to *all* of them, while they exist, the reverence of the subject is due, on the same principle which binds him to respect and to maintain the social order. Nature has provided for human happiness, in this instance, in a manner precisely analogous to her general economy. Those simple and indispensable rules of *right* and *wrong*, of *just* and *unjust*, without which the fruits of the earth could not be converted to the use of man, nor his existence maintained even in the rudest form of the social union, she has engraved on the heart as an essential part of the human constitution, — leaving men, as society advances, to employ their gradually improving *reason* in fixing, according to their own ideas of expediency, the various regulations concerning the acquisition, the alienation and transmission of property, which the more complicated interests of the community may require.

It is also beautifully ordered, that, while a regard for legal property is thus secured, among men capable of reflection, by a sense of general utility, the same effect is accomplished, in the minds of the multitude, *by habit and the association of ideas ;* in consequence of which, all the inequalities of fortune are sanctioned by mere prescription, and long possession is conceived to found a *right of property* as complete as that which, by the law of nature, an individual has in the fruits of his own industry.

In such a state of things, therefore, as that with which we are connected, the right of property must be understood to derive its origin from *two* distinct sources: the one is that natural sentiment of the mind which establishes a moral connection between labor and an exclusive enjoyment of the fruits of it; the other is the municipal institutions of the country where we live. These institutions everywhere take rise partly from ideas of natural justice, and partly (perhaps chiefly) from ideas of supposed utility, — two principles which, when properly understood, are, I believe, always in harmony with each other, and which it ought to be the great aim of every legislator to reconcile to the utmost of his power. Among those questions, however, which fall under the cognizance of positive laws, there are many on which natural justice is entirely silent, and which, of consequence, may be discussed on principles of *utility* solely. Such are most of the questions concerning the regulation of the succession to a man's property after his death; of some of which it may perhaps be found that the determination ought to vary with the circumstances of the society, and which have certainly, *in fact*, been frequently determined by the caprice of the legislator, or by some principle ultimately resolvable into an accidental association of ideas. Indeed, various cases may be supposed, in which it is not only useful, but necessary, that a rule should be fixed; while, at the same time, *neither* justice nor utility seems to be much interested in the particular decision.

In examining the questions which turn on considerations of *utility*, some will immediately occur, of which the determination is so obvious, and which, at the same time, are so universal in their application, that the laws of all enlightened nations on the subject may be expected to be the same. Of this description are many of the questions which may be stated with respect to the effects of *priority of occupancy* in establishing *permanent* rights. These questions are of course frequently confounded with questions of *natural law;* and in *one* sense of that phrase they may not improperly be comprehended under the title, but the distinction between them and the other class of questions is essential; for wherever considerations of utility are involved, the political union is supposed, whereas the principle of *justice*, properly so called (of that justice, for example, which respects the right of the laborer to enjoy the fruit of his own industry), is inseparable from the human frame.*

Section IV.

OF VERACITY.

I. *Importance and Foundation of Veracity.*] The important rank which *veracity* holds among our social duties appears from the obvious consequences that would result if no foundation were laid for it in the constitution of our nature. The purposes of speech would be frustrated, and every man's opportunities of knowledge would be limited to his own personal experience.

Considerations of utility, however, do not seem to be the only ground of the approbation we bestow on this disposition. Abstraction made of all regard to consequences, there is something pleasing and amiable in sincerity, openness, and truth, — something disagreeable and disgusting in duplicity, equivocation, and falsehood. Dr. Hutcheson himself, the great patron of that theory which resolves all moral qualities into benevolence, confesses this; for he speaks of a *sense* which leads us to approve of *veracity*, distinct from the *sense* which approves of qualities useful to mankind.† As this, however, is at best but a vague way of speaking, it may be proper to analyze more particularly that part of our

---

* On the right of property and its limitations, see Mill's *Principles of Political Economy*, Part II. Chap. I., II. — Ed.

† *Philosophiæ Moralis Institutio Compendiaria*, Lib. II. Capp. IX., X. Aristotle expresses himself nearly to the same purpose. *Ethic. Nicomach.*, Lib. IV. Cap. VII. Various passages of a similar import occur in Cicero.

constitution from which our approbation of veracity arises.

That there is in the human mind a natural or instinctive principle of veracity has been remarked by many authors, the same part of our constitution which prompts to social intercourse prompting also to sincerity in our mutual communications. Truth is always the spontaneous and native expression of our sentiments; whereas falsehood implies a certain violence done to our nature, in consequence of the influence of some motive which we are anxious to conceal.

II. *Truth and the Love of Truth.*] With respect to the *nature of truth* various metaphysical speculations have been offered to the world, and various definitions have been attempted, both by the ancients and moderns. These, however, have thrown but little light on the subject, which is not suprising, when we consider that the word *truth* expresses a simple idea or notion, of which no analysis or explication is possible. The same observation may be made with respect to the words *knowledge* and *belief*. All of them express notions which are implied in every judgment of the understanding, and which no being can form who is not possessed of a rational nature. And, by the way, these notions deserve to be added to the list formerly mentioned, as exemplifications of the imperfection of the account commonly given of the origin of our ideas. They are obviously not derived from any particular sense; and they do not seem to be referable to any part of our constitution, but to the *understanding;* or, in other words, to those rational powers which distinguish man from the brutes. This language, I know, will appear to be very loose and inaccurate to those who have familiarized their minds to the common doctrine; but it is a plain and indisputable statement of the fact.

To acquire knowledge or to discover truth is the proper object of *curiosity;* — a principle of action which is coeval with the first operations of the intellect, and which in most minds continues through life to have a powerful influence, in one way or another, on the character and the conduct. It is this principle which puts the intellectual faculties in motion, and gives them that exercise which is necessary for their development and improvement; and which, according to the direction it takes, and the particular set of faculties it exercises, is the principal foundation of the *diversities* of genius among men. And as the *diversities* of genius proceed from the different directions in which curiosity engages the attention, so the *inequalities* of genius among individuals may be traced in a great measure to the different degrees of ardor and perseverance with which the curiosity operates. When I say this, I would not be understood to insinuate that the different capacities of individuals are the same; a supposition contradicted by obvious facts, and contrary to what we should be led to conclude from the analogy of the body. I only wish to impress on all those who have any connection with the education of youth the great importance of stimulating the curiosity, and of directing it to proper objects, as the most effectual of all means for securing the improvement of the mind: I may add, as one of the most effectual provisions that can be made for the happiness of the individual, in consequence of the resources it furnishes when we are left to depend on ourselves for enjoyment; and in consequence, also, of the progressive vigor with which it operates to the very close of life, in proportion to the enlargement of our experience and the extent of our information.

In order, however, to prevent misapprehensions of my meaning, it is necessary for me again to remark, that the curiosity on which I lay so great a stress is that curiosity alone which has *truth* for its object. "There are many men," says Butler, "who have a strong curiosity to know what is *said*, who have no curiosity to know what is *true*"; — men who value knowledge only as furnishing an employment to their memory, or as supplying a gratification to their vanity in their intercourse with others. It is a weakness which we may presume has prevailed more or less in all ages, but which has been much encouraged in modern Europe by that superstitious admiration of antiquity which has withdrawn so much genius and industry from the pursuits of science to those of erudition. No prejudice can be conceived more adverse to the progress of useful knowledge, not only as it occasions an idle waste of time and labor which might have been more profitably employed, but as it contributes powerfully to destroy that simplicity and modesty of temper which are the genuine characteristics of the true philosopher.

I think it of importance to add, that the love of truth, where it is the great motive of our intellectual pursuits, gains daily an accession of strength as our knowledge advances. I have already said, that it is an ultimate fact in our nature, and is not resolvable into views of utility. Its extensive effects on human happiness are discovered only in the progress of our experience; but when this discovery is once made, it superadds to our instinctive curiosity every stimulus which self-love and benevolence can furnish. The connection between error and misery, between truth and happiness, becomes gradually more apparent as our inquiries proceed, and produces at last a complete conviction, that, even in those cases where we are unable to trace it, the connection subsists. He who feels this as he ought will consider a steadfast adherence to the truth as an expression of benevolence to man, and of confidence in the righteous administration of the universe, and will suspect the purity of those motives which would lead him to advance the good of his species, or the glory of his Maker, by deceit and hypocrisy.

III. *Means of inculcating and enforcing the Duty of Veracity.*] In offering these remarks, I shall no doubt be thought to have taken a very wide circuit in order to illustrate the nature of that veracity which is incumbent on us in our intercourse with our fellow-creatures.

But it appears to me that the most solid of all foundations for the uniform and the scrupulous exercise of this virtue is to cherish the love of truth in general, and to impress the mind with a conviction of its important effects on our own happiness and on that of society. There is, indeed, a sort of gross and ostensible practice of this duty, which is secured by what we call the *point of honor* in modern Europe, which brands with infamy every palpable deviation from the truth in matters of *fact*. The law of honor here operates in the case of veracity, in some measure, as the law of the magistrate operates in the case of justice. But as in the latter case a man may be unjust in the sight of God and of his own conscience without transgressing the letter of any statute, so, in the former, without forfeiting his character as a gentleman, he may often incur all the guilt of a liar and an impostor. Is it, in a moral view, more criminal to misrepresent a fact, than to impose on the world by what we know to be an unsound or a fallacious argument? Is it, in a moral view, more criminal to mislead another by a *verbal* lie, than by actions which convey a false idea of our intentions? Is it, in a moral view, more criminal, or is it more inconsistent with the dignity of a man of true honor, to defraud men in a private transaction by an incorrect or erroneous statement of circumstances, than to mislead the public to their own ruin by those wilful deviations from truth into which we see men daily led by views of interest or ambition, or by the spirit of political faction? Numberless cases, in short, may be fancied, in which our only security for truth is the virtuous disposition of the individual, and where the restraint of public opinion has little or no influence. Perhaps I should not go too far were I to affirm, that, as there is no duty of which the gross and ostensible practice is so effectually secured by the manners of modern times, so there is none to the obligation of which mankind seem in general to be so insensible, considered as moral agents, and accountable to God for their thoughts and intentions.

Among the various causes which have conspired to relax our moral principles on this important article, the facility which the press affords us in modern times of addressing the world by means of *anonymous* publications is probably one of the most powerful. The salutary restraint which a regard to character imposes, in most cases, on our moral deviations, is here withdrawn; and we have no security for the fidelity of the writer, but his disinterested love of truth and of mankind. The palpable and ludicrous misrepresentations of facts, to which we are accustomed from our infancy in the periodical prints of the day, gradually unhinge our faith in all such communications; and what we are every day accustomed to see, we cease in time to regard with due abhorrence. Nor is this the only moral evil resulting from the licentiousness of the press. The intentions of nature in appointing public esteem as the reward of virtue, and infamy as the punishment of vice, are in a great measure thwarted; and while the fairest characters are left open to the assaults of a calumny which it is impossible to trace to its author, the opinions of the public may be so divided by the artifices of hireling flatterers, with respect to men of the most profligate and abandoned lives, as to enable them, not only to brave the censures of the world, but to retaliate with more than an equal advantage on the good name of those who have the rashness to accuse them.

In a free government like ours, the liberty of the press has been often and justly called the palladium of the constitution; but it may reasonably be doubted whether this liberty would be at all impaired by a regulation, which, while it left the press perfectly open to every man who was willing openly to avow his opinions, rendered it impossible for any individual to publish a sentence without the sanction of his name. Upon this question, however, considered in a *political* point of view, I shall not presume to decide. Considered in a *moral* light, the advantages of such a regulation appear to be obvious and indisputable, and the *effect* could scarcely fail to have a most extensive influence on national manners.*

Besides that love of truth which seems evidently to be an original principle of the mind, there are other laws of our nature which were plainly intended to secure the practice of veracity in our intercourse with our fellow-creatures. There are others, too, which, as they suppose the practice of this virtue, may be regarded as intimations of that conduct which is conformable to the end and destination of our being. Such is that *disposition to repose faith in testimony*, which is coeval with the use of language. Without such a disposition, the education of children would be impracticable; and accordingly, so far from being the result of experience, it seems to be, in the first instance, unlimited, — nature intrusting its gradual correction to the progress of reason and of observation. This remark, which I think was first made by Dr. Reid, has been since repeated and enforced by Mr. Smith, in his *Theory of Moral Sentiments.* This author observes, further, that, "notwithstanding the lessons of caution communicated to us by experience, there is scarcely a man to be found who is not more credulous than he ought to be, and who does not, upon many occasions, give credit to tales which not only turn out to be perfectly false, but which a very moderate degree of reflection and attention might have taught him could not well be true. The natural disposition is always to believe. It is acquired wisdom and experience alone that teach incredulity, and they very seldom teach it enough. The wisest and most cautious of us all frequently gives credit to stories which he himself is afterwards both ashamed and astonished that he could possibly think of believing." This disposition to repose faith in testimony bears a striking analogy, both in its origin and in its final cause, to our instinctive expectation of the continuance of those laws which regulate the course of physical events.

* For the political aspects of this subject, see Lord Brougham's *Political Philosophy*, Part III. Chap. XXI. — Ed.

In infancy the principle of veracity is by no means so conspicuous as that of credulity, and it sometimes happens that a good deal of care is necessary to cherish it. But in such cases it will always be found that there is some indirect motive combined with the desire of social communication, such as fear, or vanity, or mischief, or sensuality. The same principle which prompts to social intercourse and to the use of speech prompts also to veracity. Nor is it probable that there is such a thing as falsehood uttered merely from the love of falsehood.

If this remark be just, it suggests an important practical rule in the business of education; — not to attempt the cure of lying and deceit by general rules concerning the duty of veracity, or by punishments inflicted upon every single violation of it, but by studying to discover and remove the radical evil from which it springs, whether it be cowardice, or vanity, or mischief, or selfishness, or sensuality. Either of these, if allowed to operate, will in time unhinge the natural constitution of the mind, and produce a disregard to truth upon all occasions where a temporary convenience can be gained by the breach of it.

From these imperfect hints, it would appear that every breach of veracity indicates some latent vice or some criminal intention, which an individual is ashamed to avow. And hence the peculiar beauty of openness or sincerity, uniting in some degree in itself the graces of all the other moral qualities of which it attests the existence.

CHAPTER III.

OF THE DUTIES WHICH RESPECT OURSELVES.

Prudence, *temperance*, and *fortitude* are no less requisite for enabling us to discharge our social duties than for securing our own private happiness; but as they do not necessarily imply any reference to our fellow-creatures, they seem to belong most properly to this third branch of virtue.

An illustration of the nature and tendency of these qualities, and of the means by which they are to be improved and confirmed, although a most important article of ethics, does not lead to any discussions of so abstract a kind as to require particular attention in a work of which brevity is a principal object. It is sufficient here to remark, that, independently of all considerations of utility, either to ourselves or to others, these qualities are approved of as right and becoming. Their utility, at the same time, or rather necessity, for securing the discharge of our other duties, adds greatly to the respect they command, and is certainly the chief ground of the obligation we lie under to cultivate the habits by which they are formed.

A steady regard, in the conduct of life, to the happiness and perfection of our own nature, and a diligent study of the means by which these ends may be attained, is another duty belonging to this branch of virtue. It is a duty so important and comprehensive, that it leads to the practice of all the rest, and is therefore entitled to a very full and particular examination in a system of moral philosophy. Such an examination, while it leads our thoughts "to the end and aim of our being," will again bring under our review the various duties already considered; and, by showing how they all conspire in recommending the same dispositions, will illustrate the unity of design in the human constitution, and the benevolent wisdom displayed in its formation. Other subordinate duties, besides, which it would be tedious to enumerate under separate titles, may thus be placed in a light more interesting and agreeable.

SECTION I.

OF THE DUTY OF EMPLOYING THE MEANS WE POSSESS TO SECURE OUR OWN HAPPINESS.

ACCORDING to Dr. Hutcheson, our conduct, so far as it is influenced by self-love, is never the object of moral approbation. Even a regard to the pleasures of a good conscience he considered as detracting from the merit of those actions which it encourages us to perform.

That the principle of self-love (or, in other words, the desire of happiness) is neither an object of approbation nor of blame is sufficiently obvious. It is inseparable from the nature of man as a rational and a sensitive being. It is, however, no less obvious, on the other hand, that this desire, considered as a principle of action, has by no means a uniform influence on the conduct. Our animal appetites, our affections, and the other inferior principles of our nature, interfere as often with self-love as with benevolence, and mislead us from our own happiness as much as from the duties we owe to others.

In these cases, every spectator pronounces that we *deserve* to suffer for our folly and indiscretion; and we ourselves, as soon as the tumult of passion is over, feel in the same manner. Nor is this remorse merely a sentiment of regret for having missed that happiness which we might have enjoyed. We are dissatisfied, not only with our condition, but with our conduct, — with our having forfeited by our own imprudence what we might have attained.*

It is true, that we do not feel so warm an indignation against the neglect of private good as against perfidy, cruelty, and injustice. The reason probably is, that imprudence commonly carries its own punishment along with it, and our resentment is disarmed by pity. Indeed, as that habitual regard to his own hap-

* See Butler's *Dissertation on the Nature of Virtue.*

piness, which every man feels, except when under the influence of some violent appetite, is a powerful check on imprudence, it was less necessary to provide an additional punishment for this vice in the indignation of the world.

From the principles now stated, it follows, that, in a person who believes in a future state, the criminality of every bad action is aggravated by the imprudence with which it is accompanied.

It follows, also, that the punishments annexed by the civil magistrate to particular actions render the commission of them more criminal than it would otherwise be; insomuch, that, if an action, in itself perfectly indifferent, were prohibited by some arbitrary law, under a severe penalty, the commission of that action (unless we were called to it by some urgent consideration of duty) would be criminal, not merely on account of the obedience which a subject owes to established authority, but on account of the regard which every man ought to feel for his life and reputation. To forge the handwriting of another with a fraudulent intention is undoubtedly a crime, independently of positive institutions; and it becomes still more criminal in a commercial country like ours, on account of the extensive mischiefs which may arise from it. It is a crime, however, not of greater magnitude than many other kinds of commercial fraud that might be mentioned. If the king, for example, grants his patent to a subject for a particular invention, and another counterfeits it, and makes use of his name, stamp, and coat of arms, he not only injures an individual, but imposes on the public. Abstraction made, therefore, of positive law, the criminality of the latter act is fully as great as that of the former. As the law, however, has made the one act capital, and the other not, but only subjected the person who commits it to pecuniary damages to the individual he has injured, the forgery of a deed becomes incomparably more criminal, in a moral view, than the counterfeit of a patent invention. A good man, indeed, will neither do the one nor the other.

But the man who adds to a fraudulent disposition an imprudent disregard to his own life and character is, undoubtedly, the more guilty of the two, and meets his fate with much less sympathy from others than he would receive if he had committed the same act without knowing its consequences.

Section II.

OF THE DIFFERENT THEORIES OF HAPPINESS.

I. *General Observations.*] The most superficial observation of life is sufficient to convince us that *happiness* is not to be attained by giving every appetite and desire the gratification it demands; and that it is necessary for us to form to ourselves some plan or system of conduct, in subordination to which all other objects are to be pursued.

To ascertain what this system ought to be is a problem which has, in all ages, employed the speculations of philosophers. Among the ancients, the question concerning the *sovereign good* was the principal subject of controversy which divided the schools; and it was treated in such a manner as to involve almost every other question of ethics. The opinions maintained with respect to it by some of their sects comprehend many of the most important truths to which the inquiry leads, and leave little to be added but a few corrections and limitations of their conclusions.

These opinions may be all reduced to three: those of the Epicureans, of the Stoics, and of the Peripatetics; and, indeed, it does not seem possible to form a conception of any scheme of happiness which may not be referred to one or other of these three systems.

II. (1.) *The Epicurean.*] The fundamental principle of the Epicurean system was, that *bodily pleasure* and pain were the sole ultimate objects of desire and aversion. These were desired and shunned on their own account; every thing else, from its tendency to procure the one of these or to save us from the other. *Power*, for example, *riches*, *reputation*, even the *virtues* themselves, were not desirable for their own sake, but were valuable merely as being instrumental to procure us the objects of our natural desires. "They who place the *sovereign good* in *virtue* alone, and who, dazzled by words, overlook the intentions of nature, will be delivered from this greatest of all errors, if they will only listen to Epicurus. As to these rare and excellent qualities on which you set so high a value, who is there that would consider them as objects either of praise or of imitation, unless from a belief that they are instrumental in adding to the sum of our pleasures? For as we prize the medical art, not on its own account, but as subservient to the preservation of health, and the art of the pilot, not for the skill he displays, but as it diminishes the dangers of navigation, so, also, *wisdom*, which is the art of living, would be coveted by none if it were altogether unprofitable, whereas now it is an object of general pursuit, from a persuasion that it both guides us to our best enjoyments, and points out to us the most effectual means for their attainment."*

All the pleasures and pains of the *mind* (according to Epicurus) are derived from the recollection and anticipation of *bodily* pleasures and pains; but this recollection and anticipation he considered as contributing much more to our happiness or misery on the whole, than the pleasures and pains themselves. His philosophy was, indeed, directed chiefly to inculcate this truth, and to withdraw our solicitude from the pleasures and pains themselves, which are not in our power, to the regulation of our recollections and anticipations, which depend upon ourselves. He placed happiness, therefore, in *ease of body* and *tranquillity of mind*, but much more in the latter than in the former, insomuch that he affirmed a wise man might be happy in the midst of bodily torments. "Hear," says Cicero, "the language

* Cicero, *De Fin.*, Lib. I. 13.

of Epicurus on his death-bed. 'Epicurus to Hermachus, greeting. — While I am passing the last day of my life, and *that* the happiest, I write this epistle, oppressed, at the same time, with so many and such acute maladies, that it is scarcely possible to conceive that my sufferings are susceptible of augmentation. All these, however, are amply compensated by the mental joy I derive from the recollection of the reasonings and discoveries of which I am the author.' " The concluding sentence of this letter does more honor to Epicurus than any other part of it. " But *you*, as is worthy of your good-will towards me and philosophy, let it be your business to consider yourself as the guardian and protector of the children of Metrodorus." *

Epicurus himself is represented as a person of inoffensive and even amiable manners. He is said to have taught his philosophy in a garden, where he lived a temperate and quiet life, enjoying what Thomson calls " the glad poetic ease of Epicurus, — seldom understood." He died at an advanced age, and was so much beloved and esteemed by his followers, that his birthday was annually celebrated as a festival. His private virtues, however, were probably, in a great measure, the effect of a happy natural constitution ; for his philosophy, besides destroying all those supports of morality that religion affords, tended avowedly to recommend a life of indolent and selfish indulgence, and a total abstraction from the concerns and duties of the world. Accordingly, we find that many of his disciples brought so much discredit on their principles by the dissoluteness of their lives, that the word *Epicurean* came gradually to be understood as characteristical of a person devoted to sensual gratifications.

The influence which these principles had on the manners of the later Romans has been remarked by many writers ; and it is not a little curious, that it was clearly foreseen, ages before, by their virtuous and en-

* *De Fin.*, II. 30. The same letter is also found in Diogenes Laertius, Lib. X.

lightened progenitors. This fact, which has not been sufficiently attended to, deserves the serious consideration of those who are disposed to call in question the effect of speculative opinions on national character.

It was in the year of Rome 471, and during the consulate of Fabricius, that the Romans seem to have received the first notice of the Epicurean doctrines. At that period the Tarentines had the address to instigate the Samnites, and almost all the other Italian states, to take arms against the republic, and also prevailed on Pyrrhus, king of Epirus, to give them his assistance. In the course of the war, Fabricius, with two other persons of high rank, was sent to Pyrrhus's court, to treat with him about an exchange of prisoners; and it was at a public entertainment given to them upon that occasion that Cineas, his minister and favorite, gave the Roman ambassadors a general idea of the philosophical principles which Epicurus had begun to teach at Athens about twenty years before. The effect which this conversation had on the minds of the Roman ambassadors is an instructive fact in the history of philosophy.

"I have frequently heard from some of my friends, who were much my seniors," says Cato to Scipio and Lælius, "a traditionary anecdote concerning Fabricius. They assured me, that, in the early part of their life, they were told by certain very old men of their acquaintance, that, when Fabricius was ambassador at the court of Pyrrhus, he expressed great astonishment at the account given him by Cineas of a philosopher at Athens, who maintained that the love of pleasure was universally the leading motive of all human actions. My informer added, that, when Fabricius related this fact to M. Curius and Titus Coruncanius, they both joined in wishing that Pyrrhus and the whole Samnite nation might become converts to this extraordinary doctrine, as the people who were infected with such unmanly principles could not fail, they thought, of proving an easy conquest to their enemies. M. Curius had been intimately connected with Publius Decius, who in his fourth consulate (which was five years before the former entered upon that office) gloriously sacrificed his life to the preservation of his country. This generous patriot was personally known both to Fabricius and to Coruncanius; and they were convinced, by what they experienced in their own breasts, as well as by the illustrious example of Decius, that there is in certain actions an intrinsic rectitude and obligation which, with a noble contempt of what the world calls *pleasure*, every great and generous mind will steadily keep in view as a sacred rule of conduct, and as the chief concern of life." *

III. (2.) *The Stoic.*] In opposition to the Epicurean doctrines already stated on the subject of happiness, the Stoics placed the supreme good in *rectitude of conduct*, without any regard to the event. They did not, however, as has been often supposed, recommend an indifference to external objects, or a life of inactivity and apathy. On the contrary, they taught that nature pointed out to us certain objects of choice and of rejection, and amongst these some to be *more* chosen and avoided than others; and that virtue consisted in choosing and rejecting objects according to their intrinsic value. They admitted that health was to be preferred to sickness, riches to proverty; the prosperity of our family, of our friends, of our country, to their adversity; and they allowed, nay, they recommended,

* Cicero, *De Senect.* The system of morals generally ascribed to Epicurus is said to have been borrowed from Aristippus, who also taught that happiness consisted in bodily pleasure; but it is probable, as Mr. Smith observes, that his manner of applying his principles was altogether his own. Indeed, we have the testimony of Diogenes Laertius that Aristippus taught that happiness consisted in the *present* pleasures of the body, and not in any mental refinements on these pleasures, according to the system of Epicurus. — Lib. II. 187. The life of Epicurus has been written in modern times by Gassendi (who also attempted to revive his philosophy, *Syntagma Philosophiæ Epicuri*), and by Bayle. Heineccius also mentions a book entitled, Jacob Rondellus, *De Vita et de Moribus Epicuri*, which has never fallen in my way. [For more modern authorities, see the general histories of philosophy by Tennemann, Ritter, and Degerando. Also, Warnekros, *Apologie und Leben Epicurs.* Steinhart in *Ersch u. Gruber. Allgem. Encyclop.*, Vol. XXXV. p. 459 *et seq.*]

the most strenuous exertions to accomplish these desirable ends. They only contended that these objects should be pursued, not as the constituents of our happiness, but because we believe it to be agreeable to nature that we should pursue them; and that, therefore, when we have done our utmost, we should regard the event as indifferent.

That this is a fair representation of the Stoical doctrine has been fully proved by Mr. Harris, in the very learned and judicious notes on his *Dialogue concerning Happiness;* a performance which, although not entirely free from Mr. Harris's peculiarities of thought and style, does him so much honor, both as a writer and a moralist, that we cannot help regretting, while we peruse it, that he should so often have wasted his ingenuity and learning upon scholastic subtilties, equally inapplicable to the pursuits of science and to the business of life.

"The word πάθος," he observes, "which we usually render *a passion*, means, in the Stoic sense, *a perturbation*, and is always so translated by Cicero; and the epithet ἀπαθής, when applied to the *wise man*, does not mean an exemption from passion, but an exemption from that perturbation which is founded on erroneous opinions. The testimony of Epictetus is expressed to this purpose.. 'I am not,' says he, 'to be apathetic like a statue, but I am withal to observe relations, both the natural and the adventitious; as the man of religion, as the son, as the brother, as the father, as the citizen.' And immediately before, he tells us, that 'a perturbation in no other way ever arises, but either when a desire is frustrated, or an aversion falls into that which it should avoid.' In which passage," says Harris, "it is observable that he does not make either desire or aversion πάθη, or perturbations, but only the cause of perturbations when erroneously conducted."

From a great variety of passages, which it is unnecessary for me to transcribe, Harris concludes that "the Stoics, in the character of their *virtuous man*, included rational desire, aversion, and exultation; included love and parental affection, friendship, and a general benevolence to all mankind; and considered it as a duty arising from our very nature not to neglect the welfare of public society, but to be ever ready, according to our rank, to act either as the magistrate or as the private citizen."

Nor did they exclude wealth from among the objects of choice. The Stoic Hecato, in his treatise *Of Offices*, quoted by Cicero, tells us, that "a wise man, while he abstains from doing any thing contrary to the customs, laws, and institutions of his country, ought to attend to his own fortune. For we do not desire to be rich for ourselves only, but for our children, relations, and friends, and especially for the commonwealth, inasmuch as the riches of individuals are the wealth of a state." * "Nay," says Cicero, on another occasion, "if the *wise man* could mend his condition by adding to the amplest possessions the poorest, meanest utensil, he would in no degree contemn it." †

From these quotations it sufficiently appears that the Stoical system, so far from withdrawing men from the duties of life, was eminently favorable to active virtue. Its peculiar and distinguishing tenet was, that our happiness does not depend on the *attainment* of the objects of our choice, but on *the part that we act;* but this principle was inculcated, *not* to damp our exertions, but to lead us to rest our happiness only on circumstances which *we ourselves could command.* "If I am going to sail," says Epictetus, "I choose the best ship and the best pilot, and I wait for the fairest weather that my circumstances and duty will allow. Prudence and propriety, the principles which the gods have given me for the direction of my conduct, require this of me, but they require no more; and if, notwithstanding, a storm arises, which neither the strength of the vessel nor the skill of the pilot is likely to withstand, I give myself no trouble about the consequences. All that I had to do is done already. The directors of my con-

* *De Off.* III. 15. † *De Finibus*, IV. 12.

duct never command me to be miserable, to be anxious, desponding, or afraid. Whether we are to be drowned or come to a harbour is the business of Jupiter, not mine. I leave it entirely to his determination, nor ever break my rest with considering which way he is likely to decide it, but receive whatever comes with equal indifference and security."

We may observe further, in favor of this noble system, that the scale of desirable objects which it exhibited was peculiarly calculated to encourage the social virtues. It represented, indeed (in common with the theory of Epicurus), *self-love* as the great spring of human actions; but in the application of this erroneous principle to practice, its doctrines were favorable to the most enlarged, nay, to the most disinterested benevolence. It taught that the prosperity of two was preferable to that of *one;* that of a city to that of a family; and that of our country to all partial considerations. It was upon this very principle, added to a sublime sentiment of piety, that it founded its chief argument for an entire resignation to the dispensations of Providence. As all events are ordered by perfect wisdom and goodness, the Stoics concluded that whatever happens is calculated to produce the greatest good possible to the universe in general. As it is agreeable to nature, therefore, that we should prefer the happiness of many to a few, and of all to that of many, they concluded that every event which happens is precisely that which we ourselves would have desired, if we had been acquainted with the whole scheme of the Divine administration. "In what sense," says Epictetus, "are some things said to be according to our nature, and others contrary to it? It is in that sense in which we consider ourselves as separated and detached from all other things. For thus it may be said to be the nature of the foot to be always clean. But if you consider it as a foot, and not as something detached from the rest of the body, it must behoove it sometimes to trample in the dirt, and sometimes to tread upon thorns, and sometimes, too, to be cut off for the sake of the whole body; and if it refuses this, it is no longer a foot. Thus, too, ought we to conceive with respect to ourselves. What are you? A man. If you consider yourself as something separated and detached, it is agreeable to your nature to live to old age, to be rich, to be in health. But if you consider yourself as a man, and as a part of the whole, upon account of that whole it will behoove you sometimes to be in sickness, sometimes to be exposed to the inconveniency of a sea voyage, sometimes to be in want, and at last, perhaps, to die before your time. Why, then, do you complain? Do you not know that by doing so, as the foot ceases to be a foot, so you cease to be a man."

In the writings, indeed, of some of the Stoics, we meet with some absurd and violent paradoxes about the perfect felicity of the *wise man* on the one hand, and the *equality of misery* among all those who fall short of this ideal character on the other. "As all the actions of the *wise man* were perfect, so all those of the man who had not arrived at this supreme wisdom were faulty, and *equally* faulty. As one truth could not be more true, nor one falsehood more false, than another, so an honorable action could not be more honorable, nor a shameful one more shameful, than another. As, in shooting at a mark, the man who had missed it by an inch had equally missed it with him who had done so by a hundred yards, so the man who, in what appeared to us the most insignificant action, had acted improperly, and without a sufficient reason, was equally faulty with him who had done so in what appeared to us the most important; the man who had killed a cock, for example, improperly, and without a sufficient reason, with him who had murdered his father.

"It is not, however," continues Mr. Smith, "by any means probable that these paradoxes formed a part of the original principles of Stoicism, as taught by Zeno and Cleanthes. It is much more probable that they were added to it by their disciple, Chrysippus, whose genius seems to have been more fitted for systematizing the doctrines of his preceptors, and adorning them with the imposing appendages of artificial definitions and divisions, than for imbibing the sublime spirit which they breathed."

This apology, however, it must be confessed, will not extend to all the errors of the Stoical school. In particular, it will not extend to the notions it inculcated on the subject of *suicide*, and, in general, on the air of defiance and gayety with which death was to be met. But to account even for these, in some measure, by the peculiar circumstances of the times when this philosophy arose, Mr. Smith observes: — "The different republics of Greece were at home almost always distracted by the most furious factions, and abroad involved in the most sanguinary wars, in which each sought, not merely superiority or dominion, but either completely to extirpate all its enemies, or, what was not less cruel, to reduce them into the vilest of all states, — that of domestic slavery. The smallest of the greater part of those states, too, rendered it to each of them no very improbable event, that it might itself fall into that very calamity which it had so frequently inflicted or attempted to inflict on its neighbours. In this disorderly state of things, the most perfect innocence, joined to the highest rank and the greatest services to the public, could give no security to any man, that, even at home and among his fellow-citizens, he was not, at some time or other, from the prevalence of some hostile and furious faction, to be condemned to the most cruel and ignominious punishment. If he was taken prisoner of war, or if the city of which he was a member was conquered, he was exposed, if possible, to still greater injuries. As an American savage, therefore, prepares his *death-song*, and considers how he should act when he has fallen into the hands of his enemies, and is by them put to death in the most lingering tortures, and amidst the insults and derision of all the spectators, so a Grecian patriot or hero could not avoid frequently employing his thoughts in considering what he ought both to suffer and to do in ban ishment, in captivity, when reduced to slavery, when put to the torture, when brought to the scaffold. It was the business of their philosophers to prepare the death-song which the Grecian patriots and heroes might make use of on the proper occasions; and of all the different sects, the Stoics, I think it must be acknowledged, had prepared by far the most animated and spirited song." *

After all, it is impossible to deny that there is some foundation for a censure which Lord Bacon has somewhere passed on this celebrated sect. "Certainly," says he, "the Stoics bestowed too much cost on death, and by their preparations made it more fearful." At least, I suspect this may be the tendency of *some* passages in their writings, in such a state of society as that in which we live; but in perusing them, we ought always to remember the circumstances of those men to whom they were addressed, and which are so eloquently described in the observations just quoted from Mr. Smith. The practical reflection which Bacon adds to this censure is invaluable, and is strictly conformable to the spirit of the Stoical system, although he seems to state it by way of contrast to their principles. "It is as natural," says he, "to die, as to be born; and to a little infant perhaps the one is as painful as the other. He that dies in an earnest pursuit is like one that is wounded in hot blood, who for a time scarce feels the hurt; and therefore a mind fixed and bent upon somewhat that is good doth best avert the dolors of death." †

"Hi mores, hæc duri immota Catonis
Secta fuit, servare modum, finemque tenere,
Naturamque sequi, patriæque impendere vitam;
Nec sibi, sed toti genitum se credere mundo." ‡

---

* *Moral Sentiments*, Part VII. Sect II. Chap. I.

The preceding extracts from Epictetus are also taken from the same chapter, and given in Mr. Smith's translation.

† *Essays or Counsels, Civil and Moral*, Essay II.

‡ Lucan. *Phars.*, Lib. II. l. 380. See the fragments of this school, published in Gale's *Opuscula Mythologica, Physica, et Ethica.* [Also, the general histories of philosophy mentioned above; Ritter and Preller in their *Historia Philosoph. Græco-Roman.*; the articles on Zeno in Bayle, *Dict.*. and in *Biographie Universelle.*]

IV. (3.) *The Peripatetic.*] The doctrine of the *Peripatetics* on this subject appears to have coincided with that of the Pythagorean school, who defined *happiness* to be "*the exercise of virtue in a prosperous life*" (χρῆσις ἀρετῆς ἐν εὐτυχίᾳ); a definition, like several others transmitted to us from the same source, which unites in a remarkable degree the merits of conciseness and of philosophical precision.

In confirmation of this doctrine, the Pythagorean school observed that it was not the *mere possession*, but the *exercise*, of virtue that made men happy. And for the proper exercise of virtue, they thought that *good fortune* was as necessary as light is for the exercise of the faculty of sight. The utmost length, accordingly, which they went, was to say, that the virtuous man in adversity was *not miserable;* whereas the vicious and foolish were miserable in all situations of fortune. In another passage they say that the difference between God and man is, that God is perfect in himself, and needs nothing from without; whereas the nature of man is imperfect and defective, and dependent on external circumstances. Although, therefore, we possess virtue, that is but the perfection of *one* part, namely, the mind; but as we consist both of body and mind, the body also must be perfect of its kind. Nor is that alone sufficient; but the prosperous exercise of virtue requires certain *externals;* such as wealth, reputation, friends, and, above all, a *well-constituted state;* for without that the rational and social animal is imperfect, and unable to fulfil the purposes of its nature.

The difference between the Peripatetics and Stoics in these opinions is beautifully stated by Cicero, in a passage strongly expressive of the elevation of his own character, as well as highly honorable to the two sects, whose doctrines, while he contrasts them with each other, he plainly considered as both originating in the same pure and ardent zeal for the interests of morality. "Pugnant Stoici cum Peripateticis: alteri negant quidquam bonum esse nisi quod honestum sit; alteri, plurimum se, et longe, longeque plurimum attribuere honestati, sed tamen et in corpore, et extra esse quædam bona. Certamen honestum, et disputatio splendida, omnis est enim de virtutis dignitate contentio." *

SECTION III.

MEANS OF PROMOTING AND SECURING HAPPINESS.

I. *Introductory Remarks.*] From the slight view now given of the systems of philosophers with respect to the Sovereign Good, it may be assumed as an acknowledged and indisputable fact, that *happiness arises chiefly from the mind.* The Stoics undoubtedly expressed this too strongly when they said, that to a wise man external circumstances are indifferent. Yet it must be confessed, that happiness depends much less on these than is commonly imagined; and that, as there is no situation so prosperous as to exclude the torments of malice, cowardice, and remorse, so there is none so adverse as to withhold the enjoyments of a benevolent, resolute, and upright heart.

* *De Finibus*, Lib. II. 21. "The Stoics oppose the Peripatetics: one sect denies that any thing can be good unless it is virtuous; while the other, after allowing very exalted and distinguished qualities to virtue, still thinks that there are some bodily and external circumstances which are good in some degree. The contest is generous; the difference is glorious; for all the dispute is who shall most ennoble virtue." See Arist., *Ethic. Nicom.*, Lib. I.

[Cousin, in his *Fragments Philosophiques*, Tome I. p. 279, observes: — "Not only do we unceasingly aspire after happiness as sensitive beings, but when we have done well, we judge, as intelligent and moral beings, that we are *worthy* of happiness. Hence the necessary principle of merit and of demerit, the origin and foundation of all our ideas of reward and punishment; — a principle continually confounded either with the desire of happiness or with the moral law.

"Behold why it is that the question of the *sovereign good* has never been resolved. Philosophers have sought a simple solution for a complex question, not having the two principles which, together, are capable of resolving it completely.

"Epicurean solution: — the satisfaction of the desire of happiness.

"Stoical solution: — the fulfilment of the moral law.

"The *true* solution is found in the harmony existing between virtue, and happiness as merited by it; for the two elements in this duality are not equal. Happiness is the consequent; virtue is the principle. Virtue though not the sole element of the sovereign good, is always the chief." — ED.]

If, from the sublime idea of a perfectly wise and virtuous man, we descend to such characters as the world presents to us, some important limitations of the Stoical conclusions become necessary. Mr. Hume has justly remarked, that, " as in the bodily system a toothache produces more violent convulsions of pain than phthisis or a dropsy, so, in the economy of the mind, although all vice be pernicious, yet the disturbance or pain is not measured out by nature with exact proportion to the degree of vice; nor is the man of highest virtue, even abstracting from external accidents, always the most happy. A gloomy and melancholy disposition is certainly to our sentiments a vice or imperfection; but as it may be accompanied with a great sense of honor and great integrity, it may be found in very worthy characters, though it is sufficient alone to embitter life, and render the person afflicted with it completely miserable. On the other hand, a selfish villain may possess a spring and alacrity of temper, a certain *gayety of heart*, which is rewarded much beyond its merit, and, when attended with good fortune, will compensate for the uneasiness and remorse arising from all the other vices."

However this may be, it is certain that various mental qualities, which have no immediate connection with moral desert, are necessary to insure happiness. In proof of this remark, it is sufficient to consider how much our tranquillity is liable to be affected, —

1. By our temper;
2. By our imagination;
3. By our opinions; and
4. By our habits.

In all these respects the mind may be influenced to a great degree by original constitution or by early education; and when this influence happens to be unfavorable, it is not to be corrected at once by the precepts of philosophy. Much, however, may be done, undoubtedly, in such instances, by our own persevering efforts; and therefore the particulars now enumerated deserve our attention, not only from their connection with the speculative question concerning the essentials of happiness, but on account of the practical conclusions to which the consideration of them may lead.

II. (1.) *Influence of the Temper on Happiness.*] The word *temper* is used in different senses. Sometimes we apply to it the epithets *gay*, *lively*, *melancholy*, *gloomy;* on other occasions, the epithets *fretful*, *passionate*, *sullen*, *cool*, *equable*, *gentle*. It is in the *last* sense we use it at present, to denote the habitual state of a man's mind in point of *irascibility;* or, in other words, to mark the habitual predominance of the *benevolent* or *malevolent* affections in his intercourse with his fellow-creatures.

The connection between this part of the character of an individual and the habitual state of his mind in point of happiness is obvious from what was formerly observed concerning the pleasures and pains attached respectively to the exercise of our benevolent and malevolent affections. As Nature has strengthened the social ties among mankind, by annexing a certain charm to every exercise of good-will and of kindness, so she has provided a check on all the discordant passions, by that agitation and disquiet which are their inseparable concomitant. This is true even with respect to resentment, how justly soever it may be provoked by the injurious conduct of others. It is always accompanied with an unpleasant feeling, which warns us, as soon as we have taken the necessary measures for our own security, to banish every sentiment of malice from the heart. On the due regulation of this part of our constitution, our happiness in life materially depends; and there is no part of it whatever where it is in our power, by our persevering efforts, to do more to cure our *constitutional* or our *acquired* infirmities.

Resentment was formerly distinguished into *instinctive* and *deliberate*. In some men the animal or instinctive impulse is stronger than in others. Where this is the case, or where proper care has not been taken in early education to bring it under restraint, a quick or irascible temper is the consequence. This fault is frequently observable in affectionate and generous characters, and impairs their happiness, not so much by the effects it produces on their minds as by the eventual misfortunes to which it exposes them. The sentiments of ill-will which such men feel are only momentary, and the habitual state of their mind is benevolent and happy; but as their reason is the sport of every accident, the best dispositions of the heart can at no time give them any security that they shall not, before they sleep, experience some paroxysm of insanity, which shall close all their prospects of happiness for ever. A frequent and serious consideration of the fatal consequences which may arise from sudden and ungoverned passion cannot fail to have some tendency to check its excesses. It is an infirmity which is often produced by some fault in early education; by allowing children to exercise authority over their dependents, and not providing for them, in the opposition of their equals, a sufficient discipline and preparation for the conflicts they may expect to struggle with in future life.

When the animal resentment does not immediately subside, it must be supported by an opinion of bad intention in its object; and, consequently, when this happens to an individual so habitually as to be characteristic of his temper, it indicates a disposition on *his* part to put unfavorable constructions on the actions of others, or (as we commonly express it) *to take things by the wrong handle*. In some instances this may proceed from a settled conviction of the worthlessness of mankind; but in general it originates in self-dissatisfaction, occasioned by the consciousness of vice or folly, which leads the person who feels it to withdraw his attention from himself by referring the causes of his ill-humor to the imaginary faults of his neighbours. Such men do not wait till provocation is given them, but *look out* anxiously for occasions of quarrel, creating to themselves, by the help of imagination, an object suited to that particular humor they wish to indulge; and, when their resentment is once excited, they obstinately refuse to listen to any thing that may be offered in the way of extenuation or apology. In feeble minds, this displays itself in peevishness, which vents itself languidly upon any object it meets. In more vigorous and determined minds, it produces violent and boisterous passion. For, as Butler has well remarked, both of these seem to be the operation of the same principle, appearing in different forms, according to the constitution of the individual. "In the one case, the humor discharges itself *at once;* in the other, it is continually discharging."

There is, too, a species of misanthropy, which is sometimes grafted on a worthy and benevolent heart. When the standard of moral excellence we have been accustomed to conceive is greatly elevated above the common attainments of humanity, we are apt to become too difficult and fastidious (if I may use the expression) in our *moral taste;* or, in plainer language, we become unreasonably censorious of the follies and vices of the age in which we live. In such cases it may happen that the native benevolence of the mind, by being habitually directed towards ideal characters, may prove a source of real disaffection and dislike to those with whom we associate. The only effectual remedy for this evil (as I have had occasion to observe in another connection*) is society or business, together with a habit of directing the attention rather to the improvement of our own characters, than to a jealous and suspicious examination of the motives which influence the conduct of our neighbours.

This last observation leads me to remark, further, that one great cause of this perversion of our nature is a very common and fatal prejudice, which leads men to believe that the degree of *their own* virtue is proportioned to the justness and the liveliness of their moral *feelings;* whereas, in truth, virtue consists neither in liveliness of feeling nor in rectitude of judgment

---

* See page 266 of this volume.

but in an habitual regard to our sense of duty in the conduct of life. To enlighten, indeed, our conscience with respect to the part which we ourselves have to act, and to cultivate that quick and delicate sense of propriety which may restrain us from every offence, how trifling soever it may appear, against the laws of morality, is an essential part of our duty; and what a strong sense of duty, aided by a sound understanding, will naturally lead to. But to exercise our powers of moral judgment and moral feeling on the character and conduct of our neighbours is so far from being necessarily connected with our moral improvement, that it has frequently a tendency to withdraw our attention from the real state of our own characters, and to flatter us with a belief, that the degree in which we possess the different virtues is proportioned to the indignation excited in our minds by the want of them in others. That this rule of judgment is at least *not infallible* may be inferred from the common observation (justified by the experience of every man who has paid any attention to human life), that the most scrupulous men in their own conduct are generally the most indulgent to the faults of their fellow-creatures. I will not go quite so far as to assert, with Dr. Hutcheson, (although I believe his remark has much foundation in truth,) that "men have commonly the good or the bad qualities which they ascribe to mankind." I shall content myself with repeating, after Mr. Addison, that, "among all the monstrous characters in human nature, there is none so odious, nor, indeed, so exquisitely ridiculous, as that of a rigid, severe temper in a worthless man"; * — an observation which, from the manner in which he states it, evidently shows that he did not consider this union as a very *rare* occurrence among the numberless inconsistencies in our moral judgments and habits.

But what we are chiefly concerned at present to remark is the tendency of a censorious disposition with

* *Spectator*, No. 169.

respect to our own *happiness*. That favorable opinions of our species, and those benevolent affections towards them which such opinions produce, are sources of exquisite enjoyment to those who entertain them, no person will dispute. But there are two very different ways in which men set about the attainment of this satisfaction. One set of men aim at modelling the world to their own wish, and repine in proportion to the disappointments they experience in their plans of general reformation. Another, while they do what they can to improve their fellow-creatures, consider it as *their* chief business to watch over their own characters; and as they cannot succeed to their wish in making mankind what they ought to be, they study to accommodate their views and feelings to the order of Providence. They exert their ingenuity in apologizing for folly and misconduct, and are always more disposed to praise than to blame; and when they see unquestionable and unpardonable delinquencies, they avail themselves of such occurrences, not as occasions for venting indignation and abuse, but as lessons of admonition to themselves, and as calls to attempt the amendment of the delinquent by gentle and friendly remonstrances. Of these two plans, it is easy to see that the one, while it appears flattering to the indolence of the individual (because it requires no efforts of self-denial), must necessarily engage him in impracticable and hopeless efforts. The other, although it requires force of mind to put it in execution, is within the reach of every man to accomplish in a degree highly important to his own character and to his own comfort. This, indeed, I apprehend, is the *great secret* of happiness, — to study to accommodate our own minds to things external, rather than to accommodate things external to ourselves; and there are no instances in which the practice of the rule is of more consequence than in our intercourse with our fellow-creatures. Let us do what we can to amend them, but let us trust for our *happiness* to what depends on ourselves. Nor is there any delusion necessary for this purpose; for the fairest views of human character are in truth the justest; and the more intimately we know mankind, the less we shall be misled by the partialites of pride and self-love, and the more shall we be disposed to acknowledge the merits and to pardon the frailties of others.

Another expedient of very powerful effect is to suppress, as far as possible, the *external signs* of peevishness or of violence. So intimate is the connection between mind and body, that the mere imitation of any strong expression has a tendency to excite the corresponding passion; and, on the other hand, the suppression of the external sign has a tendency to compose the passion which it indicates. It is said of Socrates, that whenever he felt the passion of resentment rising in his mind, he became instantly *silent;* and I have no doubt, that, by observing this rule, he not only avoided many an occasion of giving offence to others, but added much to the comfort of his own life, by killing the seeds of those malignant affections which are the great bane of human happiness.

Something of the same kind, though proceeding from a less worthy motive, we may see daily exemplified in the case of those men who are peevish and unhappy in their own families, while in the company of strangers they are good-humored and cheerful. At home they give vent to all their passions without restraint, and exasperate their original irritability by the reaction of that bodily agitation which it occasions. In promiscuous society the restraints of ceremony render this impossible. They find themselves obliged to conceal studiously whatever emotions of dissatisfaction they may feel, and soon come to experience, in fact, that gentle and accommodating temper of which they have been striving to counterfeit the appearance.

The influence of the temper on happiness is much increased by another circumstance; that the same causes which alienate our affections from our fellow-creatures are apt to suggest unfavorable views of the course of human affairs, and lead the mind by an easy transition to gloomy conceptions of the general order of the universe. In this state of mind, when, in the language of Hamlet, "*Man delights me not*," the sentiment of misanthropy seldom fails to be accompanied with that dark and hopeless philosophy which Shakspeare has, with such exquisite knowledge of the human heart, described as springing up with it from the same root. "This goodly frame, the earth, appears a sterile promontory; — this majestical roof, fretted with golden fire, a foul and pestilent congregation of vapors; — and Man himself, — noble in reason, infinite in faculties, — this beauty of the world, this paragon of animals, — seems but the *quintessence of dust*." Such a temper and such views are not only to the possessor the completion of wretchedness, but, by the proofs they exhibit of insensibility and ingratitude towards the Great Source of happiness and perfection, they argue some defect in those *moral feelings* to which many men lay claim, who affect an indifference to all serious impressions and sentiments. They argue at least what Milton has finely called a "*sullenness against Nature*," — a disposition of mind which no man could possibly feel whose temper was rightly constituted towards his fellow-creatures. How congenial to the best emotions of the heart is the following sentiment in his *Tractate on Education!* "In those vernal seasons of the year, when the air is soft and pleasant, it were an injury and sullenness against Nature not to go out and see her riches, and partake in her rejoicings with heaven and earth."

III. (2.) *Influence of the Imagination on Happiness.*] One of the principal effects of a liberal education is to accustom us to withdraw our attention from the objects of our present perceptions, and to dwell at pleasure on the past, the absent, and the future. How much it must enlarge in this way the sphere of our enjoyment or suffering is obvious; for (not to mention the recollection of the past) all that part of our happiness or misery which arises from our *hopes* or our *fears* derives its existence entirely from the power of imagination.

It is not, however, from education alone that the differences among individuals in respect of this faculty seem to arise. Even among those who have enjoyed the same advantages of mental culture, we find some men in whom it never makes any considerable appearance, — men whose thoughts seem to be completely engrossed with the objects and events with which their senses are conversant, and on whose minds the impressions produced by what is absent and future are so comparatively languid, that they seldom or never excite their passions or arrest their attention. In others, again, the coloring which imagination throws on the objects they conceive is so brilliant, that even the present impressions of sense are unable to stand the comparison; and the thoughts are perpetually wandering from this world of realities to fairy scenes of their own creation. In such men, the imagination is the principal source of their pleasurable or painful sensations and their happiness or misery is in a great measure determined by the gay or melancholy cast which this faculty has derived from original constitution, or from acquired habits.

When the *hopes* or the *fears* which imagination inspires prevail over the present importunity of our sensual appetites, it is a proof of the superiority which the intellectual part of our character has acquired over the animal; and as the course of life which wisdom and virtue prescribe requires frequently a sacrifice of the *present* to the *future*, a warm and vigorous imagination is sometimes of essential use, by exhibiting those lively prospects of solid and permanent happiness which may counteract the allurements of present pleasure. In those who are enslaved completely by their sensual appetites, imagination may indeed operate in anticipating future gratification, or it may blend itself with memory in the recollection of past enjoyment; but where this is the case, imagination is so far from answering its intended purpose, that it establishes an unnatural alliance between our intellectual powers and our animal desires, and extends the empire of the latter, by filling up the intervals of actual indulgence with habits of thought more degrading and ruinous, if possible, to the rational part of our being, than the time which is employed in criminal gratification.

In mentioning, however, the influence of imagination on happiness, what I had chiefly in view was the addition which is made to our enjoyments or sufferings, on the whole, by the predominance of *hope* or of *fear* in the habitual state of our minds. One man is continually led, by the complexion of his temper, to forebode evil to himself and to the world; while another, after a thousand disappointments, looks forward to the future with exultation, and feels his confidence in Providence unshaken. One principal cause of such differences is undoubtedly the natural constitution of the mind in point of *fortitude.*

It may be worth while here to remark, that what we properly call *cowardice* is entirely a *disease of the imagination.* It does not always imply an impatience under present suffering. On the contrary, it is frequently observed in men who submit quietly to the evils which they have actually experienced, and of which they have thus learned to measure the extent with accuracy. Nay, there are cases in which *patience* is the offspring of *cowardice*, the imagination magnifying future dangers to such a degree, as to render present sufferings comparatively insignificant. Men of this description always judge it safer to "bear the ills they know, than fly to others that they know not of," and, of consequence, when under the pressure of pain and disease, scruple to employ those vigorous remedies, which, while they give them a chance for recovery, threaten them with the possibility of a more imminent danger. The brave, on the contrary, are not always patient under distress; and they sometimes, perhaps, owe their bravery in part to this impatience. We may remark an apt illustration of this observation in the two sexes. The male is more courageous, but more impa-

35

tient of suffering; the female more timid, but more resigned and serene under severe pain and affliction.

Allowance being made for constitutional biases, the two great sources of a desponding imagination are *superstition* and *skepticism.* Of the former, the unhappy victims are many, and have been so in all ages of the world, although their number may be expected gradually to diminish in proportion to the progress and the diffusion of knowledge. All of us, however, have had an opportunity of witnessing enough of its effects in those remains which are still to be found, in many parts of this country, of the old prejudices with respect to apparitions and spectres, to be able to form an idea of what mankind must have suffered in the ages of Gothic ignorance, when these weaknesses of the uninformed mind were skilfully made use of by an ambitious priesthood as an engine of ecclesiastical policy. *Skepticism,* too, when carried to an extreme, can scarcely fail to produce similar effects. As it encourages the notion that all events are regulated by chance, if it does not alarm the mind with terror, it extinguishes at least every ray of hope; and such is the restless activity of the mind, that it may be questioned whether the agitation of fear be a source of more complete wretchedness, than that listlessness which deprives us of all interest about futurity, and represents to us the present moment alone as ours. Nor is this all. A complete skepticism is so unnatural a state to the human understanding, that it was probably never realized in any one instance. Nay, I believe it will generally be found, that, in proportion to the violence of a man's disbelief on those important subjects which are essential to human happiness, the more extravagant is his credulity on other articles, where the fashion of the times does not brand credulity as a weakness; for the mind must have something distinct from the objects of sense on which to repose itself; and those principles of our nature on which religion is founded, if they are prevented from developing themselves under the direction of an enlightened reason, will infallibly disclose themselves, in one way or another, in the character and the conduct.

Of this no stronger proof can be produced, than that the same period of the eighteenth century, and the same part of Europe, which were most distinguished by the triumphs of a skeptical philosophy, were also distinguished by a credulity so extraordinary, as to encourage and support a greater number of visionaries and impostors than had appeared since the time of the revival of letters. The pretenders to animal magnetism, and the revivers of the Rosicrucian mysteries, are but two instances out of many that might be mentioned.

Such, then, are the miseries of ill-regulated imagination, whether arising from constitutional biases or from the acquisition of erroneous opinions; and they are miseries which, when they affect habitually the state of the mind, are sufficient to poison all the enjoyments which fortune can offer. To those, on the contrary, whose education has been fortunately conducted, this faculty opens inexhaustible sources of delight, presenting continually to their thoughts the fairest views of mankind and of Providence, and, under the deepest gloom of adverse fortune, gilding the prospects of futurity.

I have remarked, in the first volume of my *Philosophy of the Human Mind*, that what we call *sensibility* depends in a great measure on the degree of imagination we possess; and hence, in such a world as ours, checkered as it is with good and evil, there must be in every mind a mixture of pleasure and of pain, proportioned to the interest which imagination leads it to take in the fortunes of mankind. It is even natural and reasonable for a benevolent disposition, (notwithstanding what Mr. Smith has so ingeniously alleged to the contrary,*) to dwell more habitually on the gloomy than on the gay aspect of human affairs; for the fortunate stand in no need of our assistance; while, amidst the distractions of our own personal concerns, the wretched require all the assistance which our imagina-

* *Theory of Moral Sentiments*, Part III. Chap. III.

tion can lend them, to engage our attention to their distresses. In this sympathy, however, with the general sufferings of humanity, the pleasure far overbalances the pain; not only on account of that secret charm which accompanies all the modifications of benevolence, but because it is they alone whose prospects of futurity are sanguine, and whose confidence in the final triumph of reason and of justice is linked with all the best principles of the heart, who are likely to make a common cause with the oppressed and the miserable. This, therefore, (although we frequently apply to it the epithet *melancholy*,) is, on the whole, a happy state of mind, and has no connection with what we commonly call *low spirits*, — a disease where the pain is unmixed, and which is always accompanied, either as a cause or an effect, by the most intolerable of all feelings, a sentiment of self-dissatisfaction; whereas the temper I have now alluded to is felt only by those who are at peace with themselves and with the whole world. Such is that species of *melancholy* which Thomson has so pathetically described as exerting a peculiar influence at that season of the year (his own favorite and inspiring season) when the "dark winds of autumn return," and when the falling leaves and the naked fields fill the heart at once with mournful presages, and with tender recollections.

"He comes! he comes! in every breeze the *Power*
Of *philosophic melancholy* comes!
His near approach the sudden starting tear,
The glowing cheek, the mild, dejected air,
The softened feature, and the beating heart,
Pierced deep with many a virtuous pang, declare.
O'er all the soul his sacred influence breathes;
Inflames imagination; through the breast
Infuses every tenderness; and far
Beyond dim earth exalts the swelling thought."

It will not, I think, be denied, that an imagination of the cast here described, while it has an obvious tendency to refine the taste and to exalt the character, enlarges very widely, in the man who possesses it, the sphere of his enjoyment. It is, however, no less indisputable, that this faculty requires an uncommon share of good sense to keep it under proper regulation, and to derive from it the pleasures it was intended to afford, without suffering it either to mislead the judgment in the conduct of life, or to impair our relish for the moderate gratifications which are provided for our present condition.

The inconveniences of an ill-regulated imagination have appeared to some philosophers to be so alarming, that they have concluded it to be one of the most essential objects of education to repress as much as possible this dangerous faculty. But in this, as in other instances, it is in vain to counteract the purposes of Nature; and all that human wisdom ought to attempt is to study the ends which she has apparently in view, and to coöperate with the means which she has provided for their attainment. The very argument on which these philosophers have proceeded justifies the remark I have now made, and encourages us to follow out the plan I have recommended; for surely the more cruel the effects of a deranged imagination, the happier are the consequences to be expected from this part of our constitution, if properly regulated, and if directed to its destined purposes by good sense and philosophy. It is justly remarked by an author in the *Tatler*,* as an acknowledged fact, that, "of all writings, licentious poems do soonest corrupt the heart. And why," continues he, "should we not be as universally persuaded that the grave and serious performances of such as write in the most engaging manner, by a kind of Divine impulse, must be the most effectual persuasive to goodness? The most active principle in our mind is the *imagination*. To it a good poet makes his court perpetually, and by this faculty takes care to gain it first. Our passions and inclinations come over next, and our reason surrenders itself with pleasure in the end. Thus the whole soul is insensibly betrayed into morality, by bribing the fancy with beautiful and agreeable images of those very things that, in the books of

* No. 98.

the philosophers, appear austere, and have at the best but a kind of forbidding aspect. In a word, the poets do, as it were, strew the rough paths of virtue so full of flowers, that we are not sensible of the uneasiness of them, and imagine ourselves in the midst of pleasures, and the most bewitching allurements, at the time we are making a progress in the severest duties of life."

Even in those men, however, whose education has not been so systematically conducted, and whose associations have been formed by accident, notwithstanding the many acute sufferings to which they may be exposed, I am persuaded that (except in some very rare combinations of circumstances) this part of our constitution is a more copious source of pleasure than of pain. After all the complaints that have been made of the peculiar distresses incident to cultivated minds, who would exchange the sensibility of his intellectual and moral being for the apathy of those whose only avenues of pleasure and pain are to be found in their animal nature, — who "move thoughtlessly in the narrow circle of their existence, and to whom the falling leaves present no idea but that of approaching winter"?

I shall conclude these very imperfect hints on a most important subject with remarking the inefficacy of mere *reasoning* or *argument*, in correcting the effects of early impressions and prejudices. More is to be expected from the opposite associations, which may be gradually formed by a new course of studies and of occupations, or by a complete change of scenes, of habits, and of society.

IV. (3.) *Influence of Opinions on Happiness.*] By opinions are here meant, not merely speculative conclusions to which we give our assent, but convictions which have taken root in the mind, and exert a constant and abiding influence on our dispositions and conduct.

Of these opinions a very great and important part are, in the case of all mankind, interwoven by education with their first habits of thinking, or insensibly imbibed from the manners of the times.

Where such opinions are erroneous, they may often be corrected to a great degree by the persevering efforts of a reflecting and vigorous mind; but as the number of minds capable of reflection is comparatively small, it becomes a duty on all who have themselves experienced the happy effects of juster and more elevated views, to impart, as far as they are able, the same blessing to others. The subject is of too great extent to be here prosecuted; but the reader will find it discussed at great length in a very valuable section of Dr. Ferguson's *Principles of Moral and Political Science.**

Of the doctrines contained in this section, the following abstract is given by the same writer in his *Institutes of Moral Philosophy.*

" It is unhappy to lay the pretensions of human nature so low as to check its exertions. The despair of virtue is still more unhappy than the despair of knowledge.

" It is unhappy to entertain notions of what men actually are, so high as, upon trial and disappointment, to run into the opposite extreme of distrust.

" It is unhappy to rest our own choice of good qualities on the supposition, that we are to meet with such qualities in other men; or to apprehend that want of merit in other men will dispense with that justice or liberality of conduct which *we* ought to maintain.

" It is unhappy to consider perfection as the standard by which we are to censure others, not as the rule by which we are to conduct ourselves.

" It is a wretched opinion, that happiness consists in a freedom from trouble, or in having nothing to do. In consequence of this opinion, men complain of what might employ them agreeably. By declining every duty and every active engagement, they render life a burden, and then complain that it is so. By declining business to go in search of amusement, they reject

* Part II. Chap. I. Sect. VIII.

what is fitted to occupy them, and search in vain for something else to quicken the languor of a vacant mind.

"It is therefore unhappy to entertain an opinion, that any thing can amuse us better than the duties of our station, or than that which we are in the present moment called upon to do.

"It is an unhappy opinion, that beneficence is an effort of self-denial, or that we lay our fellow-creatures under great obligations by the kindness we do them.

"It is an unhappy opinion, that any thing whatever is preferable to happiness." *

On the other hand, "it is happy," continues the same author, "to value personal qualities above every other consideration, and to state perfection as a guide to ourselves, not as a rule by which to censure others.

"It is happy to rely on what is in our own power; to value the characters of a worthy, benevolent, and strenuous mind, not as a form merely to be observed in our conduct, but as the completion of what we have to wish for in human life, and to consider the debasements of a malicious and cowardly nature as the extreme misery to which we are exposed.

"It is happy to have continually in view, that we are members of society, and of the community of mankind; that we are instruments in the hand of God for the good of his creatures; that, if we are ill members of society, or unwilling instruments in the hand of God, we do our utmost to counteract our nature, to quit our station, and to undo ourselves.

---

* In illustration of this last remark, Dr. Ferguson quotes in a note the following passage from the *Tatler:* — "There is hardly a man to be found, who would not rather be in pain to appear happy, than be really happy to appear miserable."

The author of the *Fable of the Bees* (see Remark *M.*) has also said, — "There is nothing so ravishing to the proud," (he should have said to the *vain*,) "as to be *thought* happy."

Does not this general anxiety to assume the appearance of happiness proceed from the universal conviction of the connection between happiness and virtue? By counterfeiting the outward signs of happiness, a vain man, without any offensive violation of modesty, lays claim indirectly to all those moral qualities of which happiness is commonly understood to be the fruit and the reward.

" '*I am in the station which God has assigned me*,' says Epictetus. With this reflection, a man may be happy in every station; without it, he cannot be happy in any. Is not the appointment of God sufficient to outweigh every other consideration? This rendered the condition of a slave agreeable to Epictetus, and that of a monarch to Antoninus. This consideration renders any situation agreeable to a rational nature, which delights not in partial interests, but in universal good."

This excellent passage contains a summary of the most valuable principles of the Stoical school. *One* of their doctrines, however, I could have wished that Dr. Ferguson had touched upon with his masterly hand; I mean that which relates to the *inconsistencies* which most men fall into in their expectations of happiness, as well as in the estimates they form of the prosperity of others. The following quotation from Epictetus will explain sufficiently the doctrine to which I allude.

" What is more reasonable, than that they who take pains for any thing should get most in that particular for which they take pains? They have taken pains for power, you for right principles; they for riches, you for a proper use of the appearances of things. See whether they have the advantage of you in that for which you have taken pains, and which they neglect. If they are in power and you not, why will you not speak the truth to yourself, that you do nothing for the sake of power, but that they do every thing? 'No, but since I take care to have right principles, it is more reasonable that I should have power.' Yes, in respect to what you take care about, — your principles. But give up to others the things in which they have taken more care than you. Else it is just as if, because you have right principles, you should think it fit that, when you shoot an arrow, you should hit the mark better than an archer, or that you should forge better than a smith."

Upon the foregoing passage a very ingenious and elegant writer, Mrs. Barbauld, has written a commentary so full of good sense and of important practical morality, that I am sure I run no hazard of trespassing on the patience of the reader by the length of the following extracts.

"As most of the unhappiness in the world arises rather from disappointed desires than from positive evil, it is of the utmost consequence to attain just notions of the laws and order of the universe, that we may not vex ourselves with fruitless wishes, or give way to groundless and unreasonable discontent. . . . . . We should consider this world as a great mart of commerce, where fortune exposes to our view various commodities, riches, ease, tranquillity, fame, integrity, knowledge. Exery thing is marked at a settled price. Our time, our labor, our ingenuity, is so much ready money, which we are to lay out to the best advantage. Examine, compare, choose, reject; but stand to your own judgment, and do not, like children, when you have purchased one thing, repine that you do not possess another which you did not purchase. Such is the force of well-regulated industry, that a steady and vigorous exertion of our faculties, directed to one end, will generally insure success. Would you, for instance, be rich? Do you think that single point worth the sacrificing every thing else to? You may, then, be rich. Thousands have become so from the lowest beginnings, from toil and patient diligence, and attention to the minutest articles of expense and profit. But you must give up the pleasures of leisure, of a vacant mind, of a free, unsuspicious temper. If you preserve your integrity, it must be a coarse-spun and vulgar honesty. Those high and lofty notions of morals which you brought with you from the schools must be considerably lowered, and mixed with the baser alloy of a jealous and worldly-minded prudence. You must learn to do hard, if not unjust, things; and as for the nice embarrassments of a delicate and ingenuous spirit, it is necessary for you to get rid of them as fast as possible. You must shut your heart against the Muses, and be content to feed your understanding with plain household truths. In short, you must not attempt to enlarge your ideas, or polish your taste, or refine your sentiments, but must keep on in one beaten track, without turning aside either to the right hand or to the left. 'But I cannot submit to drudgery like this; I feel a spirit above it.' 'T is well: be above it then; only do not repine that you are not rich. . . . . .

"'But is it not some reproach upon the economy of Providence, that such a one, who is a mean, dirty fellow, should have amassed wealth enough to buy half a nation?' Not in the least. He made himself a mean, dirty fellow for that end." *

V. (4.) *Influence of Habits on Happiness.*] The effect of habit in reconciling our minds to the inconveniences of our situation was formerly remarked, and an argument was drawn from it in proof of the goodness of our Creator, who, besides making so rich a provision of objects suited to the principles of our nature, has thus bestowed on us a power of accommodation to external circumstances, which these principles teach us to avoid.

This tendency of the mind, however, to adapt itself to the objects with which it is familiarly conversant, may, in some instances, not only be a source of occasional suffering, but may disqualify us for relishing the best enjoyments which human life affords. The habits contracted during infancy and childhood are so much more inveterate than those of our maturer years, that they have been justly said to constitute a *second nature;* and if, unfortunately, they have been formed amidst circumstances over which we have no control, they leave us no security for our happiness but the caprice of fortune. To habituate the minds of children to those occupations and enjoyments alone, which it is in the power of an individual at all times to command, is the most solid foundation that can be laid for their future tranquillity.

* *Works*, Vol. II. p. 21.

Dr. Paley, with that talent for familiar and happy illustration for which he is so justly celebrated, has said: —"The art in which the secret of human happiness in a great measure consists is, to *set* the habits in such a manner that every change may be a change for the better. The habits themselves are much the same; for whatever is made habitual becomes smooth and easy, and nearly indifferent. The return to an old habit is likewise easy, whatever the habit be. Therefore the advantage is with those habits which allow of indulgence in the deviation from them. The luxurious receive no greater pleasure from their dainties than the peasant does from his bread and cheese; but the peasant, whenever he goes abroad, finds *a feast*, whereas the epicure must be well entertained to escape disgust. Those who spend every day at cards, and those who go every day to plough, pass their time much alike; intent upon what they are about, wanting nothing, regretting nothing, they are both for the time in a state of ease; but then whatever suspends the occupation of the card-player distresses him, whereas to the laborer every interruption is refreshment; and this appears in the different effect that *Sunday* produces on the two, which proves a day of recreation to the one, but a lamentable burden to the other. The man who has learned to live alone feels his spirit enlivened whenever he enters into company, and takes his leave without regret. Another, who has long been accustomed to a crowd, experiences in company no elevation of spirits, nor any greater satisfaction than what the man of a retired life finds in his chimney-corner. So far their conditions are equal; but let a change of place, fortune, or situation separate the companion from his circle, his visitors, his club, common room, or coffee-house, and the difference of advantage in the choice and constitution of the two habits will show itself. Solitude comes to the one clothed with melancholy; to the other it brings liberty and quiet. You will see the one fretful and restless, at a loss how to dispose of his time till the hour come round that he can forget himself in bed;

the other easy and satisfied, taking up his book or his pipe as soon as he finds himself alone, ready to admit any little amusement that casts up, or to turn his hands and attention to the first business that presents itself, or, content without either, to sit still and let his trains of thought glide indolently through his brain, without much use, perhaps, or pleasure, but without *hankering* after any thing better, and without irritation. A reader who has inured himself to books of science and argumentation, if a novel, a well-written pamphlet, an article of news, a narrative of a curious voyage, or the journal of a traveller, comes in his way, sits down to the repast with relish, enjoys his entertainment while it lasts, and can return when it is over to his graver reading without distaste. Another, with whom nothing will go down but works of humor and pleasantry, or whose curiosity must be interested by perpetual novelty, will consume a bookseller's window in half a forenoon, during which time he is rather in search of diversion than diverted; and as books to his taste are few and short, and rapidly read over, the stock is soon exhausted, when he is left without resource from this principal supply of harmless amusement." *

As a supplement to the remarks of Paley, I shall quote a short passage from Montaigne, containing an observation relative to the same subject, which, although stated in a form too unqualified, seems to me highly worthy of attention. "We must not rivet ourselves so fast to our humors and complexions. Our chief business is to know how to apply ourselves to various customs. For a man to keep himself tied and bound by necessity to *one* only course is but bare existence, not living. It was an honorable character of the elder Cato, — 'So versatile was his genius, that, whatever he took in hand, you would be apt to say that he was formed for that very thing only.' Were I to choose for myself, there is no fashion so good that I should care to be so wedded to it as not to have it in my power to

* *Moral Philosophy*, Book I. Chap. VI.

disengage myself from it. Life is a motion, uneven, irregular, and ever varying its direction. A man is not his own friend, much less his own master, but rather a slave to himself, who is eternally pursuing his own humor, and such a bigot to his inclinations that he is not able to abandon or to alter them." *

The only thing to be censured in this passage is, that the author makes no distinction between *good* and *bad* habits; between those which we are induced to cultivate by reason, and by the original principles of our nature, and those which reason admonishes us to shun, on account of the mischievous consequences with which they are likely to be followed. With respect to these two classes of habits, considered in contrast with each other, it is extremely worthy of observation, that the former are incomparably more easy in the acquisition than the latter; while the latter, when once acquired, are (probably in consequence of this very circumstance, the difficulty of overcoming our natural propensities) of at least equal efficacy in subjecting all the powers of the will to their dominion.

Of the peculiar difficulty of shaking off such inveterate habits as were at first the most repugnant to our taste and inclinations, we have a daily and a melancholy proof in the case of those individuals who have suffered themselves to become slaves to tobacco, to opium, and to other intoxicating drugs, which, so far from possessing the attractions of pleasurable sensations, are in a great degree revolting to an unvitiated palate. The same thing is exemplified in many of those *acquired tastes* which it is the great object of the art of cookery to create and to gratify; and still more remarkably in those fatal habits which sometimes steal on the most amiable characters, under the seducing form of social enjoyment, and of a temporary respite from the evils of life.

I am inclined, however, to think that Montaigne meant to restrict his observations chiefly, if not solely,

---

* *Essays*, Book III. Chap. III.

to habits which are indifferent, or nearly indifferent, in their *moral* tendency, and that all he is to be understood as asserting amounts to this, — that we ought not, in matters connected with the *accommodations* of human life, to enslave ourselves to one set of habits in preference to another. In this sense his doctrine is just and important.*

---

* On the subject treated of in this section, see Degerando, *Du Perfectionnement Moral et de l'Education de soi-même.* It has been translated into English with this title: *Self-Education; or the Means and Art of Moral Progress.* Also, Carpenter's *Principles of Education,* and Combe's *Constitution of Man.* — Ed.

BOOK IV.

OF THE NATURE AND ESSENCE OF VIRTUE.

CHAPTER I.

OF THE GENERAL DEFINITION OF VIRTUE.

HAVING taken a cursory survey of the chief branches of our duty, we are prepared to enter on the general question concerning the *nature and essence of virtue.* In fixing on the arrangement of this part of my subject, it appeared to me more agreeable to the established rules of philosophizing, to consider, first, our duties in detail; and, after having thus laid a solid foundation in the way of analysis, to attempt to rise to the *general idea* in which all our duties concur, than to circumscribe our inquiries, at our first outset, within the limits of an arbitrary and partial definition. What I have now to offer, therefore, will consist of little more than some obvious and necessary consequences from principles which have been already stated.

The various duties which have been considered all agree with each other in one common quality, that of being *obligatory* on rational and voluntary agents; and they are all enjoined by the same authority,—*the authority of conscience.* These duties, therefore, are but different articles of *one law*, which is properly expressed by the word *virtue.*

As all the virtues are enjoined by the same authority, (the authority of conscience,) the man whose ruling principle of action is a sense of duty will observe all the different virtues with the same reverence and the same zeal. He who lives in the *habitual* neglect of any one of them shows plainly, that, where his conduct happens to coincide with what the rules of morality prescribe, it is owing merely to an accidental agreement between his duty and his inclination; and that he is not actuated by that motive which can alone render our conduct meritorious. It is justly said, therefore, that to live in the habitual practice of any one vice is to throw off our allegiance to conscience and to our Maker, as decidedly as if we had violated all the rules which duty prescribes; and it is in this sense, I presume, that we ought to interpret that passage of the sacred writings in which it is said, "Whosoever shall keep the whole law, and yet offend in one point, he is guilty of all." *

The word *virtue*, however, (as I shall have occasion to remark more particularly in the next section,) is applied, not only to express a particular course of external conduct, but to express *a particular species or description of human character.* When so applied, it seems properly to denote a *habit* of mind, as distinguished from *occasional acts* of duty. It was formerly said, that the characters of men receive their denominations of covetous, voluptuous, ambitious, &c., from the particular active principle which prevailingly influences the conduct. A man, accordingly, whose ruling or habitual principle of action is a sense of duty, or a regard to what is right, may be properly denominated virtuous. Agreeably to this view of the subject, the ancient Pythagoreans defined virtue to be Ἕξις τοῦ δέοντος,† *the habit of duty*, — the oldest definition of virtue of which we have any account, and one of the most unexceptionable which is yet to be found in any system of philosophy.

This account of virtue coincides very nearly with what I conceive to be Dr. Reid's, from some passages in his *Essays on the Active Powers of the Human Mind.* Virtue he seems to consider as consisting "in a fixed purpose or resolution to act according to our sense of duty." "We consider the moral virtues as inherent

* James ii. 10.

† Gale's *Opuscula Mythologica*, p. 690.

in the mind of a good man, even where there is no opportunity of exercising them. And what is it in the mind which we can call the virtue of justice when it is not exercised? It can be nothing but a fixed purpose or determination to act according to the rules of justice when there is opportunity."

With all this I perfectly agree. It is the fixed purpose to do what is *right*, which evidently constitutes what we call *a virtuous disposition.* But it appears to me that virtue, considered as an attribute of character is more properly defined by the *habit* which the fixed purpose gradually forms, than by the fixed purpose itself. It is from the external habit alone that other men can judge of the purpose; and it is from the uniformity and spontaneity of his habit that the individual himself must judge how far his purposes are sincere and steady.

These observations lead to an explanation of what has at first sight the appearance of paradox in the ethical doctrines of Aristotle, that where there is self-denial there is no virtue. That the merit of particular actions is increased by the self-denial with which they are accompanied cannot be disputed; but it is only when we are *learning* the practice of our duties that this self-denial is exercised (for the practice of morality, as well as of every thing else, is facilitated by repeated acts); and therefore, if the word *virtue* be employed to express that *habit* of mind which it is the great object of a good man to confirm, it will follow, that, in proportion as he approaches to it, his efforts of self-denial must diminish, and that all occasion for them would cease if his end were completely attained.

The definition of virtue given by Aristotle, as consisting in "right practical habits, *voluntary in their origin*," is well illustrated by what Plutarch has told us of the means by which he acquired the mastery over his irascible passions. "I have always approved," says he, "of the engagements and vows imposed on themselves from motives of religion, by certain philosophers, to abstain from wine, or from some other favorite indulgence, for the space of a year. I have also approved of the determination taken by others not to deviate from the truth, even in the lightest conversation, during a particular period. Comparing my own mind with theirs, and conscious that I yielded to none of them in reverence for God, I tasked myself, in the first instance, not to give way to anger upon any occasion for several days. I afterwards extended this resolution to a month or longer; and having thus made a trial of what I could do, I have learned at length never to speak but with gentleness, and so carefully to watch over my temper as never to purchase the short and unprofitable gratification of venting my resentment at the expense of a lasting and humiliating remorse." *

I must not dismiss this topic without recommending, not merely to the perusal, but to the diligent study, of all who have a taste for moral inquiries, Aristotle's *Nicomachean Ethics*, in which he has examined, with far greater accuracy than any other author of antiquity, the nature of *habits* considered in their relation to our moral constitution. The whole treatise is indeed of great value, and, with the exception of a few passages, almost justifies the warm and unqualified eulogium pronounced upon it by a learned divine (Dr. Rennel) before the University of Cambridge; in which he goes so far as to assert, that "it affords not only the most perfect specimen of scientific morality, but exhibits also the powers of the most compact and best constructed system *which the human intellect ever produced upon any subject;* enlivening occasionally great severity of method, and strict precision of terms, by the sublimest, though soberest, splendor of diction." †

---

* *De Ira.*

† We have several English translations of this work; one by Dr. Gillies; another by Thomas Taylor; another, the best, by R. W. Browne, in Bohn's Classical Library. — Ed.

CHAPTER II.

ON AN AMBIGUITY IN THE WORDS RIGHT AND WRONG, VIRTUE AND VICE.

THE epithets *right* and *wrong*, *virtuous* and *vicious*, are applied sometimes to *external actions*, and sometimes to the *intentions of the agent*. A similar ambiguity may be remarked in the corresponding words in other languages.

This ambiguity is owing to various causes, which it is not necessary at present to trace. Among other circumstances, it is owing to the association of ideas, which, as it leads us to connect notions of elegance or of meanness with many arbitrary expressions in language, so it often leads us to connect notions of right and wrong with *external actions*, considered abstractly from the motives which produced them. It is owing (at least in part) to this, that a man who has been involuntarily the author of any calamity to another can hardly by any reasoning banish his feelings of remorse; and, on the other hand, however wicked our *purposes* may have been, if by any accident we have been prevented from carrying them into execution, we are apt to consider ourselves as far less culpable than if we had perpetrated the crimes that we had intended. It is much in the same manner that we think it less criminal to mislead others by hints, or looks, or actions, than by a verbal lie; and, in general, that we think our guilt diminished if we can only contrive to accomplish our ends without employing those external *signs*, or those external *means*, with which we have been accustomed to associate the notions of guilt and infamy. Shakspeare has painted with philosophical accuracy this natural subterfuge of a vicious mind, in which the sense of duty still retains some authority, in one of the exquisite scenes between King John and Hubert: —

> "Hadst thou but shook thy head, or made a pause,
> When I spake darkly what I purposed;

Or turned an eye of doubt upon my face,
As bid me *tell my tale in express words;*
Deep shame had struck me dumb, made me break off,
And those thy fears might have wrought fears in me.
But thou didst understand me *by my signs,*
And didst *in signs again parley with sin.*"

As this twofold application of the words *right* and *wrong* to the intentions of the mind, and to external actions, has a tendency, in the common business of life, to affect our opinions concerning the merits of individuals, so it has misled the theoretical speculations of some very eminent philosophers in their inquiries concerning the principles of morals. It was to obviate the confusion of ideas arising from this ambiguity of language that the distinction between *absolute* and *relative* rectitude was introduced into ethics; and as the distinction is equally just and important, it will be proper to explain it particularly, and to point out its application to one or two of the questions which have been perplexed by that vagueness of expression which it is our object at present to correct.

An action may be said to be *absolutely* right, when it is in every respect suitable to the circumstances in which the agent is placed; or, in other words, when it is such as, with perfectly good intentions, under the guidance of an enlightened and well-informed understanding, he would have performed.

An action may be said to be *relatively* right, when the intentions of the agent are sincerely good, whether his conduct be suitable to his circumstances or not.

According to these definitions, an action may be right in one sense and wrong in another; — an ambiguity in language, which, how obvious soever, has not always been attended to by the writers on morals.

It is the relative rectitude of an action which determines the moral desert of the agent; but it is its absolute rectitude which determines its utility to his worldly interests, and to the welfare of society. And it is only so far as absolute and relative rectitude coincide, that utility can be affirmed to be a quality of virtue.

A strong sense of duty will indeed induce us to avail

ourselves of all the talents we possess, and of all the information within our reach, to act agreeably to the rules of absolute rectitude. And if we fail in doing so, our negligence is criminal. "Crimes committed through ignorance," as Aristotle has very judiciously observed, "are only excusable when the ignorance is involuntary; for when the cause of it lies in ourselves, it is then justly punishable. The ignorance of those laws which all may know if they will does not excuse the breach of them; and neglect is not pardonable where attention ought to be bestowed. But perhaps we are incapable of attention. This, however, is our own fault, since the incapacity has been contracted by our continual carelessness, as the evils of injustice and intemperance are contracted by the daily commission of iniquity and the daily indulgence in voluptuousness. For such as our actions are, such must our habits become." *

Notwithstanding, however, the truth and the importance of this doctrine, the general principle already stated remains incontrovertible, that in *every particular instance* our duty consists in doing *what appears to us to be right at the time;* and if, while we follow this rule, we should incur any blame, our demerit does not arise from acting according to an erroneous judgment, but from our previous misemployment of the means we possessed for correcting the errors to which our judgment is liable.†

From these principles it follows, that actions, although materially right, are not meritorious with respect to the agent, unless performed from a sense of duty. Aristotle inculcates this doctrine in many parts of his *Ethics.* ‡ To the same purpose, also, Lord Shaftesbury:—"In this case alone it is we call any creature *worthy* or *virtuous,* when it can attain to the

* Aristotle's *Ethics,* by Gillies, p. 305.

† A distinction similar to that now made between absolute and relative rectitude was expressed among the schoolmen by the phrases *material* and *formal virtue.*

‡ See *Ethic. Nic.,* Lib. IV. Cap. I.; Lib. VI. Cap. V.

speculation or sense of what is morally good or ill, admirable or blamable, right or wrong. For though we may vulgarly call an ill horse *vicious*, yet we never say of a good one, nor of any mere changeling or idiot, though never so good-natured, that he is *worthy* or *virtuous*. So that if a creature be generous, kind, constant, and compassionate, yet if he cannot reflect on what he himself does or sees others do, so as to take notice of what is worthy and honest, and make that notice or conception of worth and honesty to be an object of his affection, he has not the character of being virtuous, for thus, and no otherwise, he is capable of having a sense of right or wrong." *

CHAPTER III.

OF THE OFFICE AND USE OF REASON IN THE PRACTICE OF MORALITY.

I FORMERLY observed, that a strong sense of duty, while it leads us to cultivate with care our good dispositions, will induce us to avail ourselves of all the means in our power for the wise regulation of our external conduct. The occasions on which it is necessary for us to employ our *reason* in this way are chiefly the three following: —

1. When we have ground for suspecting that our moral judgments and feelings may have been warped and perverted by the *prejudices of education.*

* *Inquiry concerning Virtue*, Book I. Part II. Sect. III. Dr. Price, in his *Review*, Chap. VIII., has made a number of judicious observations on this subject; and Dr. Reid, in his *Essays on the Active Powers*, has a particular chapter allotted to the consideration of this very question, "Whether an action deserving moral approbation must be done with the belief of its being morally good ?" in which the doctrine he endeavours to establish is precisely the same with that which has been now stated. Compare Hume's *Treatise of Human Nature*, Book III. Part II. Sect. I., where this conclusion is disputed.

I formerly showed that the moral faculty is an original principle of the human constitution, and not the result (as Mandeville and others suppose) of habits superinduced by systems of education planned by politicians and divines. The moral faculty, indeed, like the faculty of reason, (which forms the most essential of its elements,) requires care and cultivation for its development; and, like reason, it has a gradual progress, both in the case of individuals and of societies. But it does not follow from this that the former is a fictitious principle, any more than the latter, with respect to the origin of which I do not know that any doubts have been suggested by the greatest skeptics.

Although, however, the moral faculty is an original part of the human frame, and although the great laws of morality are engraven on every heart, it is not in this way that the greater part of mankind arrive at their first knowledge of them. The infant mind is formed by the care of our early instructors, and for a long time thinks and acts in consequence of the confidence it reposes in their superior judgment. All this is undoubtedly agreeable to the design of Nature; and, indeed, if the case were otherwise, the business of the world could not possibly go on; for nothing can be plainer than this, that the multitude, (at least as society is actually constituted,) condemned as they are to laborious employments inconsistent with the cultivation of their mental faculties, are wholly incapable of forming their own opinions on the most important questions which can occupy the human mind. It is evident, at the same time, that, as no system of education can be perfect, many prejudices must mingle with the most important and best ascertained truths; and as the truths and the prejudices are both acquired from the same source, the incontrovertible evidence of the one serves, in the progress of human reason, to support and confirm the other. Hence the suspicious and jealous eye with which we ought to regard all those principles which we have at first adopted without due examination, — a duty doubly incumbent on those whose opinions are likely, from their rank and situation in society, to influence those of the multitude, and whose errors may eventually be instrumental in impairing the morals and the happiness of generations yet unborn.

2. A second instance in which the exercise of *reason* may be requisite for an enlightened discharge of our duty occurs in those cases where there appears to be an interference between *different duties*, and where of course it seems to be necessary to sacrifice one duty to another.

In the course of the foregoing speculations, I have frequently taken notice of the coincidence of all our virtuous principles of action in pointing out to us the same line of conduct; and of the systematical consistency and harmony which they have a tendency to produce in the moral character. Notwithstanding, however, this general and indisputable *fact*, it must be owned that cases sometimes occur in which they seem at first view to interfere with each other, and in which, of consequence, the exact path of duty is not altogether so obvious as it commonly is. Thus, every man feels it incumbent on him to have a constant regard to *the welfare of society*, and also to *his own happiness*. *On the whole*, these two interests will be found, by the most superficial inquirer, to be inseparably connected: but, at the same time, it cannot be denied that cases may be fancied in which it seems necessary to make a sacrifice of the one to the other.

In such cases, when the public happiness is very great, and the private comparatively inconsiderable, there is no room for hesitation; but the former may be easily conceived to be diminished, and the latter to be increased, to such an amount as to render the exact propriety of conduct very doubtful; more especially when it is considered, that, *cæteris paribus*, a certain degree of preference to ourselves is not only justifiable, but morally *right*. In like manner, the attachments of nature or of friendship, or the obligations of gratitude, of veracity, or of justice, may interfere with private or public good; and it may not be easy to say, whether *all* of these obligations may not sometimes be superseded by paramount considerations of *utility*. At least, these are points on which moralists have been arguing for some thousands of years, without having yet come to a determination in which all parties are agreed. It is much in the same manner that the different foundations of *property* may give rise to different *claims*; and it may be exceedingly difficult to determine, among a variety of *titles*, which of them is entitled to a preference over the others.

The consideration of these nice and puzzling questions in the science of *ethics* has given rise in modern times to a particular department of it, distinguished by the title of *casuistry*.

3. When the ends at which our duty prompts us to aim are to be accomplished by means which require choice and deliberation.

Even if the whole of virtue consisted in following steadily one principle of action, still reason would be necessary to direct us to the means. The truth is, nature only recommends certain ends, leaving to ourselves the selection of the most efficient means by which these ends may be obtained. Thus all moralists, whatever may be their particular system, agree in this, that it is one of the chief branches of our duty to promote to the utmost of our power the happiness of that society of which we are members; but the most ardent zeal for the attainment of this object can be of no avail, unless reason be employed both in ascertaining what are the real constituents of social and political happiness, and by what means this happiness may be most effectually advanced and secured.

It is owing to the last of these considerations that the study of *happiness*, both *private* and *public*, becomes an important part of the science of ethics. Indeed, without this study, the best dispositions of the heart, whether relating to ourselves or to others, may be in a great measure useless.

The subject of happiness, so far as relates to the individual, has been already considered. The great extent and difficulty of those inquiries which have for their object to ascertain what constitutes the happiness of a community, and by what means it may be most effectually promoted, make it necessary to separate them from the other questions of ethics, and to form them into a distinct branch of the science.

It is not, however, in this respect alone that politics is connected with the other branches of moral philosophy. The provisions which Nature has made for the intellectual and moral progress of the species all suppose the existence of the political union; and the particular form which this union happens in the case of any community to assume, determines many of the most important circumstances in the character of the people, and many of those opinions and habits which affect the happiness of private life.

These observations, which represent *politics* as a branch of *moral philosophy*, have been sanctioned by the opinions of all those authors, both in ancient and modern times, by whom either the one or the other has been cultivated with much success. Among the former it is sufficient to mention the names of Plato and Aristotle, both of whom, but more especially the latter, have left us works on the general principles of policy and government, which may be read with the highest advantage at the present day. As to Socrates, his studies seem to have been chiefly directed to inculcate the duties of private life; and yet, in the beautiful enumeration which Xenophon has given of his favorite pursuits, the science of politics is expressly mentioned as an important branch of the philosophy of human nature. "As for himself, *man*, and what related to man, were the only subjects on which he chose to employ himself. To this purpose, all his inquiries and conversations turned on what was pious, what impious; what honorable, what base; what just, what unjust; what wisdom, what folly; what courage, what cowardice; what a state or political community; what the character of a statesman or a politician; what a government of men, what the character of one equal to such a government. It was on these and other matters of the same kind that he used to discourse, in which subjects those who were knowing he used to esteem men of honor and goodness, and those who were ignorant, to be no better than the basest of slaves." *

APPENDIX TO BOOK IV.

SINCE the publication of Mr. Stewart's work, two theories on the nature of virtue have appeared and attracted considerable notice in England and this country; one by Sir James Mackintosh, and the other by Jouffroy. A succinct account of each will be given in this Appendix.†

SECTION I.

SIR JAMES MACKINTOSH'S THEORY OF MORALS.

I. *His Distinction between the Theory of Moral Sentiments and the Criterion of Morality.*] Mackintosh has, with great propriety, insisted upon the importance of a distinction of two parts of moral philosophy which

---

* *Memor.*, Lib. I. Cap. I.

[By *reason*, in this chapter, we are to understand the *discursive* reason, or *reasoning*. We have seen that Mr. Stewart, after Price, is disposed to refer the *origin* of moral distinctions to the *intuitive* reason. — ED.]

† The first is taken from Dr. Whewell's Preface to his edition of Mackintosh's *Dissertation on the Progress of Ethical Philosophy;* the second from Jouffroy himself, mostly from the twenty-ninth and thirtieth Lectures of his *Cours de Droit Naturel*, being part of the third volume, published since his death, and not yet translated into English. His criticism of other theories is taken from the twenty-second Lecture.

The object of this work does not lead me to notice German speculations on ethics not yet naturalized amongst us. Those who wish to pursue the study in that direction must read Kant, *Grundlegung zur Metaphysik der Sitten;* and *Critik der praktischen Vernunft.* (Most of Kant's ethical writings have been translated into English by J. W. Semple, under the title of *The Metaphysic of Ethics.*) Schleiermacher, *Entwurf eines Systems der Sittenlehre.* Hegel, *Grundlinien der Philosophie des Rechts.* — ED.

are often confounded; — the *theory of moral sentiments*, and the *criterion of morality*. The question of the independent existence and character of the moral faculty belongs to the former division of the subject; the construction of our system of ethics flows from the latter. There is no necessary collision between doctrines on these two points. We may hold that morality is an original quality of actions, and may still form our rules of morality by tracing the consequences of actions.

This distinction has often been neglected. Those who hold that utility constitutes morality often call upon the advocates of a moral sense to show how the assertion of such a faculty leads us to distinguish right from wrong, or how it can supersede the criterion of general utility. To this it may be replied, that the existence of a moral conscience in man is an important truth, but that this truth alone cannot be expected to replace all the principles and deductions by which a sound system of philosophical ethics is to be produced; that the construction of such a system is undoubtedly a difficult problem, but that we shall inevitably obtain an erroneous solution of the problem, if we do not take into our account the operation of the moral faculty. The criterion of utility cannot safely be applied without acknowledging the independent value of morality, any more than the moral faculty can always decide well without the consideration of consequences. For among the most important results of actions, we must include their effect upon the moral habits and feelings of men; and must consider these effects as claiming attention for their own sake. The promotion of human virtue must be our aim, as well as the augmentation of human happiness. We cannot by any analysis exclude the former of these ends; happiness depends on the exercise of the virtuous affections, far more clearly than virtue depends on the pursuit of happiness. The most wise and moderate of the utilitarian moralists do, accordingly, apply their method in this manner. Thus Paley, in estimating the guilt of corrupting a person to the commission of one offence, states it as one ground of condemnation, that such seduction is the destruction of the person's moral principle.* And it appears, at present, to be generally allowed, that the utilitarian doctrine cannot be applied without considering the effect on the moral feelings of men as among the important consequences of action. "It often happens," it is said, "that an essential part of the morality or immorality of an action, or a rule of action, consists in its influence on the agent's own mind." "Many actions, moreover, produce effects on the characters of other persons besides the agents." The effects here spoken of are, in fact, effects on the moral habits of thought; and thus the existence of the moral attributes of the mind, as original and independent objects of the attention of the ethical philosopher, is *presupposed* in this mode of applying the utilitarian scheme.

If, indeed, we take *such* good and bad consequences into the account, — if, among the useful effects of actions, we conceive the most useful to be the improvement of man's moral character, — if we frame our rules so that they shall conduce as much as possible to virtuous feeling as well as to beneficial action, to purity of heart as well as to rectitude of conduct, — if we aim at man's general well-being, and not merely at his gratification, — I know not what moralist would object to a criterion of morality so drawn from consequences, or would deny that the promotion of human happiness, and that of human virtue, require the same practical rules. Mackintosh would undoubtedly have assented to this; for he not only allows the universal coincidence of virtue with utility in the largest sense, but founds his recommendation of the highest forms of virtue on the advantage of virtuous habits and feelings, both to the possessor and to the community; as when he speaks of the trite example of Regulus, of the character of Andrew Fletcher, and of the virtue of courage.† If we

* *Moral Philosophy*, Book III. Part III. Chap. III.

† See the extract from him on the followers of Bentham in this volume.

could take into due account the whole value of right principles, and the whole happiness produced by virtuous feelings, we could commit no practical error in making the advantageous consequences of actions the measure of their morality.

But this can happen only by considering moral good as a primary object, valuable for its own sake; not by supposing that virtue is aimed at, as subservient to some other purpose of more genuine utility: and no sagacity or fairness in estimating useful consequences can stand as a substitute for the love of right itself. It is true that honesty is the best policy; but he who is honest only out of policy does not come up even to the vulgar notion of a virtuous man. If a man were tempted by the opportunity of gaining a large estate through a safe but fraudulent proceeding, the utilitarian doctrine would seem to recommend him to weigh both sides well, though it would direct him in conclusion to decide in favor of probity; but the common judgment of mankind would hardly deem him honest *if he hesitated at all.* And in like manner in regard to other temptations, the safety of virtue appears to consist so little in tracing all possible consequences, that it has been held that to deliberate is to be lost, and that the only secure protection is that purity of mind which will not look at the prospect of sensual pleasure when it forms one side of the account. We cannot help saying, with Cicero, "Hæc nonne est turpe dubitare philosophos, quæ ne rustici quidem dubitent?" *

Indeed, it appears to be acknowledged by the advocates of the rule of utility, that it is not safe to apply the principle separately in each particular case. Mr. Bentham has urged, with great beauty of expression,† the propriety of framing general rules, and conforming our practice invariably to these, so as to avoid the temptations of our frailty and passion in particular

* *De Off.*, Lib. III. 19. "Is it not base for philosophers to doubt where even peasants do not hesitate?"

† *Deontology*, Part II. Chap. I.

instances. If a reverence for general maxims of morality, and a constant reference to the common precepts of virtue, take the place, in the utilitarian's mind, of the direct application of his principle, there will remain little difference between him and the believer in original moral distinctions; for the practical rules of the two will rarely differ, and in both systems the rules will be the moral guides of thought and conduct.

But though the two schools agree so far, there still will be found a deficiency on the part of the consistent utilitarian. A persuasion that moral good is something different from, and superior to, mere pleasure, is requisite to give to our preference of it that tone of enthusiasm and affection which belongs to virtuous feeling. To approve a rule as right, is different from liking it as profitable; to admire an act of virtuous self-devotion as we are capable of admiring, is a feeling so different from the apprehension of any usefulness the act may have, that the comparison of the two things is altogether incongruous. The moral faculty converts our perception of the quality of actions into an affection of the strongest kind; nor can we be satisfied with any account of our moral sentiments which excludes this feature in the process. Thus, as we hold the affections to be motives of an order superior to the desires which have reference to ourselves only, we maintain the moral faculty, the conscience, the affection towards duty, to be a principle of action of an order superior both to the desires and to the other affections. Without the acknowledgment of this subordination, the language and feelings of men when they compare the claims of personal pleasure, of social affection, and of duty, are altogether unintelligible and absurd.

II. *He refers the Formation of our Active Principles to the Association of Ideas.*] I proceed to notice another principle which enters into Mackintosh's philosophy, and which, in the way in which he holds it, constitutes one of his leading peculiarities. He assents, in a great measure, to the explanation suggested by Hume and Smith, but more fully developed by Hartley, of *the formation of our passions and affections, and even of our sentiments of virtue and duty, by means of the association of ideas.*

1. But into this view, as usually understood, he introduces several modifications; and, in particular, he asserts that the effect of such "association" may be something very different from the mere juxtaposition of the component elements. Thus he says that the result may be so entirely a single sentiment, that "the originally separate feelings can no longer be disjoined"; and, moreover, that "the compound may have properties not to be found in any of its component parts"; as constantly happens, he observes, in material compounds.

It is clear that this view of the effect of the "association of ideas" may give results very different from those often founded upon that doctrine. If we say that gratitude, or compassion, or patriotism, are *only* certain trains of pleasurable associations, we are generally understood to assert that we can again resolve those feelings into the constituent and associated elements; and that by so doing we may hope to reason upon them most philosophically and exactly. But Mackintosh's mode of considering these and other emotions would allow of neither of these inferences. He supposes "association" to be employed in the education rather than in the creation of our moral sentiments; in awakening affections rather than in connecting notions.

2. The ideas or the feelings which are concerned in this process are said to be *associated;* but this is, he declares, a very inadequate word to express the "complete combination and fusion" which occur. This association presupposes laws and powers of the mind itself, according to which the conjunction produces its results. The celebrated comparison of the mind to a sheet of white paper is not just, except we consider that there may be in the paper itself many circumstances which

affect the nature of the writing. A recent writer, however, appears to me to have supplied us with a much more apt and beautiful comparison. Man's soul at first, says Professor Sedgwick, is one unvaried blank, till it has received the impressions of external experience. "Yet has this blank," he adds, "been already touched by a celestial hand; and, when plunged in the colors which surround it, it takes not its tinge from accident, but design, and comes out covered with a glorious pattern." * This modern image of the mind as *a prepared blank* is well adapted to occupy a permanent place in opposition to the ancient sheet of white paper.

3. Not only the word *association*, but also the word *ideas*, in the Lockian expression, appears to Mackintosh to be unsuited to its purpose, since an association takes place "of thoughts with emotions, as well as with each other." Our author has indeed shown great solicitude to bring into clear view that part of our nature which he here distinguishes from thought; — "that other part of it, hitherto without any adequate name, which feels, and desires, and loves, and hopes, and wills." After balancing the various terms which may be used to express the aggregate of such feelings, he inclines finally to call it the *emotive* part of man.

Thus the "association of ideas," according to Mackintosh, would more properly be termed *the composition of ideas and emotions.* In his view of the composite, as losing all trace of apparent composition, the author wâs, in some measure, following Hartley, though he justly claims the credit of seeing more distinctly than his predecessors the important truth, that the compound may have properties not found in any of its component parts.

4. Mackintosh maintains that this is by no means a modification of the selfish system; for the "affections and the moral sentiments, though educed by association, only become what they are when they lose all trace of self-regard." "If the affections be *acquired*,

---

* *Discourse on the Studies of the University*, p. 54.

they are justly called *natural;* and if their origin be personal, their nature may and does become *disinterested.*"

III. *His Theory of Conscience.*] But we must now consider another peculiarity of Mackintosh's system: I speak of what he names his *theory of conscience.*

1. The agreeable or painful sentiment, naturally attending certain emotions, is transferred, by association of ideas, to the volitions and acts which they produce; and thus, in the end, these *volitions* and *acts* become the *immediate* objects of our love or repugnance. According to Mackintosh's theory, the moral faculty consists of this class of secondary desires and affections which have dispositions and volitions for their sole object. This description of our moral sentiments will, he conceives, explain their peculiar character and attributes. He expresses the relation which he wishes to ascribe, by saying that the moral sentiments are *in contact with the will;* or, as he further elucidates this, "they may and do stand between any other practical principle and its object, while it is absolutely impossible that any other shall intercept their connection with the will." The conscience requires virtuous acts and dispositions to action; and by such requisition it can check and control any desires of external objects; but no desire of any outward gratification can prevent the conscience from demanding a virtuous direction of the will; and this mental relation explains and justifies, Mackintosh conceives, that attribution of supremacy and command to the conscience on which moral writers have often insisted.*

* In his remarks on Butler he says: — "The truth seems to be, that the moral sentiments, in their mature state, are *a class of feelings which have no other object but the mental dispositions leading to voluntary action, and the voluntary actions which flow from these dispositions.* We are pleased with some dispositions and actions, and displeased with others, in ourselves and our fellows. We desire to cultivate the dispositions, and to perform the actions, which we contemplate with satisfaction. These objects, like all those of human appetite or desire, are sought for their own sake. The peculiarity of these desires is, that their gratification *requires the use of no*

2. Thus conscience consists in, or rather results from, the composition of *all* those sentiments of which the final object is a state of the will, intimately and inseparably blended, and held in a perfect state of solution; and the conscience being thus represented as analogous to the desires, it implies, in the same way as other desires, a *sense* of what is grateful, and a faculty of dwelling, in thought, on the gratification so obtained.

3. But if, in order further to develop this theory, it be asked *what* states of the will are thus agreeable to

---

means. Nothing (unless it be a volition) is interposed between the desires and the voluntary act. It is impossible, therefore, that these passions should undergo any change by transfer from the end to the means, as is the case with other practical principles. On the other hand, as soon as they are fixed on these ends, they cannot regard any further object. When another passion prevails over them, the end of the moral faculty is converted into a means of gratification. But volitions and actions are not themselves the end, or last object in view, of any other desire or aversion. Nothing stands between the moral sentiments and their object. They are, as it were, in contact with the will. It is this sort of mental position, if the expression may be pardoned, that explains, or seems to explain, those characteristic properties which true philosophers ascribe to them, and which all reflecting men feel to belong to them. Being the only desires, aversions, sentiments, or emotions which regard dispositions and actions, they *necessarily extend to the whole character and conduct.* Among motives to action, they alone are justly considered as *universal.* They may and do stand between any other practical principle and its object; while it is absolutely impossible that another shall intercept their connection with the will. Be it observed, that, though many passions prevail over them, no other can act beyond its own appointed and limited sphere; and that the prevalence itself, leaving the natural order undisturbed in any other part of the mind, is perceived to be a disorder, when seen in another man, and felt to be so by the mind disordered, when the disorder subsides. Conscience may forbid the will to contribute to the gratification of a desire. No desire ever forbids will to obey conscience.

"This result of the peculiar relation of conscience to the will justifies those metaphorical expressions which ascribe to it *authority* and the right of *universal command.* It is *immutable;* for, by the law which regulates all feelings, it must rest on *action,* which is its object, and beyond which it cannot look; and as it employs no *means,* it never can be transferred to nearer objects, in the way in which he who first desires an object, as a means of gratification, may come to seek it as his end Another remarkable peculiarity is bestowed on the moral feelings by the nature of their object. As the objects of all other desires are outward, the satisfaction of them may be frustrated by outward causes. The moral sentiments may always be gratified, because voluntary actions and moral dispositions spring from within. No external circumstance affects them. Hence their *independence.* As the moral sentiment needs *no means,* and the desire is instantaneously followed by the volition, it seems to be either that which first suggests the

the conscience, or, in other words, what, according to this system, is the general character of the dispositions and actions which we consider good and right, Mackintosh's answer would be, that the conscience, being educated and awakened by certain processes of association, is thus composed of various elements, and finds good under various forms; — that the beneficial volitions are delightful, and that, therefore, they strongly attract those affections which regard the will, and thus give rise to some of the elements of conscience;* —

relation between *command* and *obedience*, or at least that which affords the simplest instance of it. It is therefore with the most rigorous precision that authority and universality are ascribed to them. Their only unfortunate property is their too frequent weakness; but it is apparent that it is from that circumstance alone that their failure arises. Thus considered, the language of Butler concerning conscience, that, "had it strength as it has right, it would govern the world," which may seem to be only an effusion of generous feeling, proves to be a just statement of the nature and action of the highest of human faculties. The union of universality, immutability, and independence with direct action on the will, which distinguishes the moral sense from every other part of our practical nature, renders it scarcely metaphorical language to ascribe to it unbounded sovereignty and awful authority over the whole of the world within, — shows that attributes, well denoted by terms significant of command and control, are, in fact, inseparable from it, or rather constitute its very essence, — justifies those ancient moralists who represent it as alone securing, if not forming, the moral liberty of man; and finally, when religion rises from its roots in virtuous feeling, it clothes conscience with the sublime character of representing the Divine purity and majesty in the human soul. Its title is not impaired by any number of defeats; for every defeat necessarily disposes the disinterested and dispassionate by-stander to wish that its force were strengthened: and though it may be doubted whether, consistently with the present constitution of human nature, it could be so invigorated as to be the only motive to action, yet every such by-stander rejoices at all accessions to its force, and would own that man becomes happier, more excellent, more estimable, more venerable, in proportion as conscience acquires a power of banishing malevolent passions, of strongly curbing all the private appetites, of influencing and guiding the benevolent affections themselves."

* To illustrate this more fully, we cite what he says in his "General Remarks": — "When the social affections are thus formed, they are naturally followed in every instance by the will to do whatever can promote their object. Compassion excites a voluntary determination to do whatever relieves the person pitied. The like process must occur in every case of gratitude, generosity, and affection. Nothing so uniformly follows the kind disposition as the act of will, because it is the only means by which the benevolent desire can be gratified. The result of what Brown justly calls 'a finer analysis' shows the mental contiguity of the affection to the volition to be much closer than appears on a coarser examination of

that our anger against those who disappoint our wish for the happiness of others, when in like manner detached from persons and transferred to dispositions, becomes a sense of justice, another element of conscience; — that courage, energy, decision, when tamed by the society of the affections, and considered as dispositions only, become magnanimity, and gratify the moral sense; — and that even those habits which mainly affect our own good, as temperance, prudence, when they become disposition and not calculation, are, for like reasons, added to the constituents of conscience.

4. Thus the view of the nature of conscience here presented explains how it is that the private desires and the social affections alike fall under the authority of the moral faculty. The explanation of this community of rule in sentiments of so widely different nature, Mackintosh considers a strong confirmation of the justice of his opinion.

IV. *Inferences deduced from this Theory.*] Without pronouncing a judgment on the truth of this theory, I

---

this part of our nature. No wonder, then, that the strongest association, the most active power of reciprocal suggestion, should subsist between them. As all the affections are delightful, so the volitions, voluntary acts which are the only means of their gratification. become agreeable objects of contemplation to the mind. The habitual disposition to perform them is felt in ourselves, and observed in others, with satisfaction. As these feelings become more lively. the absence of them may be viewed in ourselves with a pain, in others with an alienation, capable of indefinite increase. They become entirely independent sentiments; still, however, receiving constant supplies of nourishment from their parent affections. which, in well-balanced minds, reciprocally strengthen each other; unlike the unkind passions, which are constantly engaged in the most angry conflicts of civil war. In this state, we desire to experience these *beneficent volitions*, to cultivate a disposition towards them, and to do every correspondent voluntary act. They are for their own sake the objects of desire. They thus constitute a large portion of those emotions, desires, and affections, which regard certain dispositions of the mind and determinations of the will as their sole and ultimate end. These are what are called the moral sense, the moral sentiments, or best, though most simply, by the ancient name of *Conscience;* which has the merit, in our language, of being applied to no other purpose, which peculiarly marks the strong working of these feelings on conduct, and which, from its solemn and sacred character, is well adapted to denote the venerable authority of the highest principle of human nature" hope I have faithfully represented the author's meaning. But he draws from the theory certain inferences, of which I may say a few words.

1. Mackintosh, as we have seen, maintains that, though the moral faculty is formed or educed by intercourse with the external world, it is a law of our nature; yet he allows that what this law prescribes agrees with the rule, rightly understood, of bringing forth the greatest happiness. He was, therefore, naturally called upon to account for this coincidence. If moral approval be a different sentiment from the estimation of general happiness, why does the moral sense of man invariably approve that which increases the happiness of his species? If this theory account for this phenomenon, such a circumstance will, he conceives, be a strong argument in its favor.

He replies to this inquiry, that all the separate objects which conscience approves, the social affections, the decisions of justice, the maxims of enlightened prudence, tend to the happiness of some part of the species, and that thus the general rules of conscience must agree with the rules of the general happiness. All the acts which the moral faculty sanctions promote the welfare of some part of mankind, and all that reason has to do is to add up the items of the account. All the principles of which conscience is composed converge towards the happiness of man; and therefore this may be taken as its central point. And thus the coincidence just noticed is not accidental, but is a necessary consequence of the theory.

I will add, as a corollary to what Mackintosh has said, that a system of ethics, rightly constructed on the principle of promoting, in the greatest degree, the happiness of mankind, will coincide, in most of its rules of action, with a system founded on the supreme authority of conscience; but that, in order to apply safely and well the eudemonist principle, we must recollect that happiness consists rather in habits of the mind than in outward gratifications, and is to be sought rather by forming moral dispositions than by prescribing acts. In Paley's *Moral Philosophy*, we have a work framed on the eudemonist basis, which has for some time possessed considerable authority in this country, and has probably in no small degree influenced men's reasonings on such subjects in recent times. Without examining here how far Paley has always applied his principle under due conditions, and traced his consequences with a sufficiently enlarged survey, we may observe that there prevails through the work a tone of practical sagacity, good sense, and good feeling, which neutralizes most of its theoretical defects.

2. Some other bearings of Mackintosh's theory may be noticed, and especially the view it offers of the relation of religion and morality. This agrees nearly with the doctrine of Butler, and many English divines, that conscience is one of the ways in which the commands of God are conveyed to us. "The completeness and rigor acquired by conscience, when all its dictates are revered as the commands of a perfectly good and wise Being, are so obvious, that they cannot be questioned by any reasonable man, however wide his incredulity may be. It is thus that conscience can add the warmth of an affection to the inflexibility of principle and habit." Not only are we bound to accept all the precepts for the moral government of the will, disclosed either by revelation or by reason, as undeniable rules for our feelings and actions; but the relations between man and his Maker which religion teaches us tend to make this a work of love, no less than of duty, and bestow on that improvement of our inward nature to which conscience is constantly urging us an aspect of hope and joy, which human morality, without such aid, can hardly assume, and seldom long retain.

3. I will only refer to one other consequence of this theory of conscience of Mackintosh; — the view it appears to him to supply of the celebrated question of free will. Since conscience contemplates those dispositions only which depend on the will, it excludes all consideration of the cause in which the will originated: hence the voluntary dispositions appear as the first link

of the chain; and, in the eye of conscience, will is the independent cause of action. Reason, on the other hand, must consider occurrences as bound together by the connection of cause and effect, and thus sees only the strength of the necessitarian system. Thus, while speculation appears to show that our actions are necessary, practice convinces us that they are free. The advocates of necessity and of free will look at the question from different points of view; — that of the understanding and that of the conscience. But the conscientious view, being strengthened by the moral sympathy of mankind, is by far the most generally and strongly entertained.

Section II.

JOUFFROY'S THEORY OF MORALS.

I. *His Criticism of other Theories.*] Observation attests, and reason conceives, that every human action must have a motive and an end. In seeking to determine what are the distinct ends of human action, we find that they may be reduced to three: first, the peculiar object of some one natural desire; secondly, the complete satisfaction of our whole nature, or the pleasure which accompanies this satisfaction; thirdly, that which is good in itself. We find, also, that all the distinct motives of human action may be reduced to three, which correspond to these three ends: first, some natural instinct; secondly, a desire of secondary formation, which we call self-love, or the desire of happiness; thirdly, obligation. From these arise three simple forms of determination, not to speak of those mixed forms which result from the different possible combinations of these three ends and motives.

This being premised, we apply the name of *good* to the following things: —

1. The objects of the different instincts of our nature, — such as food, riches, power, glory, esteem, friendship, — each of which we call good. *Good*, in this first

acceptation, signifies whatever is fitted to satisfy some desire; so that there are as many varieties of good as there are desires.

2. The greatest satisfaction of our nature; which is, in other words, either its greatest good or its greatest happiness, according as we consider its satisfaction in itself, or the consequence of this, which is pleasure. Here, the word *good* represents no longer the object of a desire and its satisfaction, but the greatest satisfaction of all our desires. Different persons may understand this good in their own way, but each has the idea of such a good.

3. Good in itself. By *good*, in this last acceptation, we mean, not that which is good in reference to ourselves, but that which is good independently of ourselves and of every human being, — good in itself, and absolutely. There can be but one such good as this, although there may be as many kinds of good of the second class as there are beings, and as many of the first as there are desires in individuals.

4. The conformity of the voluntary action of a free and intelligent being to absolute good. The word *good*, in this last acceptation, represents that quality of the conduct of intelligent and free individuals which makes it conformable to absolute good. This is virtue, morality, moral good.

Such are the facts, at least as they appear to me. Ethical systems become false by misconceiving or mutilating these facts more or less. The system that mutilates them the most is the selfish system; for it entirely effaces the distinctions just pointed out, and reduces all these facts to one, — a voluntary and determined pursuit of personal good. The instinctive or sentimental system is less at variance with the truth. It recognizes two ends and two motives, — the end and motive of instinct, and the end and motive of self-love; — but, in all else, it misconceives the reality. The system maintained by Price and Stewart comes much nearer to the truth. This recognizes three motives and three ends; but it gives a false description of the third, and alters its nature by overlooking the distinction between *absolute good* and *moral good*. It confounds these two facts, which, though united, are distinct, and forms of them a single fact, that retains the qualities of neither the one nor the other exclusively, and thus, by blending them, mutilates both.

According to Price and Stewart, the idea of *good* is only an idea of *a quality in actions recognized by intuitive reason;* so that, beyond actions, there is nothing that is good, and, if there were no actions, good would cease to be.

In my opinion, this is true only of *moral good*. I grant the idea of moral good is the idea of a certain quality in actions,—a quality which really exists in them, and which my reason discovers. If there were no actions, this quality, and consequently moral good, would have no existence. The idea alone would exist, and this would be the idea of a possible quality of possible actions. But, in my opinion, moral good, or this particular quality, is not an intrinsic attribute of certain actions, as a round form is of certain bodies. It is, on the contrary, *a relation existing between actions and an end, namely, absolute good;* these actions may or may not tend to this end, by relation to which they are good when they tend towards it, and bad when they do not. This *end* is good in itself; it is the only *absolute good*, and whatever else is good derives this character merely from being related to it. This end is the reality which the word *good* represents; the idea of it is perfectly equivalent to the idea of *good*, and, in fact, these two ideas are identical.

In what way, according to my view, is good perceived? The process is as follows: As good and evil, in conduct and actions, depend upon their conformity or their nonconformity to absolute good, it is evident that, for me, they have no such character, unless I have attained to the idea of this absolute good. It is on the occasion of actions, to be sure, that this idea of good is conceived, and the conception may be more or less clear in my mind; but, clear or obscure, this idea must still precede any judgment as to particular actions. Thus, in my system, moral conceptions must necessarily originate in the idea of *good in itself*.

II. *His Account of the Origin of our Ideas of Absolute Good and of Moral Obligation.*] The solution of the moral problem is found in certain self-evident truths, conceived *a priori* by the reason, the immediate consequence of which is a clear definition of *good*, and this supplies us with a precise method for determining in what it consists for every possible being. What the truths are, and how they lead to this double consequence, I am going briefly to indicate.

The first of these truths is the principle, that *every being has an end;* it has all the evidence, all the universality, all the necessity, of the principle of causality, and our reason is as unable to conceive of an exception to one as to the other. It has, also, the fecundity; for, having penetrated into our intelligence, it gives birth to other truths contained impliedly in it, and these cast on the end of things the same light which the truths emanating from the principle of causality cast on their origin.

Indeed, if it is true that every being has an end, then it is true that I have one, that you have one, that there is no created being which has not one. Now in casting our eyes over the world, or over that part of it with which we are acquainted, we perceive that, if all beings have an end, this end is not uniform for all; for, as far as our observation extends, each class of beings develops itself in its own way, and aspires to an end peculiar to itself. As soon, therefore, as we have conceived that every being has an end, we gather from experience another truth, namely, that this end differs in different beings, *each being having an end peculiar to itself.*

And this second discovery is not slow to introduce a third, namely, that a relation exists between the end of each being and its nature, the diversity or peculiarity in the end corresponding to the diversity or peculiarity in the nature. Clearly, if each being has its appropriate end, it must have received an organization adapted to this end, and apt to attain it. It would be a contradiction to suppose an end to be imposed on a being whose nature did not contain the means of realizing it. Experience teaches us that no such contradiction exists in creation; it shows us everywhere the nature of beings in harmony with their destination, and a perfect parallelism between diversity of natures and that of ends; so that this third truth, that *the end of each being is conformed to its nature*, is invested in our intelligence with the same guaranties of universali ty as the other two.

By its light you perceive the method for determining what the true end of any being is. Though the end of beings is a pure conception, invisible to the observer, their nature is a reality which we can analyze and investigate; and, as the nature of every being is adapted to its end, we can find in the first a revelation of the second. There is, then, a way for discovering the destiny of beings, — namely, by the study of their nature; whenever the latter is possible, the former can be determined.

To these truths are soon added two others, which equal, in evidence and reach, the first. If each being has its end, then *creation itself, which embraces all beings, has one.* Creation, it is true, cannot be comprehended by us in its totality; we can take in only a fragment of it, and this fragment we know in a moment only of its duration. The work of God fills space and duration, while all that we can directly seize pertains to but a point in one, and a moment in the other. Still, though infinite, and to endure for ever, the same principle applies to it, assuring our reason invincibly that it has an end.

Moreover, this truth is revealed to us in connection with the preceding truths, and all together generate still another. If creation has an end, if each being has its own end, and if creation is nothing but the assemblage of all beings, it follows that the relation which exists between the whole and its parts must also exist between the end of the whole and the end of each of the parts of the whole. *The end of each being is, therefore, an element of the end of creation.* The end of creation is only the resultant of the particular ends of all the beings that people and compose the universe, while these, in their turn, are only the diverse means which concur in the accomplishment of the total and supreme end. This last conception is not less evident or less necessary than the rest, flowing, like them, from the absolute principle that every thing has an end. By an invincible relation, it attributes the end of all possible beings to a consequence of the creation, and forms out of all these scattered ends an harmonious whole, the concurrence of which aspires to a single aim, — that, even, which God proposed to himself, when he allowed the universe to escape from his hands.

This is not all. Other ideas and truths issue from this principle, that all has an end. The next which I shall signalize is *the idea of order.* The idea of order is, indeed, but an emanation, a natural and inevitable consequence of the idea of an end. If creation has an end, and if this end is nothing but the resultant of the particular ends of the beings which compose it, then the life of creation is nothing else but its movement towards this supreme end, and the movement itself, in its turn, may be resolved into the several movements of all created beings towards their respective ends. From the accomplishment of all particular ends, — accomplishment which is effected simultaneously in all points of space, and successively in all moments of duration, by the harmonious concurrence of all beings, executing, each in its sphere and at its hour, the part with which it has been charged, — results evidently the universal life, or the accomplishment of the total end of creation. Now this universal and eternal movement of each thing towards the end which God has assigned to it, and of all things towards the supreme, single, and definitive end of creation, — this movement, evidently regular, since it has an aim, is precisely what we call *order*. The only difference between the end of creation and universal order is, that the end is the aim, while the order is the regular movement of all in accordance with this aim.

Thus far nothing has been said of morality. The conceptions just announced to you are only speculative truths, which reveal to our reason what is, without teaching it what ought to be done. Such, however, is their nature, that, when they have appeared in our intelligence, the idea of what is good, and consequently of what ought to be done, necessarily follows. It is impossible for our reason not to pass from this idea of an end to the idea of good in itself, and from the idea of order to that of moral good. If there exist in the world intelligent and free beings, these beings resemble all others in having an end which has been assigned them, and a nature fitted to that end; in other terms, like all other beings, they are fragments of creation, and their end is an element of the absolute end of things. At the same time, they differ from other creatures, by being endowed with intelligence and liberty; — a difference which produces in them special and peculiar phenomena. Being intelligent, it is given them to comprehend this world of which they make part; to conceive that it has an end, that all beings have one, and that the end of each being is an element of the end of all. Being free, it is also given them to realize voluntarily this end, of which they have formed a conception, and thus to concur in the accomplishment of the absolute end of things, and contribute their part to the absolute order, that is to say, to the universal movement of all things towards an end. Now that which has been given to these privileged beings to do, — to these beings endowed by exception with intelligence and liberty, — is precisely what they ought, what they are required, what they are obliged, to do.

To the eye of reason there is a perfect, absolute, necessary equation between the idea of *end* and the idea of *good*. If it is true that the world has an end, it is equally so that this end is absolute good. If it is true that each being has a special end, then it is true that the good proper to this being is this end. Again, if it is true that between the end of each being and the end of all there is a correlation, so that the end of each being is only an element of the end of all, then it is true that the good of each being is an element of absolute good, and that thus the end of each being has the same nature and the same value as absolute good itself. Now to what is the idea of obligation invincibly attached? To the idea of that which is *good in itself and absolutely.* What we were ignorant of we now know; we have a clear conception of it. Good in itself is no other thing than the end of God in creation, than the absolute end of things. Henceforth, this end appears to us as sacred, and with it all the diverse ends which are the elements of it, and among these our own, which is one of them. The accomplishment of our end, or of our good, with which we are charged by being made free and intelligent, and that of the end or the good of others in so far as we are able to concur in it, — behold our duty, our rule, our legitimate law. Here, gentlemen, is morality; we sought it; behold it found.

I pretend not to say, that all these conceptions, which constitute logically the foundations of morality, are distinctly unfolded to all minds. Far from it. All *a priori* conceptions, though absolute and universal in themselves, reveal themselves and manifest their authority and force, in the first instance, in particular applications. Afterwards, what is universal and absolute in these particular applications is disengaged for some minds, and considered and understood by itself in the form of necessary and absolute conceptions; for others it is not. A majority do but take the first step; they pronounce a particular course of conduct to be according to their nature; that is to say, in conformity with their end; that is to say, again, what they were made for. What is common to all minds is the habit of thus applying these conceptions in particular cases, and this supposes that there is something which they all feel in common. This something is a confused idea, a confused sentiment of order, and of the respect which every reasonable being should pay to it. The proper and true name of moral good and evil is *order* and *disorder*. When I do evil, I feel myself at war with order. The least developed, the most darkened consciences, have this sentiment, as well as the most enlightened. When I do evil, I feel myself out of order, in hostility with order; when I do good, I feel myself in harmony with order; that is to say, in harmony with the absolute and common law of creation. I am "in the ways of God," as the Scriptures say; for the ways of God are his designs, the laws that govern the universe and lead it to its end.

III. *His View of the Destiny of Man.*] According to a preceding formula, we are to determine what a man's destiny is by the study of his nature; what he was made for, by considering how he is made. Now by observation we discover that there are in man instincts, tendencies, desires, by which his nature expresses itself and reveals itself primitively, and as long as it lives in this world. He also has faculties, that is, instruments, answering to his desires and tendencies, and evidently intended to be the means of satisfying these desires and tendencies. Again, he possesses a faculty of comprehension, the function of which is to enlighten him respecting the objects of his desires, and also on the best way of proceeding in order to satisfy these desires. Finally, there is in him a directive force, called the will, or the power of self-control, whose office it is, under the superior authority of reason and intelligence, or the comprehending faculty, to direct his instrumental faculties in the best manner for the attainment of the satisfaction of his nature.

Such being the constitution of human nature, we see that every thing looks to the legitimate, harmonious, and complete satisfaction of our whole nature; that is to say, of all its primary and fundamental desires and

39

tendencies. This, therefore, speaking absolutely, is its destiny, its *end.*

Here, however, we encounter a fact of great moment. Our condition, in this world is such, that not one of the desires and tendencies of our nature is ever completely satisfied on earth, either in the individual, or in the race considered collectively. Take curiosity, for example, or the desire or tendency to know, — its complete satisfaction would be absolute knowledge; or sympathy, — its complete satisfaction would be the perfect union and harmony of all beings: neither of which is ever realized in this world. Let no one object that a different and more perfect organization of society might bring about these results. Undoubtedly a different and more perfect organization of society would augment the sum of the satisfactions of each and of all the desires and tendencies of our nature; still, absolute knowledge and a perfect and harmonious union of all beings in this world would be impossible.

From this incontestable fact, two conclusions of the highest importance follow.

In the first place, it follows that the absolute end of man, as determined by his nature, is never realized in this world, and consequently, that he is not placed here for the accomplishment of this end.

The question respecting the end of man comes up, therefore, in another form. What is the end of man *in this life?* Why is he placed amidst a constitution of things where the free and spontaneous development of his desires and tendencies is obstructed and hindered, — where nature around him is not in harmony with his own nature, making his existence here a perpetual struggle, a perpetual conflict? Here, again, we must determine the end by considering the tendency, and accordingly we ask, What is the tendency of this constitution of things, as regards man? Evidently it is to call out, exercise, and strengthen his self-directing, self-controlling power, his personal power, that which makes him to be a *person,* and not a *thing,* — capable of virtue, capable of coöperating with God. Suppose we had been placed in a condition in which nothing opposed or obstructed the accomplishment of our true end; we should have gone to that end passively, if I may use such a term in speaking of an active being. We should have been like the main-spring of a watch, which, after having been wound up by the hand of its owner, goes on gradually unwinding itself, marking the hours until night; but the main-spring has no proper participation in the effect produced. Whence comes it that we elevate ourselves from the humble condition of a being which is only a thing to the sublime condition of a person? It comes from this, that the world is made as it is; fr m the rigorous law, under which we are born, that we make not a single step towards the accomplishment of our final destiny but by the sweat of our brow.

The present life, therefore, with all its difficulties and obstacles, with all its physical and moral evils, is not a mistake or an accident. It has not only been explained, but justified; but the justification brings into view a second consequence, equally important, from the fact above mentioned. We have seen what the true and absolute end of man is; we have also seen that this is not and cannot be accomplished in this life: hence we conclude that *this life is not all.* My nature was made what it is. By virtue of its organization, I feel desires which have an aim and an end; I have intelligence which comprehends all the reach of these desires, and sensibility to suffer pain and anguish when they die impotent and without satisfaction; and I also have faculties clothed with power to satisfy these desires, even in the face of difficulties and obstacles. All this I comprehend in respect to my nature. When unhappy in my present condition, I explain to myself this condition; I see the necessity and suitableness of it; — all, however, on an hypothesis which my whole nature cries out for. Is this hypothesis to be regarded as a fanciful chimera? Impossible! The life to come may be one, or multiple. What we feel authorized to affirm, under penalty of condemning to absurdity the universe, the world, the present life, God, every thing, is that this life is not all. Another life will dawn upon us, in which the accomplishment of what we have seen to be man's true and absolute destiny will be possible, — will be complete.

THE END.

www.ingramcontent.com/pod-product-compliance
Lightning Source LLC
LaVergne TN
LVHW020934110826
845150LV00004B/866